LONDON, CANADA

By Frederick H. Armstrong

Photo Research by John H. Lutman

"Partners in Progress" by Richard M. Pearce

Produced in Cooperation with
the London Chamber of Commerce

Windsor Publications, Ltd.

The FOREST CITY

AN ILLUSTRATED HISTORY OF

LONDON, CANADA

To my family: Joan, Dale, and Irene,
and also, at their insistence,
to Mugsy the cat.

Windsor Publications—History Book Division

Publisher: John M. Phillips
Editorial Director: Teri Davis Greenberg
Design Director: Alexander D'Anca

Staff for *The Forest City: An Illustrated History of London, Canada*
Editor: Jerry Mosher
Assistant Editors: Laura Cordova, Marilyn Horn
Director, Corporate Biographies: Karen Story
Assistant Director, Corporate Biographies: Phyllis Gray
Editor, Corporate Biographies: Judith Hunter
Production Editor, Corporate Biographies: Una FitzSimons
Layout Artist, Corporate Biographies: Mari Catherine Preimesberger
Sales Representative, Corporate Biographies: Maria Pender
Editorial Assistants: Kathy M. Brown, Marcie Goldstein, Pamela Juneman, Pat Pittman
Proofreader: Susan J. Muhler
Layout and Design: J.R. Vasquez

Library of Congress Cataloging in Publication Data
Armstrong, Frederick Henry.
The forest city.

"Produced in cooperation with the London Chamber of Commerce"
Bibliography: p. 328
Includes index.
1. London (Ont.)—History. I. Lutman, John.
II. London Chamber of Commerce (Ont.) III. Title.
F1059.5.L6A74 1986 971.3'26 86-23434
ISBN 0-89781-180-1

Published 1986
Printed in Canada
First Edition

Frontispiece: *For much of London's history, few buildings other than church steeples poked their tops above the canopy of trees; only in recent years has London sprouted the skyscrapers of commerce. Here the City Centre emerges from a blanket of green along the banks of the Thames River. Photo by John Bliss*

Contents

The original London District Courthouse, constructed between 1827 and 1829, still stands as a majestic reminder of the city's heritage. Photo by John Bliss

Foreword

There is a continuing tendency when attempting to introduce any work to lapse into street parlance and say "It's about time," for London long has lacked an up-to-date history of this nature.

The Forest City: An Illustrated History of London, Canada represents the first major effort to present a definitive history of London since Archie Bremner produced *Illustrated London* in the dying days of the Victorian era—a period which even today is both lauded and criticized but an era which in some facets is evident in the London of today.

Since the Bremner work appeared, the scene has witnessed changes so widespread and dramatic that some were not even mere dreams in the minds of the more romantic writers at the end of the nineteenth century. London, the railway, commercial, and wholesale distribution centre of Bremner's day, has developed into a major financial, educational, and research complex. It has assumed a major cultural role through the art gallery and theatre.

Not one development alone has contributed to this status. The motor vehicle, electric power, the airplane, and radio and television have united to bring changes which have affected every household, every business. The basic concept of merchandising is different—major conglomerates dominate where once the individual home town merchant held sway. Few of these survive. Shopping malls, with their parking facilities, draw business from the core-area establishments, many of them on streets constructed in the horse-and-buggy day.

Fred Armstrong has shown how London has developed down the years, how the little bushland settlement, which an early lieutenant-governor viewed as his provincial capital, has become the major centre of an area in which agriculture once dominated. Through the pages move the names of those who helped London grow great. Along with them are the names of some who "distinguished" themselves in anything but a laudable sense.

The London as portrayed throughout *The Forest City* is not the London as many see it today—a city with major educational and hospital facilities, huge shopping complexes, paved highways, and the continuing sight of a new street coming into existence while once-valuable farmland continues to fall to the developer's bulldozer.

In the beginning, London was a hamlet surrounding the administrative building (courthouse) for the district. In succession, the community was to become a British military centre—an imperial outpost in the bushland of a new world, a railway centre. Rail communication opened east and west, was followed by that to Lake Erie, Port Stanley, and by a line into the developing area north of London. Because of strategic location, the community became a major distribution centre.

There have been business booms and depressions. The oil industry—producing kerosene for lighting purposes—provided a major impetus in the 1860s and 1870s, although, correctly speaking, the refineries were located outside the city proper in a separate municipality. London, though, as a whole developed from their existence, and numerous fortunes have been attributed to their operation. Ultimately, the oil industry moved elsewhere and now remains largely forgotten as does another—cigar making, again once a major employer here. Until the automobile appeared, London sometimes was known as a "carriage town" because of the high standard of the vehicles turned out in a series of plants. Similarly, it was sometimes a "stove town"—McClary products went far and wide and in the developing days of the Canadian West entire trainloads were shipped there.

With this book, Fred Armstrong has proven a worthy successor to earlier London historians W. G. Moncrieff, Dr. Clarence T. Campbell, Archie Bremner, Sir John Carling, Sam Baker (for many years city clerk), Dr. Edwin Seaborn, Dr. Fred Landon, and a host of others. *The Forest City: An Illustrated History of London, Canada* is eminently worthy of your consideration.

Les N. Bronson
Looking Over Western Ontario columnist
London Free Press

Introduction

The triangular Southwestern Peninsula of Ontario forms a natural region, on the east separated from the rest of the province by the sweeping arc of the Niagara Escarpment and on the south and the west bounded by the waters of the Great Lakes. With its rich agricultural land this region promised to provide a fertile base for a prosperous economy and burgeoning cities. Yet, for the early settlers moving in from the east in the dying years of the eighteenth century and the opening decades of the nineteenth century, access to the lands was difficult. Their inland route westward was impeded by the escarpment and the dense forests; thus settlement had to make its way around Niagara Falls and then along the north shore of Lake Erie. This was a coastline that offered few good harbors and none with navigable rivers leading into the interior; the Thames River, which drains the central and western parts of the peninsula, flows far to the west before emptying into Lake St. Clair. Lake Erie literally presented no site for the growth of a future metropolitan centre.

Thus the establishment of an urban focal point for Southwestern Ontario—or western Upper Canada and then Western Ontario as it was long generally known—had to wait for colonization to begin filling in the interior. This situation did not arise until the third decade of the nineteenth century, when the inland townships were sufficiently opened to require the selection of an administrative centre to provide local government both for them and the frontier as it expanded to the north. By that time there were several potential candidates for the dignity of "district town," but thanks to a good location at the main forks of the Thames River, to the blessing of an early governor, and to a bit of luck, London was chosen and began its rise to hegemony over the peninsula in 1826.

As time passed and the hinterland became established, economic factors compounded the town's administrative ascendency. London became the entrepot for its northward-spreading region. Then, with the Rebellion of 1837, it gained additional prestige and economic advantage by being chosen as a garrison centre. Simultaneously, the town had another factor playing in its favor: it was not only centrally located but potentially on the main communication lines, halfway between Toronto/Hamilton and Detroit, and after only a short trail directly across the lake from Cleveland. London was also fortunate in that it had reached a place of importance before the road system was complete, and before the coming of the railways. Londoners were to direct both these networks to their benefit; being in the right position before the invention of technology can be of great advantage to a city.

One final factor should be noted in London's success: the magnet effect which draws people to a rising city from both its hinterland and from the stream of colonists immigrating to an opening continent. London did well in attracting those whom the nineteenth century called "men of capital and enterprise." With these forces moving in its favor it was not surprising that, by the late nineteenth century, it was the largest inland city in Canada and its settled hinterland one of the richest regions.

These positive factors which had been responsible for its rise could also have their negative side. Being the primate city of a region means prosperity when the region is expanding; however, when it is fully developed how does the city extend its influence beyond its immediate territory? The problem is especially acute when it is not a political capital, with all the organizational and legislative powers that the dignity brings. The situation can also be rendered difficult when it does not have direct lines of communication to any newly opening frontiers. For London this meant that it was secondary to the political influence of Toronto, and that it had to ship its goods to the growing West, or the established East, through either the American railways, or through Toronto and its lines. Here the magnet effect could equally play against London for the pastures of Toronto might look greener to both its entrepreneurs and its corporations. Thus, further advance in Canada basically had to be in rivalry to the great metropolitan centres of Toronto and Montreal, with many of the cards

After the "Great Fire" of April 13, 1845, which destroyed most of the town's frame buildings, the Town Council passed a municipal bylaw in 1850 compelling Londoners to rebuild with brick and stone. Dundas Street, here viewed west of Talbot Street circa 1875, became defined by two symmetrical rows of three-storey, Georgian-style commercial blocks built of local white brick. Courtesy, The University of Western Ontario (UWO)

now stacked in their favor. That London did so well is a tribute to both the strength and attractiveness of its region and to the enterprise of its men of affairs.

The rise of London is thus a double story: the growth of a city and the expansion of a region, each dependent on the other, the two growing up together. The combination is the usual one for a successful city, but the lines of geographic and political demarcation are rarely so obvious. This factor is one that is all too often passed over too briefly by historians; in essence, urban development is first of all based on geographic conditions. Given these conditions, however, as in the case of London, the citizens will seize the opportunity to build a successful city, taking advantage of the benefits of nature, and the advantages of improving technology. And, hopefully, they will be assisted a little by luck, or the element of the fortuitous, if one prefers. London has had more than its share of good geographic conditions, enterprising people, technological advantages, and good luck. As a result it has met its challenges well not only in the development phase of the nineteenth century, but also in more modern times as conditions changed.

A dense, formidable forest greeted the London District pioneer. Armed only with an axe, he cleared the land to plant his first crops between the stumps. The Springwater Conservation Area near London has never been altered by man and is thus representative of the vegetation—sugar maple, sassafras, black cherry, and white elm—that covered the area before settlement. Photo by Alan Noon

CHAPTER I

The Setting and the Governor: London to 1826

BACKGROUND TO THE CITY: THE LONDON REGION BEFORE 1700

The configuration of the rich agricultural lands of the Southwestern Peninsula of Ontario was created by the retreat of the last glacier some 15,000 years ago. As the ice melted gaps appeared which gradually developed into spillways between shrinking glacial lobes. One of these, stretching from around Amherstburg northeastward toward the Orangeville region, marked the beginnings of the Thames River valley. The moraines, or mounds of debris left behind by the retreating glacier, formed the hills which line parts of the upper Thames valley. Some of the pits left by the glacier filled with water in which moss grew to form bogs, of which the present-day Byron Bog is a survivor.

After the glaciers melted northward, the nomadic Paleo-Indian peoples followed migrating herds of caribou into the area. By 7500 B.C. the climate had warmed sufficiently for the modern temperate forests to replace the tundra vegetation. The Indians of this Archaic period evolved new techniques in response to the changing conditions, which presented more varied types of game to hunt and wider food gathering possibilities. Trade routes also began to develop. The Archaic peoples' success in adapting to the new conditions is shown by a growing number of archaeological finds which indicate an increase in population.

The succeeding Woodland period, which lasted from about 1000 B.C. to A.D. 1550, witnessed a division of cultures and again an expanding technology, which now included pottery making. By around A.D. 500 some of the Southern Ontario cultures had begun experimenting with corn growing and later this was augmented with squash and bean cultivation. The diet was still supplemented by fishing and hunting and the bow and arrow became the standard weapon. The increasingly agricultural economy meant a more settled existence and villages formed as a year-round base for at least some of the people.

By the fifteenth century when the Lawson Prehistoric Indian Village (London's largest Indian site) flourished, the Southwestern Peninsula was divided between two Iroquoian peoples. To the north, occupying the area around Georgian Bay, were the Hurons; the southern section was the home of the Neutrals, whose territory included the London region. The latter gained their name by trying to avoid the wars between the Hurons and the Iroquois of modern upstate New York. Their village at the Lawson site was occupied for about thirty years and housed approximately 1,000 people. It consisted of a cluster of longhouses, some nearly 100 feet in length, interspersed with middens, or garbage dumps, and surrounded by a defensive multiple palisade. The partial restoration of the site and the construction of the adjacent Museum of Indian Archaeology through the generosity of the Lawson family provide the visitor with an excellent opportunity to study the life of this first London.

By the turn of the sixteenth century the Indians were developing the trade patterns and alliances with the Europeans which were to have a shattering effect on their culture and organizations. Confederations were formed, such as the Iroquois Confederacy, which were designed to both coordinate trade between the villages and provide defensive alliances. As the French moved westward from Quebec, and the Dutch and then the English penetrated northward from New York City, their European conflicts inevitably became intertwined with local rivalries, all being made more bloody by the new European weaponry. The Southwestern Peninsula saw the Hurons in the north, who were allied with the French, battling with the British-supported New York-area Iroquois Confederacy. In 1649 the Iroquois wiped out the Hurons, the survivors fleeing eastward to Quebec, and then turned on the Neutrals who were dispersed by 1651. The Iroquois then retreated back to their home base, leaving the Southwestern Peninsula virtually empty. The remaining members of the defeated groups, already reduced by European diseases, generally migrated and were absorbed into other Indian tribes.

EUROPEAN CONTACT AND IMPERIAL CONFLICT, 1700-1791

Although the major fur trade routes from Quebec to the west followed the Ottawa River, by the opening of the eighteenth century French trading posts were beginning to appear along the Great Lakes. In 1701 the Sieur de la Cadillac founded a French settlement at Detroit. This westward spread of French colonization was a logical step toward welding the French Empire from Louisiana to Quebec into one great arc of settlement; however, such an empire inevitably conflicted with both the desires of England and the expansionist aspirations of its colonists along the Atlantic coast of what was to become the United States. As a result, especially during the frequent periods of French-English warfare which occupied much of the century, both the British and French empires began to establish chains of forts in the lower Great Lakes and along the American frontier.

As far as direct military action was concerned, what is now London's Southwestern Ontario hinterland was little affected by these wars; nevertheless, the political fate of the region was dictated by these engagements. In 1759-1760, following the British capture of Quebec and Montreal, this remote, largely uninhabited territory of New France automatically passed into British hands. The Province of Quebec, which Britain now established in the former French territories, initially did not include Southern Ontario. Rather, the region became part of an Indian Territory, which was to be controlled directly from Britain. The very action of establishing such a territory, however, further stirred up Britain's seaboard colonies which saw the West as their natural area of expansion. The Indian Territory also failed to function from an administrative point of view. As a result, on the eve of the American Revolution, a new constitution—the Quebec Act of 1774—reunited Southern Ontario and what was to become the American Midwest, the Northwest as it was then called, with Quebec. Coming at the same time as the "Intolerable Acts," which were levied against Massachusetts after the Boston Tea Party, the Quebec Act helped to trigger the American Revolution.

The battles of the Revolutionary War, like those of the earlier British conquest, were fought far from these western regions of Quebec and at the end of the war the land remained in British hands. Never-

This reconstructed Neutral Indian longhouse at the Lawson Prehistoric Indian Village is built on a frame of saplings supported by large interior posts, and is covered with sheets of elm bark. Openings are left for doors at either end and in the roof to allow the smoke from hearth fires to drift out. Photo by Alan Noon

This scene along the Catfish Creek within the Springwater Conservation Area east of London is reminiscent of travellers' descriptions of the Thames River before settlement in 1826. Large trees draped their boughs into the flowing waters, ducks existed in scores, and the river abounded with numerous varieties of fish. Photo by Alan Noon

Opposite page: *The Lawson Prehistoric Indian Village is Canada's only ongoing excavation and reconstruction of a prehistoric site, retracing the lives of the Neutral Indians who inhabited the five-acre site 500 years ago. This view shows a partially reconstructed longhouse interior. Courtesy, Museum of Indian Archaeology*

theless, under the peace treaty signed at Paris in 1783 the Old Northwest and the British-held parts of upstate New York were ceded to the United States. The actual transfer, however, was delayed—partly because of the region's great value to the fur trade. Despite the remoteness of the territory it was obvious that, as American settlement pushed westward, the British retention of the land would be impossible. Immediately, in 1783, what is now all of Southern Ontario and the neighboring United States, although still virtually unsettled, remained as the western portion of Quebec. For local administrative purposes it was included in the District of Montreal.

The settlement of Loyalists along the St. Lawrence River and Lake Ontario began in 1784, their farms stretching from the end of the French seigneurial grants, just west of Montreal, to what is now Prince Edward County halfway along Lake Ontario. As well, in the Niagara Peninsula the small farming community dating from the revolutionary era spread out as new settlers arrived. Although desirous of remaining under British rule, these Loyalists were far from happy with an administration at Quebec City. Before long they were demanding a separate government for the evolving western region.

The granting of this government in the West took place in two stages: first local, then provincial. Up until the 1840s local government in what is now Ontario was based on large districts which were long administered by appointed justices of the peace, rather than on counties as today. Since the western territories beyond the Ottawa River were far too remote for Montreal to provide the Loyalists with any real government, what is now all of Southern Ontario was separated from the Montreal District in 1788, and four new administrative districts were established there. These centred around the four main points of settlement—Cornwall, Kingston, Niagara, and De-

Five hundred years ago, a palisade entirely surrounded the Lawson Prehistoric Indian Village, which was occupied by the Neutral Indians. The tall rows of posts, here in a partial state of completion, were interwoven with branches to form solid walls running parallel to each other. Breaks in the walls were staggered to create a complex, maze-like entrance. Photo by Alan Noon

troit. The districts were initially given German names in honor of the royal family, but English names were substituted in 1792. The Southwestern Peninsula and the Old Northwest fell mainly within the District of Hesse, later the Western District, with its district town at Detroit. The eastern boundary of this vast territory ran from a line drawn from the Penetanguishene area on Georgian Bay to the tip of Long Point in Lake Erie. Thus it included the future site of London and most of the city's later economic hinterland.

Although these districts helped solve localized administrative problems, they did not resolve the difficulties arising from the remoteness of the Quebec government, or the settlers' dislike of the French administration and civil law. To deal with this problem, in 1791 Great Britain separated these western districts from Quebec, establishing the present Quebec-Ontario border as the boundary. The two new provinces thus created by dividing Quebec were renamed Lower Canada and Upper Canada, the latter covering the whole of the western lands. Although sharing a common governor, the two provinces were provided with separate legislatures based on that of Great Britain, each having a lieutenant-governor, an Executive Council (the equivalent of our modern cabinet), a Legislative Council (rather like today's Senate), and an elected lower house, or Legislative Assembly, the ancestor of the modern legislatures of Quebec and Ontario. With its huge territory, poor communications, and population of only some 10,000 people gathered around a few hamlets, Upper Canada's first great problem was going to be surviving in face of the spreading wave of American westward expansion.

THE GOVERNOR ARRIVES, 1792-1796

Fortunately for Upper Canada, John Graves Simcoe, Britain's first appointment as lieutenant-governor, was a man of unusual energy. Despite the fact that some of his ideas were decidedly overambitious, he possessed a great deal of good, practical sense and a realization of what the colony needed. Although resident in Upper Canada only for a brief four years from 1792 to 1796, Simcoe indelibly laid his impression on all aspects of colonial life. The province's road system, its urban pattern, and, indeed, much of what might be called the Ontario ethos, were planted before he was transferred to command in the Caribbean where Britain was fighting France.

Simcoe, with his military, English Tory, Church of England (Anglican) background, was quite typical of the governors who were sent out by Britain to rule its colonies in the late eighteenth and early nineteenth centuries. Thanks to the coincidence of two of his friends, Henry Dundas and Sir George Yonge, being in the British Cabinet, Simcoe obtained the appointment as first lieutenant-governor of Upper Canada, although the overall governor of Canada, Sir Guy Carleton, Baron Dorchester, preferred another candidate. Characteristically, Simcoe named what were to become two of Ontario's main streets—Dundas Street and Yonge Street—in his patrons' honor. As lieutenant-governor his Toryism fitted in well with the outlook of the settlers; yet some of the policies he helped establish, such as granting special privileges and lands to the Church of England, were to be major issues in the reform campaigns of later years.

Simcoe was already planning the defence of his colony before he left England in 1791. He carefully studied the available maps of Upper Canada and decided that, everything considered, the most satisfactory place for a capital would be in the Southwestern Peninsula on a site well inland. It would thus be protected from American attacks, strategically located to help hold and defend the western territories, guard the Indians against American influence, and encourage the development of the fur trade. The Forks of the Thames, where London is now situated, seemed the best possibility, while the future sites of Toronto and Chatham could be naval arsenals for the lower and upper Great Lakes respectively.

By 1793, with Britain and America's former ally France at war, the final transfer of the Old Northwest had to be dealt with quickly. Fortunately, the Americans did not want conflict. In 1794 United States Chief Justice John Jay led a mission to England, where he negotiated a treaty which made arrangements for the transfer in 1796. This meant that Niagara-on-the-Lake, selected as the first, temporary capital of Upper Canada, would soon be indefensible with the Americans occupying the opposite bank of the Niagara River. Kingston, the largest centre in the colony and the major commercial entrepot, would also be endangered. To the west Detroit would have to be surrendered and the Southwestern Peninsula would be virtually surrounded by hostile American territory.

By the time the war broke out Simcoe had already inspected his western territories and confirmed the capital site. His expedition, which left Niagara on February 2, 1793, and went as far as Detroit, occupied him until March 10th. Accompanying Simcoe was a party which included Major Edward Littlehales

JOHN GRAVES SIMCOE

John Graves Simcoe was born February 25, 1752, in Cotterstock, Northamptonshire, England. Like his father, who died during the Quebec expedition of 1759, Simcoe embarked on a military career. With a formal education which he received from the Exeter Grammar School and Eton College, and an appreciation of his father's emphasis on industry, duty, morality, and military education, Simcoe underwent a year of military tutoring. Yet, it was the prominence and wealth of his mother's family through which he received a commission as ensign with the 35th Regiment of Foot in 1770.

Simcoe's regiment arrived in Boston shortly after the Battle of Bunker Hill. Later, during the siege of the city, he bought a captain's commission in the 40th Regiment of Foot. With this corps Simcoe saw distinguished service during the American tour and was promoted to the rank of lieutenant-colonel. Early in the Revolution Simcoe participated in the Long Island campaign and also in the capture of New York City. In 1776-1777 he assisted in the New Jersey campaigns as well as the Battle of Brandywine, the Pennsylvania campaign of 1778, the raid on Richmond, Virginia, and the Yorktown campaign. Simcoe was wounded three times during the war and was captured in 1779. In 1781 he was invalided back to England, which spared him the humiliation of the British surrender at Yorktown a short time later.

Back in England Simcoe convalesced and on December 30, 1782, married Elizabeth Postuma Giwillim, an heiress to a considerable estate. In the following years Simcoe dabbled in politics and was elected to the House of Commons. In 1790 he was promised the position of lieutenant-governor over the proposed new province of Upper Canada, although he wanted to be appointed minister to the United States. Nevertheless, he enthusiastically prepared for his new responsibility and arrived in Upper Canada in June of 1792, ready to speedily transform the province into a model of England.

Simcoe believed that the American Revolution had its root in the democratic excess of the colonies. But he was not so doctrinaire as to believe that new settlers to the province would come simply in order to live beneath the Crown. He realized that undoubtedly the best way to achieve a loyal populace was to tie the settlers to the land and to familiar laws and institutions. All this he attempted by instituting a good land granting system and establishing a solid base for English law and government. Unfortunately, he had his opponents, particularly Guy Carleton, Lord Dorchester, who acted as governor-in-chief of both Canadas and was Simcoe's superior. Carleton, with some English officials, effectively blocked many of Simcoe's plans for the fledgling province of Upper Canada.

Londoners today remember Simcoe as the governor who visited the future site of London in March 1793; the military and civil prospects of the site confirmed his idea that it should be the future capital of Upper Canada. It has been a general misconception for years that Simcoe planned his capital to be located between the Forks of the Thames, where the town plot was later surveyed. Actually, he favored the south bank and for many years the area stretching as far as the coves was reserved for his metropolis.

Simcoe quickly set his plans in motion and in May 1793 ordered his Queen's Rangers to cut a road from Burlington Bay to the Thames River, to be known as Dundas Street. Beginning this grand road to London was the main thing that he accomplished with regard to his London; the site remained in its pristine state years later. Of course, Simcoe's general idea was eventually, in a limited way, achieved in 1826 when Mahlon Burwell laid the grid survey for the new capital of the London District, centred directly east of the Forks.

In July 1796 Simcoe, who was suffering from neuralgia, gout, malaria, and no doubt Upper Canadian political fatigue, was granted a leave of absence. During this time he governed part of the troubled island of St. Domingo (today's Haiti), but ill health forced him to leave in 1797. Subsequently, in 1798 he resigned his governorship of Upper Canada. For several years he had command of the Western District at Exeter, England. In 1806 he was appointed commander-in-chief in India. Taken ill at Lisbon on the way out, he returned to England and died October 26, 1806, at Exeter.

John Graves Simcoe, first lieutenant-governor of Upper Canada (1791-1799), selected the site of London as the future capital. A visit to the Forks of the Thames in March 1793 confirmed his opinion of the site; however, Toronto was chosen instead as temporary capital. Courtesy, Metropolitan Toronto Library, 927.1

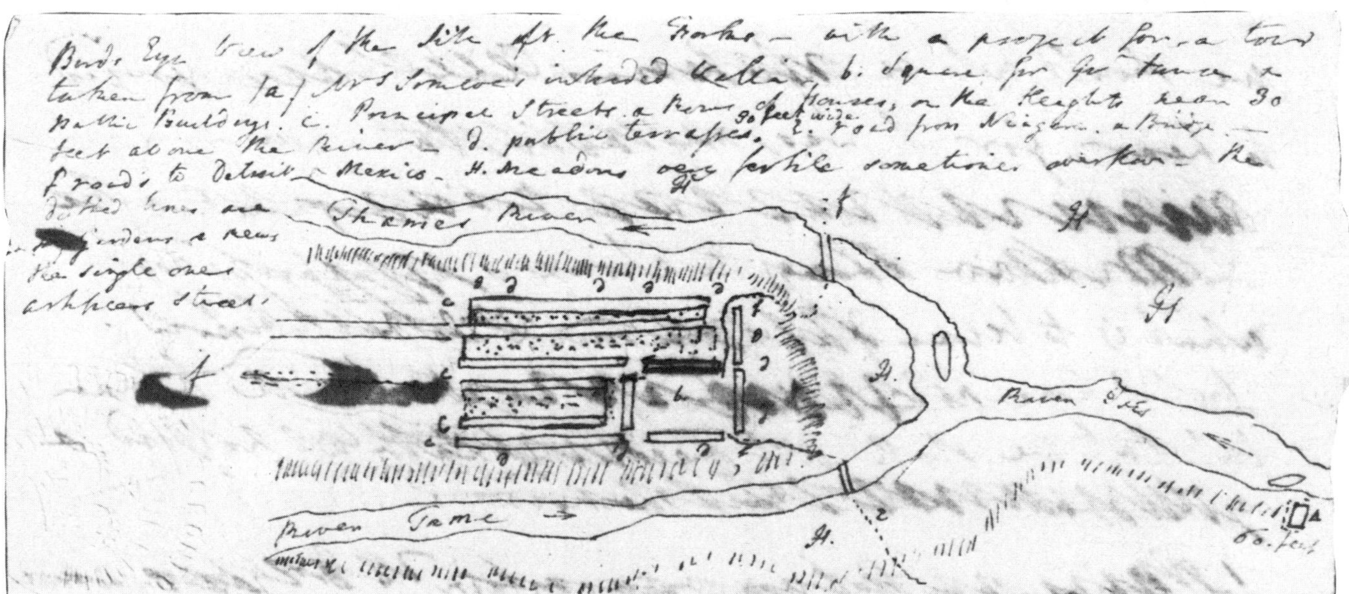

Top left: *Major Edward B. Littlehales, Simcoe's military secretary, accompanied the governor on his 1793 expedition to Detroit, which on the return journey included the visit to the site of London on March 2. From Littlehales' journal of the trip comes the earliest description of London. Courtesy, Metropolitan Toronto Library, T16339*

Above: *Sketched in 1793 by Mrs. Elizabeth Simcoe* (top right*)*, *wife of the lieutenant-governor, this "Birds Eye View of the site at the Forks—with a project for a town . . ." was intended as a rough plan for the proposed capital of Upper Canada. The new town centre would have been located southwest of the Forks. The distortion of the Thames is explained by Mrs. Simcoe's lack of familiarity with the site. Courtesy, Public Archives of Ontario*

and Lieutenant Thomas Talbot, who later became the father of much of the colonization along the Lake Erie shore region, including London itself. Reaching the future site of London in early March, the Simcoe party traversed land heavily forested with pines, completely covered with snow, and criss-crossed with the tracks of deer, wolves, bears, otters, and other animals. Despite its isolation and the wintery clime, Simcoe enthusiastically confirmed that the Forks met his expectations and would be the ideal spot for a safe, inland capital. Major Littlehales recorded the governor's feelings in his diary:

We walked over a rich meadow and at its extremity reached the forks of the river. The Governor wished to examine this situation and its environs, and we therefore stopped here a day. He judged it to be a capital situation, eminently calculated for the metropolis of all Canada. Among many other essentials, it possesses the following advantages: Command of Territory—internal situation—central position—facility of water communication up and down the Thames—superior navigation for boats to near its source, and for small crafts, probably to the Moravian settlement [near Bothwell]—to the Southward by a small portage [sic] to the water flowing into Lake Huron, by a carrying place into Lake Ontario and the River St. Lawrence—the soil is luxuriously fertile and the land capable of being easily cleared and soon put into a state of agriculture. A Pinery upon an adjacent high knoll, other timber on the height, well calculated for the erection of the public buildings, climate not inferior to any part of Canada. To these natural advantages, an object of great consequence is to be added, the enormous expence of the Indian Department would be greatly diminished, if not abolished. The Indians in all probability would be induced to become the carriers of their own peltries [furs], and they would find a ready, contiguous, commodious, and equitable mart, honorably advantageous to Government and the community in general, without their becoming a prey to the monopolizing and unprincipled trader.

Selecting the site for the capital was one thing; the actual establishment of the city was quite another. As Richard Cartwright, the greatest merchant of Kingston, jealously asserted, to get to his new capital Simcoe would have to import one of the balloons which had just been invented by the Montgolfier brothers in France. Cartwright was not the only one who was unimpressed with the possibility of locating a capital at the Forks; Dorchester in Quebec did not want the government moved so far west. With the gathering American threat to Niagara, Simcoe was forced to choose an interim site immediately and established a "temporary capital" at Toronto, renamed York, which was to have merely been his long-term Lake Ontario naval base. At Toronto the capital has remained.

Although unable to begin work on his capital as he had hoped, Simcoe took several steps that were eventually to lead to the development of the city. The first of these was securing the site. The area south of the Thames, now partly in the Township of Westminster, had been purchased from the Chippewa, Ottawa, and Potawatomi nations in 1790. Later, in September 1796, the territory to the north of the river stretching from the lower forks of the Thames at London to the upper forks at present-day Woodstock was purchased from the Chippewas for trade goods worth 1,200 pounds in the local currency. The perimeter of this latter purchase was surveyed by Abraham Iredell in November 1796 and the western part became the Township of London. Following Simcoe's idea, 3,850 acres were eventually set aside at the Forks as a Crown Reserve for the site of the future provincial capital.

To provide road communications to the western territory Simcoe began the building of Dundas Street, which was planned to stretch from Dundas adjacent to Hamilton, westward to the Forks of the Thames. Later, of course, the street was to be extended eastward to Toronto. Simcoe had construction work begun at Dundas by his Queen's Rangers Regiment in 1794, but the road—still known today as the Governor's Road—only reached modern-day Paris by the time he left the colony. It was many years before the route was completed.

Simcoe left two other legacies. One was the idea that London would some day be a capital and even though nothing was done to start work, this legend lingered. He also provided the necessary nomenclature for a capital city. No admirer of either French or Indian names, Simcoe virtually wiped the Upper Canadian slate clear, renaming everything with English names which could easily be spelled and pronounced by the settlers. Take, for instance, the county system, which he established in 1792 to create ridings for the first elections, as the counties were then electoral, not administrative, units. His method of nomenclature was a simple one: starting at what is now Windsor and moving eastward, he named the Upper Canadian counties after the English counties moving northward up the east coast of that island, beginning with Kent and Essex and running to Durham and Northumberland. With a few changes these are basically the Ontario names today. The Loyalist settlers, who had shown their opinion of French institutions with the first two laws passed in this province (which respectively substituted English civil law for the French code, and English weights and measures for French ones), raised no objections to these designations.

The area at the Forks of the Thames fell within Suffolk County. For the river itself, Simcoe fancied neither the Indian "Askunesippi" (antlered river) or the French "La Tranche"—however much it was appropriate he could hardly be blamed for not wanting a river named "the ditch" in the middle of his capital—and in July 1792 he changed the name to the Thames River. The designation London itself was not applied to the site immediately. Simcoe had originally planned to name his new capital "Georgina" in honor of George III. That appellation was fortunately forgotten almost immediately; he was referring to it as "New London" by March 1793 and as simply "London" by September 1793. Thus, when Simcoe departed Upper Canada in 1796, he had laid the basis for a city of the future, although with the site's remoteness, it would be many years before settlers moved into the area and the foundation of a town became possible.

THE LONG YEARS OF WAITING, 1796-1826

Although a few Loyalist settlers came to the Long Point area in the 1780s, the population of southwestern Upper Canada remained very sparse until the end of the eighteenth century. Administratively, however, great changes took place right across the province. The Upper Canadian government tried to provide administrative services to new areas as soon as they became fairly well populated. Basically, the officials wanted to establish a local administrative centre, or district town, with its courthouse and market within one day's travel of all settled parts of the district. In the early days, this was more an ideal than a fact. In 1798 the government, urged on by this need, as well as by the fact that a very confused system of partially overlapping townships, districts, and counties had evolved, passed a new statute regularizing all local administration in the province. Henceforth individual townships were not divided between two counties or counties split between two districts.

The legislation further created such new counties and districts as were required. The centre of the Southwestern Peninsula was sufficiently remote from Sandwich (Windsor), which had succeeded Detroit as district town, to merit the establishment of a separate administrative district. The new legislation created the District of London, which was mainly cut out of the Western District, with a smaller portion taken from the Home District to the east. At the same time the County of Suffolk was abolished and a new County of Middlesex, appropriately named after the country then surrounding London, England, was put in its place. From the time these revisions came into effect on January 1, 1800, the central Southwestern Peninsula had its own district town in Norfolk County, first at the town plot for Charlotteville Township and, after the War of 1812, at Vittoria. The County of Middlesex was virtually uninhabited, even though it included what is now the lakeshore County of Elgin, which was not separated until 1851. To the southwest Middlesex did not include Lobo, Mosa, Ekfrid, or Caradoc townships until 1821, and northward Biddulph and McGillivray townships were not added until 1863.

The real settlement of the area began only in 1803 with the arrival of Simcoe's one-time staff member Colonel Thomas Talbot, scion of an Anglo-Irish noble family. Although he became an eccentric, crusty, and rather alcoholic old gentleman, Talbot maintained excellent connections at both the provincial capital at York and in London, England. He was eventually to be given the agency for opening no fewer than twenty-nine townships stretching eastward from the Detroit River two-thirds the length of Lake Erie, and the townships south of the Thames up to London. In his project of developing the western territories Talbot was often assisted by one of the most active surveyors of the province, Colonel Mahlon Burwell of Dunwich Township, who was to lay out much of the land now in Middlesex, as well as serve the county in other capacities, such as registrar and member of the legislature.

The official settlement of what was to become London's hinterland began ceremoniously with Thomas Talbot chopping down the first tree in his "principality" on May 21, 1803. He quickly established a land system under which, for every 200 acres he was granted as agent, he gave 50 acres to a settler to open up on a location ticket, and kept the other 150 acres for himself. These lands he sold for tidy sums when the farms had been improved and the roads had been opened. The settlers received their land virtually free, but the system certainly enabled Talbot to build up a vast personal empire, which was

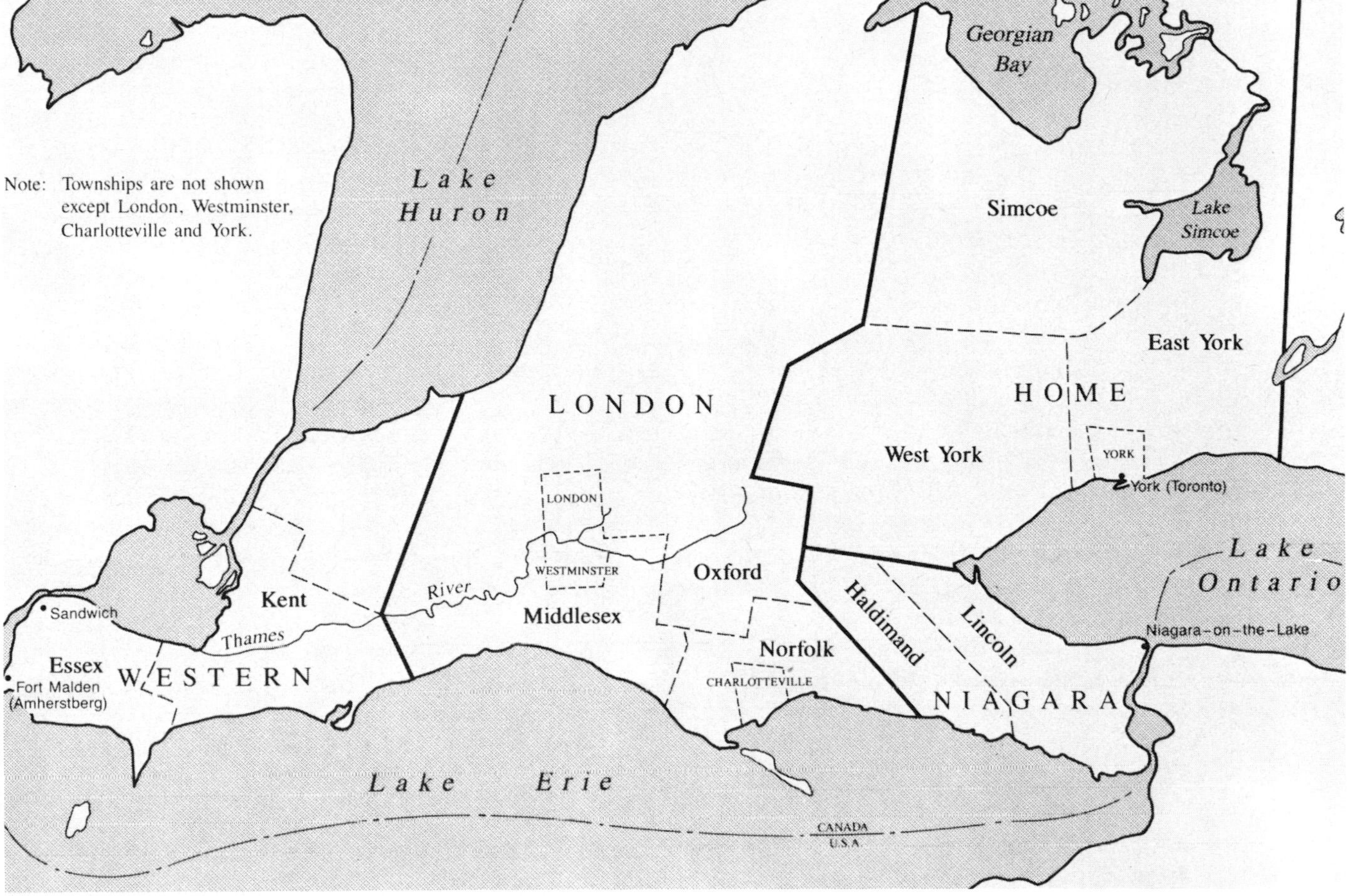

In 1800 the London District was carved out of the Western District and a small portion of the Home District to the east. The centre of the Southwestern Ontario Peninsula was sufficiently remote from Sandwich (Windsor), the district capital, to merit a separate administrative unit. Courtesy, P. Chalk

estimated at 38,500 acres in the late 1830s. However, in spite of all his powers as a settlement leader, Talbot never completely controlled his lands; squatters would frequently move onto good locations and begin to open a farm. The government at York tended to be quite generous when deciding their rights; very often if they developed the land squatters could end up with title to at least part of the property.

In the years following the beginning of Talbot's colonization of the lakeshore there was very little activity in the inland areas. In 1794 an American settler named Ebenezer Allan, along with several associates, started to open Delaware Township just west of modern London. The settlement gradually grew, although Allan developed a reputation for dishonesty and finally deserted to the American side during the War of 1812. Another colonizer, Lord Selkirk, and his party passed through in June 1804, when they stopped at the "Forks," as it quickly came to be known, en route to found a new settlement at Baldoon (near modern Wallaceburg) to the west. There was also some lumbering activity, using the Thames

THOMAS TALBOT

Of all the individuals who figured prominently in the establishment and early development of London and its region, none is more fascinating than Colonel Thomas Talbot. Often perceived today as a gruff, alcoholic old reprobate bent on acquiring a large estate at the expense of the poor and ignorant settlers, Talbot, for all his faults, did have a certain paternal feeling for the people with whom he populated the Crown lands of twenty-nine townships. He barred the land speculators who retarded the progress of many other Upper Canadian settlements and was responsible for a road network which was unrivalled anywhere in the colony. Altogether he provided the framework for the prosperous region we too often take for granted today.

Talbot, who was born into the Irish aristocracy, began his eventful life in Malahide Castle, Dublin County, Ireland on July 19, 1771. At the tender age of eleven, his family provided him with an army commission, as was often done in that period. During the course of his early military career Talbot was fortunate in becoming friends with Arthur Wellesley, later the Duke of Wellington, a connection that was to prove very helpful in his later career. In 1790 Talbot joined the 24th Regiment of Foot at Quebec and was soon selected by Lieutenant-Governor Simcoe as his private secretary. In 1793 he accompanied the governor to Detroit, and on their return they stopped over at the future site of London. The expedition was not only Talbot's first visit to what later became London, but also his first tour of the region he would one day dominate. The next year he left Upper Canada to participate in the struggle against Napoleon; but, unlike Wellesley, his military career was short-lived. In 1800 he surprised his friends by selling his commission and sailing back to Canada.

With visions of founding his own estate, Talbot obtained a large grant of land on the shore of Lake Erie in what is now Elgin County. On May 21, 1803, on the site of Port Talbot, he marked the beginning of his "principality" by felling the first tree. From this headquarters he soon began issuing location ticket permits to settle on his land. Once applicants became abundant, however, the colonel developed a reputation for being obnoxious, and miserly with the Crown lands. On one occasion his rudeness backfired and he was thrown to the ground by an incensed "land pirate." Shortly afterward, Talbot devised his notorious audience window as a personal safety measure. Land applicants stood at the window, which opened from the inside, and waited for the interview to begin with a gruff "What do you want?" If Talbot suspected a drifter, speculator, or Yankee, or if he just disliked the look of the face peering in at him, the window was slammed shut and the interview thus concluded.

Talbot was also equally notorious for his autocratic system of recording settlers' locations for land under his jurisdiction. Rather than issuing a location ticket, which was later superseded by a Crown patent once the settlement duties were performed and the fees paid, Talbot merely penciled the settler's name on a map. Settlers who neglected their duties were, quite literally, erased.

Talbot's popularity fared poorly during the War of 1812. When news of the conflict reached him he dashed off a patriotic letter to General Isaac Brock suggesting surrender to the Americans at Detroit with special provision for the protection of his property! With such a defeatist attitude it is not difficult to understand his subsequent inability to raise the local militia. American forces raided Port Talbot several times during the war, and eventually laid waste to the estate. There was nothing terribly strategic about Port Talbot and later instigators believed that the bulk of the raids were made by local traitors seeking revenge. Talbot, however, always managed to escape. Naturally, he had little use for political reformers, denouncing reform meetings as "damned cold water drinking societies" because many reformers were also temperance society members. Later, during the Rebellion of 1837, Talbot had better success rallying "his people," but took little part in quelling the rebellion.

As Talbot grew old he desired an heir for his land, and having no children himself, he looked to his nephews, Richard and Julius Airey. Julius arrived in 1834, but found country life so to his dislike that in 1841 he returned to Ireland. In 1847 Richard came to live with Uncle Thomas at Port Talbot. Their relationship soured by 1850 and Talbot moved out of his old home, gave half of his estate to Airey, and then began a European tour. In 1851 when the Aireys left Port Talbot he hastened back to his beloved home.

By then he was becoming something of a legend in his own

time, and the anniversary of his founding of the settlement was celebrated by a Talbot Dinner at St. Thomas. He visited London periodically for such occasions as the sod turning for the first railway. In 1852 his loyal servant and friend, George Macbeth, and Macbeth's wife Anne, brought an ailing Talbot to live with them at London. He died there February 5, 1853, logically disinheriting the Aireys and leaving the other half of his estate to the Macbeths.

Colonel Thomas Talbot, pictured in a circa 1850 painting by James B. Wandesforde, supervised the surveying of roads and the settlement of twenty-nine Southwestern Ontario townships and many towns, including London. Courtesy, UWO

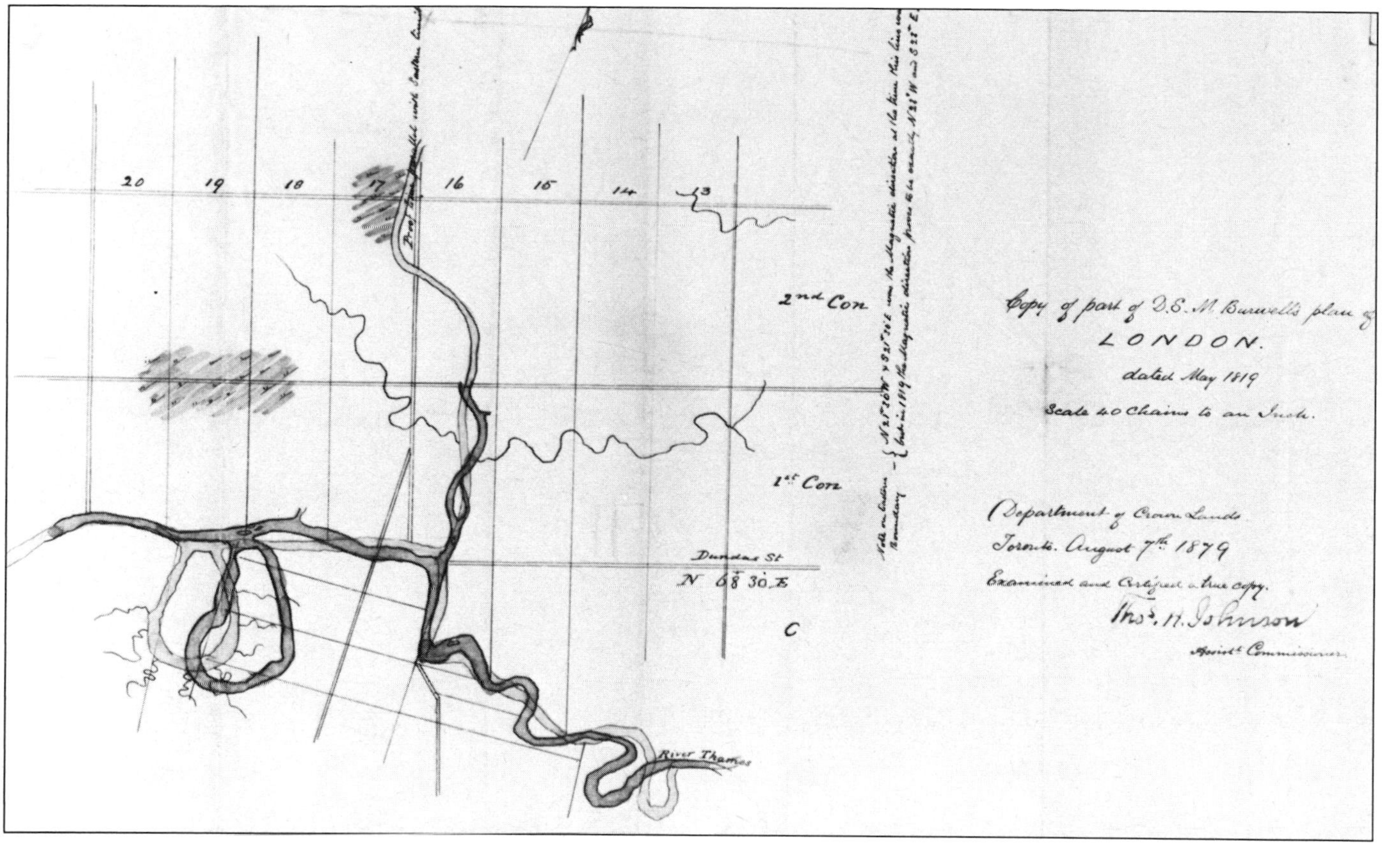

River to float the logs down from the Dorchester area.

The actual site of the Forks was first opened for white settlement in 1808, although there had been Indian cornfields there at an earlier period. In October Mahlon Burwell surveyed a 1,000-acre tract, which was already held under license of occupation by Joshua Applegarth on condition that he cultivate hemp, which was needed to make rope for the British navy in the Napoleonic Wars. For some years the Upper Canadian government subsidized the production, without much success. Applegarth soon built a comfortable log house, ploughed some ten acres of the river flats three-quarters of a mile below the Forks, and sent some hemp to the English market. However, he left in 1819 and the license was rescinded in 1822.

By that time the basic road system connecting the towns of the Southwestern Peninsula was evolving, although there was no road which we would regard as more than a bad trail. The "Western Road" between Niagara and Sandwich, also called the "Detroit Path" and soon named Commissioners Road at London, was open for sleighs by 1799, but really was not passable until about 1828. Communications across

Above: *The Crown Reserve of London, lying north of the Thames River, was surveyed by Mahlon Burwell in 1810 as part of the general survey of London Township. This 1819 Crown lands map of the Forks area indicates the first and second concessions and numbered lots 13 to 20. Courtesy, UWO*

Opposite page: *In Ontario the sixty-six-foot chain, consisting of 100 links, was the basic unit of measurement used by surveyors for the concessions, road allowances, and lots of the province's townships and townsites. This chain and surveyor's reel were employed by Deputy Provincial Surveyor Mahlon Burwell (pictured) to survey much of Colonel Thomas Talbot's domain. Photo by Alan Noon. Courtesy, London Historical Museums*

Travellers regarded the vegetation of Southwestern Ontario as extraordinary. In particular, they remarked on the enormous size of the trees. Philip John Bainbrigge's 1840 painting, "Button Wood Tree . . .," depicts a tree eighteen feet in circumference, in the bush near Chatham, Ontario. A pathway, shaded from the sun by overhanging foliage, can be seen winding its way through the gloom of the forest. Courtesy, Public Archives of Canada, C11883

the Thames began about 1818 with a ferry operated three-quarters of a mile below the Forks by a family named Montague.

The surveying of townships in the London area was also progressing. The section of Westminster Township south of the Thames River, which is now the Byron area of London, was surveyed in 1810 by Simon Zelotes Watson. He had received approval as a settlement leader from the provincial government but soon fell afoul of Colonel Talbot and ended up losing the settlement leadership to that worthy. In the same year Mahlon Burwell surveyed the south part of London Township. In 1818 Colonel Talbot was granted the superintendency of settlement in the township and Burwell was instructed to complete the survey.

By the end of that year there were more than 100 settlers, about half of them Church of England adherents from Tipperary County, Ireland, brought in by Richard S. Talbot. Their arrival acted as a catalyst and the development of the London town plot soon gained momentum. On January 4, 1819, the first town meeting for London Township was held in Joshua Applegarth's house. Shortly afterward the first recorded religious services were conducted by a Wesleyan Methodist circuit rider, the Reverend Samuel Belton. In 1822 the first Church of England missionary, the Reverend Charles James Stewart, a son of the Earl of Galloway and later the second bishop of Quebec, preached to a congregation of nearly 250 in a barn in the township. His activities are usually taken as marking the beginning of St. John's Church in Arva, north of the townsite, where the first church building was built about 1822.

Members of the future London establishment were also beginning to make their appearance. In 1824 John Kent, London's first major landowner, purchased a 200-acre farm straddling the Thames River. It spread from Wharncliffe Road North to Richmond Street north of present-day Carling Street. After 1826 Kent was selling off this land at a very good profit. The Carling family was also present. Thomas Carling and his betrothed, Margaret Rautledge, posted the notice of their intention to wed on a tree in 1820, the closest the settlers were able to come to posting their banns, given the primitive conditions of the region. Their son, the future Sir John Carling, one of London's greatest citizens, was born in January 1828. By that year, however, there was a very different settlement at the Forks, for London had been proclaimed the regional capital.

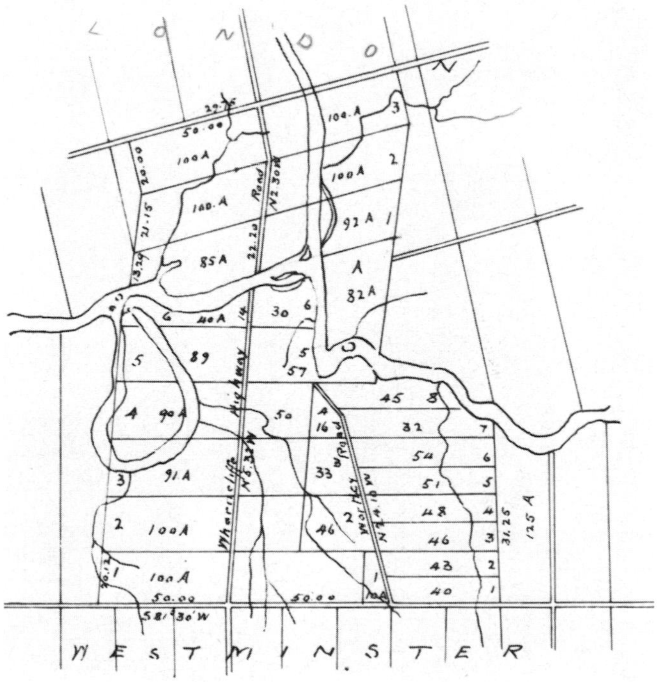

A substantial part of the Crown Reserve was prepared for settlement in 1824 when Thomas Talbot instructed Mahlon Burwell to survey the Wharncliffe Highway (Wharncliffe Road North and South) through the Crown Reserve to link Commissioners Road, the principal route of east-west travel, to the Proof Line Road (Richmond Street) which served London Township. Lots of varying sizes on both sides of the Wharncliffe Highway were laid out. Courtesy, UWO

Built of brick and faced with stucco, the original London District Courthouse, constructed between 1827 and 1829, was designed in the Gothic Revival style by Toronto architect John Ewart. As described in the Middlesex County Atlas *of 1878, "it was then considered a stately and imposing pile, and was the pride of the neighbouring settlers." Courtesy, UWO*

CHAPTER II

The Town of London, 1826-1840

T

HE FOUNDING OF LONDON

By the mid-1820s the spread of settlement had shifted the center of population to the north and west away from the district town at Vittoria. Norfolk County was no longer the major focus of settlement; Oxford County to the north with more than 4,000 people was slightly larger, and Middlesex to the west with a population of more than 9,000 was more heavily settled than the two put together. Also, in 1824 the British government chartered the Canada Land Company to open up for its settlers what are now Huron and Perth counties to the north. It was obvious that very soon something would have to be done to provide services and administration from a more central point than any town in Norfolk County. At this juncture the courthouse at Vittoria was badly damaged in a fire and the provincial government began the quest for a better location to the northwest.

The site at the Forks of the Thames was not necessarily the obvious one for a new district town. St. Thomas to the south was a flourishing center and there were other locations such as the Village of Delaware, or the site of Dorchester to the east. Though the Dorchester site had a reserve similar to London, also set aside by Simcoe, it was not given consid eration. St. Thomas was much more of a rival; how ever, that community had shown decided signs of political radicalism in the 1824 provincial election,

Above: *Along with Thomas Talbot, Mahlon Burwell, and others, James Hamilton (1792-1858) was appointed a commissioner to oversee the erection of the courthouse and gaol in 1826. He served as sheriff of the London District and later Middlesex County (1837-1858). From Bremner,* Illustrated London, *1900. Courtesy, UWO*

Above right: *As surveyor-general of Upper Canada from 1810 to 1829, Thomas Ridout was responsible for overseeing the surveys of the London District. Under his aegis Colonel Mahlon Burwell surveyed the townsite of London in 1826. Courtesy, Public Archives of Canada, C127113*

Opposite page: *The turreted London District Courthouse purportedly was modelled after Malahide Castle, County Dublin, Ireland, ancestral home of the Talbots, where Thomas Talbot was born on July 19, 1771. This contemporary view of Malahide Castle shows a marked similarity to the eastern facade of architect John Ewart's original courthouse design. Courtesy, UWO*

when Colonel Mahlon Burwell had been defeated for the riding of Middlesex despite the strong support of Colonel Talbot. In addition, St. Thomas really was not much further north from the lake than Vittoria.

A committee was set up to select the new site. It was composed of Captain John Mathews, a successful candidate for the Middlesex riding; Daniel Springer, a magistrate from Delaware; and Ira Schofield, another magistrate from London Township. These gentlemen first considered the Delaware settlement, but there was no Crown Reserve at that location. Further, the leading landowner with whom they negotiated, Dr. Oliver Tiffany, refused to consider a reasonable offer for the purchase of the land for a courthouse square and other requirements. Rather than buy up land at an exhorbitant price, the commission decided to turn to Simcoe's Crown Reserve at the Forks for the settlement. The only real drawback to the site was the lack of good roads. Once such thoroughfares as Hamilton Road were completed this problem would be overcome.

The committee's decision was well received by the provincial authorities at York. Lieutenant-Governor Sir Peregrine Maitland and his chief advisor, the Reverend Dr. John Strachan, who was Church of

England Rector of York as well as the virtual prime minister of the province, felt that a conservative centre of government could grow up here. Time has not proved them wrong.

On January 30, 1826, Governor Maitland signed the act transferring the district town to the Forks; London was at last underway. The studied choice of Governor Simcoe and his early preparations in the far west had had their results, even if not at as exalted a level as he had planned. With its designation as a district town London achieved the first real impetus in its development as the administrative centre of the entire Southwestern Peninsula, with an area at its command that stretched north from Lake Erie to Lake Huron and Georgian Bay, west to what is now the Lambton-Kent boundary, and east nearly to Brantford.

The exact location of the townsite was left open by the legislation, which only specified "within some part of the reservation heretofore made for the site of a town, near the forks of the river Thames, in the townships of London and Westminster, in the county of Middlesex." Simcoe had probably intended to use a site on the south side of the Thames between the coves and the Forks; however, Mahlon Burwell, who was deputed to do the actual survey by provincial Surveyor-General Thomas Ridout, selected the present site to the northeast of the Forks, where the courthouse was built atop the rising hillside. In all Burwell surveyed an area which spread from the river on the south and west to Wellington Street on the east and the line of present-day Queens Avenue and Carling Street on the north. The many streams, marshy areas, and bogs made the survey very difficult for the party.

The survey was undertaken in May and June of 1826 and the new streets named in a burst of loyalty typical of the period. Dundas Street, of course, was the end of Simcoe's road from the east. The other names, except for North Street (Queens Avenue), chiefly commemorated prominent people of the settlement or in England. From west to east these honored Surveyor-General Thomas Ridout; Thomas Talbot; a former Governor of Canada, the Duke of Richmond; and the Duke of Clarence, a brother of the king. Going south from Dundas Street, streets were named for King George IV; the Duke of York, another brother; Colonial Secretary Lord Bathurst; Colonial Under-Secretary Robert Wilmot-Horton; and, of course, Lieutenant-Governor Simcoe.

While the courthouse was under construction, a temporary squared-log structure was erected on the northeast corner of the courthouse block. Here the first Court of Quarter Sessions for the London District was held on January 29, 1827. On completion of the courthouse in 1829 the building was moved to the southwest corner of the block, where it served as the London District Grammar School and as a storehouse until it was demolished circa 1929. Courtesy, London Historical Museums

As well as surveying streets for the town it was necessary to build a new district courthouse. This was a multi-purpose building for all government services. It was used as an office for the district officials, as a meeting place for the magistrates who governed the London District, as a courthouse for both the local hearings of the provincial high court, and for the sessions of the District Court. Finally, it was a jail. Even before the actual survey Mahlon Burwell had begun meetings with the committee appointed to supervise the construction of the courthouse. This was composed of Burwell; Thomas Talbot; James Hamilton, later to be the sheriff of the district; Charles Ingersoll, a brother of Laura Secord; and again Captain John Mathews. Convening in St. Thomas, the committee selected the partnership of John Ewart and Thomas Parke to design the building and superintend the work. Ewart, who rarely came to London, was one of the leading Toronto builders, his designs including the original part of Osgoode Hall. Parke, who actually superintended most of the work, settled in London and later became a member of the Legislative Assembly and a newspaper proprietor.

To honor Colonel Thomas Talbot the construction committee decided to erect a Gothic courthouse supposedly copying his ancestral home, Malahide Castle, just north of Dublin, Ireland. Ewart accordingly drew up the plans for the courthouse, which is the west half of the present building. One hundred feet long from north to south, fifty feet wide, and fifty feet high with octagonal towers fourteen feet in diameter at each corner, it was built of brick plastered over with cement on a stone foundation. The plan included offices for the government, the courtroom, and cells for prisoners in the basement. Originally it faced west toward the river. The large bay in the middle of the west side, which may still be seen rising over the later jail, contained the entrance door. Construction brought in a good number of workers, many of them skilled, including Torontonians William Hale, who came to make brick using the clay dug up on nearby Ridout Street, and Robert Carfrae, a carpenter, who later became one of London's early land speculators and had two streets named in his honor. Work started in the middle of 1827 and was mostly completed by 1829. The structure cost 4,000 pounds plus 50 pounds for some alterations.

While the courthouse was underway, local government was set up in a temporary, two-storey, frame structure in 1827. Located at the northwest corner of King and Ridout streets, the building immediately provided a home for the Quarter Sessions, and housed the jailer and any prisoners who were in custody. As well, a two-storey frame house, a barn, and a stable were built on the southeast corner of Dundas and Ridout streets as a residence for the courthouse workers.

SETTLING IN

Settlers soon began to make their appearance, particularly as the government was offering free lots, subject only to the payment of an eight-pound fee for a patent giving land title and the erection of a twenty-four-foot by eighteen-foot cabin. Among the first arrivals was Peter McGregor, a chain-bearer on the survey, who moved to London in October 1826. He built a log shanty, serving as both a house and a tavern, on the southwest corner of King and Ridout streets. He was soon joined by Abraham and John Yerex, who also erected a log cabin. Another early settler was George Jervis Goodhue, who received the first actual land patent in September 1830 for the northeast corner of Dundas and Ridout streets. A Yankee immigrant from New England who had earlier operated a general store along Commissioners Road, Goodhue was to eventually become London's first "millionaire."

The hamlet's road connections began to improve rapidly with the increasing stream of settlers. An American squatter was already operating a ferry across the Thames at York Street before Levi Merrick built the first bridge there in 1826; possibly the first Ridout Street Bridge was built about the same time. Streets were improved and hills were graded to permit teams to pass up and down; logs were laid in rows to form corduroy roads and gravel and broken stone surfaces followed soon after. Outside the city to the west, Wharncliffe Road was surveyed northward in 1824 and the first Blackfriars Bridge opened in 1831.

In 1835 Lieutenant-Governor Sir John Colborne granted London the right to hold a public fair or market, and before long two excellent wells were dug in the market square. There were also pumps before many of the town's hotels. When the Reverend Benjamin Lundy visited the village in 1832, he reported that it had a courthouse, two houses of public worship, three hotels, six general stores—altogether some 130 buildings, almost all of them frame—two doctors, two lawyers, craftsmen, and a newspaper called *The Sun.* He estimated the total population at 300. London was quickly becoming an example of the instant city of the frontier.

GOVERNMENT-ADMINISTRATION

While construction workers, would-be entrepreneurs, and ordinary settlers were glad to flock to the new site, the officials of the London District, who had comfortable homes in the long-settled lakeshore area near Vittoria, were far from ready to move. The opening of London repeated what had happened at York in 1793, when Simcoe transferred the capital from Niagara-on-the-Lake and many district and provincial officials had had to be practically moved by force. Typical of the London District officials was

GEORGE JERVIS GOODHUE

The career of George Jervis Goodhue, London's first large general merchant, land speculator, and mortgage broker, shows how a fortune could be made on the frontier and demonstrates the mobility of nineteenth-century society. Born in Putney, Vermont on August 1, 1799, the son of a medical doctor and grandson of a Congregationalist minister, Goodhue came from a family that was well educated, fairly well off financially, and active in the community. Two of George's three brothers trained as doctors and all three were elected to office after they left New England, becoming respectively members of the legislative assemblies of Lower Canada (Quebec) and Georgia, and the first Chicago City Council. His four sisters ranged less widely; but they married well to an extensive landowner in the Ottawa valley, a New Hampshire state senator, a Vermont member of the United States House of Representatives, and yet another medical doctor.

After some education in Amherst, Massachusetts, Goodhue migrated west in 1820 and settled in Westminster Township in what is now the Byron area of London. Probably with the help of family funding, he opened a general store where he "sold everything the settlers wanted and bought everything they had to sell." He also operated a distillery and made potash for export. By 1825 he was well enough established to visit home, where he married Maria Fullerton of Chester, Vermont who died in 1828, leaving him with one daughter. Fullarton Street is named in her memory. After the establishment of London, Goodhue moved his store to the courthouse square about 1830, the same year in which he was appointed postmaster, an office which he retained until 1852 and which was a real asset to any pioneer merchant's operation. In 1832 he formed a partnership with Lawrence Lawrason. Their business must have been a very profitable one, for when they wound it up amicably in 1840 Goodhue is reported to have received $40,000 as his share.

By that time he was finding investment in land and mortgages a lucrative occupation. He had begun purchasing land at Byron, invested extensively at London, and, after the Rebellion of 1837, picked up some rebel estates around the region. Like most merchants Goodhue and Lawrason were active in lending money for mortgages, and they acted as agents for the Bank of Upper Canada until it opened a London branch in 1836. Both were later elected directors of the bank, Goodhue holding a directorship from 1848 to 1856. He was also involved with the 1830s railway promotions, but after that he stayed out of developmental projects. However, he invested in British bonds and Canadian bank stock, and was a shareholder in the Huron & Erie Loan and Savings Society.

Goodhue showed little interest in politics, except for offices which would confer a certain dignity, or could be used to forward his business interests. In 1840 he successfully ran for office in the only contest of his life and was elected councillor for St. George's Ward in the first London Council. His fellow councillors then chose him as the first town president (mayor). In 1831 he married a local girl, Louisa Mathews, whose father was Captain John Mathews, an MLA who had sat on the early commissions establishing London and in his eccentric way was a Reformer in politics. This placed Goodhue at least theoretically in the Reform, or Liberal, camp. That group included many other American immigrants, such as Hyman and the Leonards. In 1841, with the first Reform government in power provincially, he was appointed a justice of the peace. When a legislative councillor (senator) was needed for the southwestern region, he was an obvious candidate. Now a member of the Church of England, Goodhue, who was not given to charity, made the Methodists a considerable gift, reportedly fifty dollars, and there was no opposition to his appointment. Thus he became the "Honorable George J. Goodhue." With the decline in his health in the mid-1860s, possibly caused by tuberculosis, he ceased to attend and was not appointed to the new Canadian Senate in 1867.

When Goodhue died in London on January 11, 1870, he left an estate estimated at about $650,000. His will, which provided that his money should not be distributed after his wife's death, was hotly contested by his children and their spouses, who attempted to have it broken by provincial statute. The money was finally distributed after Louisa's death in 1880 and went partly to build several huge mansions, including "Waverley" and what is now the Central Baptist Church in London, which are no longer associated with his name. Today his only memorial is a stained glass window in the sanctuary of St. Paul's Cathedral. In London's folk memory he has gone

George Jervis Goodhue died as London's wealthiest citizen. On the city's founding he immediately established himself as a general merchant; the bulk of his fortune, however, was made in land speculation and mortgages. From Campbell, Pioneer Days in London, *1921. Courtesy, UWO*

down as a tight-fisted millionaire, who made his money by charging heavily on mortgages. His career typified a phase of any frontier community when the pioneer merchant was at the centre of business and among the most important men in the city.

Sheriff Daniel Rapelje, who came to London to take the oath of office and then handed the duties over to his son as deputy. The town had no regular sheriff until James Hamilton was appointed in 1837. The case of the District Court judge was much the same. James Mitchell, the incumbent, an old school buddy of Dr. Strachan's at the University of Aberdeen, remained in the southern regions until he was finally ousted.

Significantly, those who came more quickly were appointed to office by the District Quarter Sessions, not, as in the case of the legal officials, by the remote provincial government at York. Most outstanding of these early Londoners was John Harris, treasurer of the district since 1821, who quickly obtained a land grant to the north of the courthouse. In 1834 Harris built the oldest part of "Eldon House," which was to remain the family home until the heirs presented it to the City of London in 1960. The Harris mansion rapidly became the center of social life in the village. There John, his wife Amelia Ryerse, who was related to the old Lake Erie shore families, and their many daughters and sons organized a wide variety of entertainments: balls, parties, and such sporting events as sleighing expeditions. The district clerk of the peace, Jean-Baptiste Askin, descendant of the local squirearchy of the Windsor-Detroit region, moved to Westminster Township where he built a comfortable mansion at Wortley Road and Elmwood Avenue overlooking the south branch of the Thames River.

Although townships were allowed to elect their own minor officials, who handled matters such as road allowances, fence lines, and assessments, the government of any district was basically in the hands of the appointed justices of the peace of the Quarter Sessions, so named because they met four times a year. The Quarter Sessions handled all major administrative and financial questions of district government, as well as minor criminal cases. Other cases were attended to by the District Court with its judge; but important cases such as murders were reserved for the Assizes, circuit hearings presided over by one of the justices of the Court of the King's Bench from York, who travelled around the province at specified times.

The first meeting of the Quarter Sessions at London took place on January 9, 1827, under the chairmanship of Colonel Samuel Ryerse, Amelia Harris' father, who came up to London for the meeting. With their broad administrative and judicial power, the magistrates' actions were the most important factor governing the lives of the settlers. Much of their

Above: *Erected for John Harris in 1834 and designed in the Regency style of architecture, "Eldon House" remains one of the oldest surviving buildings in London. During the city's early history, it was the centre of the social and cultural elite of the fledgling town, which from 1838 included the officers of the British Garrison. Courtesy, London Historical Museums*

Opposite page: *This caricature, one of several drawn in the 1840s by Middlesex County Judge William Elliot (1812-1905), carries the caption, "They've got up a thing they call moral force, but I believe there's nothin' equal to the lock & key after all." It depicts London District gaoler Samuel H. Parke, who had little sympathy for legal reform. Significantly, this drawing is the only known depiction of the interior of the first London District gaol, located in the basement of the 1827-1829 courthouse. Courtesy, UWO*

work was routine—assessments, road and bridge construction and repair—but there were periodic emergency situations.

One of the worst was the cholera outbreak of 1832, which was the first really major epidemic to hit Upper Canada and showed the difficulties faced by public health authorities in a crisis situation. The Asiatic cholera, which had been sweeping across Europe for some years, was brought to North America on the immigrant ships in 1832. The whole Great Lakes basin was very badly affected with a mortality rate of probably 10 percent. Since the cause of the disease was unknown—contaminated water was one of the main sources of infection—quarantine was poorly enforced. As usually happened, the disease spread more rapidly among the poor and the intemperate. In London the cholera broke out in July and by August 2 the *London Sun* reported that there had been forty-seven cases and thirteen deaths. The obituaries of the deceased were frequently given in a blunt man-

ner typical of the period: "An industrious old man, but rather intemperate," or, "very intemperate."

Before long, people were fleeing to the countryside and the town was virtually deserted. It was reported that twenty-seven men and their families were all who remained and that twenty houses were closed on Dundas Street alone. By the end of July sixteen people were dead, including Dr. Patrick Donnelly, a Royal Naval surgeon who attempted to treat the sick. A cholera hospital was established on Hamilton Road east of the city and at least fifteen died there, although the overall total may have been two or three times that number. In October, with the coming of cold weather, the disease died away and people returned to the town. There were, however, serious repetitions in 1849 and 1854.

COURTS, LAWYERS, AND CRIME

With the three levels of court hearings at the Quarter Sessions, District Court, and Assizes, the town quickly became a focus for lawyers and litigants.

As well there were the unhappy jurors whose condition has been well described by Dr. Clarence T. Campbell, one of London's first historians:

People attending the first courts did not find it by any means comfortable. Hotel accommodation was limited—extremely—and jurors and suitors were well off who could locate themselves in some neighboring farmer's barn, and find a bed in the hay loft. Of course, there was always the woods to camp in. They brought with them their own meals—boiled pork and bread, or sausages, and hard-tack of any description, with, of course, whiskey to drink. Springs on the river bank provided them with delicious cool water; but in most cases that was only required to dilute the whiskey of those who did not take the booze in its full strength. It is said that sometimes, after the trial of a case, the jury would retire to the courtyard and have a smoke, while they considered their verdict. If the

Above: *"Thornwood" is one of the survivors of the great country estates built in London in the boom years of the 1850s. Erected in 1852 for London lawyer Henry C.R. Becher, it was pleasantly perched on the edge of a bluff overlooking the Thames River valley. This great Gothic Revival mansion on St. George Street remained with Becher descendants until sold in 1984. Courtesy, UWO*

Right: *Arriving in London in 1835, Henry Corry Rowley Becher (1817-1885) became a protege of the Harris family of "Eldon House." He studied law in the office of John Wilson and was admitted to the bar in 1841. Although unsuccessful in politics, he was for nearly a half-century one of London's leading lawyers, acting as executor of the Thomas Talbot and George Jervis Goodhue estates. Courtesy, UWO*

Opposite page: *Considered the ablest lawyer in Southwestern Ontario, John Wilson built a lucrative practice. He also held a variety of local offices, including that of London District superintendent of education. "Honest John Wilson's" personal popularity resulted in his election to the Legislative Assembly both as a Conservative and as a Reformer. He was appointed Judge of the Court of Common Pleas in 1863. Courtesy, London Room*

court happened to be short of constables, one would take the prisoner out and chain him to a stump; then seat himself in a position where he could watch the jury with one eye, and the prisoner with another.

In early days both judges and juries collected their payment in the form of fees and at times both suffered equally from not getting paid by unscrupulous lawyers. The jurors, who received a sum equivalent to twenty cents for District Court cases and twenty-five cents for the Assizes cases, no matter how long the trial lasted, did have a hold over the lawyers. If it looked as if their fee would not be paid they simply held up their verdict until they had first received their money. Similarly, the judge, who was paid by fees only, would refuse to sign his name to the record until he received his one-dollar due.

On the evidence of eyewitness accounts the District Court judges for the London area were not a particularly competent group. David L. Hughes, a young lawyer who later became County Judge of Elgin, described a case before Judge James Mitchell. The lawyer involved was James Givens, an important early citizen.

I remember a case in which a witness bearing the name of Barnard Mackleroy was called to give evidence on behalf of one of the suitors, when the lawyer conducting the case asked the judge to take down the evidence the witness was giving. The judge had not been taking any notes at all.

"Will your honor please take that down?"

"Yes, Mr. Givins, I will take that down." With that he began fumbling with his pen in his book.

"Now, will your honor be pleased to read what you have taken down?"

"Yes, Mr. Givins, I have taken down that the witness says Barnard Mackleroy is dead."

"But your honor, the witness is Barnard Mackleroy."

"I cannot help that. If the witness chooses to swear that he is dead, I cannot help it."

So the case proceeded.

When it came to the judge's charge, he said:

"Gentlemen of the jury, you have heard the evidence, and I have not. The fact is, I am a little deaf in my left ear (the jurors sat on that side) but, gentlemen of the jury, I must tell you that if you think the evidence adduced on the part of the plaintiff is the more satisfactory, it will be your duty to find a verdict for the plaintiff for such damages as you think him justly entitled to, but if, on the contrary, gentlemen, you think the evidence adduced on

the part of the defence preponderates, and is the more convincing it is my duty as an upright and just judge to tell you that, regardless of consequences, it is your duty to find a verdict for the defendant."

"Your honor, is that the charge?"

"Yes, Mr. Givins, that is the charge."

"Short and sweet, your honor."

Some of London's early lawyers were later to play a leading role in the affairs of the city and province. John Wilson, who came from Eastern Ontario where he had fought one of Upper Canada's last duels, was not only a leading barrister, but also one of the most prominent members of parliament. Henry Corry Rowley Becher arrived from England about 1835 as a protege of the Harris family. Within the year he was articling with Wilson. He later married Sarah E. Leonard, a member of the prominent iron founding family. Their 1852 home, "Thornwood," which still stands on St. George Street, originally had an estate of some thirteen acres. Becher held many prominent legal posts, including a benchership of the provincial Law Society, and was executor of several important estates, including those of Thomas Talbot and George Jervis Goodhue. Still, despite being a good friend of Sir John A. Macdonald, Becher himself was

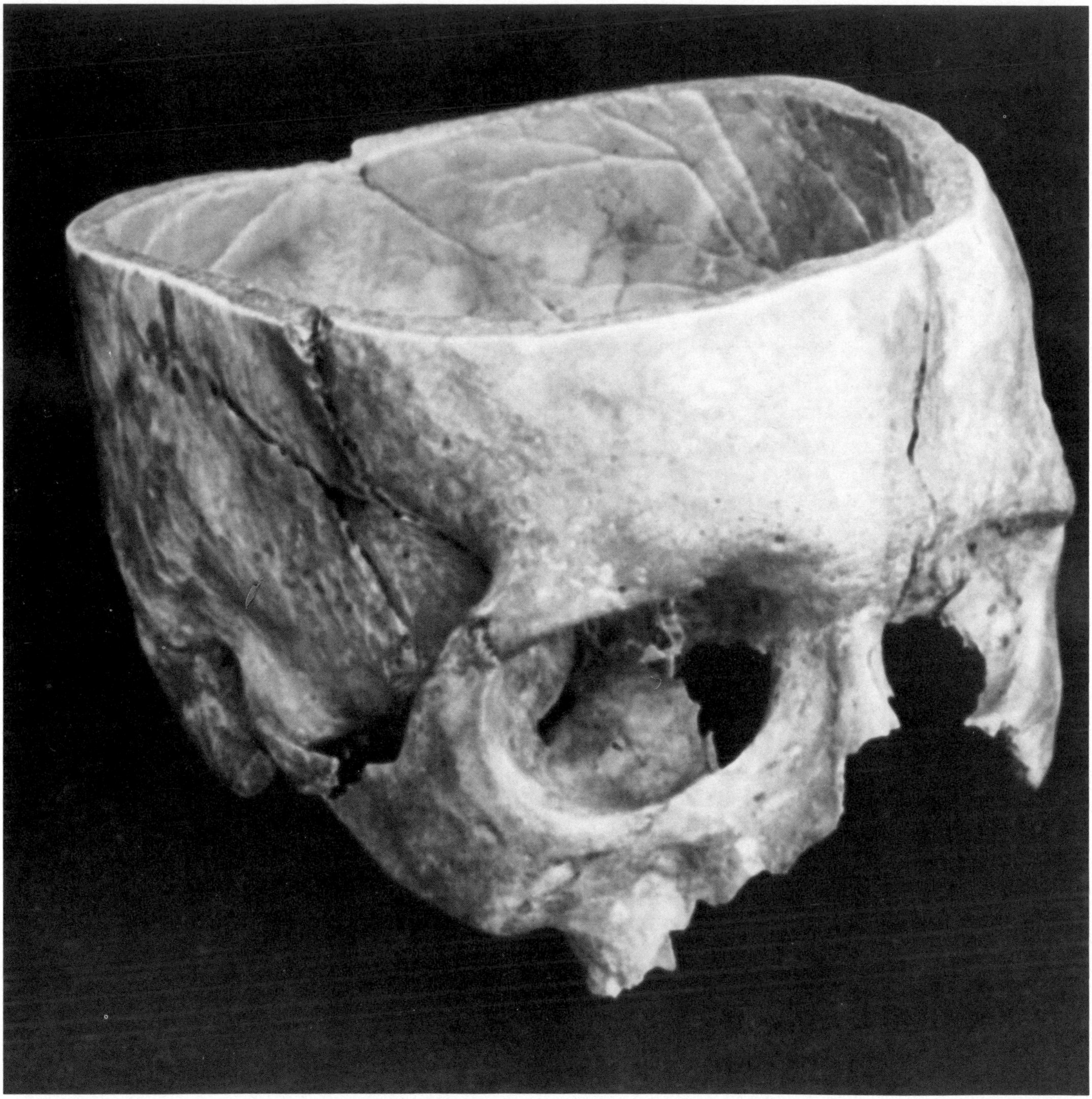

Orson Squire Fowler, a Yale medical student who had examined Cornelius Burley before his execution, determined that his varying skull thickness ("bumps") revealed criminal tendencies. On the night of the hanging, and in subsequent global tours, Fowler lectured on the pseudo-science known as phrenology with the aid of the skull. Returning to London in the 1880s, he gave the skull to the Harris family of "Eldon House," where it is exhibited today. Courtesy, London Historical Museums

Opposite page: *Cornelius Burley was found guilty of the murder of Constable Timothy C. Pomeroy, whom he allegedly shot on September 16, 1829. Dropping from the scaffold erected in the courthouse square, Burley entered criminal history as the first and second man to be hanged in London—the rope broke on the first try. Before his death, Burley twice confessed his crime to Rev. James Jackson. The* Gore Balance *printed the confession in handbill form. Courtesy, London Historical Museums*

never successful in his attempts to attain political office.

From the very first London has had some spectacular murder trials, beginning with that of Cornelius Alverson Burley, charged in 1830 with the murder of Constable Timothy Conklin Pomeroy. Burley was tried before the Assizes, with Judge James Buchanan Macaulay presiding, and found guilty on his own confession. Yet, what really happened remains a mystery. Burley, a pathetic, illiterate, unintelligent individual, was associated with a notorious family called the Ribbles; there was some question whether he had committed the murder, or if one of the Ribbles was responsible. Nevertheless, the Reverend James Jackson, a Wesleyan Methodist clergyman who appears to have been the Ribbles' minister, persuaded Burley to confess after he had been sentenced to death. It is not known whether Jackson deliberately contorted the case or just enjoyed publicity.

Burley's hanging in August 1830 was the first in London, and like all executions in the city until 1868 it was done publicly. A mob of about 3,000 assembled at the courthouse square to enjoy the proceedings, partly spurred on by the antics of the Reverend Mr. Jackson, who from the scaffold read a confession obtained after the conviction. He later had 1,000 copies printed as a handbill and sold them. The first rope broke; but fortunately for Burley the grizzly scene ended when the second rope proved sound. As a final indignity, visiting Yale medical student Orson Squire Fowler—who went on to become a millionaire phrenologist and designer of octagonal houses to catch healthful winds—obtained Burley's skull after the ensuing public dissection. For many years he demonstrated it around the continent, pointing out the bumps on a murderer's head; what is left today rests in "Eldon House." London's second murder case followed shortly when the Assizes of August 1832 tried Henry Sovereene for the murder of his wife and seven children and ordered him hanged. Sovereene, an unsavory character who had already been mixed up with various forms of petty larceny such as shooting a horse, was duly executed.

Fortunately, most crimes were of a relatively minor nature. London's first recorded offence occurred during the building of Westminster Bridge when a workman was caught stealing an axe belonging to one of his fellows. An impromptu jury decided that the culprit should be banished or whipped, although it is not clear what punishment was inflicted. The seamy side of the pioneer town, quick to develop as always, is shown by the trial of John McDonald, a grocer, who in April 1838 was found guilty at the Quarter Sessions of keeping London's earliest known "disorderly house." The largest number of convictions seem to have been for simple debt. At that time a debtor could still be committed to jail, but if he obtained bail posted by two competent men he could be released to limited freedom within certain established limits. These were set by six-inch-square posts painted red, which were placed on each major road one mile from the town. They bore a legend in large white letters, "JAIL LIMIT 1 MILE." If the debtor made the mistake of going further he was to be quickly returned to his cell.

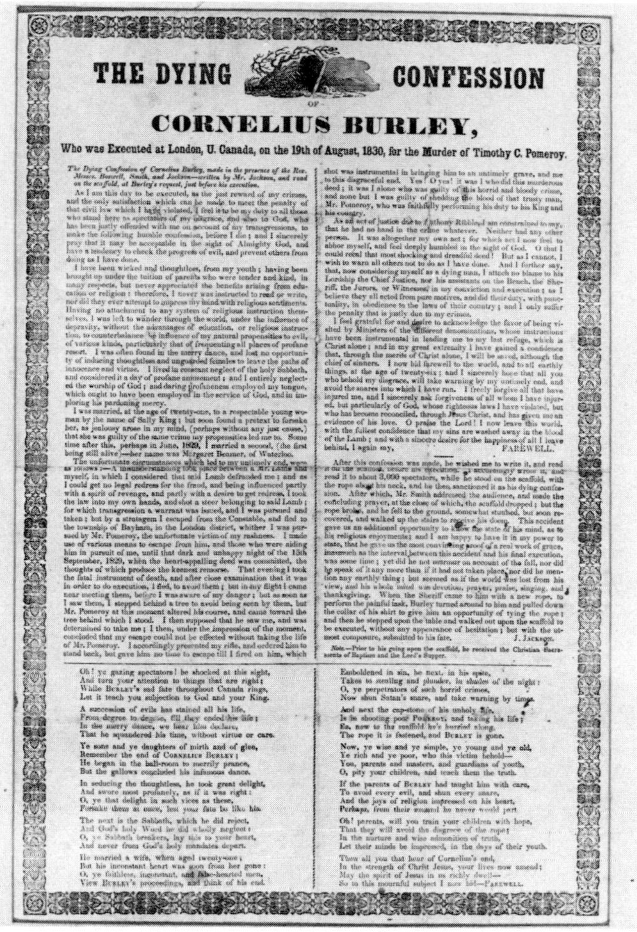
THE DYING CONFESSION

OF

CORNELIUS BURLEY,

Who was Executed at London, U. Canada, on the 19th of August, 1830, for the Murder of Timothy C. Pomeroy.

The Dying Confession of Cornelius Burley, made in the presence of the Rev. Messrs. Boswell, Smith, and Jackson—written by Mr. Jackson, and read on the scaffold, at Burley's request, just before his execution.

As I am this day to be executed, as the just reward of my crimes, and the only satisfaction which can be made to meet the penalty of that civil law which I have violated, I feel it to be my duty to all those who stand here as spectators of my disgrace, and also to God, who has been justly offended with me on account of my transgressions, to make the following humble confession, before I die; and I sincerely pray that it may be acceptable in the sight of Almighty God, and have a tendency to check the progress of evil, and prevent others from doing as I have done.

I have been wicked and thoughtless, from my youth; having been brought up under the tuition of parents who were tender and kind, in many respects, but never appreciated the benefits arising from education or religion: therefore, I never was instructed to read or write, nor did they ever attempt to impress my mind with religious sentiments. Having no attachment to any system of religious instruction themselves, I was left to wander through the world, under the influence of depravity, without the advantages of education, or religious instruction, to counterbalance the influence of my natural propensities to evil, of various kinds, particularly that of frequenting all places of profane resort. I was often found in the merry dance, and lost no opportunity of inducing thoughtless and unguarded females to leave the paths of innocence and virtue. I lived in constant neglect of the holy Sabbath, and considered it a day of profane amusement; and I entirely neglected the worship of God; and daring profaneness employed my tongue, which ought to have been employed in the service of God, and in imploring his pardoning mercy.

I was married, at the age of twenty-one, to a respectable young woman by the name of Sally King; but soon found a pretext to forsake her, as jealousy arose in my mind, (perhaps without any just cause,) that she was guilty of the same crime my propensities led me to. Some time after this, perhaps in June, 1829, I married a second, (the first being still alive)—her name was Margaret Benner, of Waterloo.

The unfortunate circumstances which led to my untimely end, were as follows:—A misunderstanding took place between a Mr. Lamb and myself, in which I considered that said Lamb defrauded me; and as I could get no legal redress for the fraud, and being influenced partly with a spirit of revenge, and partly with a desire to get redress, I took the law into my own hands, and shot a steer belonging to said Lamb; for which transgression a warrant was issued, and I was pursued and taken; but by a stratagem I escaped from the Constable, and fled to the township of Bayham, in the London district, whither I was pursued by Mr. Pomeroy, the unfortunate victim of my rashness. I made use of various means to escape from him, and those who were aiding him in pursuit of me, until that dark and unhappy night of the 15th September, 1829, when the heart-appalling deed was committed, the thoughts of which produce the keenest remorse. That evening I took the fatal instrument of death, and after close examination that it was in order to do execution, I fled, to avoid them; but in my flight I came near meeting them, before I was aware of my danger; but as soon as I saw them, I stepped behind a tree to avoid being seen by them, but Mr. Pomeroy at this moment altered his course, and came toward the tree behind which I stood. I then supposed that he saw me, and was determined to take me; I then, under the impression of the moment, concluded that my escape could not be effected without taking the life of Mr. Pomeroy. I accordingly presented my rifle, and ordered him to stand back, but gave him no time to escape till I fired on him, which shot was instrumental in bringing him to an untimely grave, and me to this disgraceful end. Yes! O yes! it was I who did this murderous deed; it was I alone who was guilty of this horrid and bloody crime, and none but I was guilty of shedding the blood of that trusty man, Mr. Pomeroy, who was faithfully performing his duty to his King and his country.

As an act of justice due to Anthony Ribble, I am constrained to say, that he had no hand in the crime whatever. Neither had any other person. It was altogether my own act; for which act I now feel to abhor myself, and feel deeply humbled in the sight of God. O that I could recal that most shocking and dreadful deed! But as I cannot, I wish to warn all others not to do as I have done. And I further say, that, now considering myself as a dying man, I attach no blame to his Lordship the Chief Justice, nor his assistants on the Bench, the Sheriff, the Jurors, or Witnesses, in my conviction and execution; as I believe they all acted from pure motives, and did their duty, with punctuality, in obedience to the laws of their country; and I only suffer the penalty that is justly due to my crimes.

I feel grateful for and desire to acknowledge the favor of being visited by Ministers of the different denominations, whose instructions have been instrumental in leading me to my last refuge, which is Christ alone; and in my great extremity I have gained a confidence that, through the merits of Christ alone, I will be saved, although the chief of sinners. I now bid farewell to the world, and to all earthly things, at the age of twenty-six; and I sincerely hope that all you who behold my disgrace, will take warning by my untimely end, and avoid the snares into which I have run. I freely forgive all that have injured me, and I sincerely ask forgiveness of all whom I have injured, but particularly of God, whose righteous laws I have violated, but who has become reconciled, through Jesus Christ, and has given me an evidence of his love. O praise the Lord! I now leave this world, with the fullest confidence that my sins are washed away in the blood of the Lamb; and with a sincere desire for the happiness of all I leave behind, I again say,

FAREWELL.

After this confession was made, he wished me to write it, and read it on the scaffold, before his execution. I accordingly wrote it, and read it to about 3,000 spectators, while he stood on the scaffold, with the rope about his neck, and he then sanctioned it as his dying confession. After which, Mr. Smith addressed the audience, and made the concluding prayer, at the close of which, the scaffold dropped; but the rope broke, and he fell to the ground, somewhat stunned, but soon recovered, and walked up the stairs to receive his doom. This accident gave us an additional opportunity to know the state of his mind, as to his religious enjoyments; and I am happy to have it in my power to state, that he gave us the most convincing proof of a real work of grace, inasmuch as the interval between this accident and his final execution, was some time; yet did he not murmur on account of the fall, nor did he speak of it any more than if it had not taken place, nor did he mention any earthly thing; but seemed as if the world was lost from his view, and his whole mind was devotion, prayer, praise, singing, and thanksgiving. When the Sheriff came to him with a new rope, to perform the painful task, Burley turned around to him and pulled down the collar of his shirt to give him an opportunity of tying the rope; and then he stepped upon the table and walked out upon the scaffold to be executed, without any appearance of hesitation; but with the utmost composure, submitted to his fate.

J. Jackson.

Note.—Prior to his going upon the scaffold, he received the Christian Sacraments of Baptism and the Lord's Supper.

Oh! ye gazing spectators! be shocked at this sight,
And turn your attention to things that are right;
While Burley's sad fate throughout Canada rings,
Let it teach you subjection to God and your King.

A succession of evils has stained all his life,
From degree to degree, till they ended his life;
In the merry dance, we hear him declare,
That he squandered his time, without virtue or care.

Ye sons and ye daughters of mirth and of glee,
Remember the end of Cornelius Burley;
He began in the ball-room to merrily prance,
But the gallows concluded his infamous dance.

In seducing the thoughtless, he took great delight,
And swore most profanely, as if it was right:
O, ye that delight in such vices as these,
Forsake them at once, lest your fate be like his.

The next is the Sabbath, which he did reject,
And God's holy Word he did wholly neglect:
O, ye Sabbath breakers, lay this to your heart,
And never from God's holy mandates depart.

He married a wife, when aged twenty-one;
But his inconstant heart was soon from her gone:
O, ye faithless, inconstant, and false-hearted men,
View Burley's proceedings, and think of his end.

Emboldened in sin, he next, in his spite,
Takes to stealing and plunder, in shades of the night:
O, ye perpetrators of such horrid crimes,
Now shun Satan's snare, and take warning by times.

And next the cap-stone of his unholy life,
Is in shooting poor Pomeroy, and taking his life;
So, now to the scaffold he's hurried along,
The rope it is fastened, and Burley is gone.

Now, ye wise and ye simple, ye young and ye old,
Ye rich and ye poor, who this victim behold—
You, parents and masters, and guardians of youth,
O, pity your children, and teach them the truth.

If the parents of Burley had taught him with care,
To avoid every evil, and shun every snare,
And the joys of religion impressed on his heart,
Perhaps, from their counsel he never would part.

Oh! parents, will you train your children with hope,
That they will avoid the disgrace of the rope;
In the nurture and wise admonition of truth,
Let their minds be impressed, in the days of their youth.

Then all you that hear of Cornelius's end,
In the strength of Christ Jesus, your lives now amend;
May the spirit of Jesus in us richly dwell—
So to this mournful subject I now bid—Farewell.

PROVINCIAL POLITICS

Although the Upper Canadian provincial government and its policies might be largely remote from London, provincial politics, and the election of members for the Legislative Assembly, played a lively role in the history of the community from the beginning. Until 1836 London voted as part of the County of Middlesex, which elected two members to the Legis-

The politics of Sir Francis Bond Head (1793-1875), lieutenant-governor of Upper Canada, encouraged the 1837 Rebellion. Virulently opposed to Reformers, branding them "The Republican party," he campaigned against them in the Legislative Assembly elections of 1836. In order to help ensure a Tory victory, Head elevated London to a separate riding, confident of the town's support. Courtesy, Public Archives of Ontario

lative Assembly. During the years before the 1837 rebellion the county returns typified the political flip-flopping from Tory (Conservative) to Reformer (Liberal) which took place in many parts of the province. The very system of holding elections contributed to the general levity of the procedures. A contest atmosphere was created by the fact that the polls were open for a week with results tabulated and published each day. Further, the polls were usually held in taverns, there was no secret ballot, and supporters of various candidates did whatever they could to either coerce or disqualify electors. An election usually verged on being a no-holds-barred contest.

Early Middlesex elections were held with a single poll at St. Thomas, so it was very difficult for anyone in the London area to vote. In 1820 Middlesex had elected two Conservatives, Mahlon Burwell and John Bostwick; but in 1824 the county reversed itself, voting for Dr. John Rolph, a leading Reformer who would have been president of the Republic of Upper Canada had the rebellion succeeded, and Captain John Mathews, a member of various commissions for establishing London. In 1828 Rolph and Mathews again carried the field, with 340 and 317 votes respectively, thus defeating Burwell with 305, and future sheriff James Hamilton, who received 275.

In 1830 the county, like much of the province, voted Tory and Mahlon Burwell was back, this time with Roswell Mount. The events at the 1834 contest give a good idea of the level of provincial politics. As Mount had died, Burwell had a new running mate, Colonel Joseph Brant Clench of Muncey Town. Opposing them were Reformers Thomas Parke of London, the courthouse builder, and Elias Moore. With the province again swinging to Reform a very tight election was obviously coming up. Someone in the Tory camp conceived the ingenious idea of nominating Reform merchant George Jervis Goodhue, who was visiting Montreal and thus was not in a position to decline the nomination. The intent, of course, was to split the Reform vote; but the Reformers quickly rallied their ranks and the perfidious attempt failed to fool anyone. Goodhue received no votes whatsoever, Burwell 372, Clench 346, Parke 518, and Moore 502. Despite the Tory attempt at subterfuge the opposition sat in their seats.

London was not involved in the 1836 county contest, for Lieutenant-Governor Sir Francis Bond Head, out to make sure of a Tory victory, had elevated the village to the status of a separate riding as it now had an adequate population. Besides, he had been assured that he could count on a Tory victory!

MAHLON BURWELL

Colonel Mahlon Burwell surveyed a large part of the twenty-nine townships of the Talbot Settlement in Southwestern Ontario, including the townsite of London in June 1826. Courtesy, UWO

Mahlon Burwell is remembered today as the man whose surveying talents expedited the orderly colonization of a large portion of the Talbot settlement, including the town plot of London. Much of his activity as a surveyor was connected with the colonization efforts of Colonel Talbot, and Burwell was Talbot's associate, good friend, and obedient ally for most of their careers. Only once did he publicly oppose Talbot: when in 1817 the people of the settlement organized the first anniversary dinner for their founder, Burwell surprisingly objected, as he believed honors were only to be bestowed on the dead. As Colonel Talbot's right-hand man he contributed much to the region and gained a degree of prominence almost equal to that of his patron.

Mahlon Burwell was born in New Jersey, on February 18, 1783. After the American Revolution, the Burwell family came to Canada as United Empire Loyalists and took up land in the Niagara Peninsula. As a youth Burwell studied land surveying and was licensed by the government in 1809, the year he established himself at Port Talbot. His surveys included London Township and central London. From 1811 until 1843, when he passed the office to his son Hercules, he was the district land registrar for Middlesex County. He was also collector of customs for Port Talbot from 1820. Much of his time was spent surveying townships and laying out roads, his activities often resulting in heated disputes with Surveyor-General Thomas Ridout. These clashes of authority were all too frequent, as Talbot's routes for the proposed roads invariably differed with those of Ridout, much to the former's benefit. In every such case Burwell naturally obeyed his patron.

During the War of 1812 Burwell was a lieutenant-colonel of the local militia. In 1814, when a marauding band of Americans raided Port Talbot, Burwell almost managed to make his escape through a back door although he was very ill at the time. Before he was able to do so, however, a severe coughing spell betrayed him and he was immediately taken prisoner. Before departing, the Americans torched his property, leaving his wife, family, and aged parents homeless. Burwell was taken to the United States where, as was customary at the time, he was released on parole after pledging his word of honor that he not attempt an escape.

After the war Burwell resumed surveying as well as his other duties, but as he grew older he devoted much of his time to politics. He first entered the political arena in 1812 when, with Talbot's unrestrained and highly improper support, he defeated Benajah Mallory as the member of parliament for Middlesex and Oxford. Years later it was alleged that when Mallory and his supporters arrived at the polls (which were held in Yarmouth, sixty miles from Oxford!), they found Talbot energetically handing out location tickets for land to any, and all, who would vote for his candidate. Burwell remained in the legislature for twelve years until he was ousted in favor of a Reformer. In 1830 he was returned by the voters of Middlesex County, but again defeated in 1834. In 1836 the Reformers held the county, but Burwell was elected as the first representative of the Town of London. Unfortunately, the elections, which were held in London, were marred by violence; on the last day mobs of London Township Orangemen roamed the streets looking for Reformer prey. It was later reported, with good evidence, that the Tories instigated the violence. Burwell maintained his seat for only one parliament, retiring in 1841. As parliament occupied little time in those days he also continued with his surveying and other duties.

Unlike many of his fellow pioneers, Burwell constantly attempted to further his classical education, which was doubtless a challenge on the frontier. Yet, his knowledge did manifest itself—particularly at his sons' expense, who, for the most part, were named for such heroic figures as Leonidas, Hannibal, and Alexander. He also had two daughters, who must have been christened by their mother, as they were named Louise and Mary. Burwell died in London on January 25, 1846, and he was buried at St. Stephen's Cemetery, Dunwich Township. He deeded London its first park on Stanley Street, but it was unfortunately put to use as a potato patch or pasture field and finally cut up into building lots by the city.

London, at last with its own poll, was put on its mettle to show the governor that it could produce. Since it received only one member, as was customary for "urban" areas, Mahlon Burwell, Tory as ever, ran against Reformer John Scatcherd for the honor of first representative of the village. The resulting election was unusually riotous. As one account notes:

When the vote was over Burwell had finally carried the riding by a vote of 37 to Scatcherd 27; London had vindicated Sir Francis' confidence. It had also got itself an investigating committee appointed by the Legislative Assembly to find out what had happened, Anglican clergyman Benjamin Cronyn being a particular object of attention. The investigation accepted the argument that the rioting was not as bad as on militia training day on June 4th—an argument which was probably quite accurate.

THE RISE OF THE BUSINESS COMMUNITY

As the local government was established London's business community expanded to provide the goods and services needed by both the growing town and the increasingly settled hinterland. Thus the settlement early moved to appropriate the roles that were to make it rich: the centre of commerce and manufacturing, and the focal point of distribution and economics in Southwestern Ontario.

Establishing a business community, despite the central location at the Forks and the fact that communications were rapidly improving, was not an easy task. London faced the problems of pioneer settlements right across the eastern seaboard of the continent. The economic growth of any pioneer community was a fragile process, for the frontier tended to become overextended very easily and very quickly. Further, the frontier financial base was always shaky, built as it was on the successful crop production of the farmer, the availability of the goods that had to be shipped over long distances at widely fluctuating prices, and the frequently precarious financial positions of the merchants, their suppliers, and the provincial government. All these problems were intensified by the wild economic swings of the nineteenth century. As an outpost of the British Empire and as a North American city, London was very much subject to a whiplash effect from the waves of expansion and recession spreading out from both the world metropolitan capital at London, England, and the growing continental commercial focus at New York City. Both frequently overexpanded in speculative bursts of development, and London-in-the-Bush, like other frontier posts, was badly hit when the successive bubbles broke.

The village's first years of growth were marked by the general boom which followed the election of President Andrew Jackson and his Democratic party in the United States. Britain also was expanding with the first railway ventures. The result, during London's founding years, was rapid inflation and general overambition. In 1837 this boom broke suddenly and the century witnessed one of its first great financial panics and a depression that lasted for the better part of a decade. Then another boom got underway in association with further railway building. The fact that London came through this period of depression so well, despite the fact that the economic setback was accompanied by a provincial rebellion and invasion threats, is indicative of the village's excellent location.

London's first pioneer entrepreneur, hotel proprietor Peter McGregor, was soon joined by others. One of the most prominent innkeepers was Abraham Carroll, whose "Mansion House" stood on the north side of Dundas Street between Ridout and Talbot. His advertisement of November 24, 1827, in the *Gore Gazette* of Ancaster marks the beginning of London's commercial advertising. Hotel keepers were quickly joined by that extremely prominent but rarely beloved figure, the pioneer general merchant. The merchants' operations were all-embracing: they bought everything, they sold everything, they exported, they imported, they often ran ancillary businesses such as stills and mills, they acted as bankers providing loans and mortgages, and they frequently called their loans and foreclosed their mortgages. Many became extremely wealthy, ending up as vast landowners; others, possibly the more generous ones, failed and sometimes slipped into bankruptcy.

London had outstanding examples of both these types of merchant. The one who ran into periodic financial difficulties, yet has gone down well in the annals of the town, was Dennis O'Brien, whose "goodness of heart" would not allow him to pursue debtors. Taking over a vacant blacksmith's shop about 1827, O'Brien set up a general store in the usual way: he brought in some supplies and built a counter by placing a couple of casks on the floor and laying a couple of planks across their tops. Conversely, the partnership of George Jervis Goodhue and Lawrence Lawrason was a fantastic success. Goodhue established his partnership with Lawrason, a Loyalist Tory, about 1832. Their combination general store, real estate office, and post office at Dun-

das and Ridout streets did extremely well. The firm was dissolved amicably in 1840 and the two partners went on to prominent positions in the city, Goodhue becoming very unpopular through his mortgage brokering. More specialized types of mercantile business were slower to appear, as the population was not large enough to support them.

Industry soon joined commerce and provided the basis of the wealth of some of the greatest London dynasties. The manufacturers quickly demonstrated the importance of the town's location by increasingly selling their products beyond the settlement's boundaries. Both branches of the Thames provided water power sufficient to run mills, but the North Branch had more good sites. Courthouse builder Thomas Parke erected London's first grist mill in 1833 and sold it to Dennis O'Brien a year later in 1834. Named the Blackfriars Mill, it was constructed near the location of Blackfriars Bridge.

Above left: *Formerly a pedlar, Dennis O'Brien (1792-1865) located permanently in London in 1826, becoming the town's first general merchant. In 1836-1837 he erected London's first brick business block. He also engaged in land speculation, but unlike his avaricious competitor George Jervis Goodhue, O'Brien was generous with his debtors. From Campbell,* Pioneer Days in London, *1921. Courtesy, UWO*

Above right: *Lawrence Lawrason was an early London merchant, MLA, and large-scale land speculator who was in partnership with George Jervis Goodhue in a general store from 1832 to 1840. Lawrason also was president of the London and Port Stanley Railway. Bankrupted by the depression of 1857, he was police magistrate from 1866 until his death in 1882. Courtesy, UWO*

The milling of flour and grain was one of London's staple economic functions in its early history. One of the numerous mills built within the vicinity of the town along the Thames River was the North Branch Mill, or Saunby's Mill, in London West. Joseph D. Saunby and William Hilliard acquired the building in the 1860s. Courtesy, UWO

The oldest surviving London firm, now Labatt's Brewery, began in 1828 when John Balkwill opened his London Brewery at the same location where the plant still stands, southwest of Richmond and Horton streets at the Thames. The firm passed to the partnership of Eccles and Labatt in 1847 and seven years later came fully into the ownership of the Labatt family. A year after Labatt's, in 1829, future Mayor Simeon Morrill opened his tannery near Ridout and Dundas streets. It rapidly developed into a profitable business and before long Morrill was selling hides as far away as Chicago. A rival appeared in Ellis Walton Hyman's tannery, opened about 1833. Hyman went on to build a diversified business empire which dealt in shoes and leather as well as hides. He became one of London's most important financiers, as did Elijah Leonard, Jr., like Hyman an American immigrant, who had been engaged in the foundry business in St. Thomas since 1834. After the Upper Canadian Rebellion, in 1838, he moved to London and established one of the most important and long-lasting manufactories in the city's history.

For these businessmen, or indeed, for any Londoner, communicating with the world outside presented difficult problems. The roads to both Ancaster and Port Stanley were in dreadful shape at best. As well, steamship routes were just developing on Lake Erie. By the late 1820s some signs of improvement were evident. In 1827 the legislature gave permission for mail stagecoaches to run on the route from Niagara-on-the-Lake through London to Sandwich opposite Detroit. The stages began operating in July 1828, and the joys of travel are well demonstrated by the schedule. Thrice weekly the coach left Niagara at 3 a.m. for the four-day trip to Sandwich. Stopping at Queenston at 4 a.m., St. Catharines at 7 a.m., and Ancaster at 3 p.m., it hopefully reached Brantford sometime the first evening. At 4 a.m. the next day the coachman hastened on to Burford, Oxford, and finally the second night's stop in Westminster Township near London.

At London the first stagecoach inn was at Swart's Tavern, inconveniently located on Commissioners Road just west of Wellington Road far south of the town. From 1833, with London's increasing size, the coaches ran up to the downtown Hawley Brothers' King's Arms Hotel. For those Niagara passengers who wished to continue west and those Londoners travelling to the American border, the stage rattled away for a third day at 4 a.m., stopping at the Thames crossing. Finally, after yet another long day's journey, it reached Sandwich in the evening, hopefully in time for the passengers to catch a boat for Detroit. The return trip to Niagara left at the same pre-dawn hours and again took four days. It was a typical, gruelling pioneer journey, during which the schedule was frequently interrupted by bad roads, broken axles or wheels, or just the vagaries of the weather.

In 1833 the Hawley Brothers began a thrice weekly stage from London to St. Thomas, leaving the village after the mail from the east-west coach had been received. At St. Thomas the passengers and mail could transfer to the St. Thomas-Port Stanley stage. Then, at Port Stanley, the Thames Steamer was available on its twice weekly circuit to connect with the Erie Canal boats at Buffalo and eventually, New York City. For those leaving London the last part of the trip to New York along the canal's peaceful waters must have been absolute heaven after the dust and ruts of the road and the choppy crossing of Lake Erie.

The London settlement had a post office with Lawrence Lawrason as postmaster from March 1825,

In 1847 John Kinder Labatt, in partnership with Samuel Eccles, purchased John Balkwill's 1828 London Brewery. By 1854, when Labatt bought Eccles' interest, John Labatt's Brewery employed six men and had an annual capacity of 4,000 barrels. Still operating on its original Simcoe Street site, John Labatt, Ltd., is London's oldest business. Courtesy, Labatt Brewing Company, Ltd.

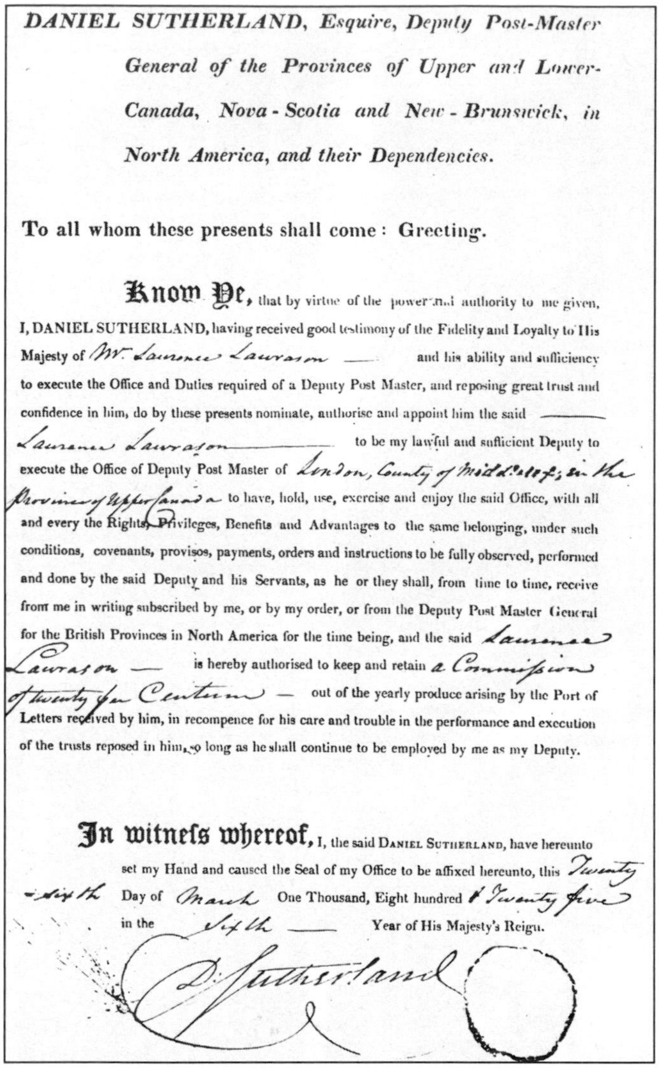

DANIEL SUTHERLAND, Esquire, Deputy Post-Master General of the Provinces of Upper and Lower-Canada, Nova-Scotia and New-Brunswick, in North America, and their Dependencies.

To all whom these presents shall come: Greeting.

Know Ye, that by virtue of the power and authority to me given, I, DANIEL SUTHERLAND, having received good testimony of the Fidelity and Loyalty to His Majesty of Mr. Laurence Lawrason and his ability and sufficiency to execute the Office and Duties required of a Deputy Post Master, and reposing great trust and confidence in him, do by these presents nominate, authorise and appoint him the said Laurence Lawrason to be my lawful and sufficient Deputy to execute the Office of Deputy Post Master of London, County of Middlesex, in the Province of Upper Canada to have, hold, use, exercise and enjoy the said Office, with all and every the Rights, Privileges, Benefits and Advantages to the same belonging, under such conditions, covenants, provisos, payments, orders and instructions to be fully observed, performed and done by the said Deputy and his Servants, as he or they shall, from time to time, receive from me in writing subscribed by me, or by my order, or from the Deputy Post Master General for the British Provinces in North America for the time being, and the said Laurence Lawrason is hereby authorised to keep and retain a Commission of twenty per Centum out of the yearly produce arising by the Port of Letters received by him, in recompence for his care and trouble in the performance and execution of the trusts reposed in him, so long as he shall continue to be employed by me as my Deputy.

In witness whereof, I, the said DANIEL SUTHERLAND, have hereunto set my Hand and caused the Seal of my Office to be affixed hereunto, this Twenty-sixth Day of March One Thousand, Eight hundred & Twenty five in the Sixth Year of His Majesty's Reign.

D. Sutherland

Above: *This document, signed by Deputy Postmaster General Daniel Sutherland on March 26, 1825, appointed Lawrence Lawrason as London's first postmaster, a year before the city's founding. The post office was located at present-day Oxford Street West and Sanatorium Road. Courtesy, UWO*

Opposite page: *This issue of* The London Sun, *dated January 26, 1832, is the earliest known London newspaper to survive the vicissitudes of time. Edited by Edward Allen Talbot, it began publication in July 1831, with the last issue appearing in December 1833. Typical of newspapers of the period, it reported the debates of the Provincial Parliament and the latest news of the Old Country. Courtesy, UWO*

though at first it was located far to the west at present-day Oxford Street and Sanatorium Road. By 1830, his partner George J. Goodhue was postmaster and the mail soon went to the convenient store of Goodhue and Lawrason. From July 7, 1831, news of the world was available through the settlement's first newspaper, *The London Sun,* published by Robert Heron and edited by Edward Allen Talbot, a son of the pioneer settlement leader of London Township. That paper ceased publication in December 1833, but from then on there was almost always at least one newspaper printed in the city, although none had a long lifespan.

The first step in London's development as one of Canada's major financial centres came in October 1835, when the Bank of Upper Canada opened an agency in the city. A year later the two-storey white brick building, which is now the southern structure of the Labatt restoration, was completed. Before the decade was out the village had received the first patent issued by the Upper Canadian government. Edward Allen Talbot, as well as being an author and newspaper editor, was an inventor; his "Atmospheric Propelling Engine" was duly registered in July 1834. Unfortunately, it was not a great success.

THE SOCIETY OF THE NEW SETTLEMENT

During the same years London's social institutions were taking shape. Although in many cases it could not be said that Upper Canadians were deeply religious, the idea of a church-state connection and the state supporting the church was carried over from Britain. Naturally, the Church of England as the state church of the Mother Country assumed a particularly important place in an administrative centre. Those Presbyterians connected with the state Kirk of Scotland had special government support too, as did the Catholics, and, later on, the Methodists.

By 1824 the Church of England missionary at St. Thomas was occasionally preaching in London Township. Then in 1829 the Reverend Edward Jukes Boswell arrived as missionary to London, staying three years. The village even received an Episcopal visitation when Charles James Stewart, then second bishop of Quebec, held a service in the temporary courthouse in August 1828. Real development of the Church of England, however, dates from the arrival of the energetic, Anglo-Irish Reverend Benjamin Cronyn in 1832; he remained in the city and eventually became the first Anglican bishop of Huron.

Finding the church site on Dundas Street unsatisfactory, Cronyn soon sold the land and obtained a

THE LONDON SUN.

VOL. 1. LONDON, U. C. THURSDAY, JANUARY 26 1832. NO 19.

THE LONDON SUN.
Is Printed and Published every Thursday, in the Town of London, by
ROBERT HURON.
E. A. TALBOT, ESQ. EDITOR
TERMS.—$3 per annum, if paid in advance; and $4 if not paid till the expiration of the year
ADVERTISING AT THE USUAL RATES.

AGENTS FOR THE SUN.
London—Wm. Robertson, Esq.
Port Talbot—Col Burwell, M. P.
Oxford West—Col Ingersol, M. P.
Oxford East—G. W. Whitehead, Esq.
Oxford—Dr C. Duncomb M. P.
...—Col. Boswick,
...

List of Letters Remaining in the ... Post Office Dec. 15th. 1831.
...
G. J. GOODHUE Postmaster.

Groceries.
Young Hyson, Twanky and Hyson Skin Teas. Loaf and Muscovado Sugar. Cloves, Alspice Nutmegs, Ginger, Pepper. Cinnamon, British Oil, ... Camphor Gum, Paregoric, Elixor Castor Oil, Arrow root, Magnesia, Camomile Flowers, Itch Ointment, &c 10 Kegs Tobacco and a few jars Mackaboy Snuff.
DYE-STUFFS
A few Barrels Ground Logwood, Fustick, Red wood. One Barrel Copperas, Allum, Salt Petre, Refined Borax, &c.
The above will be sold low for ready pay
E. S. LYMAN & Co.
London Dec. 29, 1831

SHERIFF'S SALE.
Joseph T. Barrett vs. Samuel Ryckman, and John L. Ryckman. In the Kings Bench.
BY virtue of an Execution, in the above suit, I have taken Lot No. 7 in the 4th concession of Aldboro' as belonging to Samuel Ryckman, which I shall sell at public Auction on Saturday the thirty first day of December next, 12 o'clock, noon—at the Burford House in Burford, London District
A. A. RAPELGIE Sheriff L. D.
By S. WRIGHT, Deputy
Sheriff's Office L. D. 23d September 1831.

LIVERY STABLE.
Smith Work and Farrier.
J. WILLIAMS begs leave to inform his friends and the public, that he continues to carry on the above business in its various branches and in addition to which he will in future keep a Livery Stable where can be had pleasure Waggons, Sleighs, Carts, on moderate terms by the day, month, or year.
N. B. If any damage is done to any vehicle while on hire the party will be held responsible.
London August 18th 1831.

POETRY.
From the Casket.
AN EPIC POEM.
My truant muse has shaken off her trance—
And wide awake, with renovated vigour,
I'll scale the cloud-built Casket of romance,
And cut in print no trifling figure—
Amongst the poets of those classic times
Who crowd the Casket with immortal rhymes
...

NEW GOODS.
THE subscribers beg leave to inform their ...

PROVINCIAL PARLIAMENT, OF UPPER CANADA.
On motion of Mr Boulton the petition Charles Rubridge and 274 others of Monaghan, Smith, Ennismore, Otonabee, Duro ..., Dummer and Belmont, in the Newcastle District—praying to be set off as a separate County, with Peterborough for a County Town, was read: the rule being suspended for that purpose and the said petition was refered to Messrs. Boulton, Sampson and Brown
The petition of Benjamin Woodhull, was referred to Messrs. Mount, Elliot and W. Wilson
The petition of Moses Maynard, was refered to Messrs. Buell, Attorney General and Jones.
...

Present—Messrs. Attorney General, Berczy. Bidwell, Boulton, Buell, Chisholm, Clark, Crooks, Duncomb, Eliot, A Fraser, Howard, Ingersol, Jones, Lewis, McCall, A McDonald, McMartin, McNab, Macon, Morris Mount, Norton, Perry, Randal, Robinson, Roblin, Samson, Shade, Shaver, Sol. General, Thomson, Warren, Werden, W. Wilson.
The 6th Resolution was then put and carried as follows.
Resolved—That an humble address be presented to His Majesty, setting forth the substance of the foregoing resolutions and imploring His Majesty's faithful subjects of Upper Canada, that the school lands may not be applied to any other object than that for which they were intended by His Majesty's late Royal Father.
The 7th Resolution was then put and carried as follows.
Resolved—That the Chairman be instructed to draft and report to the House an address to His Majesty founded on the foregoing Resolutions.
Agreeable to order Mr. Clark the Chairman of the Committee, reported the draft of an address which was read twice, concurred in, and ordered for a 3d reading to-morrow.
The Speaker reported that the master in Chancery had brought down 2 messages from the hon. Legislative Council.
The messages were read by the Speaker as follows.
Mr. Speaker.
The Hon. William Allan has leave to attend a select Committee of the Commons House of assembly as desired by that House in their message of this day if he thinks fit—and Grant Powell Esq. has leave to attend the same select Committee.
JOHN B. ROBINSON.
Speaker.
Legislative Council Chamber.
20th day of December 1831.
Mr. Speaker
The Legislative Council have passed the amendments made by the commons House of assembly in and to the Bill sent down from the House, entitled, "an act to remove doubts respecting the jurisdiction over offences committed upon the Lakes and Rivers in this Province.
J. B. ROBINSON.
Speaker.
Legislative Chamber,
20th day of Dec. 1831.

... The House took means to inform the country—they printed his former libels, word for word, and sent 2000 copies of the libels, and ... to the country, at the public expense—they thus appealed to public opinion, and said that your House was slandered. But this is not your House, Mr. Speaker, nor their House, it is the people's House.— They were the servants of the country, and the people their masters—and he contended that this House had no more right to expel a member than one servant in private life had to turn away a fellow servant. Nevertheless this House have done so, and although a very distant and inconvenient day was appointed for the election the 2nd of January, when the people had to attend their township meetings, still they assembled, and showed to this House a full clear, calm and deliberate expression of public opinion. ...
[Here Mr. Burwell called him to order—the House had nothing to do, he said, with the circulation of the Christian Guardian and a short discussion upon points of order ensued, when Mr. Mackenzie proceeded.]
He (Mr. Mackenzie) came to the House, not with a desire to insult but to convince hon. members, ...
...

Until the creation of the Diocese of Huron in 1857, John Strachan (1778-1867) as Bishop of Toronto provided leadership to Anglicans in Southwestern Ontario. He was a pillar of the Family Compact and fervently supported the exclusive right of the Church of England to the Clergy Reserves. Strachan opposed Rev. Benjamin Cronyn's election as first Bishop of the Diocese of Huron on the grounds of Cronyn's low church views. Courtesy, UWO

grant of four and a half acres on Richmond Street. The first St. Paul's was opened there in 1834 with a seating capacity of 400. A frame building with an unusually large tower, it had a rather brief lifespan, as it was destroyed by fire in February 1844. Cronyn also transferred the cemetery from the Dundas Street property to the St. Paul's property, where some of the early tombstones may still be seen.

In those days what is now the Anglican Church was sharply divided internally. The Church of Ireland group, as represented by Cronyn and many of his Irish colleagues in southwestern Upper Canada, believed in relatively simple forms of ritual, while the future Bishop John Strachan and many of the clergy in Toronto followed the practices of the more ceremonial Church of England. This divergence led to clashes between the two factions and was a factor in the founding of separate institutions of higher education in London. The Church of Ireland clergy, however, were the official clergy for the region, even though there was no complete liturgical agreement. When Sir John Colborne endowed some forty-four Anglican rectories just before he left Upper Canada in January 1836, two of them were St. Paul's London and St. John's Arva. Within a few years Cronyn had 400 acres of glebe or church land under cultivation. He gradually developed the properties of the church—and his own properties—through astute land speculations.

The Presbyterians, a much more dour, moralistic group, were split into many separate congregations. Their first representative in London, the Reverend William Proudfoot, arrived in 1832 and remained a dominant figure in the city until he died in 1851. His congregation, organized in 1833, evolved into the First Presbyterian Church and today forms part of First St. Andrew's United Church. Interdenominational relations were to say the least touchy. While busy founding his own church, Proudfoot attended a sermon preached by Cronyn and his comments say a great deal about ecumenism at the period: Cronyn's sermon, he noted in his diary, "beggared all description, but he seems a serious man and sound in the faith so far as he knows anything about it."

The leading figure in the Catholic Church was Dennis O'Brien, and many of the early services were held in his home by travelling missionaries. The Reverend Laurence Dempsey, the first resident Catholic priest, arrived in 1833 and shortly opened St. Lawrence's Church and Churchyard on Richmond Street at the site of the Grand Theatre. A roughcast Methodist Church was built in 1833, but at first

The Reverend Benjamin Cronyn described his sturdy Dundas Street dwelling, "The Pines" (later renamed "Woodfield"), in 1842: "The House is of stone 50 feet by 40 with a return [wing] 30 feet by 20, both two stories high. There is a basement story also, the house is throughout finished in the very best manner . . ." It was demolished in 1968. Courtesy, UWO

there was no permanent minister and it merely served as a preaching station. The Congregationalist Church, now part of the United Church, was established in London in 1837 by the Reverend William Clarke.

The elementary school system had never blossomed in Upper Canada because of funding problems and religious disagreements. London had several private schools, such as Miss Kezia Stinson's, which in 1831 was held in a one-storey log building with a fireplace; there were plenty of holes in the log walls and the branch of a tree running through one of them. As Archie Bremner commented in his *Illustrated London* at the end of the century, "there was no patent system of ventilation, but plenty of it." A boarding school for young ladies that planned to teach the more ornamental branches of female edu-

Prince

cation was opened by Mary Proudfoot, a daughter of the Reverend William Proudfoot, in 1835. Whatever the deficiencies of these ladies' schools, they were probably a considerable improvement over the first London effort, run by Peter Van Every, Jr., in the courthouse when he was not occupied with his other post as town jailer.

The Upper Canadian grammar, or high school, system provided a school for each district, but it was not until October 1837 that the District School was moved to London. The London school, first taught by Francis Wright, B.A., was supervised by a committee of trustees composed of Mahlon Burwell, John Harris, the Reverend Benjamin Cronyn, and five other ministers. On Sundays the schoolhouse was used by several different religious denominations for their services. In 1841 the Reverend Benjamin Bayly was appointed schoolmaster; under his guidance the District School gradually developed into a proper high school. Not surprisingly, both Wright and Bayly were, like Cronyn, graduates of Trinity College, Dublin—an example of how well the Anglo-Irish patronage network was operating in the region.

Beyond religion and education Londoners quickly developed a wide variety of diversions. In an economy based on agriculture the improvement of farming methods was a major interest; the earliest London District Agriculture Society was established in October 1831 at a meeting held in the village. The date of the first agricultural fair is uncertain, but it may have been as early as 1833. Two years later Lieutenant-Governor Colborne gave official authorization for a fair and a market in the community, and a fair was definitely held in October 1836. Possibly it was not a great success, for one observer noted that "there were far more sellers than buyers."

The first clubs also appeared. Masonic lodges had been formed locally as early as 1829, and a meeting was held at the Forks in 1830. By 1841 London had a lodge of its own. Sports clubs were set up for such games as curling and cricket, and sailing on the river. Swimming in the Thames was a popular activity. Archibald Ouray was the first unfortunate Londoner known to have drowned there on June 1, 1831. The earliest known ball, as dances were generally called, was held in 1833 at the King's Arms Hotel at Richmond and Dundas streets. As early as 1838 the 32nd Regiment of Foot officers performed *Hamlet,* and in 1839 the first theatre performance took place with the military participating in a double bill of *Wives and Sweethearts* and *Bombastic* [sic] *Furioso.*

The lieutenant-governors added to the life of the

Above: *William Lyon Mackenzie (1795-1861) led the Upper Canada Rebellion in the Toronto area, inspiring Dr. Charles Duncombe to lead a rebel force in the London District. After the failure of the uprisings, both fled to the United States. Unlike Duncombe, Mackenzie returned to the province after the amnesty of 1849. Courtesy, Frederick H. Armstrong*

Opposite page: *The officers and soldiers of the British Garrison often provided entertainment for London's citizens. This illustration reproduced from the* Alexander Sketchbook, 1843 *depicts a ball which the 1st Royal Scots gave at the barracks for their London and area friends. With which soldier did the young woman dance? Courtesy, Public Archives of Canada, C98802*

Above: *Colonel Allan Napier MacNab, as he appeared in the 1840s, was speaker of the House of Assembly at the time of the Rebellions. He arrived from his home in Hamilton with an additional force to suppress the insurrection. For his prompt action MacNab was knighted. Courtesy, Metropolitan Toronto Library, T13738*

Opposite page: *This detail from a London map of 1865 illustrates the British Garrison property, which extended north from Dufferin Avenue (Duke Street) to Piccadilly Street, and east from Clarence Street (Church Street) and Richmond Street to Waterloo Street. British regulars were stationed in London in 1838 in response to the Upper Canada Rebellion of 1837 and the subsequent threatened American invasion. Except for 1854-1862, they stayed until 1869. Courtesy, UWO*

city with occasional state visits. Sir Francis Bond Head arrived in September 1836 after the Tory victory in the election and attended divine service at St. Paul's. His successor, Sir George Arthur, visited the village a couple of times in 1839, once to review the military and once on a general tour of the western districts in the wake of the rebellion. Nature too played its part in the entertainment: on November 12, 1832, Londoners recorded the greatest meteor shower they had ever seen when the Leonid Meteors burst across the sky in a display that compared to descending snow or hail.

THE REBELLION OF 1837 AND ITS CONSEQUENCES

In early December 1837 the peaceful village was suddenly disrupted when rebellion, or rather two disorganized rebellions, struck Upper Canada. In Toronto (as York had been named again in 1834) and its northern hinterland, William Lyon Mackenzie led an abortive uprising which has often been seen as the only outbreak; in the Southwestern Peninsula, however, Dr. Charles Duncombe of St. Thomas led another, equally unsuccessful uprising. London was fortunate, for despite the fact that it was the district town, the rebellion's major rallyings and skirmishes took place around it, largely at Sparta near St. Thomas and to the east in modern Brant County. The southwestern Upper Canada insurrection—the Duncombe Rebellion—was basically a follow-up to events in Toronto. Because of bad communications, however, it did not begin until the Mackenzie Rebellion in Toronto was dispersed. Although there had been considerable local political disagreement, as shown by the stormy elections, the movement was no broad-based peoples' uprising. Rather, Duncombe and a few fairly prosperous individuals, a couple of them magistrates, organized some followers and attempted to take the Southwestern Peninsula, thinking Toronto had fallen.

London was completely taken by surprise. With the incredibly bad communications rumors were rampant; no one knew what was happening. The London District establishment, led by the Reverend Benjamin Cronyn and officials such as Askin and Harris, barely had time to consider possible action when the whole incident was over. Allan Napier MacNab of Hamilton, the builder of Dundurn Castle, marched west with the militia after the defeat of the Toronto rebels and snuffed out the western uprising with little difficulty. Many of the rebels were jailed at London, but none were hanged for their part in the uprising.

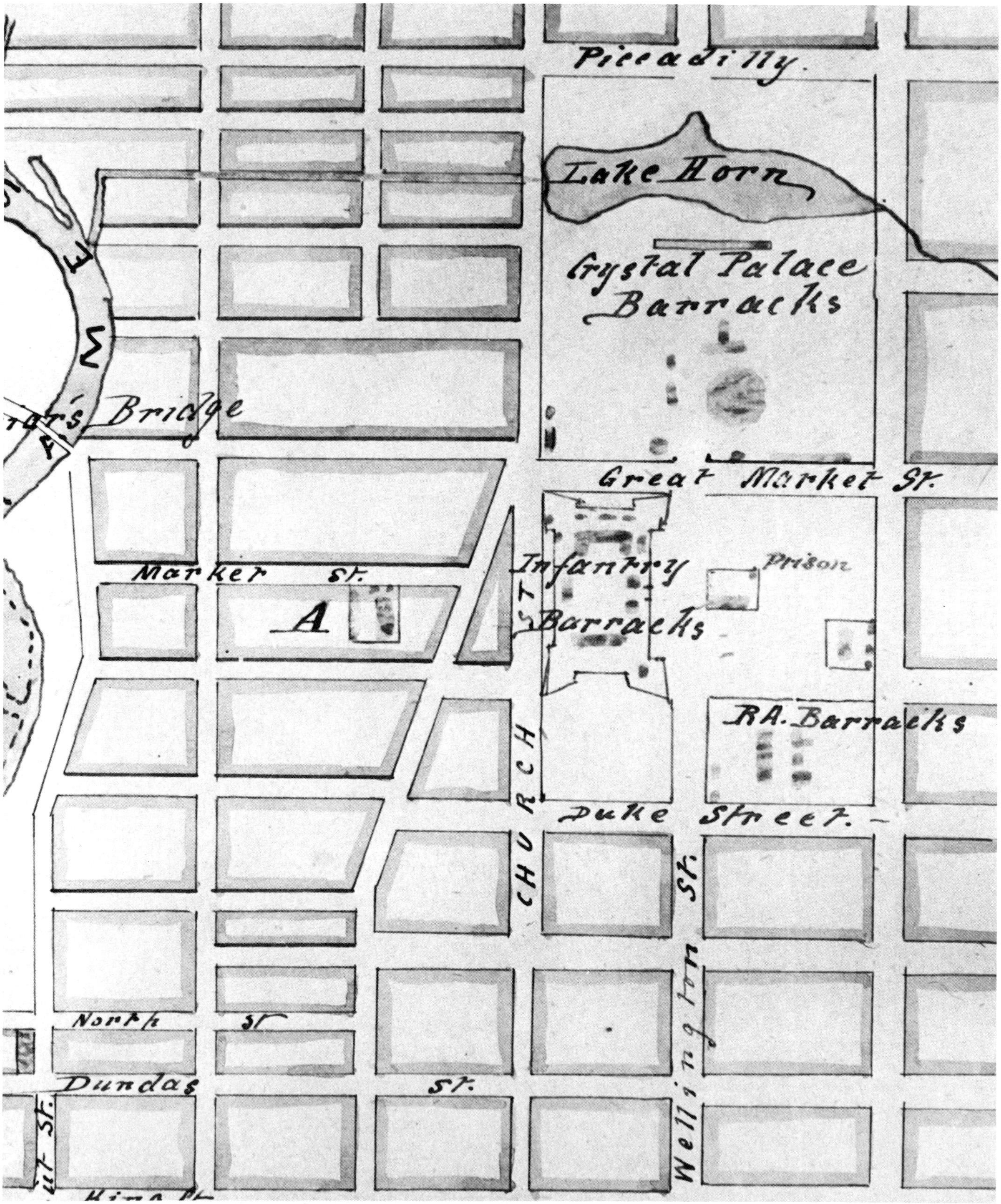
Piccadilly
Lake Horn
Crystal Palace
Barracks
Bridge
Great Market St.
Market St.
A
Infantry
Barracks
Prison
CHURCH ST
R.A. Barracks
Duke Street
Wellington St.
North St
Dundas St.

Although the London and Toronto jails were soon filled with many of their followers, as so often happens the rebel leaders Mackenzie and Duncombe escaped to the United States. From that haven they began plotting raids and excursions to overthrow the Upper Canadian government. Their plans fell on sympathetic ears, for many respectable Americans saw the rebellions as a continuation of their revolution, and a lot of not-so-respectable ones, out of work during the depression, saw a chance for free land, loot, and adventure without much danger. Most raids were easily put down, but in one of the last attacks on December 27, 1838, a large group of "Patriots" invaded at Windsor. After a day of encounters marked by unusual brutality on both sides, forty-four invaders were taken prisoner and sent to join the rebels in London jail. In the trials that followed six were sentenced to be hanged and some were exiled to Tasmania. In the post-rebellion months other individuals who had either supported the rebellion, or who were believed to have been rebel supporters, sold their property and emigrated to the United States, causing considerable dislocation in the countryside. Altogether the insurrection was a totally unnecessary tragedy which disrupted the lives of a great number of people and in the immediate term set back the cause of democratic government in Upper Canada.

GARRISON TOWN

The American raids were over by early 1839. In the long run the rebellion and its aftermath proved to be one of the most important factors in the rise of London. As a result it was made a garrison town and with this dignity took on a new social outlook and enjoyed the benefits of military spending. With the constant threat of border incursions in the post-rebellion period the British army needed an inland site for its garrison, one that could not be captured

Top right: *Until proper barracks were built, the soldiers of the British Garrison were quartered for a short time in private houses. Local builders secured the military contracts totalling approximately 150,000 pounds. The buildings, one of which is pictured here, were frame in construction and were surrounded by a palisade. Courtesy, UWO*

Bottom right: *Of all the British regiments stationed in London, the Royal Scots Regiment under its commander Colonel George A. Weatherall made a particular impression. Instead of keeping disorderly soldiers confined to barracks, Weatherall organized them to remove the huge stumps which abounded in the town's roadways. Wellington Street (north of Dundas) and the Garrison grounds were cleared, in the latter instance forming a parade square, today's Victoria Park. The stumps formed a fence around the garrison property. Courtesy, UWO*

The young officers of the British Garrison formed a Sleigh Club. On Shrove Tuesday, 1843, as described by Sir James Alexander in L'Acadie, *the club "held a sort of carnival. They dressed themselves out in fantastic attire . . . and so drove and rode about, much to their own amusement and the wonder of the peaceable inhabitants . . ." From* Alexander Sketchbook, 1843. *Courtesy, Public Archives of Canada, C98778*

easily by an American invasion. As in Simcoe's time, so in 1838, London was the ideal choice. With its central location troops could be rushed to any point on the Niagara, Lake Erie, or Lake Huron frontiers. St. Thomas was briefly considered, but that centre apparently wanted no unruly troops in its midst, so London was the winner. The garrison was to affect the city in every way imaginable. Military provisioning founded many London fortunes, for instance that of Ellis Walton Hyman, whose tannery received the British army leather contract for such items as boots and saddles. Since the garrison was paid in good solid currency their purchases not only helped expand the merchant community, but also greatly helped in turning the region from a barter to a cash economy.

With the coming of the garrison the backwoods town was linked into the imperial power structure in a way that it had never been as just a mere district capital. The various regiments travelling back and forth across the world in defence of the Empire brought a glimpse of a wider world to the settlement. Both officers and men played a great role in changing the character of the town from an American frontier community to a British outpost. The inevitable intermixing of town and garrison families sometimes led to rather sharp clashes, particularly at the taverns. Yet many soldiers married daughters of the settlers and a fair number of them remained in the town after they left the army.

The actual establishment of the garrison took place quite quickly in May 1838. Dennis O'Brien's wife Jane noted that London "is one continued sea of confusion, the city is crowded with soldiers, and many are billoted on each house." Despite the fact that her brother was jailed for supporting the rebellion, O'Brien himself did not hesitate to rent his Dundas Street block of brick stores as a temporary barracks for the 32nd Regiment. What is now Victoria Park and the blocks to its immediate north and east were rapidly prepared as a barracks and parade ground, at a considerable profit to the local contractors. An infantry barracks was built in 1839 and the garrison bell, imported from India, could soon be heard tolling the hours over town and countryside. Citizens who awoke in the night could be assured that they were protected from any foreign invasion or recurring uprising.

The garrison also played a considerable role in the town's administration and public works. The troops naturally joined in such entertainments as clubs and dances, but they also helped provide law and order when needed, assisted in the fighting of fires, and at times helped with public works. By 1843 Colonel Weatherall had soldiers convicted of minor misdemeanors removing gigantic tree stumps from the roads and using them to build a fence around the parade ground. The work was undoubtedly heavy, but the soldiers found it more acceptable than many of the methods of military discipline, which included lashing for relatively minor offences.

The officers too played an important part in the town's society. They mingled with the emerging local establishment just as the troops mingled with the people, and in many cases intermarried with local girls of the upper classes. However, unlike the troops who frequently settled in the town, the officers were generally well connected back in England and many returned with a colonial wife. The Harris family of "Eldon House" saw more than one daughter marry into the British upper classes. The officers also organized various military events, dances, and sporting entertainments such as sleighing. Those trained in drawing left some of the earliest impressions of the town. Several of the officers went on to important careers, such as Colonel Richard Airey, nephew and partial heir of Colonel Thomas Talbot, who ended up as a field marshal and a lord, but who is chiefly famous for writing the order for the charge of the ill-fated Light Brigade in the Crimean War.

Sir Richard Airey (1803-1881) was a nephew of Colonel Thomas Talbot. As Colonel of the 34th Regiment, he was stationed in St. Thomas, a short distance from his uncle's Port Talbot estate. Airey painted several views of London and the area, including London, Canada West, *featured on the dust jacket of this book. In later years he is best remembered as the officer who wrote the orders for the famous "Charge of the Light Brigade" during the Crimean War. Courtesy, Public Archives of Ontario*

This panoramic view of London, sketched in 1855 (the year of London's incorporation as a city), was drawn by the itinerant artist Edwin Whitfield, who produced numerous large topographical lithographs of North American cities. Whitfield's vantage point—Askin's Hill on Wortley Road, high above the curve of the Thames River—proved popular with artists and photographers alike. Prominent features include the newly erected Great Western Railway Bridge and the towers of the courthouse and numerous churches. Courtesy, UWO

CHAPTER III

A New City in the Railway Era, 1840-1861

LONDON BECOMES A CITY

With the settlement firmly established, London, like so many frontier towns, leaped to city status in an extraordinarily brief space of time as settlers poured into southwestern Upper Canada. Through the London District this growth of settlement had a second effect, for it meant that additional administrative districts were required for local government purposes. Thus, as London rose to city status it simultaneously lost administrative control over much of its immediate hinterland, a change which had little effect on its influence, for it retained its economic paramountcy. In 1837 Norfolk County became the Talbot District and Oxford County became the Brock District. Four years later Huron and Perth counties and the region to their north were separated, becoming the District of Huron. The London District was then reduced to what is now Elgin County and the southern two-thirds of Middlesex County. After the district system was abolished and local government transferred to the counties in 1849, Middlesex County's boundaries were changed twice: in 1851 when the southern townships were separated to form Elgin County; and in 1863 when its boundaries were extended north to their present limits.

Internally, London itself naturally required more extensive governmental powers. By 1840 the village's population had reached 1,716, not counting the garri-

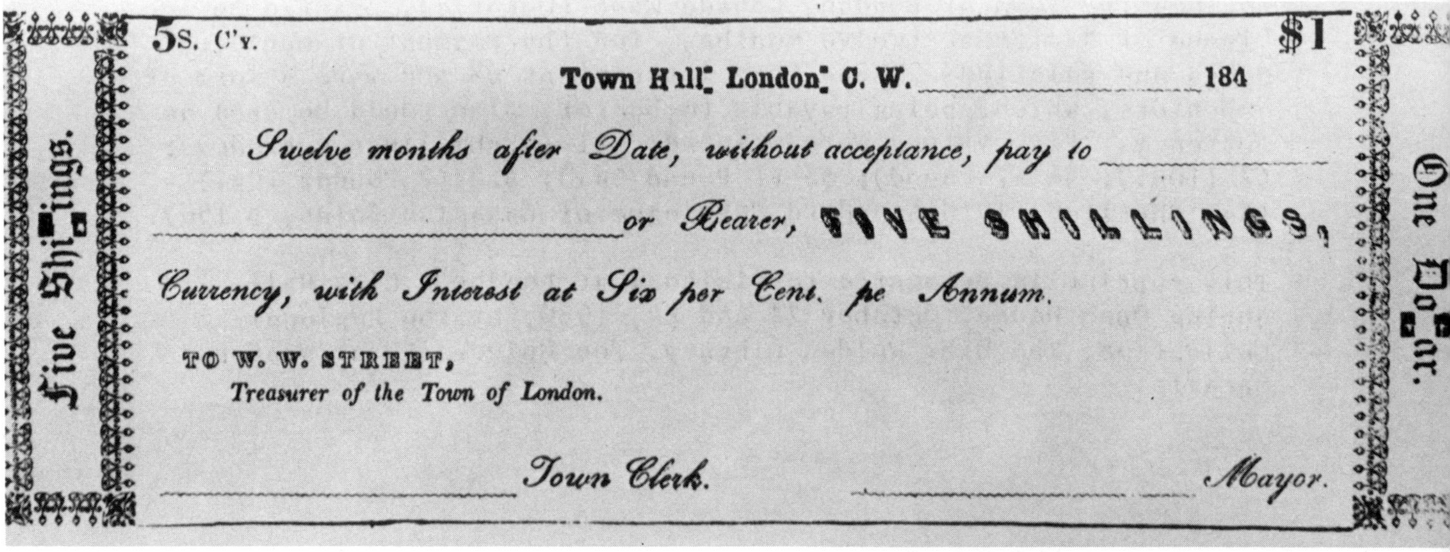

5S. C'Y. $1

Town Hall, London, C. W. ______________ 184

Twelve months after Date, without acceptance, pay to ______________

______________ or Bearer, FIVE SHILLINGS,

Currency, with Interest at Six per Cent. pe Annum.

TO W. W. STREET,
Treasurer of the Town of London.

______________ Town Clerk. ______________ Mayor.

Five Shillings. One Dollar.

Above: *In 1848 the Town of London printed its own money, called "drafts at twelve months," for the payment of municipal debts and salaries. These bore interest at 6 percent payable to the bearer, and thus could be used as currency. Five values were printed: $1 (5 shillings currency); $2 (10s.); $4 (1 pound); $5 (1 pound 5s.); and $10 (2 pounds 10s.). Courtesy, UWO*

Right: *An architect and builder, Thomas Parke (1793-1864), in partnership with John Ewart, designed and built the London District Courthouse in 1826. Settling in London, he became a member of the Legislative Assembly and was surveyor-general in the first Baldwin-La Fontaine government in the early 1840s. From* London and Its Men of Affairs, *1915. Courtesy, UWO*

L. MOELLER & Co.,
(Sign of the Indian Chief,)
Keep constantly on hand a choice stock of
CIGARS,
Meerschaum Pipes, Tubes, &c., at Wholesale and Retail; City Hotel Buildings, Dundas-St., London, Canada West.
Also, Dundas-St., nearly opposite the P. O., Woodstock.
A large and well
Selected Stock!
Of the articles always on hand, and will be sold at the lowest possible prices to defy
COMPETITION!
L. MŒLLER.
W. DESSAUER.

Cigar manufacturing was established in the city as early as 1845, and cigars, pipes, and tobacco were available at stores such as L. Moeller & Co. on Dundas Street. This advertisement appeared in Railton's Directory for the City of London. C.W., 1856-57. Courtesy, UWO

son, for the British troops and their families were never included in local census records. As a result, the provincial government granted London the first of three successive incorporations giving it the status of a town, although the new municipality's powers were more like those of a village today. The provincial act divided London into four wards named, as was customary at that time, after the four saints of the British Isles: St. George, St. Patrick, St. Andrew, and St. David.

The town council, called the Board of Police, consisted of one representative elected by each ward and a fifth chosen by the four elected councillors. The five men then elected their president from among their number. Not surprisingly, the honor of being elected first head of London's council went to the "rich Mr. George J. Goodhue," leading merchant, postmaster, and mortgage broker, who was shortly to be appointed a member of the Legislative Council, the Senate of that day. Considering that virtually ev-

The sober austerity of "Waverley Hall" reflected the personality of its entrepreneurial occupant, London's wealthy pioneer merchant George Jervis Goodhue. The house was erected in the 1840s on Bathurst Street, close to the town's manufacturing area. The view was presently made even less attractive by the Great Western Railway, which laid its tracks behind the cottages on the north side of the street in 1853, and by the nearby Hunt Bros. coal yard. The residence served as the head office of Silverwood's Dairies, Ltd., from 1917 until it was demolished in 1961. Courtesy, UWO

Opposite page: *Fourteen years after its founding in the forest, London had grown large enough for the Upper Canadian Legislature to grant it incorporation as a town with policing powers. This tattered document, dated February 28, 1840, and signed by James Hamilton, sheriff of the London District, authorized elections for representatives for the Wards of St. Patrick, St. David, and St. Andrew. A separate document provided for elections in St. George's Ward. Courtesy, UWO*

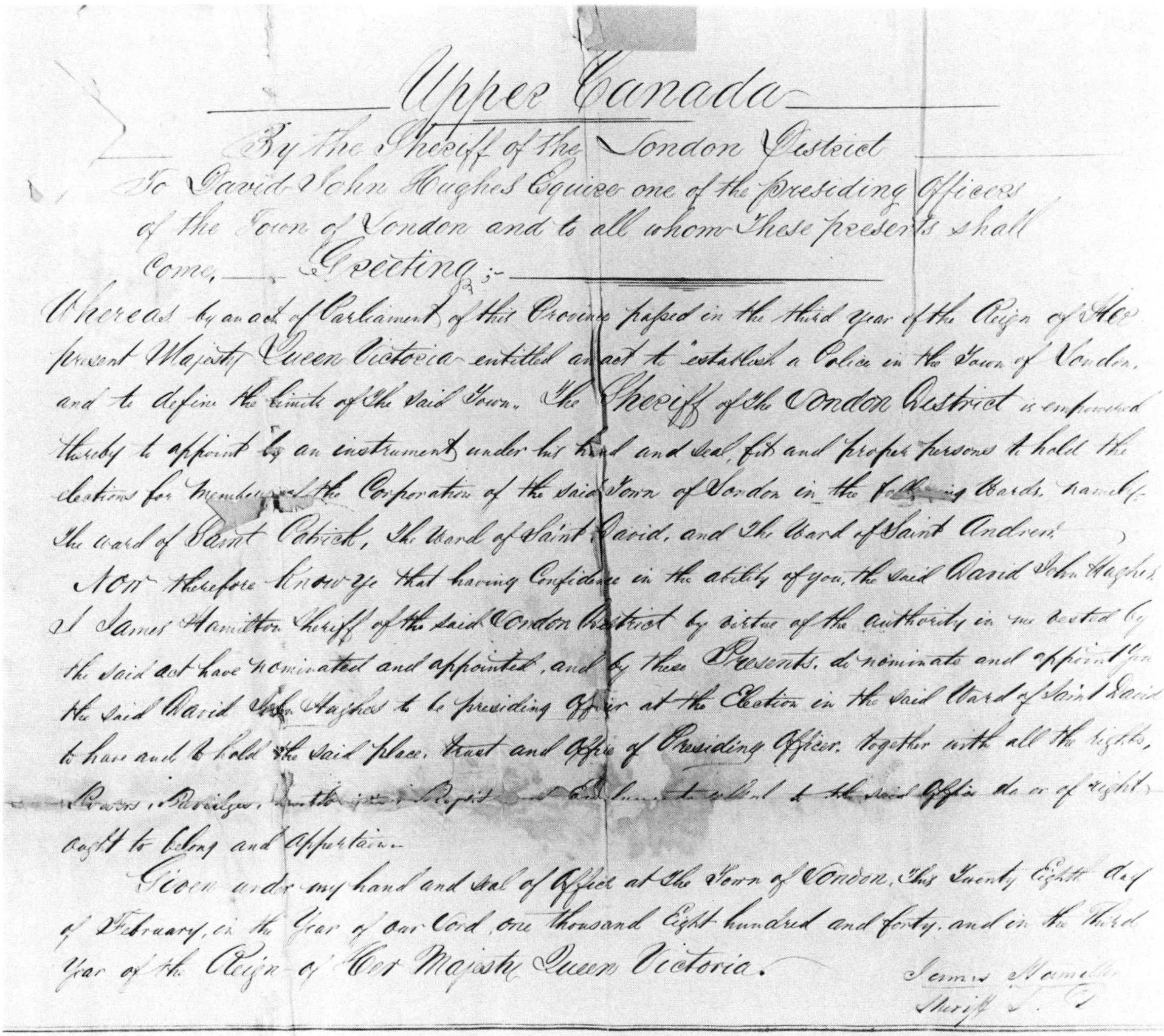

Upper Canada

By the Sheriff of the London District

To David John Hughes Esquire one of the Presiding Officers of the Town of London and to all whom These presents shall Come, — Greeting:—

Whereas by an act of Parliament of this Province passed in the third year of the Reign of Her present Majesty Queen Victoria entitled an act to establish a Police in the Town of London, and to define the limits of the said Town. The Sheriff of the London District is empowered thereby to appoint by an instrument under his hand and seal, fit and proper persons to hold the elections for members of the Corporation of the said Town of London in the following Wards, namely, The Ward of Saint Patrick, The Ward of Saint David, and The Ward of Saint Andrew.

Now therefore Know ye that having Confidence in the ability of you, the said David John Hughes, I James Hamilton Sheriff of the said London District by virtue of the authority in me vested by the said act have nominated and appointed, and by these Presents do nominate and appoint you the said David John Hughes to be presiding Officer at the Election in the said Ward of Saint David to have and to hold the said place, trust and Office of Presiding Officer, together with all the rights, Powers, Privileges, [illegible] to the said Office due or of right ought to belong and Appertain.

Given under my hand and seal of Office at the Town of London, this Twenty Eighth day of February, in the Year of our Lord, one thousand Eight hundred and forty, and in the Third Year of the Reign of Her Majesty Queen Victoria.

James Hamilton
Sheriff L. D.

ery type of municipal service was lacking, it was no surprise that the revenues were hardly adequate. Permitted assessment rates were low and further revenue from granting licences for liquor sales and taverns was limited. However, the statutes required that taxpayers provide a certain number of days' labor to help repair roads each year.

During the 1830s the original 1826 survey had been extended as the town grew. With the 1840 incorporation the boundaries were extended far beyond the area of settlement, stretching basically to Adelaide Street in the east and Huron Street in the north. The eastern boundary was to remain unchanged until 1885, the northern boundary until 1961. The new streets commemorated Field Marshal the Duke of Wellington, victor of the Battle of Waterloo; Lieutenant-Governor Colborne; Lieutenant-Governor Maitland; King William IV; and Queen Adelaide. The new incorporation soon proved inadequate as more powers were required by the council. In 1847, when a new statute established a full Town Council with a mayor effective January 1, 1848, London had a population of 3,942. A year later this had shot up to 4,668. For the first two years the mayor was elected directly by the people; then in 1850 the whole council was restructured with three aldermen for each of

Above: *Built on the west side of Richmond Street, south of Dundas, the City Hall was erected in time to accommodate the mayor and councillors of the newly incorporated City of London of 1855. The three-storey building (as seen on the left of this late 1860s photograph) was designed by London architect Samuel Peters. In the 1880s, to complement the Second Empire architecture of the adjoining Masonic Temple, the building was altered to accommodate a magnificent mansard roof. Converted to a bank in 1911, it was demolished in 1969. Courtesy, UWO*

Opposite page: *Few politicians have the honor of being elected mayor of two newly incorporated municipalities. Murray Anderson, a tin merchant, was the first mayor of the City of London in 1855 and in 1874 the first mayor of London East, a village he was instrumental in founding. Courtesy, London Historical Museums*

the four wards, who elected the mayor from among themselves. The office was first filled by tanner Simeon Morrill.

Almost immediately it again became obvious that the town corporation's powers were inadequate as the population rushed toward the magic figure of 10,000, which was required for full city incorporation. In 1854, when the local city census showed a population of 10,060, a third incorporation was obtained. London was proclaimed a city effective January 1, 1855. At Covent Garden Market Square, construction was already underway on both a market house and a City Hall at a total budget of 20,000 pounds. After considerable argument as to whether the City Hall should face east toward Richmond Street, or west to look over the market square, it was designed to face in both directions. Appropriately elegant for the dignity of the new city, the building was built of white brick—a feature that was just becoming fashionable—three cupolas on the roof, cut stone trim, and the very latest in technology, cast iron posts for interior support. The market hall was a similarly pleasing building, set to the west of the City Hall in the Covent Garden Market itself, and looking south to

King Street. The cost of the City Hall by itself was 7,501 pounds 10 shillings, with one pound then being equivalent to five dollars in the local currency or four dollars American.

The new city was divided into seven wards, fortunately numbered to avoid the proliferation of saints' names found in such places as Toronto. Each ward elected four representatives: two aldermen and two councilmen. The councilmen did not require as high a property qualification for office and did not sit as justices of the peace in the city police court. At first the mayor continued to be selected by the council, but from 1859, except for a brief period in the 1860s, he was elected by the people. Murray Anderson, a prosperous tinsmith, became London's first city mayor.

Although the powers changed, the council's membership tended to spill over from one incorporation to another; the same issues and problems carried on as well. This situation, particularly given the lively municipal politics of the nineteenth century, provided an opportunity for endless battles, which the councillors seem to have thoroughly enjoyed. The city fathers were usually substantial businessmen, sometimes on their way upward to important offices in higher levels of government. Some Canadian cabinet ministers, such as Sir John Carling, Sir Frank Smith, and Charles S. Hyman, had their political baptisms on London's city council floor. Yet the conduct of the council was often anything but businesslike; councillors were thrown out of meetings and, on one occasion, rocks were pitched through the council windows.

Two of London's mayors provided particular blazes of color: Thomas C. Dixon and Frank Evans Cornish, who will be noted in the next chapter. Dixon's career may be taken as an example of council debate at its worst. Elected mayor in one of the first direct elections in 1849, Dixon, a hatter by trade, was soon on bad terms with his councillors. At one of the first meetings he stormed out of the chamber when they passed a piece of legislation over his objections. At the next meeting he refused to sign the minutes. The year proceeded as it started, with the mayor frequently refusing to put forward motions as required and the council cheerfully censoring him and electing a chairman to do his work. Nevertheless, at the last meeting in December, possibly fortified by the cheers of the season, the council passed an almost unanimous vote thanking the mayor for his "straight forward and manly conduct" during his term of office.

MUNICIPAL SERVICES

As noted, then as now the city constantly needed expanded and improved services, but lacked the funds to carry out much that had to be done; the citizenry, while eager for extra services, was very much loath to pay the concomitant taxes. Although the town was permitted to borrow for such projects as the construction of sewers or the extension of water mains for fire protection purposes, finding a bank willing to loan money was difficult. The banks were very suspicious of the corporation's promissory notes and on occasion members of council had to assume personal liability for London's debts. While the market fees helped supplement municipal funds, the operation of the market was one of the most time-consuming problems facing the City Council. Initially there was more than one market site, but in 1846 Covent Garden was recognized as a city market and soon became the only market in London. Around it a very

active but rather unsavory business district flourished, with half the doors opening into the market square leading into saloons and taverns.

The market square itself was largely an open place for the farmers to sell their produce, but there were covered booths inside the market hall. Also, the municipal weigh scales were located there. As the lessees of stalls had to pay fees, the City Council was expected to provide them with a monopoly on sales of their produce in the city until a certain time of day. From the size of the recorded fees the annual cost of renting a market stall was roughly equivalent to $800 to $1,000, a very considerable sum for the period. Still, it was a lucrative location, for people who attempted to buy or sell goods that were not first displayed at the market ran into fairly heavy fines. As early as 1843 one citizen was fined ten shillings plus eight shillings costs ($4.50 total) for purchasing a pig which had not been offered in the market square.

Constant extensions and improvements to streets and roads were needed. A city engineer was appointed to oversee the opening of streets, the improvement of street surfaces, and the building of sidewalks. William Robinson held the office for many years. Bridges over the Thames River presented another difficulty, not only because of the spring floods, called freshets, but also because of sloppy workmanship. Wellington Street Bridge, built in 1840, was already dangerous by 1847 and had to be rebuilt the next year. In building the Ridout Street Bridge the workmen lacked the energy to drive in the piles, so they crept back at night to cut the tops off the stakes sticking up from the ground. In the morning the piles looked as if they had been driven in properly. Not surprisingly, the bridge washed out in 1848 and Londoners had to take a boat across the river until it was replaced in 1863.

Keeping the streets clear of "nuisances" was possibly the greatest ongoing problem faced by any nineteenth-century city council. The general term "nuisances" covered a wide variety of concerns ranging from people throwing garbage onto the streets, to cellar entrances with dangerous steps leading down from the street, to animals running loose. For instance, in 1843 council passed a resolution prohibiting cows from being "milked, slopped or otherwise fed on the sidewalks in the town." That such notices had to be frequently repeated shows that they had

little effect. Pigs were probably the worst nuisances of all; in 1847 a pound keeper was dismissed for taking bribes to allow pigs to run freely on the streets. In a major step toward cleaning up the town, brick sewers were run under Dundas Street from Wellington to Richmond streets and then down to King Street and the river. Street lighting was another area in which progress was made, this time by private enterprise, not by an expansion of municipal services. Until the mid-1850s, except for lanterns in front of hotels, the moon provided the only light or people carried their own lanterns. Then in 1853 the first gas company was formed and the next year gas lights were installed along Dundas Street.

The water supply presented a constant health hazard to which no easy solution was found. Most city water came from individuals' wells, or a pump in the rear of the City Hall from which water was supplied by a carter. As early as 1854 an attempt was made to bring water from the ponds at Pond Mills in Westminster, but these were found to be surface water without springs to feed them and the idea had to be dropped. The result was, of course, a great deal of illness highlighted by a typhoid epidemic in 1847 when the victims included President of the Board of Police Dr. Hiram Davis Lee. The first hospitals were connected with the garrison and by 1848 a general hospital was established there.

The immigrants coming into town presented an-

Above: *Lady Eveline-Marie Mitchell Alexander, wife of Sir James Alexander, an officer with the 14th Foot, sketched in 1842 this view of London looking west along Dundas Street from Wellington Street. It illustrated her husband's account of London, which appeared in the first volume of his* L'Acadie, *published in 1849. The tall building on the right, the first St. Paul's Church, burned on February 21, 1844. Courtesy, UWO*

Opposite page: *The Covent Garden Market was established at Talbot and King streets in 1845. Here local farmers brought their produce to supply Londoners' daily needs. In the market building, right centre in this circa 1890 view, were the basement stalls of the butchers. Note in the foreground the farmers' wagons and horses, and beyond, the mansard roofs of the City Hall and Masonic Temple. The entire block was razed in 1956 for the Covent Garden Market and Parking Building. Courtesy, UWO*

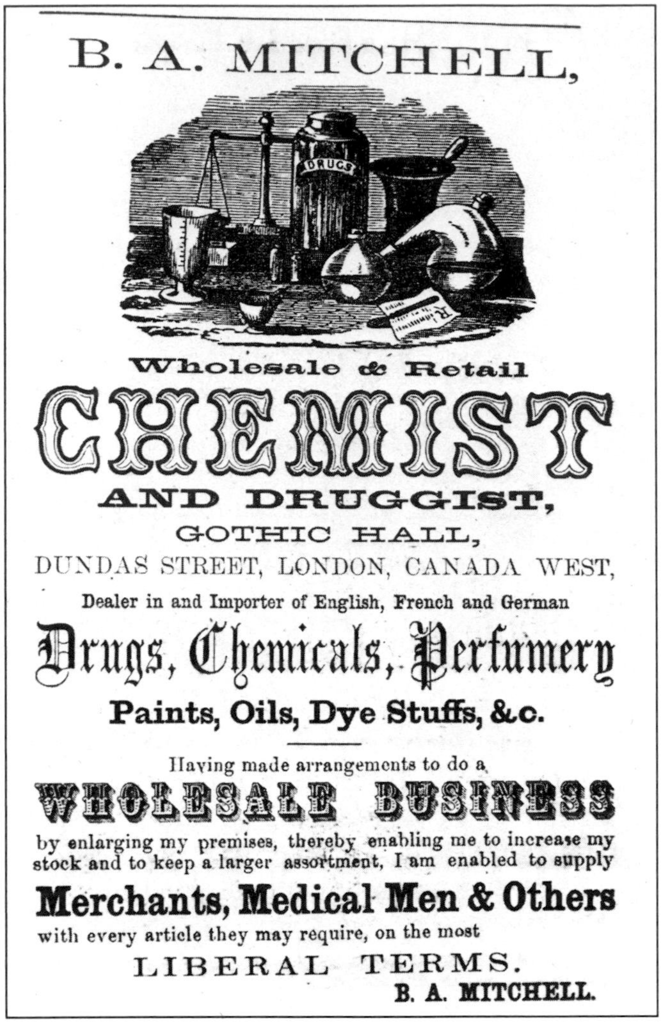

B.A. Mitchell established his pharmacy in London in 1846; the store dispensed a variety of medicinal remedies from the "Gothic Hall" on Dundas Street until well into this century. This advertisement appeared in Railton's Directory for the City of London, C.W., 1856-57. *Courtesy, UWO*

other health hazard and in 1847 a frame hospital was erected on the market square for immigrants from Scotland. The building soon burned down and the city had to periodically find shelter for victims of smallpox and various forms of immigrant fever. At one time teamsters bringing in sick immigrants were fined five pounds for each person they smuggled in. In the cholera epidemic of 1854 the immigrants arriving on the newly built railway brought the epidemic with them. A special wooden hospital was constructed on Hamilton Road for their care, but probably about a hundred died and were buried at night without services. Basically, the care of immigrants' health was an on-and-off process, for the council had neither the money nor the will to do much unless it was absolutely necessary.

In the early days policing too presented great difficulties; there was not only the shortage of funds but also no security of tenure for the Police Force, which frequently changed with elections. In 1855, however, a regular force was organized. Its task was not an easy one, for London was a typical frontier community with many taverns and a population that included a certain number of drifters. In 1859 the records show that Ann and Robert Forsyth were charged with keeping a house of ill fame and each fined $2.50 plus costs. Three months later one Ann Onion, a notorious drunkard, was charged with drunkenness and vagrancy and sentenced to three months imprisonment. On a more elevated level a London lawyer, John Stuart, obtained the first divorce of its kind granted by any British North American legislature in 1841. This was decidedly a society affair, for his wife, Elizabeth Van Rensselaer Stuart, who had run off with a Lieutenant John Grogan of the 32nd Regiment of Foot while visiting Toronto the year before, was a granddaughter of Chief Justice William Dummer Powell.

In education London lacked a public school system to supplement the Grammar (High) School under the Reverend Benjamin Bayly, a friend of Benjamin Cronyn's who did a great deal to develop education in London. With new provincial legislation a school board was set up in 1842; Cronyn himself was appointed superintendent of education and a school district was established in each ward. By 1848 John Wilson, a leading barrister in the city, was superintendent, four teachers had been hired, and a total of 362 pupils were enrolled. Until the first London Free School (later the Union School) was established in 1849 it was necessary for the parent to pay fifty pounds ($250) per annum plus fees. Further schools

were added as funds permitted and in 1857 the London Separate School Board opened a school adjacent to St. Peter's Church.

With the inadequate water supply and the presence of many frame buildings, fire was a constant threat in pioneer communities. Most towns had at least one great fire. Despite the Town Council's attempts to control fire hazards, London unfortunately suffered several bad fires. One of the earliest by-laws prohibited cigars and pipes in stables or outhouses and ordered that candles in such places be protected by a lantern. Another by-law decreed that the highly flammable "Lucifer" matches be kept in outbuildings, not stores. The council showed little patience for those who came to gawk at fires and ordered that any who refused to help with firefighting be penalized with a period in the cells. Arsonists, or incendiaries as they were called, posed another problem;

The education of early London children had been looked after by private schools or by common schools in the wards, where fees were required. After London's reincorporation as a town in 1847, all the ward schools were disbanded and unified in a single Union School, erected in 1849 and supported solely by property taxes. The school's entire student body assembled for this portrait circa 1875. Courtesy, UWO

Above: *London's "Great Fire" erupted in a hotel stable at the southeast corner of Dundas and Ridout streets on April 13, 1845. The flames spread over thirty acres and destroyed 110 mostly frame buildings, three-fourths of the town. A bylaw required all Londoners to possess a leather fire bucket such as this one and to volunteer for the bucket brigade. Photo by Alan Noon. Courtesy, London Historical Museums*

Opposite page, top: *After the "Great Fire," several wealthy Londoners fled the incendiary dangers of the town proper and relocated in remote areas. One of these was Lawrence Lawrason, who in 1846 erected "Lauriston" two blocks east of the town. Bankruptcy in 1864 forced Lawrason to sell his residence to the Roman Catholic Sisters of the Sacred Heart, who converted it to an academy for young girls. Courtesy, UWO*

Opposite page, bottom: *After the "Great Fire" destroyed most of the town's frame buildings, the Town Council passed a municipal bylaw in 1850 compelling Londoners to rebuild with brick and stone. Dundas Street, here viewed east of Talbot Street circa 1875, became defined by two symmetrical rows of three-storey, Georgian-style commercial blocks built of local white brick. Courtesy, UWO*

there were frequent accounts of buildings being deliberately fired.

In 1838 provision was made for bucket brigades, each ratepayer being required to keep leather buckets. As well, by 1843 tanks of water were placed at street corners and people forbidden to take water out of them for household use. These provisions were of little assistance, however, when fire did break out. In 1839 the first major blaze destroyed several buildings on the south side of Dundas between Talbot and Ridout streets. Then in October 1844 another fire started on the north side of Dundas Street and quickly burnt several buildings on both sides between Talbot and Ridout streets. The event induced London's largest property owner, George J. Goodhue, to give the city a fire engine in early 1845. It was not unusual for fire insurance companies or rich citizens to thus provide their town with a fire engine as a type of self-insurance, yet the value of such machines was rather questionable. As Archie Bremner noted in his history of London, Goodhue's fire engine "would be graded somewhat higher than a watering can, but lower than a lawn sprinkler."

On April 13, 1845, when London's greatest fire started in the stables of the Robinson Hall Hotel on the southeast corner of Dundas and Ridout streets, the fire engine caught fire almost immediately. Before the conflagration was extinguished or rather burnt itself out, the fire destroyed about one-fifth of the town, including some 300 buildings. The historical buildings that stretch from the courthouse to "Eldon House" today were saved because, except for destroying a shed, the fire did not cross to the west side of Ridout Street. There was one positive side, however, for brick was used in the new structures that replaced the destroyed buildings, thus rendering a repetition of the fire unlikely. As well, the town bought a new and more powerful fire engine from Quebec in 1846 and the next year erected the first fire hall to hold it. In addition, water tanks were constructed at further corners, and in 1848 London acquired its first alarm to replace the trumpet used to that time.

SOCIAL LIFE

The increasing size of the city meant a growing diversity in social life and entertainment. The 1840s saw further religious groups such as the Baptists and the Congregationalists forming in the town, and established denominations, such as the Methodists and the Presbyterians, splitting into several congregations. Some of London's largest parishes made their

URRIDGE&CO.
HARDWARE
The
W.D. McCLOCHLON

St. Paul's Cathedral, London's oldest church, was completed in 1846 to the Gothic Revival designs of William Thomas, one of Canada's greatest architects. In the early 1890s the building was enlarged from its original proportions, shown here, by the addition of transepts and an extended chancel. From W.H. Smith, Smith's Canadian Gazetteer, *1846. Courtesy, UWO*

appearance, including the Methodist North Street Church, now Metropolitan United Church, which was created by an 1850s division in the Methodist congregation and became the wealthiest Methodist church in the city. William Proudfoot's Presbyterian congregation developed into the First Presbyterian Church, and St. Andrew's Presbyterian Church was established by the Church of Scotland's Presbyterians and became the spiritual home of London's Presbyterian business community. By the 1840s increasing numbers of refugee slaves from the United States were to be found in the city and in 1852 they formed a Coloured Methodist Episcopal Congregation in the south end of the town near the river.

The growing numbers of Irish immigrants provided the Catholic Church with a great stimulus. In 1851 St. Lawrence's Catholic Church was burned by an arsonist while the parish was building a new church across Richmond Street on the present site of St. Peter's Basilica. This new St. Lawrence Church was opened in 1852. It was renamed St. Peter's in 1856 when London became the seat of a new bishopric stretching over most of southwestern Upper Canada, and encompassing the French Catholics in Windsor and Essex County. London's first bishop was the Reverend Adolphe Pinsonneault from the Montreal area. Unfortunately, he had little understanding of either his Irish flock or Upper Canada, thoroughly disliked London, and in 1859 moved the seat of the diocese to the French ambience of Sandwich (Windsor). London's loss was only temporary. With Pinsonneault's removal in 1867 his Irish successor Bishop John Walsh even more rapidly returned the bishop's seat to London, where it has remained ever since.

The Church of England was expanding and retaining its place as the establishment institution; for instance, six of the seven presidents of the council under the first incorporation were Anglicans. When St. Paul's Church on Dundas Street burned in 1844, funding was immediately made available for reconstruction. The Reverend Benjamin Cronyn selected the present site of St. Paul's Cathedral. William Thomas of Toronto, one of Canada's greatest nineteenth-century church builders, was chosen as architect. He designed a Gothic church eighty-five feet by fifty-nine feet which cost 7,000 pounds ($35,000). Clay for bricks was available nearby and construction proceeded so rapidly that the new church, with a seating capacity of 1,000, opened on Ash Wednesday, 1846, just two years after the fire. During the next few years it was embellished with chimes, gas lights, an organ, and hot air heating, all the comforts of the latest technology. This building forms the nucleus of St. Paul's Cathedral today.

In 1857, a year after the establishment of the Catholic Diocese of London, the Church of England created the Diocese of Huron, which also covered much of the Southwestern Peninsula. The selection of a bishop marked a new stage in the independence of the British North American colonial church; for the first time the bishop was elected by the clerics and representatives of the parishes in his diocese rather than being appointed by the government. The logical candidate was the Reverend Benjamin Cronyn, although his Church of Ireland beliefs displeased Bishop Strachan of Toronto, who once referred to him as "a low-church man, and better fitted for a political agitator than a bishop." The election, which was presided over by Strachan, was somewhat stormy, but Cronyn—who had equally sharp things to say about Strachan—was elected first bishop. He proceeded to England for consecration, the last Canadian bishop to do so. As bishop of Huron Cronyn was a great success, as he raised the 10,000-pound endowment required by the Crown for establishing a

THE CRONYN FAMILY

The Cronyn family is London's longest enduring dynasty, having arrived in 1832, even before John Harris settled, and remains active in the city to the present day. The name is chiefly associated with Bishop Benjamin Cronyn, one of the central figures in London's affairs for forty years; but his descendants form a large and widespread clan who have been active in London's business and social development as well as in the Church of England. The bishop's eldest son, Verschoyle, in a different way, probably contributed as much to London's growth as his father.

Benjamin Cronyn, Sr. was born in Kilkenny, Ireland in 1802, graduated from Trinity College, Dublin in 1822 and trained for the Church of Ireland priesthood. Unable to find a parish at home, he emigrated in 1832 to Upper Canada, where he and his wife, Margaret Anne Bickerstaff, were persuaded to stop at London instead of going on to the mission of Adelaide. Cronyn had trained as a clergyman in the Church of Ireland, which had a very different liturgical outlook from the Church of England, locally dominated by a Scot, John Strachan of Toronto; the result was something of a power and patronage struggle in Southwestern Ontario in which Cronyn and his Anglo-Irish colleagues were finally triumphant. The story of his energetic church-building and fundraising activities forms part of the basic history of London's growth in the text of this book, and it was through his efforts that the funds were raised for the creation of the Diocese of Huron in 1857. Despite Strachan's efforts, Cronyn was duly elected bishop and proceeded energetically to develop his church in the Southwestern Peninsula.

Almost everything was needed in the new diocese: adequate clergy, more churches, and more funding. An idea of the bishop's difficulties can be seen in his June 1859 re-

Top: *Rev. Benjamin Cronyn was elected as the first bishop of the new Anglican Diocese of Huron in 1857. Courtesy, UWO*

Above: *Verschoyle Cronyn built on his father's inheritance through extensive land speculation. Courtesy, Photographic Conservancy of Canada*

port, when he noted that he had visited eighty-four congregations, preached 130 sermons, consecrated five churches, admitted 1,453 communicants, and travelled 2,452 miles. Even considering that the railways were now stretching across the region, this was a mammoth task. In addition, with the help of Isaac Hellmuth, Cronyn raised funds and organized Huron College in 1863, and when he found that English funding was being reduced in 1867 he solicited an additional $30,000 for missionary work in the diocese. An excellent businessman, he greatly developed the church's land holdings, and in addition laid the basis of his family's fortune and extensive land holdings by the time he died on September 21, 1871.

None of his descendants were to become clergymen, but his son Verschoyle (1833-1920) followed in his footsteps as an entrepreneur. In a rather typical pattern of the second generation in the nineteenth century, the younger Cronyn trained in the law and was called to the bar in 1860. He married Sophia Eliza Blake, a daughter of Ontario Chancellor William H. Blake, and his sister married Sophia's brother Edward, later second premier of Ontario. Before long Cronyn formed a partnership with Frederick P. Betts, who later became his son-in-law. Verschoyle, like his father, speculated in land and by 1890 had some $103,500 worth of property in the city. He was also a leading figure in the establishment of the Huron & Erie, which has been described as his monument. He was an incorporator of the London Street Railway in 1873 and was its president until 1893. On his death on June 1, 1920, he left an estate of $306,606, of which $122,485 was in Huron & Erie stock—a considerable appreciation when it is considered that the entire amount contributed by the twenty-five original proprietors in 1864 was only $13,941. Evidence of Verschoyle's broad horizons was the fact that he was also investing in Brazilian Traction, Light & Power Company of Toronto (Brascan)—another long-time Ontario profit maker.

Verschoyle's younger brother Benjamin Jr. (1840-1905) became a lawyer too, and married one of the daughters of George J. Goodhue, but though he was popular in the city and was mayor in 1874-1875, he lacked the financial acumen of many members of the family and was badly hurt in the Bank of London's collapse in 1887. Afterward he left the city; however, his magnificent mansion is today the Central Baptist Church—his initials carved in the woodwork go well with the later occupancy.

In the later generations Hume Blake Cronyn (1864-1933), Verschoyle's son, again demonstrated the family's financial aptitude as president of the Huron & Erie and Canada Trust from 1926 to 1933. As well, he was elected federally in 1917. Two of his sons again achieved prominence. Verschoyle Philip (1895-1978), a great-grandson of both Bishop Cronyn and John Labatt I, was a director of the Canada Trust and Huron & Erie from 1929 and chairman from 1958 to 1968, as well as a director of John Labatt breweries from 1948 to 1960. He also had a distinguished military career, serving in the Royal Flying Corps in World War I, and was chancellor of the University of Western Ontario from 1961 to 1967. His younger brother, Hume (born 1911) made his fame in the theatre far from London.

Cronyn Memorial Church stands today as one of the main parishes of the city, but it represents only one aspect of that family's many activities.

new bishopric, and greatly increased the wealth of the Church of England, and his own wealth, by making astute land speculations as the city expanded.

In his later years he was assisted by one of London's most enigmatic figures, the Reverend Isaac Hellmuth, who, after first visiting London on educational matters, gradually worked himself into the position of Cronyn's right-hand man and successor. Hellmuth, a man of infinite energy, had been born at or near Warsaw about 1817-1820—all the sources for his life differ, apparently because he always gave different information. He was educated at the University of Breslau, and was converted from Judaism to Christianity. He then went to England and studied for the Church of England ministry. After some years at Bishops' College at Lennoxville in Quebec he settled in London, Ontario.

The larger population meant new entertainments. A variety of clubs were formed, including national societies for England, Ireland, and Scotland, and social clubs such as the Temperance Group and in 1847 the Independent Order of Odd Fellows. The Horticultural Association was revived in 1852, and the YMCA organized in 1856. In sports, cricket was at first very popular, although eventually it was replaced by baseball. As well, there was organized sleighing in the winter and the London Curling Club was established in 1849. The garrison with its cavalry was soon hunting and holding regular steeplechases, and horse racing was also popular. The militia, such as the Independent Voluntary Artillery organized by Captain Duncan Mackenzie in 1841, provided another diversion with its parades and exercises.

Cultural institutions appeared in the form of the Mechanic's Institute, which had both library and educational functions. Founded in 1835, it was revived and incorporated in 1841 with Elijah Leonard as president, and a small frame building was constructed for its use southwest of the courthouse overlooking the Forks of the Thames. A gala ball with 100 tickets at three dollars each raised funds for a porch with four Greek columns in 1843. The Institute, which was in essence an effort by the upper classes to elevate the industrious workers, regularly held drawing classes in addition to giving lectures and loaning books. Although it went through difficult periods in the late 1840s and 1850s, it was always revived and eventually it transferred its books to the public library. The building itself was eventually burned by an incendiary.

By 1844 plays were given by officers and some of the sons of the upper class who called themselves the Gentlemen Amateurs. Sometimes there were setbacks, as when Simcoe Lee, who later became a celebrated actor, was dragged off the stage by his father while playing a female role. Before long there was a permanent theatre run by John McFarlane of Detroit, whose wife Jessie danced between plays and as an "afterpiece." The Town Hall was also regularly rented out for entertainment and frequently was the scene of balls held by the garrison. By the 1850s London was becoming an overnight stop on the circuit for professional entertainers travelling from Detroit to Toronto, such as W.Y. Brunton's Varieties. P.T. Barnum arrived with his great circus, incensed the population with its memories of the rebellion by playing Yankee Doodle, and made a surreptitious departure. The success of other entertainers, such as the owner of "the learned pig" who paid thirty shillings ($7.50) for a license, is unknown.

In 1854 London was chosen as the location of the annual Provincial Exhibition, the ancestor of the Canadian National Exhibition, which then circulated between the various towns. This was a much grander event than the town's own annual fair, and London was selected to celebrate the arrival of the railway

P.T. Barnum, one of the great impresarios of the nineteenth century, not only developed the idea of a museum of curiosities and the modern circus, but also arranged soprano Jenny Lind's tour of North America in 1850. Barnum visited London more than once on his many tours of the continent. Courtesy, Frederick H. Armstrong

the year before. The Exhibition was laid out on a magnificent scale on a twenty-eight-acre site spreading from Talbot Street to the river between Oxford and Grosvenor streets. There Londoners visited halls displaying many varieties of crops, vegetables, and flowers, admired the new products of commerce and industry, and received prizes for their agricultural successes.

As well there were special occasions such as fireworks to celebrate the birthday of the Queen, or "the Forest City's Grand Civic Pic-nics" held at Port Stanley, which became London's recreation centre after the railways arrived. Visits of governors and other important figures also enlivened the city. Sometimes these were not a great success, as in 1849 when Governor-General Lord Elgin arrived despite the objections of Mayor Dixon, who opposed his liberal pol-

icies, and there was very nearly a riot. Far different was the entertainment for Albert Edward, Prince of Wales, who came in 1860 on London's first royal visit and was heartily entertained by the entire population. Two months later the town heard another future statesman at a ministerial dinner for the new attorney-general of Upper Canada, John A. Macdonald.

THE COMMUNICATIONS NETWORK

While Lieutenant-Governor Simcoe has always received full credit for his dream of a city at the Forks, a second passerby, Hamilton Hartley Killaly, who played a crucial role in the evolution of the city, has almost been forgotten. In 1841 Great Britain decided to try and solve the problems of the Canadas by reuniting Upper and Lower Canada as one province. Although the United Province of Canada was a political failure, which was to lead in turn to Confederation in 1867, the twenty-six years of its existence witnessed incredible economic and technological changes, particularly in the field of communications. While the railways are the best known of these, thanks to Killaly London had already established excellent connections with its hinterland a decade earlier.

In 1841, as one of the terms of the union, Britain loaned the new United Province the immense sum of 1.5 million pounds (7.5 million dollars) for the completion of necessary public works. Killaly, as London's member of the legislature from 1841 to 1843, was possibly the most generous of all London's generous members of parliament. He was also president of the Board of Public Works and spent almost the entire 100,000-pound ($500,000) appropriation for the first year on his own riding and its hinterland. No one could argue that London needed better roads; yet, even for the nineteenth century, this was a superb act of patronage.

With the assistance of a skilled engineer, Casimir Stanislaus Gzowski (who was later knighted and briefly became administator, or acting lieutenant-governor, of Ontario), Killaly either built or upgraded the network of roads stretching out from London in every direction except north. When he left office the city's dreadful trails to its hinterland had generally been rebuilt as plank, corduroy, or gravel roads, properly graded and provided with good drainage and substantial bridges. Eastward the roads connected London with Hamilton, westward with Chatham and Windsor/Sandwich, northwestward with Port Sarnia, and southward with St. Thomas and Port Stanley. At the last village a splendid pier and a drawbridge were erected to facilitate shipping. Northward, the only direction in which Killaly failed to make improvements, a toll road, called the Proof Line Road, was constructed in 1849-1850 by such leading entrepreneurs as Freeman Talbot, a son of the London Township settlement leader, Lawrence Lawrason, and brewers John Labatt and Thomas Carling.

Equally important changes were taking place in the city's communications. London was joined to the newly developed telegraph system, which was spreading across the eastern continent, in October 1847. In 1851 the provincial government took over the post office from Britain and provided better services. Letter delivery for a fee became available, although free delivery was not instituted until 1876. An impressive new post office was built at the southwest corner of Richmond Street and Queens Avenue in 1860. In 1854 London became a customs district and between 1870 and 1872 a Customs House was built on the northeast corner of the same intersection.

The city's newspapers continued to be short-lived until January 2, 1849, when William Sutherland published the first issue of the *Canadian Free Press.* It was sold to Josiah Blackburn in 1852 and today, as the *London Free Press,* is one of Canada's oldest newspapers. In 1856 the *Free Press* was involved in a printers' strike which Blackburn, like most newspaper proprietors of the era, won by hiring outside help and reducing the number of editions. During mid-century a rival in spreading the news to the city was still the town crier, who began his recitation of auctions, stray cattle, lost children, town meetings, and entertainments with the traditional "Oyez! Oyez!

Above: *This impressive cut stone post office was erected on the southwest corner of Richmond Street and Queens Avenue in 1858-1860. Before that the post office had been situated either in private residences or stores, near the courthouse at Ridout and Dundas streets. This new location reflected the eastward shift of London's business centre. Courtesy, UWO*

Opposez!" and ended with "God Save the Queen!"

On December 15, 1853, London entered the age of the "iron horse" when the first railway train chugged into the city. As early as 1831 the area's merchants and farmers had proposed a London and Gore (Hamilton area) Rail Road Company, but the idea had fallen victim to the depression of 1837. With the return of boom times in the mid-1840s, London and Hamilton entrepreneurs revived their railway scheme on a much more elaborate basis. Sir Allan MacNab of Hamilton, who had put down the western rebellion, was the key figure in the enterprise and among the local promoters were many familiar names in London history: Colonel Talbot, his nephew General Richard Airey, George J. Goodhue, Henry C. R. Becher, the Harris family, Sheriff Hamilton, and first city mayor Murray Anderson. Their politics were as diverse as their business interests, but all were united in the belief that the railroad would bring

Opposite page: *Arriving in Upper Canada from Dublin, Ireland, in 1834, Hamilton Killaly (1800-1874) lived at "Killaly Castle" in London Township and represented London in the Legislative Assembly from 1841 to 1844, serving on the Executive Council. A brilliant engineer, he was for periods in his life in charge of the Welland Canal, chairman of the Board of Works for the United Provinces of Canada, inspector of railways, and a member of a royal commission to report on the defenses of Canada. Courtesy, UWO*

THE HARRIS FAMILY

The progenitor of one of London's most prominent families, John Harris was born in England in 1783. At the age of sixteen he began his naval career by enlisting in the merchant navy. Later, in 1801, he either volunteered for or was impressed in the Royal Navy and eventually made his way to Upper Canada, In 1813, after qualifying as a master. During the War of 1812 he saw service, and was also wounded, on Lake Erie. Afterward, in 1815, he married Amelia Ryerse at Port Ryerse in Norfolk County. She was a daughter of Samuel Ryerse, an early settler of Long Point. For the first two years of his married life Harris continued to follow his naval calling by assisting Henry Bayfield to chart the Great Lakes. But in 1817 he retired from the navy on half pay, in order to be near his wife and, subsequently, his family.

Four years later he was appointed treasurer of the London District. He and his family lived at Vittoria until 1834, several years after it was decided to move the district capital to London. In September of the same year they moved into their recently completed home, "Eldon House." This Georgian-style house, with its Regency influence, was named in honor of the Earl of Eldon, the Lord Chancellor of England from 1801 to 1834. Here much of the district's financial business was performed, as well as a good number of the new town's social functions. The daily routines of the Harris household continued uninterrupted until the uncertain times of the Rebellion of 1837. More than one false threat of a rebel invasion caused alarm in London, and particularly in "Eldon House," which the rebels supposedly threatened to burn after they killed its master.

On one occasion, during a Sunday service in December 1837, Mrs. Cronyn, wife of the town's Anglican clergyman, discovered Amelia Harris and her children busily employed in making bullets for the militia. Although Mrs. Harris was initially embarrassed, her feeling soon subsided when she saw that her visitor was carrying a pair of bullet molds which she intended to use for the same purpose. During the same month John Harris took part in the famous *Caroline* incident at Navy Island in the Niagara River. On the 29th it was discovered that the *Caroline* was ferrying men and arms betweeen Fort Schlosser, New York and the rebel encampment on Navy Island. Determined to end this blatant example of American interference, forty-one men in seven boats left Chippewa under the command of Captain Andrew Drew. In a highly controversial raid, the Canadians boarded the vessel, which was docked on the American side, cut it free, and, as it drifted toward destruction in the rapids, set it ablaze.

One benefit of the rebellion was the decision to station the British regiments in London beginning in 1838. With them came a general economic boost to the town, evident in the free labor performed by the soldiers, the pay they spent, and the military contracts awarded locally. Socially, the dashing and worldly officers gave a much-needed boost to the local elite's balls and parties. Of course, with five attractive and eligible young ladies living under its roof, "Eldon House" was a popular place for the officers to congregate and as a result many social functions were held there. Yet, the gaiety of these events was not indicative of its entire history. In 1845, for example, as part of their planned separation from the rest of the county, the southern townships appointed their own treasurer. Harris, backed by the northern townships, refused to step down, or to turn over his books. The deadlock caused a fair bit of confusion for a time, as no one knew to whom to pay their taxes. In the end Harris won and managed to retain his office until his death on August 24, 1850.

With her husband and chief means of support suddenly gone, Amelia Harris found it increasingly difficult to find the money necessary to finish raising and educating her children, not to mention running a large house. She managed, however, until her death in 1882, but by the late 1880s the situation was becoming increasingly desperate and the loss of "Eldon House" threatened. Edward Harris, the eldest of the twelve Harris children, inherited the property but left the city, allowing his brother George, a lawyer, to take it. Coincidentally, at this time George's wife, the former Lucy Ronalds, inherited her grandmother's considerable estate, thus preserving "Eldon House." After George Harris' death in 1923, the estate passed to his daughter Amelia and her brother Ronald, who married Lorna, daughter of Sir George Gibbons. Because Amelia never married, Ronald's children, George, Lucy, and Robin, received "Eldon House" after their aunt's death in

John and Amelia Harris built "Eldon House" in 1834. Courtesy, City of London, "Eldon House"/Harris Family

1959. In 1960 they presented their family home and its contents to the people of London. "Eldon House," today a museum, stands as a monument to the London that once was, and also to one of the city's first families.

London prosperity and control over the Southwestern Peninsula.

The Great Western Rail Road (soon changed to Railway), as the enterprise was now called, was like the stagecoach to run from the Niagara frontier to Hamilton, London, Chatham, and Sandwich, where connections could be made to Detroit. A new charter was quickly obtained with the support of businessmen all along the route, and in October 1847 old Colonel Talbot presided over London's ground breaking ceremony. His presence symbolized the speed with which the frontier had developed; in one generation the site of London had passed from a forested wilderness to a nascent metropolitan centre.

There were many arguments over the exact railway route and difficulties with financing, but by 1852 the present Canadian National route had been selected and the London City Council had agreed to purchase stock as all city councils on the line were forced to do. Then on the cold, slushy December evening in 1853 the first train completed its six-hour journey from Hamilton at the fantastic speed of twenty-five miles per hour. It arrived two hours late; nevertheless, the thousand waiting people did not mind, as the majority of them were well fortified and were exuberantly celebrating the opening of a new era of prosperity for the city. Colonel Talbot, who had just died, would have thoroughly approved of the proceedings. In 1854 the line was safely extended to Windsor; soon there were four daily trains going each way through London carrying passengers, goods, and the mail. A Sarnia branch was opened in 1858.

This was only the beginning of London's rail network. In 1855 the Great Western extended its line from Hamilton to Toronto, and during the next year the Montreal-based Grand Trunk Railway was completed west to Toronto and then on to Sarnia in 1859. Meanwhile, in 1858, the company had built a spur line from St. Marys to London, thus connecting the city with a second railway system. London, however, like most centres of the period, wanted its own rail lines. The London and Port Stanley Railway was chartered in 1853 to provide quick transportation and recreational service to London's port. Urged on by many of the aldermen, including Anderson and Carling, the City Council, like the councils of St. Thomas and the County of Middlesex, invested heavily. The L&PS, as it was always called, opened in 1856 just in time for the depression.

Despite attempts to run special excursion trains, both the municipalities and the major promoters of the railway, including President Lawrence Lawrason,

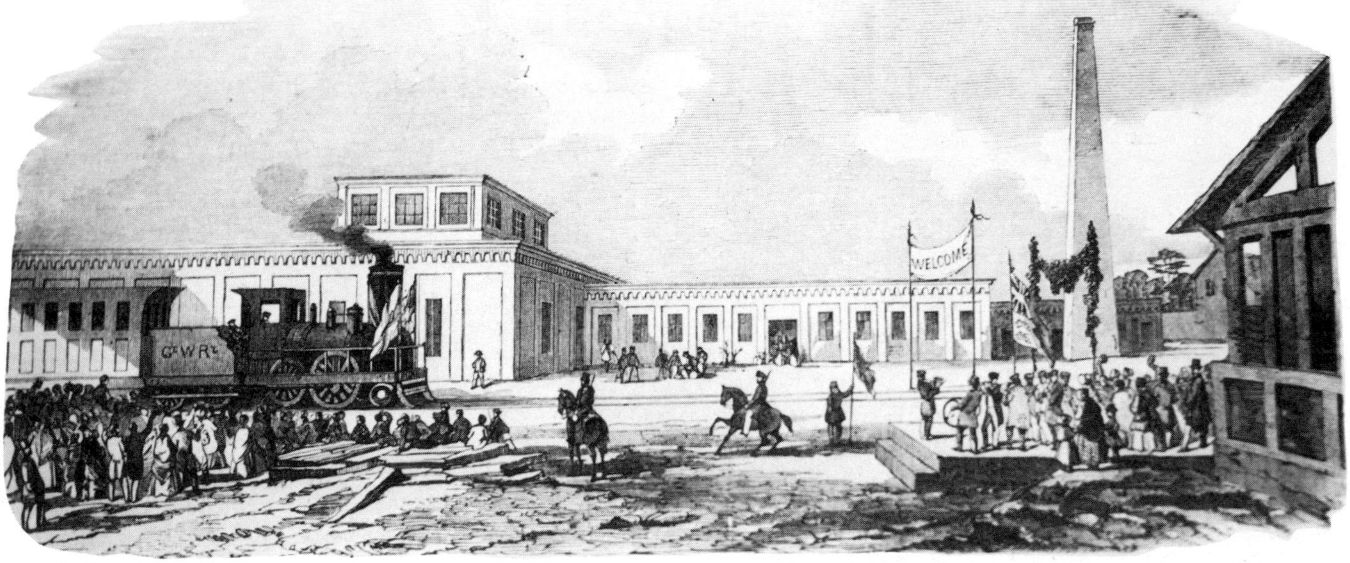

were quickly in deep financial difficulties. The effect on London's sometime rival St. Thomas was even more disastrous, as that town was turned into a way station on the railway line and within a few years its population had declined by some 50 percent. In 1872 London abandoned the operation and leased the line to the Great Western, which was itself having problems, eventually leading to its amalgamation with the Grand Trunk in 1882. Although it initially failed to make money, the London and Port Stanley, like the other railways, helped open up London to the world and gave easy access to the Lake Erie recreational area. In fact, it was probably Canada's first recreational railway. Yet, travel in that era frequently resembled an endurance test rather than a holiday, as is demonstrated by a contemporary description of an excursion from London to Cleveland:

...we left at half past four in the morning for Port Stanley, and at eight, we went on board the boat for Cleveland. There were 300 people on board, a band from Buffalo played all day, and the crowd danced. We had a thunderstorm and saw a waterspout. It was half past four when we arrived at Cleveland. We went in all the shops. We had tea at seven and went back on board again at eight. The band played all night and the crowd danced again. The gentlemen could not get berths so took the sofas out of the ladies' cabins and we gave them blankets and pillows. We got up at two o'clock in the morning as the boat arrived at Port Stanley at four. It was nine o'clock when we reached home.

THE BUSINESS PICTURE: BOOM AND BUST

With the completion of the railways the urban pattern for the eastern part of the continent was fixed; a century later the cities that had become railway centres were major nodes on the highway system and airport locations. Future cities in the West would be developed because of their value as railway locations, not because of the old pattern of waterways. For London, as the centre of a wheat-producing area which was then really the granary of Canada, the railway meant that the agricultural products of its hinterland could be shipped to eastern Canada, Europe, or the United States. Conversely, the goods needed by the hinterland were brought in through the city.

The railway also meant a change in industrial patterns. Up until this time, rather inefficient local industries could survive because of the high cost of shipping in goods; with the completion of the railway network these industries were wiped out by more efficient ones in larger centres. Thus London not only confirmed its importance as the central place of southwestern Upper Canada, but also its business community, following the spreading rail lines, began to open branches in other Canadian cities. When London was in the throes of economic depression in 1861, a local newspaper, the *Prototype,* writing to cheer up the city, noted correctly that London "is, first of all . . . a great inland Market Town—a place of resort for the wealthy and growing farming community of the disposal of produce and purchase of necessities or luxuries."

Above left and right: *Indicative of the lithographer's art, these advertisements appeared in* Railton's Directory for the City of London, C.W., 1856-57. *They reflect the increased range of goods and services available to Londoners, afforded by the railway's arrival in 1853. Courtesy, UWO*

Opposite page: *When the first train steamed into London from Hamilton on December 15, 1853, the city entered a new economic era. The event, here pictured by* The Illustrated London News, *was hailed with much festivity, including a public dinner at which Great Western Railway directors were liberally toasted by grateful local dignitaries. Courtesy, UWO*

During the boom years of the railway construction era London's position as a metropolis was consolidated in a variety of ways. Financially, the Bank of Upper Canada had been joined by the Bank of Montreal in 1844 and other major banks of the colonies soon established branches in the city. By 1858 London had its own Middlesex Mutual Insurance Society. In that same year the introduction of decimal currency greatly simplified transactions, and the first Canadian metallic coinage began to provide the province with adequate small change. The town had already begun to develop some large wholesale stores by the late 1840s and, with the advent of the railway, some of these wholesalers went on to build up very large distribution operations in a variety of goods such as hardware, dry goods, and groceries. John Birrell, who was later very active in establishing financial institutions, founded a large dry goods wholesaling operation, as did the firm of Robinson, Little and Co. With manufacturing opened up to the broader market the Morrill and Hyman tanneries expanded, and one of the city's longest lasting firms, Charles Hunt's City Mills, made its appearance in 1854.

London particularly prospered through the manufacture of railway equipment and heavy machinery. Also, carriage and wagon works and agricultural implements manufactories, which had already been important in the city's economy, expanded greatly. Many individual businesses which had been in opera-

Descended of a family of famous Massachusetts and New York iron founders, Elijah Leonard, Jr., came to Upper Canada in 1829, settling in London in 1838. Here he established E. Leonard & Sons, manufacturers of engines and boilers. Leonard played a leading role in the manufacturing and financial growth of nineteenth-century London. He was a prominent local politician and died in 1891, a respected senator of Canada. Courtesy, London Historical Museums

tion for some years were able to take advantage of the boom; Elijah Leonard, whose foundry had been prospering for some twenty years, and Mayor Murray Anderson, with his Globe Foundry and tin warehouse, are examples. They were now supplemented by new businesses, particularly specialist manufacturers. John and Oliver McClary established their McClary stove company, L.H. Perrin opened his biscuit factory in 1855, and Thomas McCormick began a similar operation in 1858. All were to flourish. Brewers like Carling and Labatt expanded and there were new specialist manufacturers such as Philo Soper's Gun Factory and Brown's Sewing Machine Company. In April 1857 London's merchants and manufacturers founded the Board of Trade, a symbol of any city's economic success.

No boom lasts forever; and as noted, the end of a boom strikes heavily in frontier communities which have overexpanded. This was most certainly the case in London, where the railway, good times, and dreams of endless wealth had resulted in a real estate boom very much like the one that struck Winnipeg thirty years later. By the early 1850s, with the railway plans unfolding, London's land prices were skyrocketing. By 1853 the city was caught up in wild real estate speculation. Surrounding forested areas which would not be built up for a generation were selling for fantastic prices, and surveyors were busy as far afield as Komoka, fourteen miles to the west, in anticipation of metropolitan expansion. The inflation in prices was nearly 300 percent between 1849 and 1856.

Then, in 1857, railway construction was fairly well finished and the Crimean War, which for two years had helped fuel growth, ended. Suddenly panic and depression swept the land as in 1837. By late 1856 a depression had begun in Britain and soon overextended businessmen were feeling the pinch across North America. During the next two years some three-quarters of London's small businesses failed and the number of debtors in the prisons increased so greatly that the laws had to be relaxed. To make matters worse there was a general crop failure on the continent with a wet spring, July frost, and wet fall. Farmers everywhere were wiped out.

In London the real estate speculators found themselves ruined as the assessment values which had gone up nearly 100 percent in four years suddenly fell back virtually to where they had started. It was to be some thirty years before prices returned to their 1850s heights. The population dropped severely: in 1855 it was estimated at 16,000; five years later it

The significance of the Globe Foundry, here pictured on a billhead dated 1861, extends far beyond its establishment by Murray Anderson in 1854, for it gave rise to the industrial community of London East. Situated on the southwest corner of Dundas and Adelaide streets on the eastern boundary of the city, the factory initially employed 100 men, who purchased cheap lots and erected houses east of Adelaide Street in London. Incorporated in 1874, London East was annexed by the city in 1885. Courtesy, UWO

was down to 11,000. The city could hardly afford to feed the poor and had to beg for private donations to enable it to keep the soup kitchen open. In order to pay its debts the City Council resorted to issuing its own city paper money backed by the market fees, taxes, licenses, and any special civic impost.

In 1860 when the legislature of the Province of Canada was meeting in Quebec, Legislative Councillor George J. Goodhue was questioned on the conditions in London and its hinterland. His answers well summed up the dismal situation:

Q.— Is there now great distress existing in the Upper Province; and if so at what period did it originate?

A.— There is very great distress existing in Canada West. Particularly so in the cities, towns and villages. Was first felt in the autumn of 1857.

Q.— What were and are the principal causes of that distress?

A.— For several years previous to 1857, large sums of money had been expended by railroad companies. Most of the municipal corporations had borrowed, and expended, very large sums for local improvements, there had been for several years good crops,

Named in honor of the Shawnee Indian chief, the Tecumseh House was one of Southwestern Ontario's great railway hotels. Situated on the southwest corner of Richmond and York streets close to the Grand Trunk Railway station, it was the largest hotel in British North America when it opened in 1856 and, until demolished in 1929, provided accommodation for royalty, Canadian prime ministers, commercial travellers, and celebrities. Courtesy, London Room

good prices, and very large discounts by several banks upon accommodation paper. These combined had led to excessive over-trading, particularly so in real estate on credit.

Q.— Has much depopulation flowed from such distress?

A.— In the City of London there has been a decrease of at least 3,000, in a population of 13,000 and I believe about the same ratio in other cities, towns and villages.

Q.— To what cause or causes do you attribute the greater depopulation of our cities and towns?

A.— Previous to 1857 there was a great demand for mechanics of every description, and very high prices were paid. This demand ceased at once, and there was followed a constant emigration of the best mechanics and labourers from the province.

Q.— To what cause can be attributed the extraordinary falling off in employment you mention in the embarrassed muncipalities?

A.— The sudden stoppage of all public and private improvements.

Q.— To what cause do you attribute the stoppage of all public and private improvements alluded to?

A.— Previous to 1857 in the cities and towns there had been a great demand for buildings of all descriptions. This ceased at once.

Q.— How does the value of real estate and the scale of rents in these localities generally compare with what they were four years ago?

A.— The value of real estate in the City of London is from 1/3 to 1/2 the price of 1857 and rents are reduced in the same proportion. I may add that in the City of London there are 40 stores not occupied, and 200 houses vacant.

Goodhue himself did not suffer badly; although his real estate holdings decreased in value he was certainly not forced to sell, and his annual rate on mortgages ran as high as 24 percent. He was a definite exception and such business leaders as his sometime partner, Lawrence Lawrason, were forced into bankruptcy. Truly, by 1861, when the *Prototype* wrote its article on the advantages of London's location, the situation in "London the Less" seemed an almost hopeless one. Nevertheless, as the journal pointed out, the basis of the city's economy was a sound one; with the return of good times prosperity was assured.

"Eldon House" was erected in 1834 for John Harris, treasurer of the London District. Successive generations occupied the mansion until, complete with furnishings, it was generously donated to the corporation of London in 1960, to be preserved as a symbol of the Harris family's contributions to London history. Photo by Alan Noon

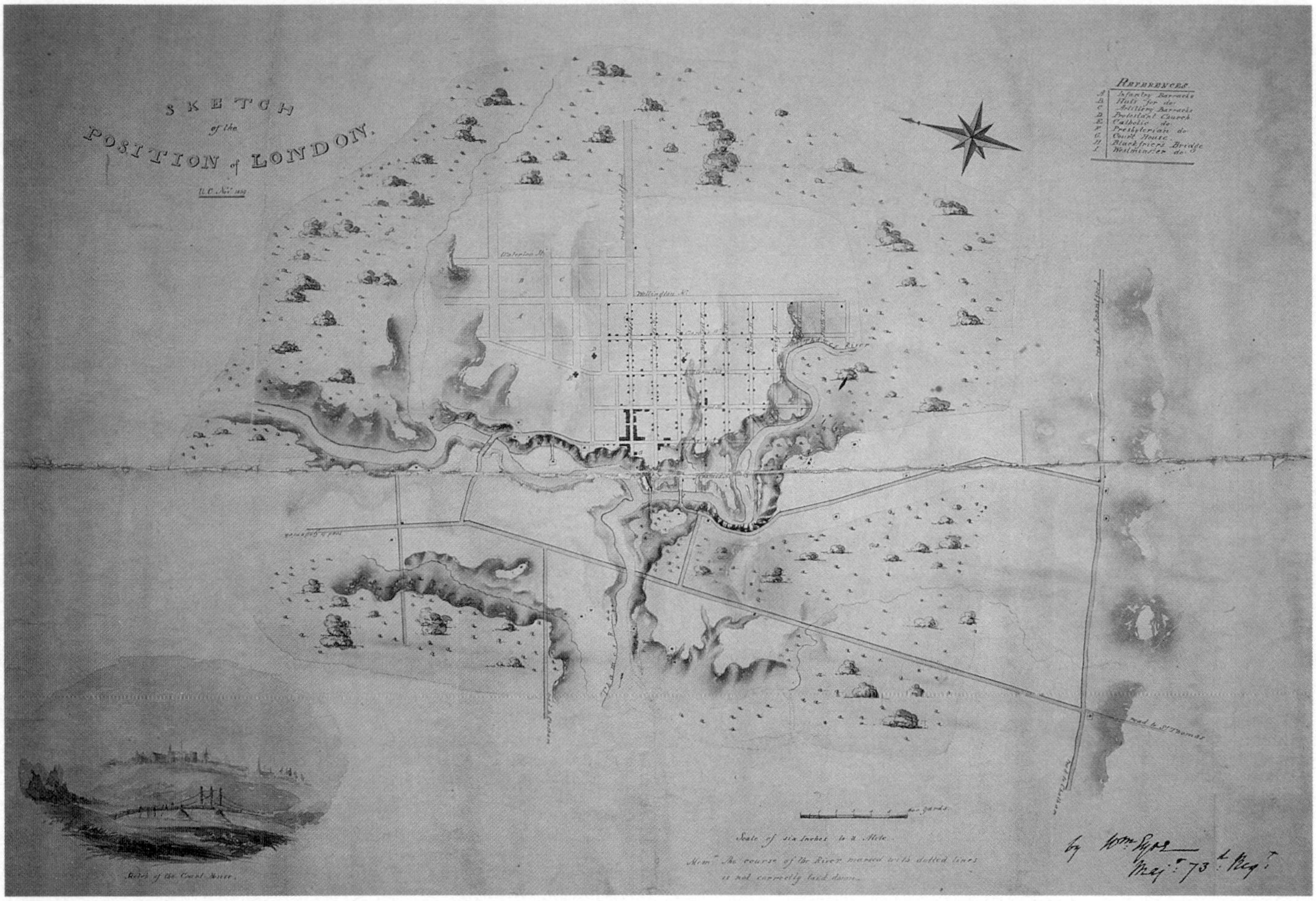

This 1839 military map of London was signed by Major William Eyre of the 73rd Regiment, then stationed at the British Garrison. It shows the position of the barracks, courthouse, major churches, bridges, and principal roads with their destinations. Settlement still remained within the original 1826 survey boundaries. The oval-shaped watercolor in the lower left corner represents the earliest glimpse of London, with the Westminster Bridge in the foreground and the courthouse beyond. Courtesy, UWO

George Russell Dartnell, surgeon-general of the British Army in Canada, was stationed in London in the early 1840s. He painted this fine view of the courthouse and surrounding buildings in 1843. With the exception of the courthouse and merchant Dennis O'Brien's three-storey brick business block (to the left of the courthouse), all the structures depicted were destroyed in the "Great Fire" of April 13, 1845. Courtesy, London Regional Art Gallery

In 1844 James Hamilton painted this tranquil watercolor scene, which looks southwest from the courthouse square. Visible among the wandering cows and ubiquitous stumps are several log and frame dwellings. In the distance, across the Thames River in Westminster Township, are the mansions of John Wilson and James Givens, two Middlesex County judges. Courtesy, Metropolitan Toronto Library

The arrival of the British military in 1838 brought London the excitement and dash that it severely lacked as a pioneer town. One of the officers was Sir James Alexander, who with his wife, Lady Eveline-Marie Mitchell Alexander, sketched extensively while stationed in Upper Canada, and later wrote of their travels. Lady Alexander depicted the first grand military steeplechase held in Canada, which took place on May 9, 1843, on the river flats west of the Forks. Courtesy, London Regional Art Gallery

BLANKETS

OXO

Opposite page: *Fanshawe Pioneer Village is in its concept a typical nineteenth-century crossroads village. Generous donations of buildings and artifacts from area residents have been gathered to re-create a fascinating impression of local pioneer life. Here the visitor can peruse a block of stores, housing a harness maker, gunsmith, barber shop, and general store (bottom). Photos by Walter Eldridge. Courtesy, Upper Thames River Conservation Authority*

In its heraldic description, the Coat of Arms, adopted in 1855 by the newly incorporated city, symbolized much of London's past history and future hopes: the deer and brown bear supporters and the beaver in the crest represent the nearby forest; the locomotive, the economic optimism generated by the arrival of the railway; and the sheaves of wheat, the agricultural base of London's hinterland. The motto freely translates as "Through Labor and Perseverance." Courtesy, City of London

Top: *This view of the Forks of the Thames from the mud flats of Petersville, or London West, is one of many watercolors of London painted by the prolific James Hamilton. Visible through the trees are the Middlesex County Courthouse and Gaol and the White Sulphur Springs Bath House. Dundas Street slopes up toward the commercial core of the city. Courtesy, Metropolitan Toronto Library*

Above: *Dated August 14, 1872, this James Hamilton watercolor depicts the Great Western Railway Coves Bridge. A steam engine, with several passenger cars in tow, journeys eastward into London. The Coves are swampy islands formed by a meander, or oxbow, of the Thames River. Courtesy, Metropolitan Toronto Library*

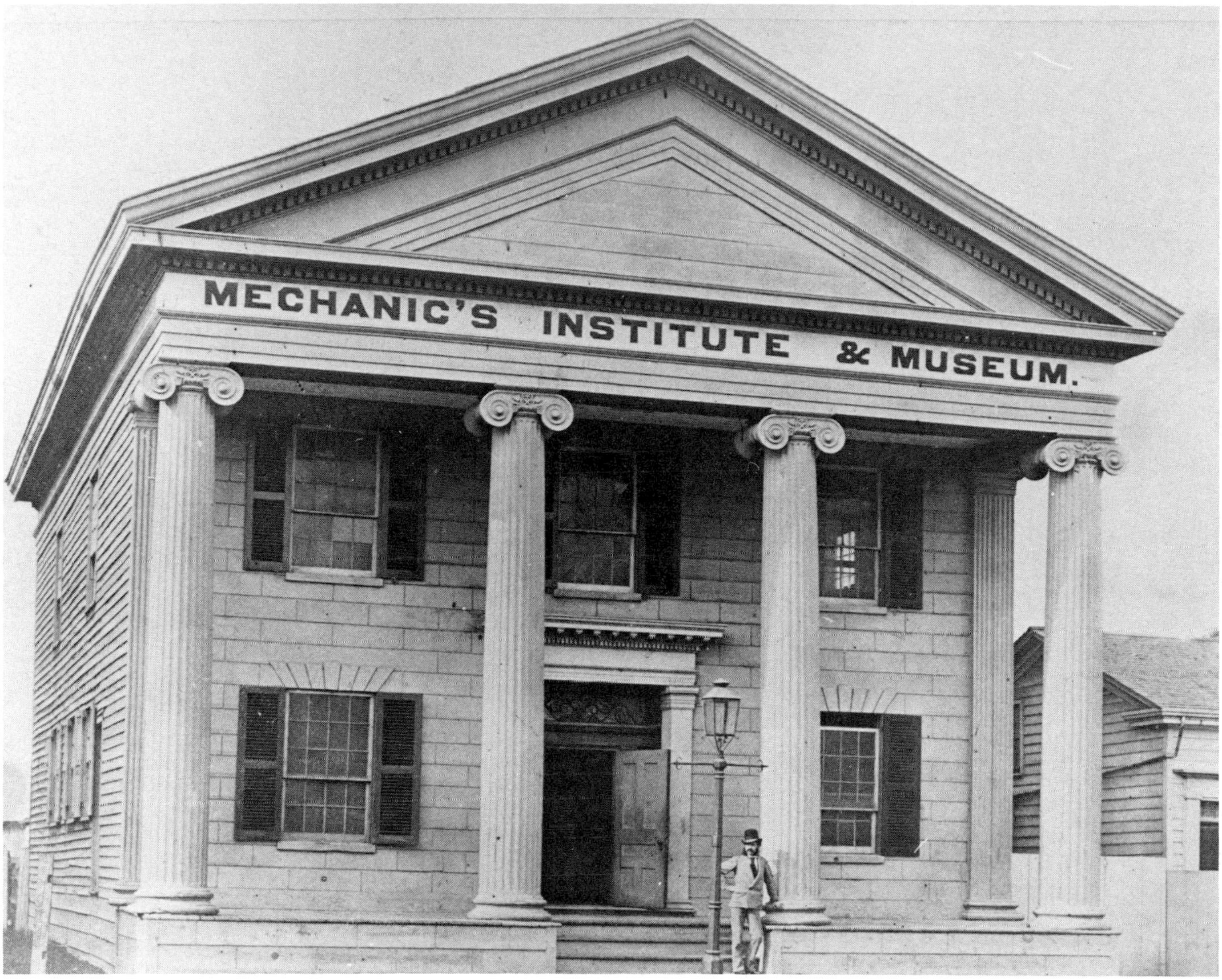

London's library system originated in the Mechanic's Institute & Museum, founded in 1842. This columned, Greek Revival temple of learning was erected on the southwest corner of the courthouse square and later moved to Talbot Street where Queens Avenue once terminated. As well as housing a lending library, the Mechanic's Institute sponsored public lectures, musical events, art exhibits, and debates. Courtesy, UWO

The substantial buildings of brick and stone in this circa 1875 photograph of Richmond Street, looking south from Fullarton Street, give evidence of the prosperity which London had attained by the 1870s as the dominant metropolitan centre of Southwestern Ontario. A visitor entering London at this point would be approaching the city's business core. Among the buildings on the east side of the street were the Customs House and Bank of British North America, and on the west side the Bank of Montreal, the Merchants Bank, and the Post Office. Courtesy, UWO

CHAPTER IV

Metropolis of Southwestern Ontario, 1861-1880

LONDON AND THE AMERICAN CIVIL WAR
London's setback was not to endure for long as the city's economy was spurred back to prosperity by two factors, one local, one international; the local event was the discovery of oil in Lambton County to the west in 1857. Once the oil boom got under way London flourished as a refining centre for two decades. The international factor, which affected the city more immediately, was the disaster of the American Civil War which broke out in 1861 and raged for four years. Upper Canada was in the ideal position of being a neutral territory which could not be damaged by the war yet could make a profit by supplying the belligerents. At the centre of British North America's greatest agricultural area, London's merchants were able to make a fortune providing wheat for the Northern armies. In addition, London's manufacturers switched over to wartime production, and its financiers speculated in American paper currency. As a result, when the war ended in 1865, the city's commercial and industrial leaders, far from being in financial difficulties, had reached new heights of affluence. In a way, London's great success in the years following was a memorial to the American Civil War. The financial institutions that were partially founded on the profits of the war and oil refining were to spread the city's influence across the nation.

London, of course, had long been involved in

directly in the growing American conflict. John Brown's Underground Railway had brought hundreds of Negro refugee slaves to Upper Canada, particularly the southwestern region and Toronto. Brown himself had drafted a constitution for the provisional government of the United States in London and Chatham in 1858, before fleeing to Kansas when his location became known. The Negro refugees provided a relief problem for the city. Since the barracks were empty because the British troops had left in 1853, a refugee camp for some 700 ex-slaves was established there in 1855. Four years later the Reverend Isaac Hellmuth, as general secretary of the Colonial Church School Society of England, had begun to make arrangements for educating both Negro children and adults. Thus London's sympathies fully backed the North and freedom for the slaves. The city's outlook showed up most strongly on April 19, 1865, at the mass meeting held at the Wesleyan Methodist Church on North Street in memory of assassinated president Abraham Lincoln.

Yet in a way there was a certain ambivalence in British North America's attitude, particularly after Britain and the North came near to clashing in 1861. Possibly also there was a certain chivalrous feeling for Southern society. The result was that in London, as in Montreal and Toronto, complex spy networks made their appearance with secret agents from both sides setting up headquarters. As far as the South was concerned this "Northwest Conspiracy" was designed to harass the North from the safety of British North America. Consequently, by 1865, although trade was not halted, international relations with the North were far from friendly. The United States cancelled its free trade, or reciprocity, treaty with British North America and threatened to militarize the Great Lakes. Fortunately the latter event never happened and tensions gradually cooled down after the Civil War.

Defence was naturally one of London's greatest problems during these years. In 1853, fifteen years after they had first been stationed in London, British troops had been withdrawn from the city with the growing threat of European conflict, which exploded into the Crimean War in 1854. With the garrison gone London began to form militia regiments for its own defence. In 1856 the 1st London Volunteer Troop of Cavalry was formed under Captain J.W.B. Rivers. After the outbreak of the Civil War in 1861 Britain sent 10,000 troops to British North America, 2,000 of whom were stationed in London.

Although the return of the troops and their fami-

lies brought joy to the merchant community, relations between the city and the garrison were frequently strained. This was partly the fault of stormy Mayor Frank E. Cornish, who, in 1863, got into a fist fight with the barracks' second-in-command at a Tecumseh House Ball. The result was a reduction in the number of troops. There were also street brawls and at least one tavern clash. Such friction was at least partially the result of rivalry between Irish settlers and English soldiers. At times the military discipline raised controversy. In July 1865 a soldier was bound to one of the guns at the barracks and given twenty-five lashes for insubordination and disrespectful conduct toward his superior officers.

In 1866, after the war, the continuing bad relations between Britain and the United States opened the way to the danger of raids by groups of Irish-American Fenians out to liberate their homeland by capturing Canada. During the summer there was actually a raid on Fort Erie and there were rumors that Sarnia had been captured and that troops were marching on

London. Both the British garrison and the militia were kept at the alert, but fortunately no real attack threatened the city. Three years later, with Canada welded into a nation by Confederation and the return of more peaceful times, the British garrison marched away for the last time in May 1869. As a result, there was some militia reorganization and in 1872 four troops in Southwestern Ontario, including London's volunteer Troop of Cavalry, were consolidated as the First Regiment of Cavalry, in 1892 renamed the First Hussars Regiment. While preparing for possible future war, the government also finally granted some financial aid to the surviving veterans of the War of 1812. In 1875 thirty veterans were examined at London. Aged seventy-eight to eighty-seven, the old soldiers, who included four Indians, were survivors of such engagements as Lundy's Lane, Fort Erie, and Stoney Creek.

The postwar period witnessed London's first spectacular kidnapping in June 1872, when two men abducted one James Simpson, rushed him to the Grand Trunk Railway Station in a cab, and hurried him across the border to the United States as a "dangerous lunatic under restraint." News soon spread through the city that Simpson was actually a Dr. James Rufus Bratton of Yorkville, South Carolina, who had been a Ku Klux Klan activist and was now hiding in the city with the South defeated. The result of the abduction was a diplomatic clash between Great Britain and the United States, and Dr. Bratton was allowed to return to London, where he practiced for some years. For his part in the affair one of the assistants to the crown attorney was given three

Above: *Much pageantry accompanied the London celebrations of Confederation Day, July 1, 1867, when Canada was granted Dominion status by Great Britain. To the accompaniment of band music, the 53rd Regiment of the British Garrison conducted a review of the parade ground (now Victoria Park). The barracks are visible in the distance. Courtesy, Photographic Conservancy of Canada*

Opposite page: *Francis Evans Cornish was the most colorful character to wear the mayor's chain of office (1861-1864). After being arrested for public drunkenness, as magistrate and mayor he fined himself four dollars in court and gave himself a severe lecture on the evils of liquor. He also bought votes with free beer. In 1872 he moved to Winnipeg, Manitoba, and won election as its first mayor in 1874. Courtesy, UWO*

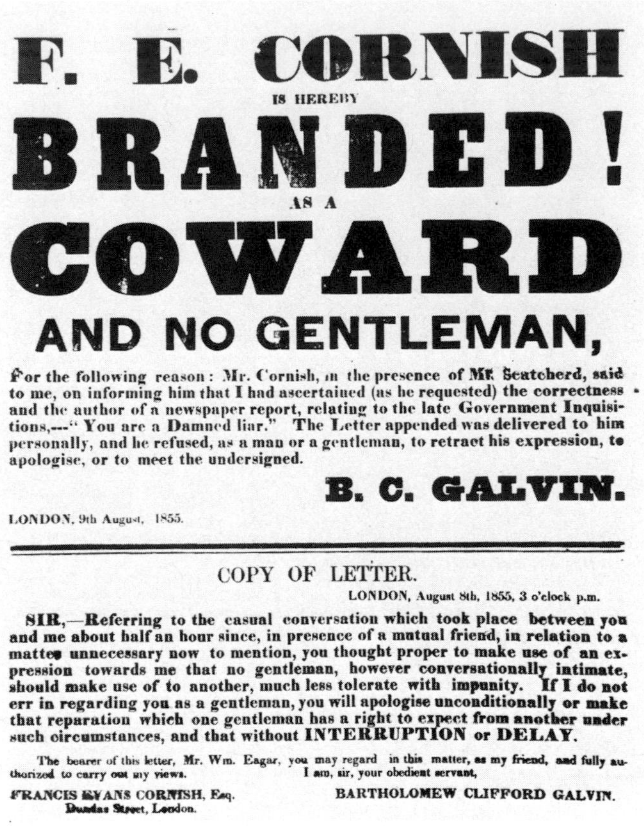

F. E. CORNISH
IS HEREBY
BRANDED!
AS A
COWARD
AND NO GENTLEMAN,

For the following reason: Mr. Cornish, in the presence of Mr. Scatcherd, said to me, on informing him that I had ascertained (as he requested) the correctness and the author of a newspaper report, relating to the late Government Inquisitions,---"You are a Damned liar." The Letter appended was delivered to him personally, and he refused, as a man or a gentleman, to retract his expression, to apologise, or to meet the undersigned.

B. C. GALVIN.

LONDON, 9th August, 1855.

COPY OF LETTER.

LONDON, August 8th, 1855, 3 o'clock p.m.

SIR,—Referring to the casual conversation which took place between you and me about half an hour since, in presence of a mutual friend, in relation to a matter unnecessary now to mention, you thought proper to make use of an expression towards me that no gentleman, however conversationally intimate, should make use of to another, much less tolerate with impunity. If I do not err in regarding you as a gentleman, you will apologise unconditionally or make that reparation which one gentleman has a right to expect from another under such circumstances, and that without INTERRUPTION or DELAY.

The bearer of this letter, Mr. Wm. Eagar, you may regard in this matter, as my friend, and fully authorized to carry out my views.

I am, sir, your obedient servant,

BARTHOLOMEW CLIFFORD GALVIN.

FRANCIS EVANS CORNISH, Esq.
Dundas Street, London.

Such incidents as alleged in this broadside of August 9, 1855, were typical of Francis E. Cornish's public antics. Although the outcome of this confrontation is unknown, Cornish once beat up a major from the British Garrison whose drunken boasting reflected on his wife's good name. The military nearly left London over the incident. Courtesy, London Historical Museums

years in the penitentiary. Fortunately there were no further incidents.

THE POLITICAL PICTURE

While London may have had relative peace on the military front, the same cannot be said for the political picture. In fact, sometimes in conjunction with the garrison, London voters were involved in some of their most acrimonious political contests during the 1860s and 1870s, and with Confederation in 1867 a third, federal arena was created in which they could do battle. It might almost be said that the introduction of the secret ballot, first federally and provincially in 1874 and then municipally in 1876, spoiled local politics. In the early 1860s the mayor of London was Frank Cornish, whose political wranglings at least equalled those of earlier mayor Thomas Dixon. Despite his battles with the barracks' second-in-command, Cornish was supposedly elected in 1861 by bribing soldiers to move into the city for twenty-four hours, thus obtaining the franchise and then voting for him in the open ballot. After his final defeat no mayor of London has, fortunately, come close to his record.

During the United Province period, which lasted from 1841 until 1867, London's representative was usually a Conservative. The members returned included the first representative from the city to hold the premiership, William Henry Draper (1845-1847), who was a resident of Toronto and had little interest in his riding. Later, "Honest John Wilson" was regarded as virtually the political owner of London until he was elevated to the bench. He managed to be elected as both a Conservative and an independent. After Confederation in 1867 John Carling, later Senator Sir John Carling, was elected as London's first representative in both the federal and the provincial parliaments. When dual representation, which allowed a man to sit in both the provincial and federal houses, was abolished in 1872, Carling decided to keep the federal office. The Londoners then elected William R. Meredith, another Conservative. He was leader of the opposition in the Ontario Legislature for most of the period before he was appointed chief justice of Ontario in 1894 and knighted shortly thereafter.

The politics of the new Dominion of Canada were not of an elevated order, as is demonstrated by the contest between Liberal Colonel John Walker and Tory John Carling. Carling remains one of the most familiar names in London's history; today Walker is virtually forgotten. A native of Scotland with a mili-

This remarkable photograph of Richmond Street, looking south between King and York streets, was taken in the late 1860s. The pioneer town of mud streets, wooden boardwalks, open gutters, and small-scale, primitive frame buildings was being changed by telegraph poles, gas street lamps, and large-scale, brick buildings, as represented in the middle distance by the Holman Opera House and the Tecumseh House. Courtesy, UWO

tary background, he had settled in Southwestern Ontario by the mid-1860s, when he fought in the Fenian raids. Walker was also involved in various speculations connected with the newly opened oil fields. Although he became a vice president of the Canadian Pacific Railway and was connected with some charitable institutions, his whole career comes through as a somewhat shady one. This is not to say that Carling's politics were always straightforward and honest; such activity would hardly have led to political survival at that period.

Originally a supporter of Carling, Walker quarrelled with him and contested the 1874 election as a Liberal, winning by about sixty votes much to the surprise of everyone. Carling contested the results and the hearings demonstrated that both sides had been purchasing votes for money, although as always it was difficult to tell how much the candidates themselves knew about this bribery. The judge decided against Walker, stating "it would be as easy to believe that one had been dipped in the lake and come out dry as to believe that so much corruption had been indulged in unknown to the candidate." Whatever the metits of his case, Walker was un-

Sir John Carling, knighted by Queen Victoria in 1893, posed for this photograph before a painted backdrop, dressed in his Windsor Castle court uniform. Courtesy, UWO

SIR JOHN CARLING

Undoubtedly one of London's best known business and political figures was Sir John Carling. His portraits present us with the image of an elder, austere, and refined statesman. This, coupled with the knowledge that he was a wealthy brewer who held numerous government positions and was also knighted, makes it difficult to appreciate his humble beginnings. John Carling was born on February 23, 1823, in London Township. His father, Thomas Carling, an early pioneer, had emigrated from England in 1818. In 1820 he married Margaret Rautledge.

The Carlings farmed until 1839, when a concern for their sons' education induced the family to move to the new town of London. There the father established a brewery, one of several such family enterprises, and ten years later he relinquished control to his son William. John, whose parents had hoped would become a lawyer, but who had apprenticed at the Hyman Tannery instead, was made a partner. John was in charge of public relations, in which his good looks and confident manner brought him much success. His public life really began a year earlier, when at the age of twenty-two he became a public school trustee for London. In 1854-1856 and 1858 he was elected a member of London Council. In 1857 Carling was persuaded to replace John Wilson, the provincial Conservative candidate, and soundly defeated Elijah Leonard by more than 600 votes. Politically, Carling fared well in the following years. In 1861 he was reelected by acclamation and in 1862 he was appointed receiver-general under the Cartier-Macdonald government. At the time of Confederation he won seats in both the federal and provincial houses, but when dual representation was abolished in 1872 Carling resigned his seat in the Ontario legislature. His first political setback came in 1874, when he narrowly lost to Colonel John Walker, who was unseated for bribery and corruption. In the by-election which followed, James Fraser was chosen as the new Conservative member.

Carling was again elected in 1878 and returned to the Cabinet in 1882 as postmaster-general. From 1885 to 1892 he was minister of agriculture. Defeated in 1891, he was appointed to the Senate, but quickly resigned in order to contest a by-election in London in which he beat his former employer's son, Charles S. Hyman. With Sir John Abbott's retirement as prime minister in 1892, having refused the lieutenant-governorship of Ontario, he became minister without portfolio. Knighted in 1893, Carling was again appointed to the Senate in 1896 just before the fall of the Conservative government.

Throughout his political career, which was truly impressive, perhaps even remarkable considering his humble beginnings, Carling seems to have kept London's (and his brewery's) best interests foremost in his mind. As a director of the Great Western, the London, Huron & Bruce, and also the London & Port Stanley railways, he realized the business potential of a good rail network. The importance of transporting Carling beer to other markets was, no doubt, at least partially responsible. Later he played a key role in bringing the Grand Trunk carshops to London and keeping them there by averting a threatened move to Brantford after they were destroyed by fire. Carling energetically assisted in the relocation of the Insane Asylum (now the London Psychiatric Hospital) from Amherstburg to London, on land he owned. He also persuaded the Canadian militia to buy more of his land for Wolseley Barracks. When London's first water commission was formed in 1878, Carling was elected chairman. The system provided plenty of clean, cheap water for London's citizenry and businesses.

Sir John Carling's long and eventful life ended on November 6, 1911, in his home on Wellington Street. His wife was Hannah, daughter of Henry Dalton of London. His contributions to London were numerous and valuable, and in politics he was correctly considered an honest, upright man. Carling never would have survived, let alone have succeeded, in nineteenth-century political life had he not understood the patronage system.

seated in 1875. Carling did not run immediately, but in 1878, in a Conservative landslide, he decisively defeated Walker and remained London's MP until 1891, when he was defeated by Charles S. Hyman, the son of Ellis W. Hyman. However, like Walker, Hyman was unseated the next year. Carling defeated him in the resulting election and remained member for London until he was elevated to the Senate.

Two campaign workers trumpet their support for Liberal Charles Smith Hyman and reform in the by-election of February 1892. They appear prepared to sweep away his opponent, Conservative John Carling. To no avail, however, for Hyman went down to defeat. Courtesy, UWO

EXPANDING AND ORGANIZING SERVICES

The continued growth of the city from 11,200 in 1860 to 19,941 in 1880 meant an increase in urban problems and also an unending need for new services. Roads were particularly important; new streets were constructed, the first macadamized pavements were laid, and a road roller was purchased for improving the streets. Stronger bridges were also needed. In 1875 the city erected its first two iron bridges: Victoria Bridge across Ridout Street, which cost $8,000; and the still-surviving $10,000 Blackfriars Bridge across the north branch of the Thames. Its lacey structure reminds us that Victorian engineering could be beautiful as well as long lasting.

For the average Londoner the great transportation breakthrough of the era, although it was the subject of endless complaints, was the London Street Railway Company, usually called the LSR, incorporated by provincial charter in 1873. In 1875, after negotiations with the city, the company was given the right to use the streets for fifty years for cars "powered by animal power." In May of that year the street railway commenced operations with three horse-drawn vehicles running on Dundas Street from Richmond to Adelaide streets. Their operators were paid one dollar per day. By the end of the year the line had been extended out to what is now the Western Fairgrounds. After an agreement with the Proof Line Road Company, which controlled upper Richmond Street, the line was extended up Richmond Street from Dundas Street to Oxford Street, opening in time for the fair which was then located north of Victoria Park. As in other cities the removal of snow from the railway tracks became a problem; shovelling it off blocked sidewalks and melting it with salt led to complaints from those travelling by sleigh. In the end the LSR ordered "buses," really covered sleighs, for periods of heavy snow. The treatment of the horses was another cause of controversy, as the company received numerous summonses for cruelty and some drivers were fined.

The city continued to suffer from a large number of fires during the Civil War, some of them appar-

The first iron bridge in London, Blackfriars Bridge ranks among Canada's most significant examples of surviving nineteenth-century engineering. Extending gracefully over the North Branch of the Thames River for an unsupported 212 feet, it was erected in 1875 by the Wrought Iron Bridge Company of Canton, Ohio. Carling's Brewery can be seen in the distance through the supports in this circa 1880 view. Courtesy, UWO

ently set by arsonists. One of the worst fires occurred on Maple Street in 1868, when troops were brought in to haul a blazing cottage to the centre of the road to stop the fire from spreading. The most spectacular fire of all was the February 1879 destruction of the huge Carling Brewery on Talbot Street. By then firefighting had become more organized with the establishment of the first permanent paid fire department in 1873 to replace the voluntary brigade.

Thomas Wastie, the first fire chief, was backed by two assistants and fourteen "call men." He resigned in 1880 to become the captain of the ill-fated steamer *Victoria.* In 1875 a telegraph fire alarm was added with sixteen alarm boxes and thirteen miles of wire spread along 237 thirty-foot poles. Despite reorganization and technological advance there were still problems. On one occasion Oliver Richardson, an original member, "borrowed" the only team of horses one summer evening to visit his sweetheart in Arva north of the city. Naturally, a fire broke out and though horses were quickly borrowed to pull the engine, Oliver was dismissed by the unromantic City Council.

In 1878, after considerable argument as to whether the city first needed a sewerage system or a water system, the latter was decided upon and an election held for a Board of Water Commissioners (the beginning of the Public Utilities Commission). The two victors were tanner Ellis W. Hyman and brewer John

Carling. City Engineer William Robinson was instructed to investigate possible sources of water and the Springbank site was selected because of the purity of its streams in which brook trout flourished. The first hydraulic pump house was built in 1879, and water was soon piped through the city.

Policing was also reorganized, as London adopted a regular police force with a chief constable in 1855. In 1866 it received its first police magistrate to try minor cases at court. Lawrence Lawrason, who had suffered financial reverses in the great panic of 1857, but still was highly respected in the city, was appointed to the post and held it until his death in 1881. The London detective force was created in 1871 and the police acquired their first vehicle, "the black Maria," and began a horse-driven patrol. Some of the sentences of that time sound strange today; in 1864 the police charged two "nymphes du pave" with disorderly conduct and gave them twelve hours to leave the city or face imprisonment for thirty days. Liquor offences posed problems even if liquor licensing acts were not very well enforced. There was practically a riot on Dundas Street in 1872, due to the arrival of a Mr. Mason from Toronto whose occupation was informing on those who sold liquor illegally.

In 1879 an unwanted visitor was a Scottish-born graduate of McGill University, Dr. Thomas Neill Cream, who later went to England where he became one of the most notorious murderers of the century. While here he apparently fatally chloroformed one of the chamber maids at the Tecumseh House with whom he had been having an affair. Cream then continued his crimes in Chicago and was eventually executed in England. The last public hanging in Lon-

Top: *London's first paid, permanent fire department was established in 1873 with a complement of seventeen men. Previously, fires were fought by volunteer brigades. With their equipment and horses, the firefighters pose in front of the King Street firehall, built by the city in 1852-1853. Courtesy, UWO*

Above: *Almost from its opening in 1829, the courthouse had endured harsh reports regarding its physical inadequacies. Finally, in 1877-1878, the building was drastically remodelled with an addition which doubled the size of the structure, extending eastward toward Ridout Street North. The new design was faithful to the original: castellated towers, Gothic pointed windows, and stuccoed walls. Courtesy, UWO*

Above: *London Asylum superintendent Richard Maurice Bucke is recognized for his early contributions to the exploration of mental health and psychological theory. He radically altered patient treatment, and improved the buildings and grounds to conform with his therapeutic principles. He was also a close friend, biographer, and literary executor of American poet Walt Whitman. Courtesy, Photographic Conservancy of Canada*

don, Ontario—Thomas Jones of Delaware for the murder of his niece—took place in December 1868. Phoebe Campbell was the first and only female to be hanged in London, executed for the 1872 murder of her husband in West Nissouri Township. On the exotic side of crime, London apparently had its own Hellfire Club in 1867. One of the members, under the pseudonym of "Slippery Jack," entered the houses of some of the leading London families on a bet and awakened the ladies by tickling their feet. Although he sometimes would break into three to four houses a night and was occasionally shot at, he was never caught. One result of his escapades was that having one's feet mysteriously tickled at night became a sort of symbol of social status for the young ladies. Legend has it that there were two individuals involved, one a British officer who returned to England and succeeded to a title.

HEALTH AND EDUCATION

London's General Hospital, now Victoria Hospital, began in connection with the garrison in 1848. In 1855 a new building was erected on Hamilton Road with four wards containing ten beds in each, but this was fired by an incendiary. Finally, in 1874, preparations were made for a move to land the city had set aside at the present South Street location. The new buildings were opened in 1875 and expanded at different times. In 1866 the City Council passed legislation providing for health officers and an appointed Board of Health. The Women's Christian Association, chartered in 1875, provided many services for the poor and needy, and friendless girls. In 1879 the Association opened a women's refuge, in 1886 a home for aged women, and in 1894 a home for incurables.

The London Asylum, now the London Psychiatric Hospital, was transferred to the city from Fort Malden at Amherstburg through the efforts of federal member John Carling in 1870. Its 300 acres of land were purchased from Carling himself; once again a London member's patronage had benefited the city. A large institution, with 1,200 inmates, it provided a decided boon to employment. So proud were Londoners of their vast new structure that in 1876, when Emperor Dom Pedro II of Brazil briefly visited the city incognito, the hospital and Carling's Brewery were selected as the subjects for the Imperial Tour! Dr. Richard Maurice Bucke, superintendent from 1877 to 1902, was one of North America's leading innovators in the treatment and training of the insane. He stopped the use of alcohol as a tranquilizer, had cottages built for those able to live with more freedom, and generally did whatever was possible to humanize the institution.

The 1870s saw a very considerable improvement in the London education system. The 1871 Educational Act of the new Province of Ontario substituted the title "high school" for the old form of grammar school and provided for commercial, scientific, and English branches within the system. In 1873 London appointed a joint Board of Trustees for both public and high schools and in 1877 the old grammar school building was sold and a new 2.6-acre site purchased for a central collegiate. The original Central Collegiate Institute was built in 1877-1878 and the students from the former Union School were transferred to the building. Ten years later laboratories were added and in 1893 the collegiate was further expanded with the addition of an auditorium. While some of London's first well-known teachers such as Nicholas Wilson and the Reverend Benjamin Bayly were still active at this time, one of London's most important educational figures of modern times also made his appearance: John I. Dearness, who began his teaching career in Middlesex County in 1869. The Western School of Art was established in 1877 under government auspices and during the next couple of decades was active in training a large number of London students, including the city's most famous artist, Paul Peel.

While the public schools were evolving, an elaborate system of Church of England high school and university education was being organized in the city. As soon as the new Diocese of Huron was formed in 1857 Bishop Cronyn had begun thinking of a theological college to train clergy locally, rather than having the seminarians go to Toronto to study at Strachan's High Church Trinity College. In 1862 the Reverend Isaac Hellmuth, by this time Cronyn's right-hand man in many endeavors, went to England and persuaded the Reverend Alfred Peache of Bristol to provide an endowment of 5,000 pounds sterling, the equivalent of about $25,000 Canadian at that time. With this money as a start, Huron College was founded in 1863.

Hellmuth himself was simultaneously developing the idea of a private high school for boys to be called

Above: *Rev. Isaac Hellmuth, a man of great vision and ambition and a converted Polish Jew, succeeded Rev. Benjamin Cronyn as Bishop of the Anglican Diocese of Huron in 1871. Hellmuth established London as a leading educational centre. He resigned amid controversy in 1883, retiring eventually to an English vicarage. Courtesy, UWO*

Opposite page, top: *London's position as the region's medical centre began in 1870 with the opening of the London Asylum, today's London Psychiatric Hospital. The original building, a massive, 800-bed structure seen here circa 1875, was erected on a drained swamp along Highbury Road, a half-mile from downtown London. The asylum formed a self-contained community with its own fire station, cottages for staff and patients, agricultural facilities, and even a railway station. Courtesy, UWO*

the London Collegiate Institute. He was able to raise sufficient funds to have the cornerstone laid in 1864 and the collegiate opened the next year. In 1868 it was renamed Hellmuth College and operated until 1877, training many sons of the city's leading families. Hellmuth also turned his thoughts to opening a girls' school. He succeeded in raising the funds to build the structure and even persuaded Prince Arthur, one of Victoria's younger sons who was visiting Canada, to preside at the official opening ceremonies in 1869. The school flourished until about 1893.

When Cronyn died in 1871 Hellmuth succeeded him as second Anglican bishop of Huron and was soon involved in several complex schemes which led his biographer to call him "the dreamer." The grand design for a new vast Anglican Holy Trinity Cathedral was probably the most spectacular of the ideas, and the chapter house was built at Richmond and Piccadilly streets in 1872-1873 with funds raised by the sale of part of St. Paul's property at the northeast corner of Richmond Street and North Street (Queens Avenue). However, his establishment of the Western University of London (since 1923 the University of Western Ontario) was certainly his most enduring contribution to the city. Hellmuth's ideas in founding the university are not entirely clear, like so many of his enterprises. Education was definitely one of his major interests; however, unlike Cronyn, he seems to have had less objection to Strachan's Trinity College in Toronto. Hellmuth organized the campaign for a university in 1877 and in 1878 obtained a charter. Meanwhile, the Sisters of the Sacred Heart had expanded the field of private education in London by founding Mount Hope Institute for Young Ladies in Lawrence Lawrason's old mansion on Colborne Street at North Street (Queens Avenue) in 1865.

Opposite page, top: *Hellmuth Boys' College was part of Bishop Isaac Hellmuth's scheme to establish schools of a denominational character in Southwestern Ontario. The institution received its first students in 1864. After its financial collapse in 1877, the school, renamed "Dufferin College," became the first home of the Western University of London, Ontario, later the University of Western Ontario, founded in 1878. Courtesy, UWO*

Bottom: *Similar to Hellmuth Boys' College, Hellmuth Ladies' College was a private preparatory school. Founded in 1867 by Bishop Hellmuth, it was briefly successful until financial difficulties likewise forced its closure. Bohuslav Kroupa, the school's art teacher, sketched this lively scene of hoop-skirted students playing croquet by the college. From* Canadian Illustrated News, *1872. Courtesy, UWO*

PARKS AND OPEN SPACES

By the 1870s the forest had been so completely cut down that the City Council began a policy of planting trees along the city streets to provide greenery. In 1871 15,000 trees were purchased in Dorchester for twenty-five cents each for this purpose. The 1860s and 1870s also witnessed a series of land transfers that resulted in the development of some of the city's major green spaces. Some of the most important of these involved the fairgrounds. There were two types of fairs held in London in the early days: the local agricultural fair, and the occasional visits of the Provincial Exhibition, which from its founding in 1846 until 1878 rotated among the major centres of the province. The Exhibition soon expanded its exhibits beyond those of an agricultural fair, incorporating displays of manufactured goods and improvements in the fine and decorative arts.

London was first chosen as a site in 1854 to celebrate the arrival of the railway and special grounds were prepared in the Oxford-Grosvenor Street area. When the exposition came back in 1861 the site chosen was the north end of the garrison grounds at Wellington Street and Central Avenue. There a new octagonal Crystal Palace was built to hold the displays; later it became the site of all of the local fairs held in London, as well as the Provincial Exhibition in 1865, 1869, 1873, and 1877. Meanwhile, the idea of developing London's own fairs into a Western Fair for the whole peninsula was raised by the local city and county agricultural and horticultural societies, and the first Western Fair was held at the garrison location in September 1868. A decade later, after the Church of England cemetery was moved from "Salter's Grove" (now Queen's Park), the fair was transferred to that location.

Victoria Park, which occupies the south-central part of the garrison grounds, also dates from this period. After the British garrison had departed and the main garrison building itself burned down, a drill shed was erected at Wellington Street and Central Avenue. Later, when arrangements were made to provide grounds for a new barracks east of Adelaide Street near Oxford Street (Woseley Barracks), the government turned the old garrison grounds over to the city as a park, although part was developed for housing. In 1874 Governor-General the Earl of Dufferin dedicated Victoria Park, and the services of the gardener who prepared the grounds for the United States Centennial Exposition at Philadelphia were secured to lay out its fifteen and a half acres.

The city's large cemeteries were opened too. St.

Above: *The annual Western Fair has been held in London every September since 1868. This 1875 engraving in* Canadian Illustrated News *depicts the first fairgrounds, located on the north half of the old British Garrison property (above today's Victoria Park). The principal exhibition building was the octagonal Crystal Palace, here festooned with flags. Courtesy, UWO*

Opposite page: *Victoria Park represents the last green space in the area once occupied by the British Garrison. Named in honor of Queen Victoria, the park was dedicated by Governor-General Lord Dufferin on August 27, 1874. Its plan, here reproduced, was developed in 1878 by William Miller, head gardener of Fairmount Park, Philadelphia. Courtesy, UWO*

Peter's Catholic Cemetery moved from the grounds around the church out to Hamilton Road, and then to Victoria Street in northeast London in 1861. St. Paul's transferred first from the churchyard to Salter's Grove, and then out to Woodland Cemetery in 1879. Mount Pleasant Cemetery, incorporated in 1875, succeeded the old Methodist Cemetery, which had been a non-denominational burying ground since 1857. The last two moves, where the old cemeteries were largely cleared, witnessed dolorous processions of coffin-laden carts and cabs crossing the city to protests from the living Londoners, who would have to travel in the same cabs. A fourth cemetery, today almost completely neglected and forgotten on the south side of Oxford Street West, was Oakland Cem-

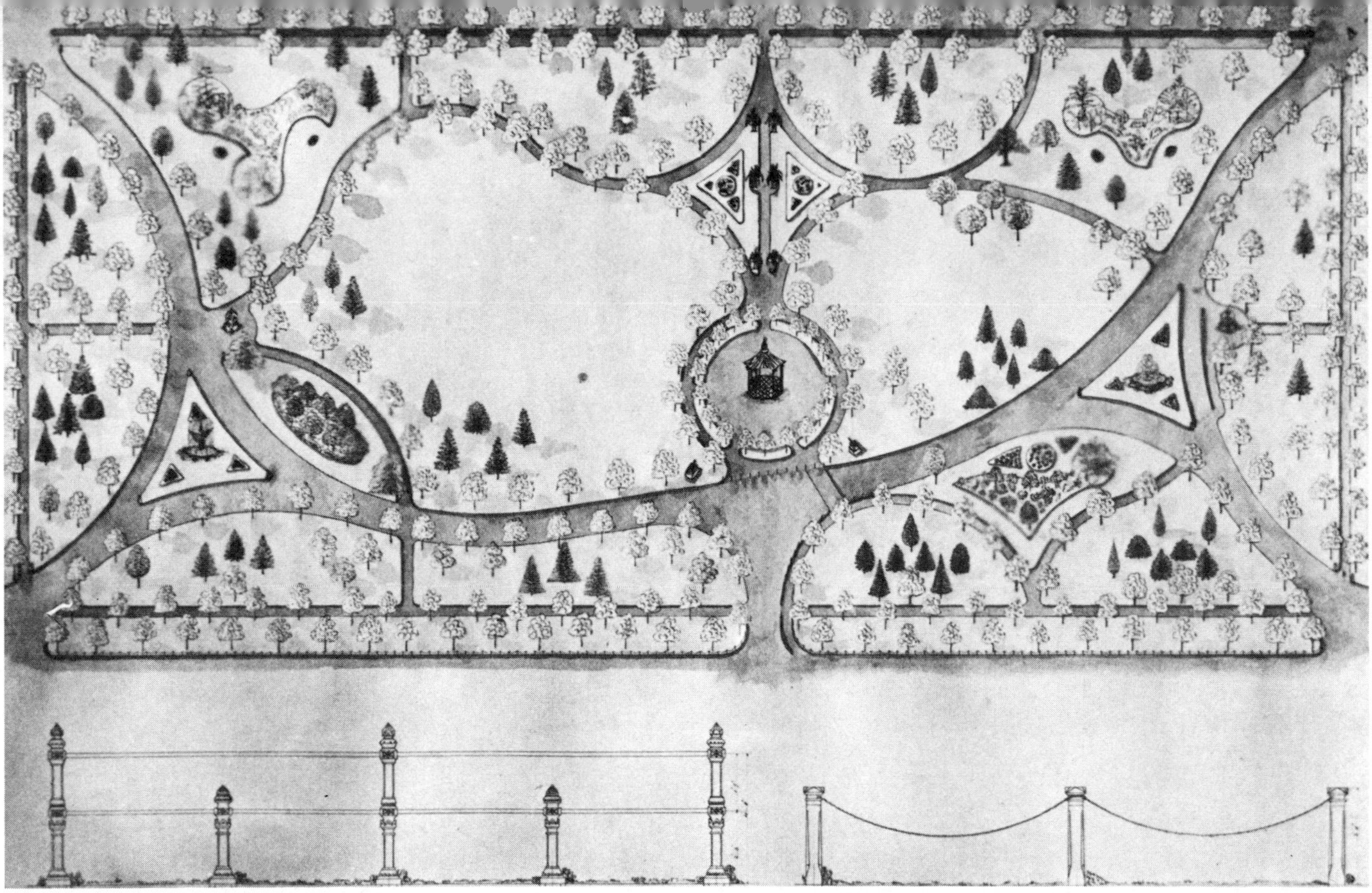

etery, which combined two earlier Methodist cemeteries and now belongs to First-St. Andrew's and Metropolitan United Churches.

In the years following, with the Victorian love for memorials, the cemeteries filled with both magnificent and curious examples of funerary architecture. Some of these were unusual in that they were cast in white bronze, a composition which, its vendor W. Webb advertised, would "out last Marble or Granite, and is not affected by age or exposure." Observing these tombstones today can confirm that the advertisement was quite honest. The most magnificent mausoleum of all, possibly the most spectacular tomb in Canada, was the one put up in Woodland for Annie Pixley, a celebrated actress on both sides of the Atlantic, who died in 1893 and is interred here with her husband and infant son. This cost no less than $50,000. In Mount Pleasant the Little family later erected a miniature Greek temple, a favorite type of mausoleum across the continent.

THE EVOLVING SOCIETY OF THE CITY

As London grew in population it became more diverse in both religion and ethnicity; new groups appeared such as the Latter Day Saints (Mormons) who built their first London church in 1875. Other denominations, such as the Congregationalists who constructed a large church on Dundas Street in 1876, were now better established, and many of the old denominations were rebuilding their churches and organizing new parishes. The Scottish Presbyterians erected present-day St. Andrew's Church in 1868. That a more liberal outlook on life was beginning to make its appearance, at least in some quarters, is shown by the dispute in that church in 1875, when the Reverend John Scott, who had been pastor for twenty-five years, was ousted after a protracted disagreement over whether or not an organ should be allowed in the building. The controversy was one that shook the Presbyterian Church badly and Scott, who resolutely supported the simple forms of worship with no instruments, retired from increasingly urban London to the small hamlet of Cromarty. In 1878 the Catholic Church established its own newspaper, *The Catholic Record,* which was published for many years by Thomas Coffey. In 1866 an English officer, who was to become London's only candidate for sainthood, was stationed in the city during the last months of his life: the Honorable Henry Edward Dormer, a young man of noble family, who was unfaltering for his ministrations to the poor and died from typhoid fever while attempting to provide aid to others.

The first Jews who practised their religion made their appearance in London in 1861 and soon were establishing their own synagogues. Other Jews, who, like Hellmuth, had changed their faith, were coming to play a prominent role in the city; several of the founders of Imperial Oil were of Jewish extraction. After the American Civil War another change took place, as many blacks began to return to the United States from the Ontario towns with the end of slavery. The Italian community was forming, with the first Italian child, of Sicilian parents, being born in the city in 1875. The long-established ethnic groups were also founding further organizations, such as the Irish Benevolent Association of London and Middlesex, established in 1877.

London native Paul Peel (1860-1892) was one of the most important Canadian artists of the nineteenth century. Studying art in Philadelphia, Paris, and London, England, he painted both in the French academic tradition and in the new Impressionistic style. His 1883 depiction of the Covent Garden Market is featured on the dust jacket of this book. Courtesy, Fanshawe Pioneer Village

Culturally, London was also becoming more active. The first artists, who had largely been members of the British garrison trained in draftsmanship, were supplemented by long-time residents of the city. London's first well-known artist (although he was hardly a professional for he was also manager of the Bank of Upper Canada and a man of considerable wealth), was James Hamilton, who left many pleasing views of London in the last century. Professional artists were also appearing, such as John Robert Peel, the father of London's famous Paul Peel, and James and John H. Griffiths, both of whom painted for a living and taught at the Western School of Art and Design. Some firms such as McClary stoves and W. J. Reid and Company chinaware employed artists to decorate their products. Several of these artists were involved in the Western Art Union which was founded in 1876 as something of a rival to the Ontario Society of Artists.

The larger city was also adding many more cultural and entertainment institutions. The Mechanic's Institute, which had declined in the 1860s, was revitalized and in 1876 moved to a new location on Dundas Street which contained a theatre for amateur stock productions. It soon had a library of 1,500 books. Further clubs, some of them with benevolent associations, were formed, such as the Maccabees of the World, a fraternal society established in 1878. The Women's Christian Temperance Union made its appearance in 1878 with Mrs. Murray Anderson as first president. At the same time the YMCA, which like the Mechanic's Institute had gone into a decline, was revived and occupied its own building in the same year. Its move to its long-time location on Wellington Street did not take place until 1897.

London was enlivened by the periodic visits of such politicians as John A. Macdonald, first prime minister of Canada, and John Sandfield Macdonald, first premier of Ontario, who jointly addressed a mass meeting in July 1867. The governors-general visited the city on ceremonial occasions, Lord Dufferin coming more than once. His successor, the Marquis of Lorne, and his wife Princess Louise, a daughter of Queen Victoria, visited the city in 1879.

The city was large enough to support its own theatres by this period. In 1866 Ellis W. Hyman rebuilt an old racket court at the corner of Richmond and York streets as London's first music hall. It had a seating capacity of 580. Five years later the new Spettigue Hall at the southwest corner of Dundas and Clarence streets, later renamed the Duffield Block, was opened with the London Philharmonic

ELLIS W. AND CHARLES S. HYMAN

The careers of the two Hymans, father and son, say a great deal about the growth of colonial cities of the frontier and the accumulation and enjoyment of North American fortunes. Ellis Walton Hyman, the founder of the family fortunes, typifies the nineteenth-century entrepreneur who moves into a new area, establishes himself in a profitable line of business, and expands as his city and its hinterland grow. He diversifies his operations, ships his products more widely as the opportunities present themselves, and finally crowns his activities by excursions into the field of finance with the profits of his basic operations. The son, Charles Smith Hyman, a man of undoubted ability and boundless energy, demonstrates how a family fortune can be used to launch a career in politics and how money, which was possibly a joy in itself to his father, can be used to enjoy life.

Ellis Walton Hyman was born in Williamsport, Pennsylvania on December 2, 1813, and was trained as a tanner. About 1835 he came to London and formed a partnership with David O. Marsh. In 1838 they obtained the boot contract for the garrison and were on the road to riches. Thus, rather ironically, Hyman based his fortune on supplying the troops sent to defend his city against American compatriots. When Marsh retired, Hyman took over the business and by 1867 was able to open a new, larger tannery on the west side of Richmond Street south of Oxford Street. He also built a shoe manufacturing plant in 1874, and a pork packing plant in London East for the English trade in 1877.

Charles Smith Hyman succeeded his father as president of the Hyman tannery in 1878. He served London politically with distinction, as an alderman, mayor, and Liberal MP. Courtesy, Photographic Conservancy of Canada

Simultaneously, Hyman was moving into other enterprises. In 1853 he was an incorporator of the L&PS and in 1871 of the London, Huron & Bruce Railway. Beyond London he was connected with the establishment of the Toronto Street Railway in 1863 and the Bank of Hamilton in 1872. Naturally, he was connected with the Board of Trade, and was an incorporator of the London Oil Company in 1866. In the same year he opened London's first theatre. In 1864 he had been one of the group who established the Huron & Erie Loan and Savings Company (the Canada Trustco of today), was its second

president from 1867 to 1871, and remained a director until 1876. Meanwhile, he helped found the London Life Insurance Company in 1874 and was a director until his death. As contemporaries said, "everything he touched turned to gold."

Hyman married twice, his second wife being Annie Maria Niles (1824-1901), a daughter of pioneer sawmill operator, lumber dealer, and MLA William Niles of Nilestown. A very decided lady, she helped advance the career of her eldest son, Charles, when Ellis died unexpectedly on April 12, 1878, shortly after being elected one of the first water commissioners for the city. The other two sons were to play only a small role in the firm's operations.

Charles Smith Hyman, born at London on August 31, 1854, was educated at Hellmuth College. He married Elizabeth, daughter of John Birrell, a leading dry goods wholesaler and Tory, though the Hymans, like most American immigrants, were Liberals. Charles' marriage, like that of his father, showed how a local family aristocracy was forming in the city. Although he expanded the tannery operation into the Northwest Territories and the Maritimes with the developing railway network, Charles left much of the management to his partners.

Unlike his father, who merely sat on the Town Council for a couple of years, Charles quickly moved into politics, becoming active in both the Board of Trade, where he was president for a year, and the city, where he was mayor in 1884. In 1900, with Carling out of the way in the Senate, Hyman won the federal election and was reelected in 1904. The next year Sir Wilfrid Laurier appointed him minister of public works and a great political career seemed underway; but then in April 1907 he suddenly resigned because of "ill-health" and left on a world tour. Charles was a famous ladies' man in London; there were rumors that the cause of the illness was a husband who came home at the wrong moment and threatened Sir Wilfrid with a scandal, which in those days would have been disastrous. Whatever the cause, Hyman's political career had ended.

"Champagne Charley," as he was known from his habit of having a special bar car attached to his trains, was active in a variety of clubs and lodges. He was also one

"Elliston," built for Ellis W. Hyman circa 1861, was considerably remodelled (as seen here) by his widow after his death in 1878. Sir Adam Beck later purchased the mansion and renamed it "Headley." Courtesy, London Historical Museums

of London's best known sportsmen, a renowned cricketer, and an excellent tennis player. As minister he had tennis courts laid out for the use of the civil servants. In addition, he probably introduced bridge to Canada. As one account said, there was "no half-heartedness about him," and he was likened to American president Teddy Roosevelt. He died October 9, 1926.

Today there is little in London to commemorate the Hymans, except an unimportant street. The tannery passed from the family in 1947, closed in 1970, and was then demolished. Ellis' magnificent residence in North London was sold to Sir Adam Beck, with whom it is associated today. However, Charles' mansion, "Idlewyld," survives on Grand Avenue, and there is a commemorative window to Ellis in the sanctuary of St. Paul's Cathedral. But possibly many of London's corporations and something of the prosperity of the city stand as their memorial.

Although baseball existed in organized form in London by 1856, the Tecumseh Base Ball Club, incorporated in 1876, was the first professional team. With a sensational series of victories, the Tecumsehs won the minor league International Base Ball Association championship in 1877. This Canadian Illustrated News *sketch shows a game on June 27, 1877, played in Tecumseh Park, now Labatt Park, between the Tecumsehs and the Guelph Maple Leafs. Courtesy, UWO*

Society performing a cantata called "The May Queen." A variety of entertainers stopped at the city. General Tom Thumb, the world's smallest man at thirty-five inches, came in 1861 and again in 1876. Professor Ayers presented a Gala Day program, highlighted by a balloon ascension which attracted 7,000 to 8,000 visitors in 1862. In 1879 P.T. Barnum, the great circus proprietor, returned—for a much better reception—with his "farewell tour" of the Greatest Show on Earth.

Sport clubs also developed. The Forest City Riding Club was formed in 1872. The earlier Tecumseh Boat Club was revived, and London's first regatta was held by the Forest City Rowing Club in 1879. Cricket continued to be a popular sport, with the London Cricket Club still active. London's most famous sporting club was formed in 1868, when the Forest City and London base ball clubs amalgamated as the Tecumseh Base Ball Club of London. The club, whose most famous player was Fred Goldsmith, had an excellent field at Tecumseh Park and developed into international champions, defeating the Pittsburgh Alleghenies to win the minor league International Base Ball Association championship in 1877. The Tecumsehs disbanded in 1878, some going to United States teams.

What probably kept the largest number of citizens in good shape was a new attraction: "velocipedemania," or, as we would say today, bicycle riding. This sport was rapidly spreading across the continent in 1868; it appeared in London in January 1869, when a youth propelled a bicycle along Dundas Street. In three years London had its own Forest City Riding Club and Tecumseh Park soon had a bi-

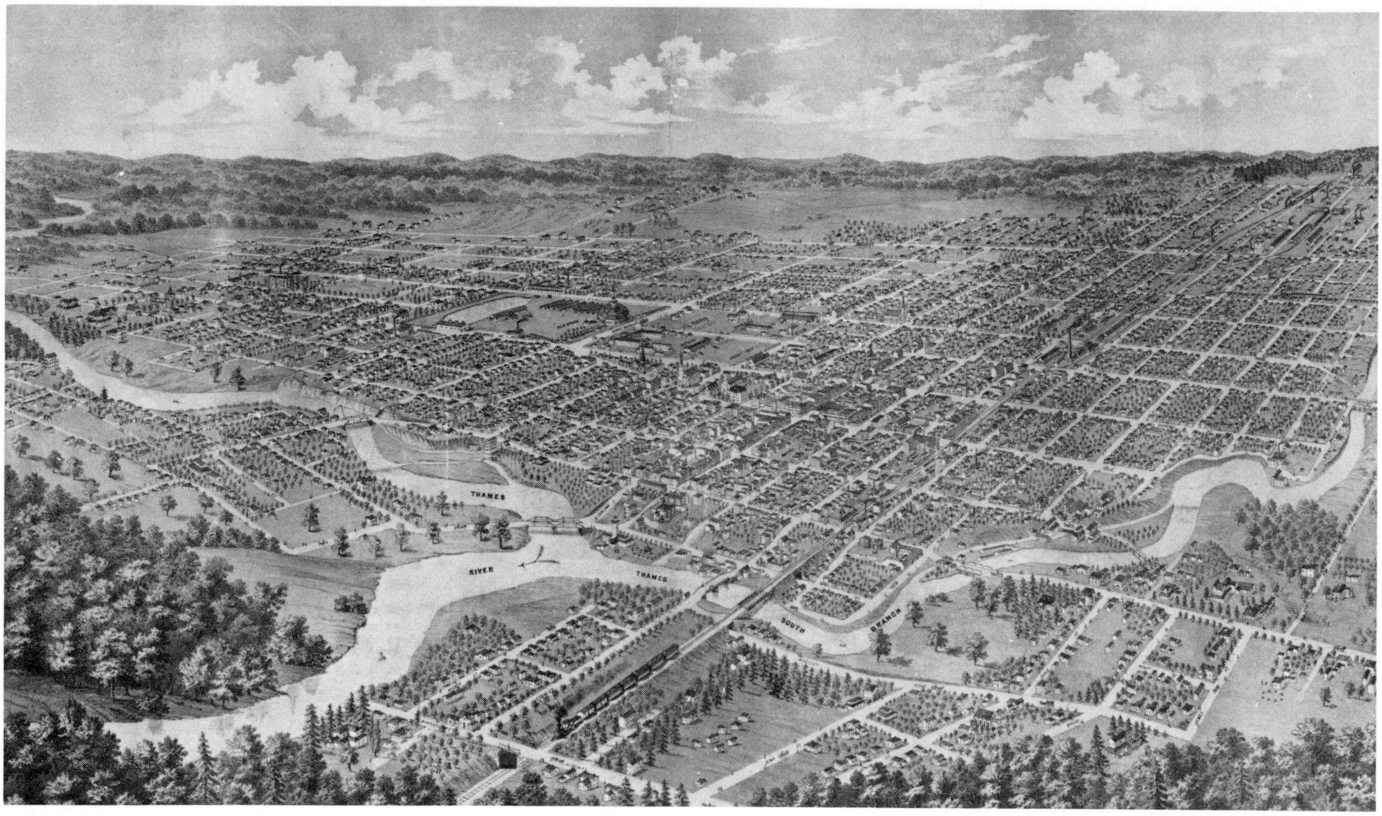

cycle track, as well as a baseball diamond, where contemporary sources asserted "the wheelmen" could be counted in the hundreds. The bicycle quickly became something more than a sporting vehicle as Londoners began to use it go to work or to make deliveries. Londoners also continued to use the railways for excursions and picnics to Port Stanley, or neighboring towns such as St. Marys, which in return held excursions to London. Ultimately these junkets led to the August civic holiday.

COMMUNICATIONS AND COMMERCE

With its railways linking it to the wider world and its hinterland now being rapidly settled, London in the years after the recovery of the early 1860s both consolidated its place as the regional metropolis of Southwestern Ontario and expanded its business connections into wider fields. With communications established in every other direction, in 1870 the city began to build its own line to the north, the London, Huron & Bruce Railway. In 1871 the citizens voted a subsidy of $100,000 for construction, which was completed in 1875. It amalgamated with the Great Western Railway the next year and was regarded as the "best railway investment London ever made." Naturally, the railroad had the full backing of the London Board of Trade. The much less successful London & Port Stanley was leased to the Great Western Railway in 1872—and was a further cause of expense as its track had to be changed to standard narrow gauge.

Communications were extended in a new way in 1877 when the London Telephone Company, which soon joined the Bell System, gave the first demonstration with a telephone call between its Richmond Street office and the Asylum, where Dr. Richard M. Bucke became the first telephone subscriber. By 1879 London had its first switchboard, the same year that a switchboard was established in London, England, and a year after Toronto's first one was installed. The newspaper network was expanded too when John Cameron brought out the first issue of his *London Evening Advertiser* in 1863. The "Tizer," as it came to be known, was to survive as the great rival to the *London Free Press* until 1936. The *Free Press* generally took a Conservative line and the *Advertiser* a Liberal one. *The Farmer's Advocate and Home Magazine* was established the following year in 1864, good evidence of London's place in its agricultural hinterland.

In another way London's growing influence as a central place for Southwestern Ontario was shown by

Above: *In this circa 1880 view, the Labatt's brewery buildings stand in the centre, the Labatt mansion to the right. The brewery at this time had a production capacity of 30,000 barrels of ale and stout per annum; the malt house held 85,000 bushels of Southwestern Ontario-grown barley. Courtesy, UWO*

Opposite page: *Spreading in a northeasterly direction toward a mythically mountainous and forested horizon, this 1872 bird's eye view of London proudly displays the city's growth and prosperity. The Forks of the Thames neatly divide London from its suburbs of South London, south of the river, and Petersville, west of the river. Courtesy, UWO*

the flourishing condition of such hotels as the Tecumseh House and the addition of such newly established hostels as Samuel Grigg's Grigg Hotel, built opposite the Great Western Railway Station in 1879. The establishment of the Western Ontario Commercial Travellers Association in 1876, which had 500 members before many years, in another way demonstrated the intricacy of its growing business connections. Commercially, business was freed from some government restrictions. In 1864 the Board of Trade began to press for the abolition of market fees, which formed an important aspect of municipal revenue. In 1882 they were successful and the fees, which were largely paid by farmers coming into town, were finally abolished in return for Middlesex County abolishing the tolls on all the roads under its control, which had put up costs for Londoners. The only tolls remaining were those charged by the Proof Line Road Company, which was finally bought out only in 1907 by joint agreement of the city, county, and township councils.

Londoners now had a wide variety of stores at which to do their shopping. These were led by Thomas F. Kingmill's emporium, opened in 1865, and the department store opened by John Bamlet Smallman and Lemuel H. Ingram in 1877, which later became Simpson's and is now owned by the Hudson's Bay Company. Long-standing London specialist firms, such as James Cowan's Hardware Company, founded in 1864, were making their appearance. In fact, the Londoner could find almost any type of shop—sometimes combined with a manufacturing operation—to suit his needs: photographers, picture framers, looking glass makers, booksellers and book binders, melodeon manufacturers, and even a marble manufacturer.

INDUSTRY AND FINANCE

In industry, where so many of London's great fortunes were made, the early entrepreneurs' manufactories were now passing to a second generation and reaching substantial proportions. Other early businesses, however, failed to keep up with changing conditions; in 1868 Simeon Morrill's tannery slipped into bankruptcy. The very prosperity of London's manufacturing base caused some difficulties in the Board of Trade. With Southern Ontario's growing industrial base, London's manufacturing interests naturally joined those of Toronto and Hamilton in pressing for a protective tariff, while these cities' commercial interests were, of course, equally interested in free trade. This division, coupled with political differences, led to a brief split in the Board of Trade from 1874 to 1881.

In 1876 *Bradstreet's Reports*, a predecessor of the Dun & Bradstreet of today, listed the Carling brothers' brewery, worth $250,000 to $300,000, and Hyman's tannery, worth between $200,000 and $250,000, as London's two largest businesses. These figures cannot be translated into modern money with any reliability, but the fact that a streetcar operator was making a dollar a day provides a fair estimate of their prosperity. Another comparison is the annual salary of female school teachers, which was raised

Above: *Third son of John Kinder Labatt, John Labatt II became brewmaster in 1864, having apprenticed in Wheeling, West Virginia. On his father's death in 1866, the brewery was left to his mother, Eliza, with John as partner. Between his assuming full control in 1872 and his death in 1915, Labatt's became one of Canada's largest breweries with an enviable reputation for quality. Courtesy, London Historical Museums*

Opposite page: *The oil industry spurred the development of London East. Beginning in 1863, Southwestern Ontario entrepreneurs erected refineries east of Adelaide Street; the Atlantic Petroleum Works, pictured here circa 1880, was among the most substantial. The barrels in the foreground were produced by the London and Petrolia Barrel Co. Courtesy, UWO*

from $220 to $250 in 1873 when butchers were selling choice roasts, steaks, and chops at twelve and a half cents per pound. The teachers could have even bought oysters at twenty-five cents a can, or fifty cents a keg (exact sizes not given); but, if they had been caught short of firewood in the great shortages of 1866 or 1870 they would have had to pay eight dollars per cord. And London could be beastly cold—on January 9, 1873, the temperature set a fifteen-year record by falling to twenty-eight degrees below zero Fahrenheit (-33 C.).

Two new types of industry made their appearance in London during the third quarter of the nineteenth century and were particularly important in the city's growth. The first of these was the now-forgotten cigar manufacturing business, which began as early as 1845 but greatly expanded about 1860. It received a great boost in 1879 when a new tariff made the cost of importing German cigars prohibitive, and only declined after the First World War. The industry, which was mostly carried on in small manufacturing plants, became one of London's largest employers. At its height, about 1912, some eighty million cigars were being manufactured annually by twenty-two factories.

Probably the first large-scale plant was George Tuckett's Tobacco Manufactory, opened in early 1861. Describing this operation, the London *Prototype* commented that tobacco manufacturing was "quite a new thing here" and was now going full blast with the firm almost immediately able to furnish fifty boxes of cigars weekly for a yearly value of about $18,000. The brands had various colorful names such as "Eldorado," "Bird's Eye," and, just to cover all political affinities, "Prince of Wales" and "Washington." Line, MacDonald and Company probably became the largest of these firms. Subsidiary industries developed too, such as the Beck Brothers Cigar Box Manufactory which moved from Toronto in 1884. Adam, later Sir Adam, Beck was to become one of the most significant figures in Ontario's history.

The other new industrial development, one that probably made more fortunes than any other single type of business in London's history, was the first Canadian oil boom which began with the discovery of oil in Lambton County about 1857. The trade that developed served to make London, Ontario known all over the new Dominion of Canada. Although the oil fields were fairly distant from London, the Board of Trade managed to obtain special railway privileges which allowed oil operators to spend their days at Bothwell in Lambton and their nights in London.

Favorable rates were also obtained for shipping oil to London for processing. Despite this yeoman work by the business community, which briefly made London the oil capital of Canada, the City Council took the rather short-sighted policy of passing legislation that moved the refineries beyond the city limits because of their unpleasant odor. As Archie Bremner wryly commented in his *Illustrated London*: "the odor remained, but taxable property was outside of the jurisdiction of city assessors."

While London may have lost taxes, its entrepreneurs certainly did not miss their opportunity. The oil refiners built their plants beyond Adelaide Street in the nascent village of London East (incorporated 1874) and in a few years, between petrochemical manufacturing of various types and the carshops of the Great Western Railway, the area was a booming if somewhat unsavory one. London itself also suffered from the waste products of the oil industry which flowed down the South Branch of the Thames across the city. Rather ironically, when the winds blew from the east the sulphuric fumes would eat the paint on the newly erected mansions of the oil barons on Queens Avenue well within the city. Probably the first oil refinery was that set up by William Spencer in 1862. He was soon joined by others and before long there were some dozen different firms operating, as well as secondary industries such as the Canada Chemical Company, established in 1867 to make the acid needed in the refining process.

Rivalry from United States refineries and rapid changes in the technical processes, however, posed too many difficulties for the small businesses to overcome. As a result, in 1880 seven of the London refineries joined together to form Imperial Oil with its headquarters in London and offices at Petrolia. Except for Isaac Guggenheim of New York, the nineteen men involved were all from London and its region. The names Engelhart, Fitzgerald, Smallman, Spencer, and Waterman were relatively new to the scene, but some of the old establishment families such as the Goodhues, Hymans, and Macbeths (Talbot's heirs) were also involved. Frederick A. Fitzgerald became the first president. The new corporation was not long domiciled in the city; the desire to have the offices and refineries close to the oil fields was too great. When the London East plant was struck by lightning and burnt down in 1883, new refineries were built closer to shipping facilities at Sarnia. The offices of the company successively moved from London to Petrolia to Sarnia to Toronto.

The general prosperity of the city during the Civil War period and the following years resulted in London developing as a major financial centre.

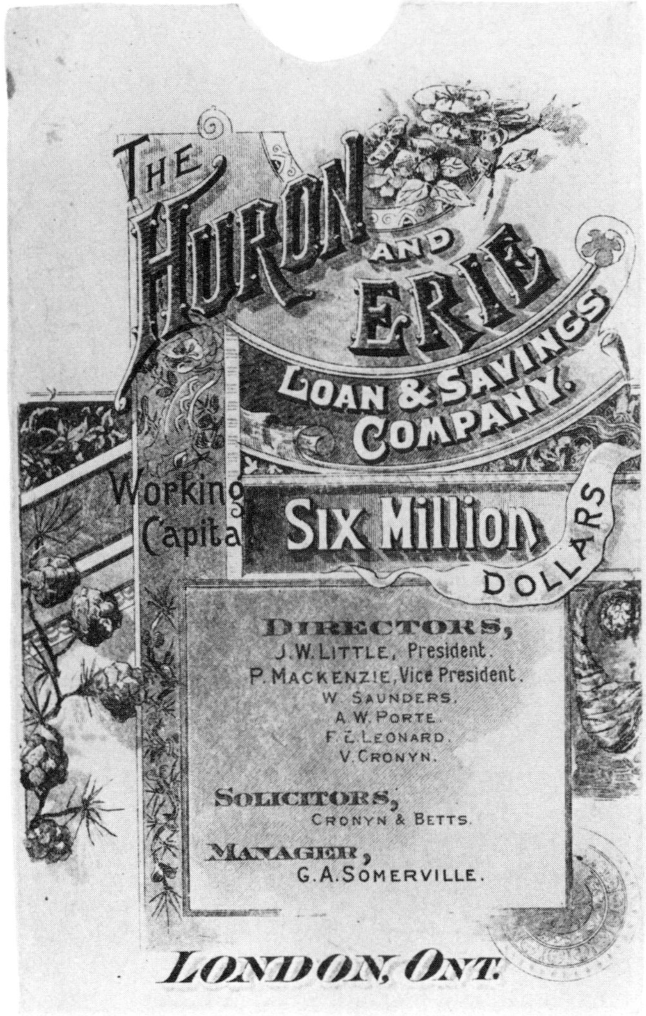

At the end of the 1860s most of the old banks of Upper Canada were swept away in a series of failures and amalgamations; however, newer banks opened branches to take their place in the city, including the Canadian Bank of Commerce, Molson's Bank, and the Bank of Toronto. With the newfound prosperity of the city, London's established families and *nouveau riche* began directing their energies toward incorporating savings, loan, and building societies to provide money for mortgages at reasonable rates of interest. Through the next few years a large number of these companies were opened in the city, and it was claimed that every lawyer had his own operation. Most did not last for many years, but several of them developed into well-established financial firms. In his last years old George J. Goodhue must have found considerable competition.

Most important of these, of course, was the Huron & Erie Loan and Savings Society which was organized in 1864 by twenty-five businessmen, including representatives of the Cronyn, Hyman, and Leonard families, and soon took in other smaller companies. This of course became the Huron & Erie Mortgage Corporation, later Canada Trust, and finally the Canada Trustco of today. Many of the old London names such as Cronyn, Leonard, Little, and Meredith long continued to be associated with its growth. The Ontario Loan & Debenture Company was founded in 1870 and remained a major firm in London for a century before being taken over by the Royal Trust Company a century later. It was first under control of the Harris family and later the Jefferys' interests. The Dominion Savings & Investment Society, established in 1872 by such families as the Merediths, Duffields, and Watermans, was also prominent for some years.

Henry Taylor, who was connected with Dominion Savings, was also prominent in the short-lived Bank of London which lasted from 1883 to 1887. In the field of insurance, the greatest development was the foundation of the London Life Insurance Company in March 1874 by much the same group of leading London businessmen. John G. Richter, who became

manager in 1883, was to make it a major force in the field. In 1877 London even had a Richmond Street stockbroker, John Wright, who quoted the Huron & Erie stock at the substantial sum of $130 to $132. Fire insurance companies such as the London Mutual Fire Insurance also were making their appearance.

REGIONAL HEGEMONY

Thus by 1880 London, building on the excellent geographic base that Simcoe had seen long before, had fully established itself as a growing metropolitan centre with all the necessary communication and business connections to control its hinterland in Southwestern Ontario (or, as it was still to be called for many years despite the addition of the north to the province, Western Ontario). The completion of the London, Huron & Bruce Railway marked the end of a stage in London's development in which first-class communications were established with all parts of its natural geographic hinterland. Its position had been quickly bolstered by an expansion of its commercial and industrial base to serve the growing population in its territories, and the establishment of the financial institutions necessary for its region.

This southwestern territory of some fourteen counties was to remain roughly the limit of London's direct influence, as was evidenced by such factors as the growth of the circulation area of the *London Free Press* and the branch college network that was later built up by the University of Western Ontario. London had attained its position as a regional metropolis; next the city would extend its business connections into wider fields along Canada's broadening railway connections, to the Maritimes in 1876 and into the West after 1885, in rivalry with Toronto and Montreal.

Above: *London's financial district had originally been located in "Banker's Row," today's "Ridout Restoration." With the shift of the principal northern route into London from Ridout Street North to Richmond Street, London's financial district relocated by the 1870s. Joining the post office at the intersection of Queens and Richmond were the Customs House, the Bank of Montreal, the Merchants Bank, and the Bank of British North America, pictured here. Regrettably, all of these buildings have been demolished. Courtesy, UWO*

Opposite page, left: *Thomas H. Smallman's Canada Chemical Manufacturing Company was one of several industries fostered by the London East oil refineries. Smallman co-founded Imperial Oil in 1880 and was a driving force in London's financial and business communities. Courtesy, UWO*

Opposite page, right: *The oil boom, the American Civil War, and the return of the British Garrison brought back prosperity after the depression of 1857. Merchants invested their profits in the founding of financial institutions, thereby making London a national financial centre. Pictured is an 1894 passbook cover from the Huron and Erie Loan & Savings Company (or Huron & Erie—the ampersand was used inconsistently). Founded in 1864, it is the Canada Trustco today. Courtesy, UWO*

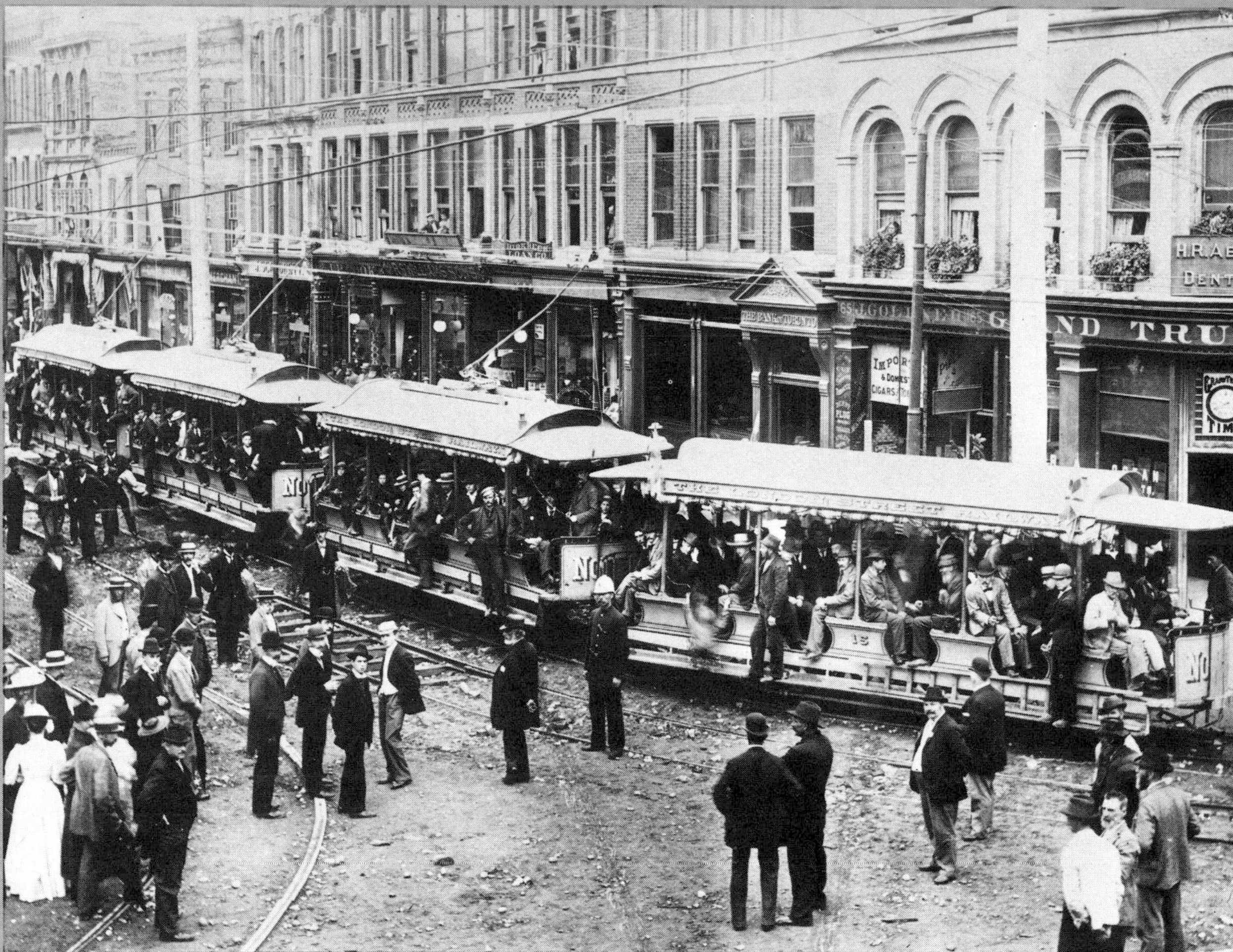

Londoners gaze at the crowded streetcars on the inaugural run of the newly electrified London Street Railway on September 12, 1895. The L.S.R. had commenced operations with horse-pulled trams on May 24, 1875. Because the first order of electric cars was delayed, the trolleys pictured here on Dundas and Richmond streets were the old horse cars converted to electricity. Courtesy, UWO

CHAPTER V

Annexation and Electrification, 1880-1912

LONDON IN 1880
The visitor to London in the early 1880s would have found little to remind him of the pioneer village that was less than a half-century in the past. In 1880 London had a population of 19,941 and an area of settlement that spread well past the boundaries of 1840 in every direction except to the north, where the far distant boundary at Huron Street would not be reached by the spreading wave of construction until the period after World War I. Downtown, the focus of the city had moved eastward from the courthouse-market square area, for once Richmond Street was connected to London's northern hinterland, Richmond and Dundas streets had become the main intersection.

Some buildings dating from the reconstruction after the great fires of the mid-1840s still stood in the west end of the downtown, but along Dundas and Richmond streets new, larger, more ornate business blocks had been built, generally three or four stories in height. Some of them had high mansard roofs, and decorative cornices of cast iron imitating wood or stone. At Richmond Street and Queens Avenue a financial district had developed, housed in fine, cut stone buildings. Here were located the head offices of the banks, the post office, and the customs house. Before long the London Club also occupied its present position.

Above: *Ranking with St. Paul's Cathedral in medieval splendor, St. Peter's Basilica is the grandest of London's churches. Erected between 1880 and 1885, its design by Toronto architect Joseph Conolly is reminiscent of the middle French Gothic period. The costs incurred in its construction, however, prevented completion according to the architect's rendering, here pictured in this lithograph. From Goodspeed,* The History of Middlesex County, *1889. Courtesy, UWO*

Above right: *In the few years he practiced his profession, George F. Durand (1850-1889) gained recognition as Southwestern Ontario's most significant nineteenth-century architect. Employing the prevailing High Victorian styles, he won important commissions in London and throughout the region. Courtesy, London Historical Museums*

Opposite page: *The McCormick mansion on Grand Avenue was among the greatest of the South London estates. Erected circa 1883 for biscuit manufacturer Thomas McCormick, the huge house was a mass of gables, dormers, verandas, and conservatories, its attic holding as many as 400 people for church and charity functions. Vacant by 1914, it was demolished when no buyer could be found. Courtesy, Photographic Conservancy of Canada*

With the lack of zoning regulations the downtown was not limited to commercial uses and both large and small factories were scattered through the area, such as the Perrin biscuit company. To the east of the City Centre, around Wellington Street, were several other large manufactories, including Perrin's rival the McCormick Manufacturing Company, the McClary stove works, and the Leonard foundry. The downtown streets, despite the efforts of the City Council to find a good surfacing material, remained messy, and the cornices of the new buildings were gradually being obscured by the telegraph and telephone poles with their festoons of wires—a hazard to firefighters—which were in a few years to be joined by those of the electric system. Some of the merchants were so incensed by their ugliness that by 1881 they were threatening to chop the lines down with axes.

Although many of the new buildings were impressive, the main feature of the downtown was once again the county courthouse, which had just been extensively rebuilt in 1877-1878 after years of com-

plaints about its inadequacy; one of the judges had noted in 1876 that it lacked such basic amenities as both water and toilets. The reconstruction doubled the size of the building, adding the whole east section facing over Ridout Street with its fine central tower and two flanking turrets. Fortunately, the design of the original building was copied exactly, as was again the case when the library wing to the south was added in 1911. The new structure, however much it copied Medieval design, had all the necessary comforts, including heating by hot air.

The present St. Peter's Cathedral, which was completed in 1885, soon came to join the courthouse as one of the most prominent structures on the skyline. The impressive French Gothic design, with its use of stone instead of brick, showed the wealth and importance of the Catholic Church in the Southwestern Peninsula, even though the construction of the towers was delayed until 1958. It was to be elevated to the status of a minor basilica in 1961. Like the Anglicans before them, the Catholics brought in a Toronto architect, Joseph Conolly, who also designed the magnificent Church of Our Lady in Guelph. Although London has tended to bring in outside designers for many of its important structures, by the 1880s the city had some very good architects of its own. Samuel Peters, Jr. and William Robinson were two of the first architects of prominence; both also worked in the capacity of city engineer. Peters had already designed the Tecumseh House, the City Hall, and the market building, and Robinson was responsible for the still-surviving St. Andrew's Church. As well as designing buildings himself, Robinson trained many other architects, including Thomas H. Tracy, George F. Durand, and John M. Moore. These men were associated in various partnerships which devel-

oped into the Ronald E. Murphy firm of today.

The increasing traffic and congestion of the downtown meant that most of those who could afford it began to move away from the city's centre. Immediately to the north, at recently landscaped Victoria Park and along Queens Avenue, the new petrochemical barons and many other city leaders had begun to build their mansions in the 1870s. Many of them are still standing today. Queens Avenue became London's showpiece and was always among the first to receive new services, such as paving. Northward a fine residential district gradually developed and beyond it the estates of many of the wealthy were to be found scattered in the countryside. Other affluent Londoners moved southward into the north end of Westminster Township, conveniently located just across the river and easily accessible once the Ridout Street Bridge was opened. Though it was never incorporated separately and lacked any special municipal services, this area of New Brighton, or London South as it became better known, gradually developed many pleasant residences. Grand Avenue with its vast mansions, of which "Idlewyld" and "Waverley" still stand, became another showpiece of the city.

To the east of the main city across Adelaide Street, London East, featuring smaller lots, workingmen's houses, many petrochemical businesses, and the Great Western Railway carshops, had developed into London's industrial suburb by this period. Incorporated in 1874, it centred along Dundas Street with its commercial heart located in the area just to the east of Adelaide Street. To the west of the city was the village of Petersville, or London West, as it renamed itself after a battle with the Peters family of "Grosvenor Lodge" in the early 1880s. Although it was upwind from the industrial fumes of the eastern factories, it was the last residential choice for most Londoners as it was located, soon to become tragically obvious, on the flood plain. Composed mostly of small residences, it lacked both services and any real taxation base.

THE ANNEXATIONS, 1885-1912

Given this situation it was not surprising that the city, seeking both expansion room and an extended taxation base, and the suburbanites, seeking more services, would soon come together to form a larger municipality. With its industry London East was the first suburb to be taken in by the city. Whereas London looked hopefully to the taxes which could be raised, London East badly needed the services, particularly an extended system of streetcar transportation along Dundas Street, a proper water supply, and fire protection. This became more than obvious in 1883 when both Imperial Oil Limited and the Great Western carshops burnt down; Imperial Oil was to move to Petrolia and Sarnia and be permanently lost to London, and the carshops were not rebuilt until 1896. With these incentives the two municipalities came to an agreement which led to amalgamation in March 1885. The section of Westminster Township

which formed London South followed in April 1890. The homeowners were largely employed in the city and again the need for clean water and other services persuaded them to accept annexation.

London West, also incorporated in 1874, had to wait much longer, not from any lack of desire for annexation, but rather because the city was far from eager to take on such an unpromising and unremunerative suburban area. As a result, London West had been a separate village for almost a quarter-century when it was finally taken over by the city in December 1897. With London West's additional 2,000 inhabitants, the population of the city nearly doubled in less than twenty years to reach a total of 38,575. The last annexation of the pre-World War I years occurred in 1912, when the city expanded eastward in a great arc around old London East. The annexation included Knollwood Park to the northeast, Ealing and Pottersburg to the east, and Chelsea Green to the southeast.

CITY GOVERNMENT AND DEPARTMENTS

In 1882 the structure of city government was altered so that there were four wards divided by Dundas and Wellington streets, each ward electing three aldermen. In 1885 a fifth ward was added for London East and in 1890 another for London South; London West did not receive separate aldermen after its an-

Above: *A London East neighborhood is depicted early in the century, fixed in the heat of a summer's day. The laundry hung out to dry, the sheds and horse barns, small garden plots, sturdy board fences, and small backyard privies re-create the forgotten commonplaces of domestic life. Courtesy, UWO*

Opposite page: *The generally working-class, low-lying suburb of London West is depicted in this 1897 view. Most of its residents were employed in London or were engaged in market gardening. Incorporated in 1874 as the village of Petersville, renamed London West in 1881, the community was annexed to London in 1897. Courtesy, UWO*

nexation. Effective 1901 the number of aldermen was cut back to twelve and, in what must have been an incredibly confusing situation for the voter, all were elected on one general ballot. The city councillors of the period were all leading businessmen, usually connected with the Board of Trade and usually active in either of the two political parties, although municipal politics continued on a non-partisan basis. Two particularly active mayors may serve as examples of the types of careers represented. Emanuel Thomas Essery (1893-1894), son of a London shoe manufacturer, was trained as a barrister and was eventually to become a K.C. Educated at the University of Toronto, he also had a military certificate from Royal Military College and had fought in the Fenian raids. Essery had broad business connections, was president of the London & Port Stanley Railway, and was a member of the St. George's Society, the Masons, and the Orangemen, as well as being grand secretary of the Canadian Order of Beavers. He was also at one time president of the Veteran's Association and a member of the Conservative party, running as an unsuccessful provincial candidate in 1894.

Mayor John W. Little (1895-1898) is possibly an even better representative of this group. With his uncle, George Robinson, who was also very important in the city, he formed the firm of Robinson, Little and Company, whose drygoods business was to expand into the Canadian Northwest and continue until recent years. Little, who died in 1913, was a Liberal, a member of the Board of Trade, and president of the Huron & Erie Loan and Savings Society. He had a city mansion on the south side of Victoria Park and a country residence, "Hazelden," on the Thames River to the west of the city. Along with Conservatives Adam Beck and George Gibbons he was one of the most important men in turn-of-the-century London. These mayors with their variety of business operations and membership in a plethora of societies are typical examples of the group of men who were coming to form a sort of medium-size, interlocking directorate of both the city and its corporations; their

descendants were to hold power until almost the present day.

The era witnessed a continuation of the organization of the municipal departments on their modern bases. Like the Fire Department, the Police Department was properly marshalled; a new police chief, W.T.T. Williams, was appointed in 1877. He was to hold office until 1920 and oversaw the development of an appropriate Police Force for the growing city. The night duty force was armed in 1878 and a year later the police began to wear helmets. The city provided funding for a new central police station on Carling Street in 1882 which was to be used until 1930. In 1898 the Police Force not only began operating the city ambulance, but also ordered a bicycle so they could apprehend cyclists who were speeding or riding on the sidewalks. The first motorized patrol wagon came in 1913, followed by the sale of the police horses. The Fire Department had its central firehall remodeled in 1890, and like the Police Force was regularly adding new equipment, such as an aerial

Above: *Throughout most of the nineteenth century, London streets, at best, were gravelled with crushed stone. The streets were periodically scraped and watered to keep down the blowing dust. Beginning in 1880, a section of the central city was paved with cedar blocks, replaced after 1895 by brick and asphalt paving. The workmen in this view of Talbot Street, north of Dundas, tar the bricked road surface. Courtesy, London Historical Museums*

Opposite page: *This circa 1890 photograph depicts city laborers, hoes and shovels in hand, scraping and levelling the dirt surface of Clarence Street, immediately north of Dundas Street, in London's business district. Courtesy, UWO*

Top: *London's selection as the site of the third provincial Normal School in 1898 solidified the city's position as the educational centre of Southwestern Ontario. Utilized from 1900 to 1958, the institution trained more than 12,000 teachers. Today, its educational function continues as the Monsignor Feeney Centre for Catholic Education. Courtesy, UWO*

Above: *From his niche high in the tower, St. Joseph blesses the new St. Joseph's Hospital of 1892. The Sisters of St. Joseph first occupied a ten-bed facility in the Judge Street mansion on Grosvenor Street in 1888. This is pictured on the extreme right of the photograph, linked by a roofed walkway. Over the decades the hospital has expanded to cover the entire block. Courtesy, UWO*

truck for fires in the new four- and five-storey buildings.

The last part of the nineteenth century saw most cities attempting to find a really satisfactory method of street paving, with the result that as many as nine different types of paving were being used simultaneously in some places. London in 1880 adopted cedar block paving for the central portion of the city, but this rotted too quickly, absorbed horse urine, and smelled. By 1895 the cedar blocks were being replaced by asphalt resting on a concrete foundation. At the turn of the century various forms of asphalt were being tested and street paving began to look very much as it does today. Sidewalks presented an equally endless problem, with plank sidewalks seeming to rot away as fast as they were put down. At the end of the century the City Council decided to switch over to various combinations of flagstones, or artificial stones, or cement. Late in the century the city began to clear the sidewalks with corporation snowplows on a "comprehensive common-sense plan."

Communications within London were also being improved by the erection of new bridges, beginning with the Oxford Street Bridge in 1881. By the turn of the century the problem of the innumerable rail crossings in the city was taken in hand and negotiations with the Grand Trunk Railway led to the construction of subways under what is now the Canadian National line both at Wortley and Wharncliffe roads in 1906. The latter subway today forms one of London's worst traffic bottlenecks. Agreement on a comprehensive system of track elevation and subways proved impossible, however, when the City Council and the Grand Trunk were unable to come to terms on a subsidy. The results are again obvious to Londoners today. The city was far more successful in the construction of a proper sewerage system. Willis Chipman was appointed consulting engineer in charge of sanitary system work in 1892 and under his supervision the sewer system was constructed in 1896-1898. A storm sewer system was built in 1912-1915.

In 1905 the Board of Education, like the City Council, began to be elected by a general vote in a system which lasted until 1980 and became progressively more unwieldy as London grew larger and the number of names on the ballot increased. With the population expansion many new schools were constructed, such as the Simcoe Street School in 1888, and in that same year the Collegiate Institute was enlarged. One of the most impressive buildings in London, the Western Ontario Normal School, which has just been refurbished as the Monsignor Feeney Centre for Catholic Education, was built in 1898-1899 for the training of teachers for London and its hinterland areas. John Dearness (1852-1954), London's longest lived prominent citizen, long played a leading role in the institution, and became one of the city's most famous educational figures.

New fields of education made their appearance. In 1887 Agnes M. Pritchard became the first kindergarten teacher and went on to become supervisor of kindergartens for the city. Manual training courses in the schools began in the first decade of the century and household science training was added in 1911. The Technical High School, now H.B. Beal Secondary School, was built in 1912. The Western School of Art and Design continued to flourish through the last decades of the century, but after provincial government funding was stopped it eventually ceased operation in 1903.

For the Western University the era was one of trials and tribulations. After Bishop Hellmuth departed in 1883 his successor, Bishop Maurice Baldwin, found some of his projects such as the university, which lacked adequate maintenance and endowment funds, and the construction of the new cathedral at Richmond and Piccadilly streets, to be far beyond the overextended finances of the diocese. Given the limited resources of both city and church and the provincial refusal to fund universities, cutbacks were necessary. The university did graduate its first B.A., Robert Franklin Sutherland, in 1883, but two years later the Arts Faculty was suspended when Huron College temporarily planned to withdraw from affiliation. The faculty remained in abeyance for a decade.

Although a law school was established briefly in 1885-1887, the survival of the university was basically a result of the development of the Medical Faculty, which had been established in 1881 and by 1888 was able to move to a new building at York and Waterloo streets. In 1895, with the support of Bishop Baldwin and the Huron College Council, which hoped it would bring a broader basis of financial support, the Faculty of Arts was revived. Under the leadership of Dr. Nathaniel C. James, who from 1901 to 1914 was head of the institution, Western began to develop into a modern university. In 1908 a new provincial charter was obtained under which the university was secularized, dissolving all connections with the Church of England, and the province and city began to make appointments to a newly created Board of Governors. Huron College remained an affiliate. With the help of funding from the city and

the provincial government, the institution could now look beyond day-to-day financing and plan a strong development program.

The story of London's hospital facilities during these years was a tale of great success. Beyond the development of medical education in conjunction with the university, a school of nursing training was added in 1883. Then in 1887 the hospital was given a formal, partly elected Board of Trustees by provincial legislation. By the mid-1890s, despite the fact that the General Hospital was only twenty years old, it became necessary to build a much-expanded building. Support was obtained from the City Council with the strong backing of Dr. John Wilson, the mayor in 1898-1899, who insisted that the poor should be able to have their own doctor and medical services without charge.

The new hospital was erected at a cost of more than $100,000. Renamed Victoria Hospital in honor of the Queen's Diamond Jubilee, the hospital had special wards for children, consumptives, and contagious diseases, and special quarters for surgeons and staff. By 1909 the isolation ward had become a separate building with sixty beds, and construction was commenced, with the support of Sir Adam Beck, on the Queen Alexandra Sanitorium for tubercular cases. The Sisters of St. Joseph began their hospital in 1888, at first in conjunction with their work at the Mount Hope Refuge. The Victoria Home for Incurables, now Parkwood Hospital, was established in 1903. Mayor J. W. Little gave an ambulance to the city and in 1896 St. John's Ambulance Brigade was organized. It was followed by the Victorian Order of Nurses in 1906, established through the efforts of the London Local Council of Women.

For all the great advances of the late nineteenth century, in London or in any other city, a lack of controlling legislation meant that many people continued relying on useless patent nostrums which were widely advertised in magazines and newspapers. For instance, in 1886 Dr. Pierce's Favourite Prescription proclaimed that it was good for "worn-out, run-down," debilitated school teachers, milliners, seamstresses, housekeepers, and overworked women generally at only one dollar per bottle. The male community also had its cure-alls. In 1889, M.B. Lubov's specific No. 8 was advertised: a positive, painless, permanent, and pleasant cure for the disease of men brought about through indiscretion, exposure, or overwork! Individual attitudes also impeded the advance of medicine, as many people refused to have anything to do with hospitals, regarding them as only a place to die. Others formed such bodies as the London Anti-Vaccination League, which was established in November 1909.

Charitable institutions were expanding in the city. Many were on a religious basis, such as those operated by the Sisters of St. Joseph, including the House of Providence and Mount Hope, which was extended in 1906 to include a home for old men. This has developed into Marian Villa. Other institutions were operated by various charitable groups, such as the 1874 Protestant Home for Orphans, Aged and Friendless (Merrymount). The McCormick Home for the aged opened in 1892 and the Children's Aid Society was established in 1893 and was able to build a new shelter by 1905. In 1896 some fifty of these charities came together to form the Charity Organization of London, Ontario, with the objective of preventing duplication of effort. It was really Canada's first community welfare council.

THE ELECTRIFICATION OF LONDON

The advent of electricity in the 1880s led to as great a revolution in city life as the railways had provided

thirty years earlier, although this time the change was of a completely different order. The development of electric power in London, as in other Ontario cities, can be broken down into two phases. During the first phase, various independent companies competed for contracts for supplying electricity and there were hopes of fantastic profits to be made in the new enterprise. The second phase began just after 1900 when various Ontario leaders, including London's Adam Beck, brought forward the idea of harnessing the power of Niagara Falls to produce electricity at a cheaper rate, and making it generally available at low cost through an Ontario government commission. Inevitably, the battles over the adoption of hydroelectricity involved not only competing corporations, but also Liberal and Conservative political rivalry, and the idea of centralizing control against localizing production.

Londoners had their first view of electricity's potential at a demonstration of Ball's Electrical Light Machine in September 1881. Almost immediately a group organized to form an electrical light company and before the end of the year Canadian patent rights were secured for the Ball system and the first machine constructed in the city. In late July 1882, 7,000 Londoners came to Victoria Park to see a demonstration of electric lights suspended from five high poles. Electric light came to London's streets in 1886 when the Ball Electric Company and the Royal Electric Company divided a three-year contract for providing street lighting. After several changes the

Top: *Prosperity enabled Smallman & Ingram, Ltd., to build a new, L-shaped, five-storey building in 1907-1908 at the southwest corner of Dundas and Richmond streets in the heart of London's business district. The store, here viewed in the 1920s, was purchased in 1944 by Robert Simpson Company, Ltd. Courtesy, London Historical Museums*

Above: *The Hunt Brothers, who took over the London Electric Company in 1898, also operated Hunt's City Mills. Described in this letterhead as "the oldest milling firm in Ontario," it was founded by Charles Hunt in 1854. First located at the foot of Talbot Street along the South Branch of the Thames River, the flour mill moved in 1917 to London East, where its six-storey building became an area landmark. Courtesy, Frederick H. Armstrong*

Opposite page: *John Bamlet Smallman (1849-1916), brother of Thomas H. Smallman, made his fortune in Smallman & Ingram, Ltd., the department store which he founded with Lemuel Hill Ingram in 1877 when they opened a small retail drygoods store on Dundas Street. New lines of goods and innovative retailing translated into annual increased profits and expanded facilities. Courtesy, UWO*

London Electric Company, operated by the Hunt Brothers, took over the street light franchise in 1898. They soon had a rival in the Helena Costume Company, owned by the Little family, which expanded from making clothing to distributing power from their plant around the downtown area. As the Littles did not have a franchise giving them the right to distribute electricity, they could not erect poles on the streets and were forced to string their wires over the roofs of buildings.

The move to bring hydro-electric power from Niagara Falls to the cities of Ontario was headed at London by Adam Beck, associated with Philip Pocock and Edgar I. Sifton. Beck's right-hand man was Dr. Edward Victor Buchanan, a Scottish engineer who had been trained in Glasgow. Buchanan later became the engineer in charge of the installation and then was manager of the Public Utilities Commission from 1915 to 1952. The battle for power focused on bringing low-cost electricity to the people of the province, but it was generally led by such manufacturers as Beck, who was opposed to the high rates charged by the various electric companies which often had Liberal affiliations. Naturally, the Tory *London Free Press* backed Beck and the Liberal *Advertiser* backed his opponents. Beck was helped a great deal by the fact that the Liberal government at Toronto had been in power for many years and was showing less and less ability to provide leadership. It was finally defeated in 1905 by the Conservatives, who were quite ready to support hydro-electric development and establish an Ontario Hydro-Electric Commission. Beck, who had been mayor of London from 1902 to 1904, was among the members of the legislature.

Beck began his campaign for hydro-electric power—"white coal," as it was often called—about 1900 and by 1903 had the support of the London City Council, which soon passed a bylaw favoring such a development. Similar action was being taken in other municipalities and in 1903 Beck attended a meeting at Berlin, Ontario (now Kitchener), at which businessmen and representatives of the various municipalities organized a group to lobby for the distribution of power from Niagara Falls. In 1906 the Tory government formed a provincial Hydro-Electric Power Commission under Beck's chairmanship and by 1908 fourteen municipalities had entered into contracts to take Niagara power. On November 30, 1910, Philip Pocock, chairman of the Board of Water Commissioners, pressed the switch bringing hydro power into London, and with it the full use of the potential of electricity became possible. Although Berlin (Kitchener) beat London in the race to be the first city to use hydro-electric power, Beck was the man who had spearheaded the development. As chairman of the Ontario Hydro-Electric Power Commission until his death in 1925, Beck directed the expansion of hydro in Ontario even during the years when he was out of power politically.

The Hydro-Electric Power Commission rapidly put an end to the excessive profits made by its rivals, who used a variety of gas, gasoline, hydraulic, and steam-generated power. Niagara Falls electric power was distributed to the province at cost, and as one London businessman stated, "lighting costs are the cheapest on the continent, and cheap power adds considerably to the profits of manufacturers." In London, power was first sold at four and a half cents per kilowatt hour, and soon dropped to two cents. There was no charge for meter rent. The London Electric Company charged nine cents, plus twenty-five cents for meter rent. Not surprisingly, that organization, which had refused to sell at what the City Council regarded as a reasonable price when it had the opportunity, went out of business in 1917.

Average citizens found life made brighter not only by the new incandescent lamps which covered the whole city, but also by the opportunity to install electricity in their own homes. Poorer Londoners could obtain financing from the company for the installation, which could be repaid in easy monthly payments. To make the advantages of electricity even more available to Londoners, in 1912 Beck decided to sell electrical appliances, as local firms were not interested in handling them. Until 1956 the Hydro operated its own appliance stores. The advertisements show that a wide variety of household aids were available: irons, toasters, fans, washing machines, sewing machines, vacuum cleaners, and stoves. The Hydro also began to install wiring and in 1915 an electrical control and inspection department was set up for those who wanted to do their own wiring. There were some problems, as in March 1922 when a sleet storm brought down hundreds of miles of wire, making the streets impassable. Beck rushed in fifty linemen from Toronto to supplement the 200-man local team and soon had the power back on, as Buchanan was happy to report, well before the telephones were back in order.

THE SOCIETY OF THE CITY

London's first Chinese appeared about 1878, although there were a few Chinese in the city in the early years. The Jewish community, on the other

hand, increased greatly with an influx from Russia in the 1880s. They soon had their own synagogue and in 1889 purchased land on Oxford Street West for a Jewish cemetery. In May 1882 the Salvation Army held in London its first open air meeting in Canada. The Catholic Church, as noted, built St. Peter's Basilica from 1880 to 1885. The influence and importance of the London bishopric can be seen in the fact that John Walsh and his two immediate successors were elevated to the archbishopric of Toronto. Just after the Canadian Pacific Railway was completed, in 1887, Bishop Baldwin moved the Anglican Cathedral back from Bishop Hellmuth's Chapter House to St.

Sir Adam Beck was determined to make cheap power available not only to industry, but to the general public so as to improve domestic living conditions. Following Beck's policy, the local Hydro-Electric Power Commission in 1912 opened a Hydro Shop on the northeast corner of Dundas and Wellington streets, the first in Ontario. Until 1956, the Hydro Shop promoted and sold a full range of electric appliances. Courtesy, UWO

SIR ADAM BECK

London's mayor and MP, Sir Adam Beck, "The Hydro Knight," gained fame as founding chairman of the Ontario Hydro-Electric Commission. Courtesy, UWO

Sir Adam Beck, one of London's most celebrated citizens, was born in Baden, Ontario, on June 20, 1857. At only fourteen years of age he began working in his father's iron foundry as a blacksmith's assistant. When the foundry folded, Beck and his brother, William, moved to Galt where they started a lumber veneering and cigar box manufacturing firm. In 1884 the business moved to London and eventually the Becks' company expanded to open branches in Montreal, Toronto, and Hamilton. Like many nineteenth-century entrepreneurs, he would often still refer to himself as "only a boxmaker."

Beck made his first venture into politics in 1898 when he ran unsuccessfully as a Conservative for a seat in the legislature. Success came four years later, in 1902, when he was elected as mayor of London and as London's member of the provincial parliament. He was mayor for three years and except for 1919-1923 was London's MLA until his death. Much of Beck's political interest soon focused on the question of hydro-electric power—an issue which would engage him for the rest of his life. During his first term in the legislature Beck led an investigation into the development and distribution of power from Niagara Falls.

In 1905, with a Conservative landslide, Beck was appointed as a minister without portfolio to the Cabinet of Sir James P. Whitney, who supported publicly owned power. The next year Beck introduced the bill creating the Hydro-Electric Power Commission of Ontario, of which he was made the first chairman. In the 1908 election Beck "guaranteed" the availability of electric power to even the poorest of citizens. Though some were sceptical, his promise was fulfilled when, two years later, hydro-electric power finally came to Kitchener, London, and the other cities of the province.

Ontario's hydro systems quickly grew to encompass an investment of more than $200 million over which Beck held responsibility. Premier Whitney became increasingly concerned about his growing dominance and attempted to put the Hydro Commission under the control of the Cabinet. Naturally, Beck clashed with the Whitney government over this issue and eventually resigned from his position in the Cabinet in 1914. This decision was not in vain, however, for in spite of much opposition Beck managed to maintain the commission's public ownership.

In 1912 Beck became a colonel in the Canadian militia and served during World War I as director of remounts, supervising the purchase of horses for the army. Two years later his many contributions were rewarded when he was knighted by King George V. While Sir Adam Beck's interests undeniably centred on the Hydro-Electric Power Commission, he and his wife Lady Lillian, who died in 1921, will be long remembered for their devotion to various humanitarian projects. In 1904 the Becks' daughter, Marion, was diagnosed as having contracted tuberculosis. Though Marion was eventually cured, the Becks decided to establish the Queen Alexandra Sanitorium in Byron to ensure the finest available facilities for the treatment of those afflicted with tuberculosis. Lady Beck herself personally oversaw the successful "rose days" in which thousands of roses were sold publicly in order to raise funds for the sanitorium. Beck and his wife continued their altruistic efforts in the pursuit of readily accessible medical assistance. In 1909 Beck was elected president of the newly established London Health Association. Five years later Lady Lillian assumed presidency of the London Red Cross Society.

In 1900 the Becks purchased the old Ellis W. Hyman residence, which they remodelled and renamed "Headley." Its extensive grounds, covering a whole city block, gave them ample room for stabling and exercising their horses. Both of the Becks were great equestrian enthusiasts and participated in numerous shows in Canada, the United States, and England, bringing back many prizes for the performance of their own breed of horses. Beck was elected director of the National Horse Show Association of America, as well as of the International Horse Show, London, 1911. He was master of the fox hounds at the London Hunt Club from 1897 to 1922.

Sir Adam Beck was often called "the poor man's friend" for his efforts to provide cheap electricity and help the sick and destitute. His fight to bring cheap and easily available electric power to Ontario also aided the province's manufacturing interests, and helped consolidate Ontario's place as Canada's industrial centre. He died in London on August 15, 1925.

On February 23, 1900, a Richmond Street fire devastated the Masonic Temple, depicted here circa 1885. The Grand Opera House, occupying the top stories, was completely destroyed in the conflagration. Courtesy, UWO

Paul's Church, where it remains today. After the destruction by fire of the Queens Avenue Methodist Church (formerly North Street Church) in 1895, the congregation began the construction of the present Metropolitan Church. The Unitarians dedicated their church on Richmond Street in 1907.

London's theatre entertainment still centred on Hyman's rebuilt squash court at the northeast corner of York and Richmond streets in the 1870s, which George Holman made into the Holman Opera House for a few years. In 1880-1881 it was replaced by the Masonic Temple Building, which had a new Grand Opera House incorporated in its plan. Seating 1,128 people, the new theatre was able to provide a large enough auditorium for London to join the professional theatre circuit. The building was described as "unexcelled in the Dominion." The theatre was leased by Colonel C.J. Whitney of Detroit and became a stopping place for many of the troupes on the Toronto-Detroit leg of the theatre circuit. The theatre proved to be very profitable for twenty years, but then burned down in February 1900 and was rebuilt as an office building without its high mansard roof. Renamed the Richmond Building in 1928, it

With the destruction of the Grand Opera House, Toronto impresario Ambrose Small quickly added London to his chain of theatres by erecting the Grand Theatre on Richmond Street in 1901. Although described on opening night by one newspaper critic as "having the appearance of a car barn with cold storage at the rear," it possessed a magnificent stage and proscenium arch. Courtesy, London Historical Museums

was finally demolished in 1967. Colonel Whitney and his associate Ambrose J. Small of Toronto replaced the theatre by constructing their own building in 1901, which is the Grand Theatre of today. One of the largest theatres in Southwestern Ontario and possessing the largest footage for acting of any theatre in Canada, it was again a definite boost to the city. The seating capacity was 1,840 and there were two balconies.

Thus from 1881 London had a first-class theatre and soon there were other smaller ones to back it up. The numbers attending became sufficiently important for the London & Port Stanley Railway to delay the departure of the last train for fifteen minutes on theatre evenings so that patrons from St. Thomas and Port Stanley could return home. In addition, by the 1890s seats could be purchased by mail, telegraph, or even by telephone. Critics, however, left the impression that the audiences to a very large extent were not quite in a class with the magnificent setting. Downstairs in the theatre one found the society and intellectual types coming possibly out of ritual and being there to be seen as much as anything. Upstairs in the balcony, or, as it was then called, "the gods," was a much less polished element, in fact one that seems to have contained a fair number of hoodlums. In 1892 the Grand Theatre was forced to prohibit "boistrous or unseemly conduct . . . whistling, cat-calling or stamping of feet." In 1900 further prohibition came against noisiness, profanity, and the spitting of tobacco juice. Finally in 1910 the last-named nuisance was prohibited under a general provincial law which forbade spitting tobacco juice in public. Obviously, the audience must have been rather diverting on occasion.

The level of entertainment was naturally on the light side. Comedy was well received and "soggy melodrama" was much favored. Possibly most popular of all were the musical melanges which were sort of a combination of comedy and light music. In 1902-1903 one can judge the seriousness of much of the entertainment by the fact that of 107 Grand Theatre performances, works by Shakespeare appeared only four times. Political speeches did have their place and in February 1891 Sir John A. Macdonald and Sir Charles Tupper addressed a Conservative rally in the city. The famous Mohawk Indian poetess E. Pauline Johnston appeared, giving a reading from her works at Victoria Hall on Clarence Street in 1893.

On the international circuit Winston Spencer Churchill, then twenty-six years old, spoke on "The Boer War and what I saw of it" in December 1900, the great Polish pianist Ignace Jan Paderewski gave a recital in April 1905, and Sarah Bernhardt appeared in London in both 1896 and 1910. In January 1882 Orson Squire Fowler was back in London to give six public lectures at the Grand Opera House; one wonders if he still was carrying poor Cornelius Burley's skull along for demonstrations. On a rather more restrained note London's own "Cy" Warman

This stuccoed, one-room, Neoclassical style building was London's first art gallery. Located in Queens Park, it was opened on September 10, 1912, during the annual Western Fair. Unheated, the gallery exhibited paintings only during the warmer months. Its inadequacy initiated the quest for a permanent facility, answered by the Elsie Perrin Williams Memorial Library and Art Museum of 1940. Courtesy, London Historical Museums

composed "Sweet Marie" in Victoria Park on a July evening in 1891. The great surprise performance of the century, however, occurred on April 1, 1898, when Joseph Tuttle was shot to death on the stage of the Music Hall on Dundas Street by rival actor William D. Emerson.

The Provincial Exhibition was now settling at Toronto, although a last provincial fair was held at London in 1881, and Londoners continued developing their own Western Fair as a regional exhibition. In 1885 the citizens voted to move the fair to its present location in Queen's Park and the land was accordingly purchased by the City Council. In 1887 the Western Fair Association was incorporated and a vast new Crystal Palace built, which was in use until it burned in 1927. The fair also contained a half-mile race track, a bandstand, and a midway with games of chance and hucksters selling a variety of goods including patent medicines. In 1895 much of the fair burned down on opening day, but tents were quickly erected and the entertainment went ahead. In 1912 culture joined the other exhibits when the Western Fair Board built the present Art Gallery, really the

Above: *The 1881 London Club has long been the social centre for London's business and professional men. The building, designed by London architect George F. Durand, still is one of the most impressive downtown structures. Courtesy, UWO*

Opposite page: *The Great Western Railway station on York Street served travellers from the arrival of the G.W.R. in the 1850s. This 1875 view from a window of the Tecumseh House on Richmond Street appeared in* Canadian Illustrated News. *Long an inadequate embarrassment, the station was replaced in 1936. Courtesy, UWO*

first art gallery in London, which was unfortunately unheated and could only be used in summer.

Library facilities were also improving. The London Public Library Board was formed in 1893 and the Mechanic's Institute merged with it in 1894. In 1895 the board opened a large library building at the corner of Queens Avenue and Wellington Street which was used until 1940. The YMCA built a new building in 1897 just eight years after the YWCA had been founded for women. The latter received a new home on Princess Avenue in 1904. London's first troop of Boy Scouts was active by 1911.

New park space for the citizens gradually developed around the waterworks at Springbank Park. The initial seventy-eight acres of land at Springbank were gradually expanded until by 1911 the Water Commission owned 546 acres of open land. At first reached conveniently only by boat, in 1896 the park was joined to the city by the street railway line, which continued to be in use until 1935. From 1897 the citizens could watch summer stock theatre performed there and in 1898 a "large and commodious" pavilion was erected at the street railway terminal.

The 1890s also witnessed a flourishing of the women's organizations. The London Local Council of Women was organized in 1893 under the patronage of Lady Aberdeen, wife of the governor-general of Canada. A non-sectarian, non-partisan association, it soon served as an umbrella group for other women's associations which retained their own identity. Mrs. E.N. English was the first president. Women were also instrumental in founding the Children's Aid Society. In 1897, again with the backing of Lady Aberdeen, the Victorian Order of Nurses was formed, and with the support of the Council of Women, a London branch was opened. The Imperial Order of the Daughters of the Empire was established in London in 1901. They were very active in providing equipment for Red Cross work during the Boer War, and for the Byron Sanitorium. The year 1905 saw the founding of the London Mother's Club which developed into the Home and School Clubs at a later date.

Many other types of associations were making their appearance. The Canadian Club of London was established in 1906, holding lectures on a variety of topics. Two fraternal groups providing life insurance, Dr. Oronhyatekha's Independent Order of Foresters and the Woodmen of the World, had their head offices at London. More sports clubs also were developing, such as the Forest City Curling Club, the London Bowling Club, and the London Gun Club. Professional and elite organizations were also coming

to the fore. In 1880 the Middlesex Law Association was formed and in 1881-1882 the London Club built its present clubhouse at the corner of Queens Avenue and Richmond Street. George F. Durand, one of London's most talented architects, designed the building. The London Hunt Club was established in 1885 for outdoor sports for both ladies and gentlemen and to encourage equestrianism. By 1889 the club had acquired the Glenmore property on the east side of Western Road, which it used until it moved to its Oakridge Park location in 1960.

TRANSPORTATION AND COMMUNICATIONS

On November 18, 1883, Londoners lost twenty-four minutes and fifty-three seconds as they advanced their timepieces to adopt the new standard time, with the world moving from sun time taken at each location to an ordered system. Invented by a Canadian, Sir Sandford Fleming, and adopted at a conference in Washington, standard time solved the railway's problem of scheduling trains with every city on a different time. So cumbersome had the old sundial system become that trains had generally started operating on standard time even before the nations approved it. For instance, if it was 4:43 in Toronto, it would be 4:40 in Hamilton, 4:35 in London, and 4:23 in Detroit. Standard time also helped the developing Bell Telephone Company's long distance system, which followed rapidly after the invention of the telephone itself. London's first long distance telephone line, stretching over the fourteen miles to St. Thomas, came into operation in 1882.

London's railway system also was undergoing change. In 1882 the Great Western Railway, which London had built along with its sister cities, was absorbed into Montreal's Grand Trunk Railway system. The Canadian Pacific Railway system was extended from Woodstock to London, the first passenger train arriving May 30, 1887, with three coaches, a baggage car, and twenty-two passengers. Construction was then continued on a line to Windsor, completed in January 1890. The new 1893 Canadian Pacific Railway Station was built with a $40,000 subsidy from the city. With CPR lines extending to the Pacific Ocean—far beyond the area serviced by the Grand Trunk route—London businesses could now ship their products across the country.

The tale of the London & Port Stanley Railway was, as usual, not as happy a story. The L&PS negotiated the right to use the Michigan Central Railway and by 1893 Londoners could reach San Francisco in four days. But relations with the Grand Trunk Railway, which had taken over the lease for operating the line when it absorbed the Great Western Railway, were not always satisfactory. In 1892, with the expiry of the lease, the Grand Trunk refused to continue. London was forced to reorganize the railway, buy out St. Thomas' stock, and make a twenty-one-year

agreement with the Erie & Detroit Railway (later the Pere Marquette Railway) to operate the line. Mayor Little made arrangements for car ferries to operate between Cleveland, Ohio and Port Stanley, and by 1910 86 percent of the freight carried was coal. By that time the railway had to face the problem of a rival line that was electrified.

This rival was the South Western Traction Company, later renamed the London & Lake Erie Railway and usually known as the "Traction Line." It was London's only real radial railway, or, as it would be called today, inter-city trolley line. Originally promoted by English businessmen, its first attempt to get a charter in 1900 was unsuccessful, but two years later a charter was granted and the railway began building southward from London. Almost immediately it ran into financial difficulties with the tracks only reaching Lambeth; it was two years before money could be raised to continue the line the twenty-eight miles down to St. Thomas, and finally in 1907 to Port Stanley. The London terminal was on Horton Street where the Salvation Army Store is now located. By 1909 the Traction Line was again in financial trouble; its creditors foreclosed and started it up again as the London & Lake Erie. The Traction Line's great triumph was its 1912 victory over the Sabbatarian forces which attempted to prevent it from running Sunday/holiday trains. Still, by 1917 it was in trouble again and the next year it was liquidated and scrapped. With all these lines running, however, London became the Canadian city with the most trains arriving and departing daily.

With the collapse of the Traction Line, the L&PS again had a monopoly on recreational traffic to Lake Erie, but the rival that was eventually to destroy it had already made its appearance: the automobile. In April 1904 a London Automobile Club caravan, consisting of five cars carrying a total party of nineteen, made its first run to Aylmer and St. Thomas via Belmont. With an increasing number of cars in the city, London's first fatality occurred in August 1910 when Anson Wallace of Richmond Street was fatally injured by a new McLaughlin Runabout. The next year Charles S. Hyman organized the London branch of the Ontario Motor League. The horseless carriage moved into commercial business when T. Whitehall of Broughdale started to bring his loads of tomatoes to the market in his automobile. At the Western Fair

in 1911 Fred C. Harding displayed his new London-built Harding Twenty Cars for the admiring public. Then, in April 1914, Miss Meta Macbeth, a prominent young lady of London society, passed her driver's examination to become London's first "chauffeuse."

Under the presidency of Verschoyle Cronyn, the London Street Railway continued to extend its networks, constructing tracks in 1888 across the Ridout Street Bridge to provide service for London South. By the 1890s it was clear that electric trams would be more efficient than horses. Accordingly, the new president of the LSR, H.A. Everett, arranged an agreement with the city under which the railway received a monopoly for fifty years and agreed to bring in an electric tram system. It was also agreed that at the end of the fifty years the city would have the right to purchase the system either immediately or at five-year intervals. The electric cars began running in September 1895 and the horses were sold at the end of the year.

Although contemporary accounts frequently present London as a scene of little labor difficulty, there had been grumblings for a good deal of time. As early as 1872 the Workingman's Progressive party had been formed and different mayors of London had been castigated for their wage policies. Mayor Charles S. Hyman, conversely, had received praise in the *Canadian Labour Courier* in 1887 when he let his employees work only nine hours a day instead of ten

Above: *In 1877 the London Asylum, today's London Psychiatric Hospital, was the city's first telephone customer. The Bell Telephone Company of Canada opened its exchange in London on Dundas Street in 1880, and in 1893 installed Canada's first metallic switchboard there, as seen in this 1896 photograph. Courtesy, Bell Canada*

Opposite page: *From the dryness of his seat, the driver of a horse-drawn grocery wagon disdainfully dismisses a passing car as it wallows its way through the axle-deep mud of Richmond Street, north of Oxford Street, circa 1913. Courtesy, UWO*

SIR GEORGE CHRISTIE GIBBONS

Sir George Christie Gibbons was born in St. Catharines on July 2, 1848, and educated at Upper Canada College. At only seventeen years of age, he received a medal for his participation in the volunteer militia during the Fenian raids.

Called to the Ontario bar in 1869, he went on to practice law in London where his firm, Gibbons, Harper and Gibbons, became one of the most important in the city. Appointed a Q.C. in 1891, he held many important positions in the profession both provincially and locally: member of the first Law Faculty at Western University; president of the London-Middlesex Bar Association; and bencher of the Law Society of Upper Canada. Like most lawyers he also was involved in various businesses, being president of both the London and Western Trusts, which he established in 1896, and the City Gas Company, as well as a director of London Life.

Gibbons was an undeniably impressive figure in London society. He was one of the founders of the London Club and held the presidencies of the London Hunt Club and the London Liberal Club. His activity in the Liberal party eventually drew him into the "Big Four," a small group of prominent London Liberals including another noteworthy figure in London's history, Charles S. Hyman. Despite his many accomplishments within the London community, it was this Liberal connection which led to Gibbons' most important work as the Canadian chairman of the International Waterways Commission. Prime Minister Sir Wilfrid Laurier appointed him to this position in November 1905, probably at the suggestion of Hyman, who had just become minister of public works.

Gibbons was immediately confronted with the issue of the American government's control over the New York electric companies which were diverting water from the Niagara River. He realized early on that a treaty for this particular problem alone would not be adequate, and, soon after his appointment, urged Laurier to pursue the negotiation of a general treaty which would dictate principles governing all boundary waters, not just those in the Niagara region. Considering Canada's total failure to gain its objectives in the 1903 Alaska boundary dispute, this was a bold suggestion. More than a year transpired before Gibbons finally made some real progress toward his goals. In 1907 his correspondence with American Commissioner George Clinton, delegated by the American secretary of state, Elihu Root, eventually led to a compromise memorandum on "Proposed Treaty Clauses." This proposal, to which Gibbons had made a most important input, strove to promote a just and equal share of the boundary waters.

After much commuting between both capitals, Gibbons finally went to Washington with a modified memorandum in 1908. Still, several months of battle with the American negotiators were needed, for they were reluctant to see their country accept any equality with a British dominion. Finally, Gibbons managed to overcome the odds, and his efforts were rewarded with the ratification of the Boundary Waters Treaty of 1909 creating the bilateral International Joint Commission with equal representation from both countries. Gibbons correctly saw this as a healthy assertion of Canadian strength. His efforts as one of the main architects of the Boundary Waters Treaty were rewarded by King George V in 1911 when he was knighted for his success in strengthening the friendship and, more importantly, guaranteeing a harmonious equality between Canada and the United States. The same year, with the fall of the Laurier government, he ceased to be a member of the commission. He was never a member of parliament.

While Sir George Gibbons helped to solidify the bounds between two of the largest and most prosperous countries in the world, he always managed to find time to turn his attentions back to London. In 1908, at the height of the treaty negotiations, he served on the original Board of Governors of the Western University. He was also honorary president of the Canadian Club of London. His wife, Lady Elizabeth Gibbons, who died in 1914, was also active in London society. She was first president of the Woman's Canadian Club in 1910, and was concerned with other charitable organizations. Sir George took ill suddenly while vacationing at St. Andrews-by-the-Sea, New Brunswick, and died at Montreal after an operation on August 8, 1918.

While "Lornehurst," the huge Gibbons mansion on the south side of Victoria Park, was demolished to make way for the London Life

Sir George Christie Gibbons was knighted in 1911 for his services as chairman of the Canadian section of the International Waterways Commission. Courtesy, Photographic Conservancy of Canada

head office, there are two memorials to the Gibbons. In 1927 their children purchased the sixty-four-acre Gibbons' Park on the North Branch of the Thames River and presented it to the city in their memory. In 1961 the heirs of his daughter, Helen B. Gibbons, cleared the way for the purchase of her estate, "Gibbons' Lodge," to the north of the city, as a residence for the president of the University of Western Ontario. It still provides a green oasis across from London's newest and largest mall.

without reducing wages. Good labor relations were certainly not the case for the London Street Railway Company. On October 21, 1898, the LSR employees became Branch 97 of the Amalgamated Association of Street Railway Employees of America. Six days later the association called its first strike which lasted until November 1. The management claimed that the union merely represented "agitators"; but, despite the fact that some of the workers continued on the job in the barns and repair sheds, the company agreed to a one-third of a cent increase to fifteen and one-third cents per hour and the strike ended.

The second LSR strike was a very different matter and stands as the worst in London's history. It began suddenly on May 22, 1899, when seventy-nine motormen and conductors walked off at 4:30 p.m. with no notice. The directors decided to hire new men to replace them, and the result was a series of riots lasting from June to September, with heavy damage to streetcars, and policemen with loaded revolvers riding the cars to prevent citizens from throwing stones. The worst scene was on July 8 when a mob of several thousand people, many of whom were curiosity seekers, took control of the downtown from about 2:30 p.m. until the militia were called out at midnight. Mayor John Wilson read the Riot Act, for the first and only time in the history of the city, and the mob was finally dispersed. The replacement employees continued to provide service; by the fall the riots had died down and in May 1900, a year after the strike had begun, the directors decided not to re-hire the striking employees. Although unsuccessful, the strike was a factor in the development of the London Trades & Labor Council in the first decade of the new century, and labor organizers had some success in electing members to the City Council in the years before World War I.

THE BUSINESS SECTOR

With its commercial and financial base well established, many of the major developments in London business were in the field of manufacturing. Many manufactories were still in the downtown area, particularly those of the older companies; however, new industries were tending to move to London East where business was being encouraged to locate by the City Council. By 1915 London had 237 manufactories, producing some seventy-four lines of goods and employing 12,000 people. The city also had a new organization, the London Industrial Bureau, which was designed by many of the chief manufacturers to encourage other industries. Manufacturers erecting plants in the eastern manufacturing section of the city were offered "fixed assessments on land value only" for a period of fifteen years. Loans were available at moderate rates of interest if the employers would agree to take on a large number of hands. The City Council, in certain cases, was also allowing exemption from building tax and completely exempting some factories from assessment. None of this was unusual in a period when many Ontario municipalities were competing to attract new industry and there was little regulation of such matters by the government.

Some of these operations were quite large, the biggest employer of all being the McClary Company with 1,500 men, which advertised that in addition to its production of stoves it also made enamelwear and operated a foundry. McClary's by this time had branches in Vancouver, Winnipeg, St. Johns, Toronto, and Montreal. The McCormick and Perrin biscuit companies were also large, each employing some 650 hands by 1915. Some very old firms also were quite sizeable: Charles S. Hyman & Company had 250 employees and Carling's Brewery employed eighty-five. Cigar manufacturing, a field in which London exceeded every other Canadian city except Montreal by the beginning of World War I, still operated from generally smaller factories, but the numbers employed were showing a definite increase, going up from 770 in 1910 to 1,205 by 1915.

One of the larger cigar factories was that owned by Jose Gaste, a native of Santiago de Chile, who had studied in Chile and the United States before opening his firm in London. By 1915 he was employing 200 hands and spending three months of the year in Cuba to study the latest developments in the cigar preparation and tobacco growing industries. Adam Beck's cigar box manufacturing company was by this time employing 175 hands, although Beck himself was heavily engaged with his Ontario Hydro work. Charles Ross Somerville had opened his highly successful paper box manufacturing firm in 1888.

The Albert E. Silverwood dairy had first appeared in London in 1903, operating a branch plant which soon developed into Silverwood's Limited with a five-storey warehouse and cold storage facility built by 1912. The Stevens and Burns iron and brass foundry was reorganized as the Empire Brass Works (now EMCO) in 1903 and quickly became the largest in Ontario with 250 employees. Kellogg's Toasted Corn Flakes Company has a more complex history. A native Londoner who long operated a business on Dundas Street, Robert Wallace, moved to Salt Lake City in 1890 and then to Battle Creek, Michigan in 1905 where, in cooperation with several other business figures, he founded the breakfast food companies that are so well known. When it came time to open a Canadian branch, he remembered his native town and the result is one of London's flourishing businesses.

One of the clearest signs of London's prosperity was the number of bank branches in the city. Every major Canadian bank was represented; the Bank of Commerce had three branches and the Bank of Toronto no less than four. Despite its obvious importance as a banking centre, London's only fantastically unsuccessful effort in the field of finance was the short-lived Bank of London. Incorporated in May 1883, the bank operated for only four years under the presidency of Henry Taylor. Then in August 1887 it suddenly suspended payments, ruining many Londoners who had invested heavily in the enterprise. A much more enduring operation was the Northern Life Assurance Company, incorporated federally in 1894 by a group of largely Liberal business figures including T.H. Purdom of the *London Advertiser;* Frank E. Leonard of the iron foundry family; F.A. Fitzgerald, the first president of Imperial Oil; and George A. Harris, a London lawyer who was then the squire of "Eldon House." London continued as headquarters of a large number of trust companies and in 1899 the Canada Trust Company was established to handle the Huron & Erie's trust business.

THE MANY FORMS OF DISASTER

Turn-of-the-century London witnessed an almost amazing series of disasters, many of them following in short order in the 1880s. The first of these in 1880, and definitely by far the best known and the most written about, was the Donnelly massacre near Lucan in Biddulph Township just north of the city.

Opposite page, top left: *One of Canada's great industrialists, John McClary (1829-1923) founded the McClary Manufacturing Company in 1847. Located in huge factories in downtown London and on Adelaide Street, the business won fame for its cookstoves, heaters, and furnaces. Courtesy, Photographic Conservancy of Canada*

Top right: *Frank E. Leonard (1846-1923) entered the family's foundry business in 1870 and became president in 1913. He engaged in the usual activities expected of a member of London's elite, becoming an alderman, director of the Huron & Erie Loan and Savings Company, and president of the London Chamber of Commerce. Courtesy, Photographic Conservancy of Canada*

Bottom: *This lithograph, printed in June 1881, illustrates the capsizing of the overloaded* Victoria *on Victoria Day, May 24, 1881, which killed 181 people. Courtesy, UWO*

VICTORIA

There on February 4, James Donnelly and four members of his family were murdered and their house set on fire in an unsuccessful attempt to hide the crime. The quarrels between the Donnellys and their neighbors went back for some quarter of a century. Indeed, they probably originated in Tipperary County, Ireland, but the squabbles were made worse by local religious, political, and business rivalries. These had already caused a considerable number of incidents, some of them centring around the operation of the stagecoach line which the Donnellys ran to London. The murders resulted in a widely publicized trial at London's courthouse which involved many of the leading figures of the province and in the end resulted in a controversial acquittal. There will never be any agreement on this decision, but the "Biddulph Tragedy" gave London more notoriety than anything else in its history.

The next disaster followed quickly on May 24, 1881, when the steamship *Victoria* capsized on the Thames River during the Victoria Day celebrations with a loss of more than 180 lives. The popularity of the new Springbank Park and the lack of roads had led to the Thames Navigation Company launching a boat service from the courthouse docks to the park in 1878, and by 1881 three boats, including the *Victoria,* were operating. At that time there were no regulations regarding safe construction of boats, or the number of passengers which they could carry. With the large crowds coming back from the park at the end of Victoria Day, the boats became dangerously overcrowded and the *Victoria* on its fatal trip was allowed to load some 600 to 800 people although it was only seventy feet long. This was criminal overcrowding, especially as there was already a considerable amount of water in the hold. As the boat was nearing the Cove Bridge it careened with a shifting of the heavy weight on the upper deck; the boiler broke loose and the upper deck collapsed on the lower one, crushing a large number of people. The ship then proceeded to sink. Of those killed, most were children and the majority of them were girls, who were unable to swim because of their heavy dresses. The captain and the owner were charged but were acquitted. The last survivor of the disaster lived to 1976.

Next, in 1882, the city awoke to find that John Brown, since 1852 the town's and then the city's treasurer, had shot himself, and there were apparently vast discrepancies in his accounting records. There had been rumors of problems in 1863, but these had blown over when one collector had been found short in payment. Although rumors had resurfaced in recent years, the suicide came as a complete surprise. In an investigation the city accounts were found to be nearly $70,000 short, a fantastic sum for the period, but not an incident that was unique, given the nineteenth-century methods of accounting and auditing.

On July 11, 1883, a tremendous electrical storm lasted some eight hours. *London Advertiser* reporter

William Thompson, returning home from a fire in the small hours of the next morning, decided to look at the River Thames and see if the rainfall had had any effect. What he witnessed was a solid wall of water sweeping through London West, smashing houses and drowning people. Thompson rushed to warn the city and the fire bell was soon tolling, but much of the damage was already done, for the flood had burst the river banks to the north of the suburb and surged with great force through its length. Sweeping the Oxford Street Bridge away as it hit, the flood inundated Blackfriars Street with three to four feet of water and proceeded to completely wash away some six acres of land and a large number of houses.

Above: *The collapse of W.J. Reid & Co.'s Crystal Hall on Dundas Street on July 16, 1907, remains one of the worst catastrophes to occur in London. During renovation to convert the upper stories to a bowling alley and pool hall, the building was weakened by windows pierced in an end wall. As a result, a large part of the structure collapsed, crushing the building next door and killing seven people. Courtesy, UWO*

Opposite page: *The severity of the damage sustained by London West during the flood of July 10-11, 1883, is dramatically apparent in this photograph of the corner of Empress Avenue and Napier Street, taken shortly after the waters had receded. Houses were ripped from their foundations and swept down the river to be dashed against bridges, trees, and other buildings. Courtesy, UWO*

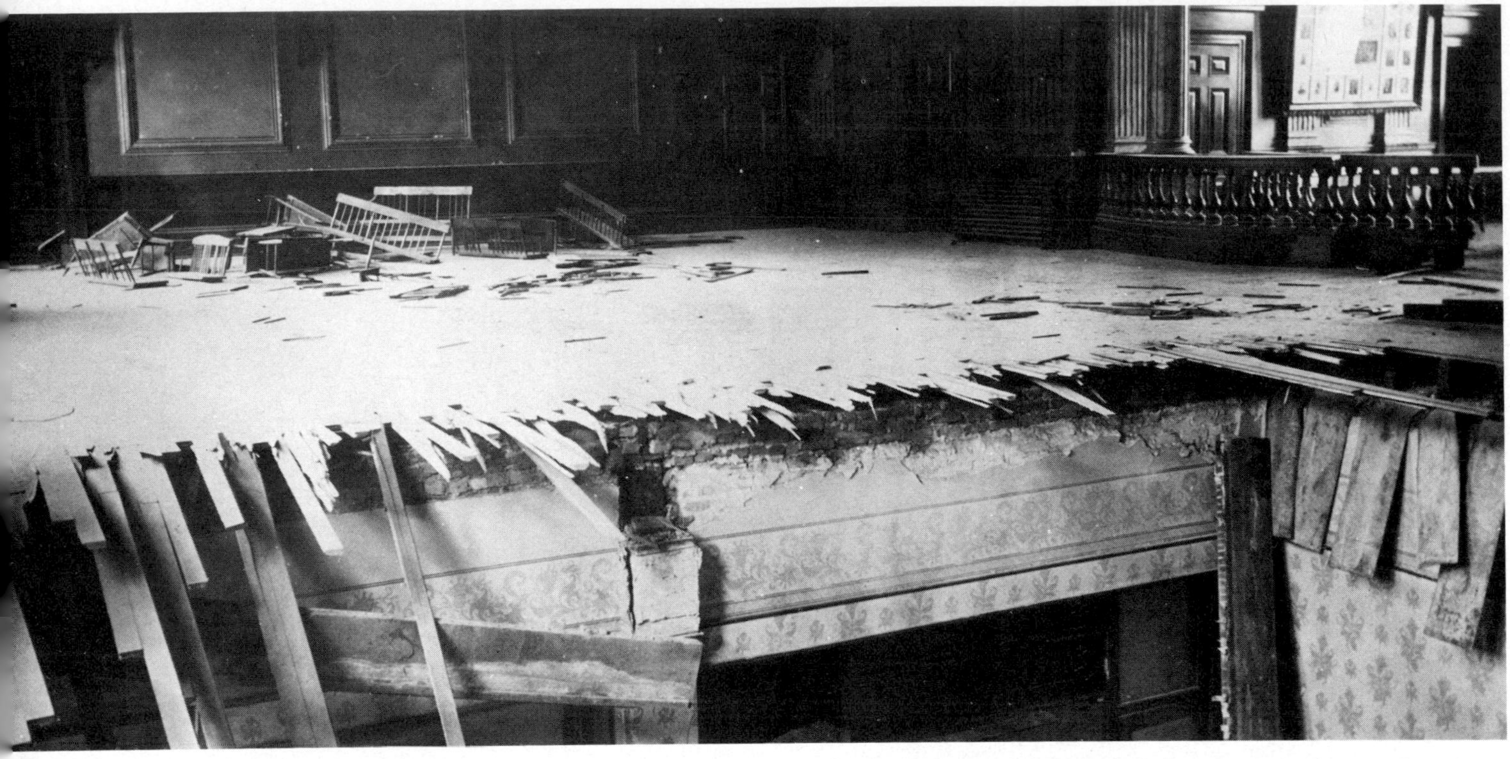

The City Hall Disaster was one of London's worst tragedies. On January 3, 1898, a section of the second floor auditorium collapsed during a victory celebration for newly elected mayor John Wilson. Of the 250 people who fell to the floor beneath, 23 died and more than 150 suffered injuries, both totals compounded by a 500-pound safe which toppled on the mass of humanity below. Courtesy, UWO

Four hundred other houses were rendered uninhabitable and seventeen people drowned. The swath of the damage spread on to Chatham and large acreages of crops were destroyed along the river's route. In a way London was paying for its carelessness in allowing people to build on the riverbanks in low-lying areas; unfortunately, however, nothing was learned from the incident. London West was restored much as it had been and despite dike building was still subject to future floods. Fortunately, a sanitary committee under Dr. Bryce of the Provincial Board of Health prevented epidemics from getting started.

After the flood, disaster took a rest for fifteen years before reappearing in a new form in 1898. In 1893 the city had passed its first building bylaw, but this was either inadequate, or neglected, when Mayor Little had the offices on the first floor of the City Hall rearranged a few years later. The election night victory rally on January 2, 1898, proceeded merrily until after midnight, when the floor of the upstairs auditorium collapsed without warning, precipitating a large number of people down to the offices below. A heavy safe and a steam radiator then fell down on top of the victims, with the result that at least twenty-three were killed and scores injured. Despite this nothing was done to stiffen building regulations to prevent a recurrence.

In 1907 the Reid Crystal Hall on Dundas Street, a large store with a warehouse above it, was being remodelled for new occupancy when the eastern end of the building suddenly collapsed across an alley into the building next door, killing several people. Investigation showed that in the course of the remodelling the eastern wall had been weakened by poking badly placed windows through it and this caused the collapse. The result was the Building Inspection Bylaw of 1908.

The line of disasters ended with two major fires. In the first of these in January 1904, the fire chief, John A. Roe, was killed by a falling wall at the Sterling Brothers Shoe Factory at York and Clarence streets, where three were injured. In the second fire, Roe's successor, Lawrence Clark, was killed with two others while fighting a fire at Westman's Hardware on Dundas Street in 1908. While they were trying to free a hose in the basement the upper floors collapsed.

The Royal Canadian Regiment has been a London military institution since 1883, and has served with distinction in the Northwest Rebellion, the Boer War, and the First and Second World Wars. The Regiment's 100th anniversary in 1983 was celebrated with a special Ceremony of Trooping the Color, its Colonel-in-Chief, Prince Philip, Duke of Edinburgh, on hand to present the colors. Photo by Alan Noon

Above: *"Return from School" was painted circa 1884 by Frederic Marlett Bell-Smith. The painting depicts students returning home from the Union School on Waterloo Street after classes were dismissed. Bell-Smith arrived in London from Hamilton, Ontario, in 1881. His particular use of bright colors reveals the artist's brilliant and uniquely Canadian palette, developed while painting the Rockies. Courtesy, London Regional Art Gallery*

Opposite page: *Sunshine streams through the glorious interior of St. Peter's Basilica, constructed in 1885. Photo by John Bliss*

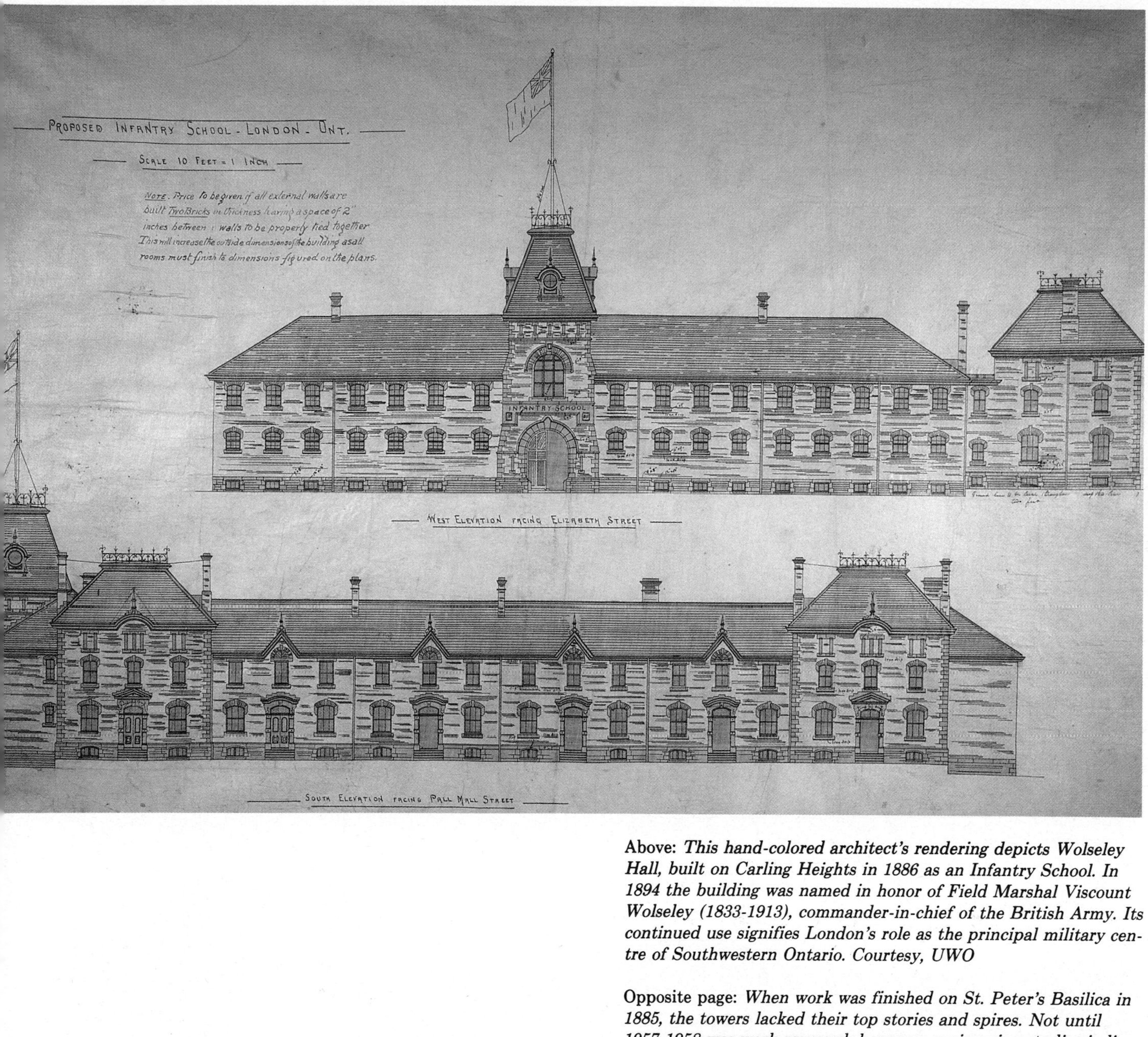

Above: *This hand-colored architect's rendering depicts Wolseley Hall, built on Carling Heights in 1886 as an Infantry School. In 1894 the building was named in honor of Field Marshal Viscount Wolseley (1833-1913), commander-in-chief of the British Army. Its continued use signifies London's role as the principal military centre of Southwestern Ontario. Courtesy, UWO*

Opposite page: *When work was finished on St. Peter's Basilica in 1885, the towers lacked their top stories and spires. Not until 1957-1958 was work resumed; however, engineering studies indicated that the foundations could not support the towers as originally intended by architect Joseph Conolly. The new designs by architect Peter Tillman of London produced towers less pretentious in scale, but in harmony with the rest of the cathedral. Photo by Alan Noon*

Right: *The Pixley-Fulford Mausoleum in Woodland Cemetery is judged among the finest funerary monuments in Canada. It was raised in 1897 in memory of Annie Pixley, a popular Canadian actress, by her husband, Thomas Fulford. The superstructure is made of Stanstead granite with an inner lining of marble. The tomb is surmounted by three lifesize granite statues, representing Victory, Music, and Drama. Photo by Alan Noon*

Below: *While London's cigar industry imported most of its tobacco from the United States and Cuba, some tobacco was grown locally for both cigars and cigarettes. Although the industry declined by the 1930s, tobacco barns such as these are still a common sight southeast of the city. Courtesy, Ross Breadner*

Opposite page: *Stirton & Dyer was one of numerous cigar manufacturers flourishing in Edwardian London. This colorful circa 1910 poster rather daringly advertised its Booster Cigar label. Made from high grade, imported Cuban and American tobacco, the Stirton & Dyer cigar obviously was smoked only by discriminating gentlemen of wealth and importance. Courtesy, UWO*

BOOSTER
CIGAR
EVERY
KNOCK
IS A
BOOST.
"EVERY KNOCK IS A BOOST."
"EVERY KNOCK IS A BOOST."
HIGH GRADE CIGAR MANUFACTURERS
STIRTON & DYER
LONDON CANADA.

Top: *University College was one of the first buildings to be erected for the new University of Western Ontario campus, then in London Township. The Collegiate Gothic style was chosen for its associations with Oxford, Cambridge, and American Ivy League colleges. The majestic tower was built as a memorial to the men and women from Middlesex County who sacrificed their lives in World War I. Photo by Alan Noon*

Centre: *The Forks of the Thames River have been a frequent subject with both artists and photographers. Mary Healey (1885-1923), one of several women who played a significant part in London's art community in the early twentieth century, executed this pastel view circa 1918. Courtesy, London Regional Art Gallery*

Bottom: *Artist Albert Templar (b. 1897) specializes in portraits and depictions of London street scenes. Painted in 1928,* The Abbott Block, *a group of stores on Dundas Street opposite the Armories, is illustrative of Templar's drawing skills and vibrant use of color. Courtesy, London Regional Art Gallery*

WAR AND NOSTALGIA

With the British army gone, the closing years of the century saw London's own troops occupied in the defence of Canada and the Empire. When the second Louis Riel rebellion broke out in the Northwest in 1885, the 7th Fuseliers were called up by a trumpeter on a bicycle and twenty-one officers with 244 noncommissioned officers and men left for Winnipeg. As the Canadian Pacific Railway was still under construction, there were "gaps" in the line and it took them so long to reach Clark's Crossing on the Saskatchewan River that the rebellion was over on their arrival. Still, they were rewarded with a triumphant reception on their return to the city. The next year provision was made for a new military school on Oxford Street East when land was purchased from John Carling for a site. The Liberal *Advertiser* was enraged at the purchase price of $727 an acre which was arranged by Carling's solicitor, Mayor Henry Becher. Wolseley Barracks was erected before the year was out and the military school was then moved to the new buildings from its site on the east side of Victoria Park. The military lands along the park were then sold off for a line of new mansions, including that of John Carling. In 1887 the Infantry School Corps, which became the Royal Canadian Regiment in 1901, was moved into the barracks, which has remained its headquarters.

By 1899, when the Boer War broke out in South Africa, London had been organized as the No. 1 Military District and Sir Wilfrid Laurier addressed the volunteers from the city at the Grand Trunk Railway Station as they departed for the war. Various members of the First Hussars, Royal Canadian Regiment, and Middlesex Regiment went to Africa where, unlike the Northwest Rebellion, they saw action before the war ended in 1902. In London, a branch of the Red Cross was organized by Mrs. Harriet Boomer to assist the soldiers. In 1908 the ladies of the Imperial Order of the Daughters of the Empire raised the $1,800 necessary to erect the Boer War Memorial which stands in Victoria Park. By that time the London military had obtained a downtown headquarters with the opening of the Dundas Street Armories in 1905 at a cost of $183,000.

Even before the Boer War the ties of affection for the Empire were clearly shown in London's celebrations of Queen Victoria's Diamond Jubilee in 1897; the city held week-long celebrations in July and there were special services in many churches. The Jubilee of Victoria's long reign reminded Londoners that they themselves lived in what was now an old city. By the 1890s only one log house from the early days remained standing and some Londoners were stimulated to try and recover the city's past before it was forgotten. Archie Bremner, a reporter with the *London Advertiser,* published the first edition of his *Illustrated London* in 1897. It proved so popular that a second edition came out in 1900.

For sixty-two years, Nicholas Wilson, "Old Nick" (1827-1909), taught in London schools. Fondly remembered by generations of London schoolchildren, he was appointed the first principal of Union School in 1849 and later became a staff member of Central School. His philosophy of education was guided by the motto that "courtesy and kindness open more doors than a crowbar." Courtesy, UWO

Another event celebrating London's past had already taken place at the Grand Opera House in March 1897 to mark pioneer schoolmaster Nicholas Wilson's completion of fifty years of teaching in the city. "Old Nick," as he was lovingly known, was given $1,000 in gold by his pupils who enclosed it in a magnificent silver casket. It was Wilson who, about this time, came up with the idea of forming a London Old Boys' Association. This was duly inaugurated in a July meeting at the Tecumseh House, where a fine dinner was served, followed by festivities at Springbank Park. The Old Boys ceremonies were so popular that they were repeated the next year and soon Old Boys chapters were formed in such places as Detroit and Chicago. The celebrations continued periodically until the 1920s, and one was held as late as 1938. On October 12, 1901, the Duke and Duchess of Cornwall, the future King George V and Queen Mary, visited London. Ten days later, stimulated by John Carling, the London & Middlesex Historical Society held its organizational meeting at the university. London was now an established city and recognized that fact.

Port Stanley, pictured in the 1920s, was not only London's principal lake port, but also its summer playground. After the London & Port Stanley Railway was established, thousands of Londoners vacationed on its beaches and danced at its pavilions each holiday season. Courtesy, UWO

CHAPTER VI

From Municipal Reform to the Roaring Twenties, 1912-1929

THEMES OF THE ERA
From the last annexation in 1912 to the onset of the Great Depression in 1929, London's population increased from 49,102 to 69,742 and the city began to take the form of a modern metropolis. In the few years before war broke out reorganization was the basic theme of London activities. Across North America there had been much discussion of the "city beautiful" movement and urban planning and these had their effect on London through the next two decades, although, unfortunately, not with too many tangible results. One change that was made, although only temporarily, was the institution of a board of control type of government. As in many other Canadian cities, such as Halifax, Londoners found that this did not increase efficiency or save money—indeed it would have been impossible to save money with wartime conditions and inflation—and the board was abolished. A much more permanent change was the organization of the modern Public Utilities Commission.

Another theme was the increasing participation of women in all types of municipal activities. During the previous two decades the traditionally retiring Victorian ladies had shown that they were first-class organizers, founding many women's groups headed

Above: *As in the rest of Ontario, most immigrants to London before 1914 traced their origin to the British Isles. This family of twelve, temporarily housed at Queens Park, came to London from England in 1913. Not until after 1945 did London receive significant numbers of immigrants from other areas of Europe. Courtesy, UWO*

Opposite page: *Dr. Fred Landon (1880-1969) throughout his long life led several careers, any one of which would have ensured him lasting fame. As a journalist, he was assistant managing editor of the* London Free Press; *as a librarian, he was chief librarian of the London Public Library and the first chief librarian of the University of Western Ontario in 1923; and as an academic, he was a noted Ontario historian and teacher. He was also a university administrator and an active community leader. Courtesy, UWO*

by the London Local Council of Women in 1893. By the second decade of the century women's organizations were active in many aspects of civic life, and the move began to have the franchise extended to females. Sir Adam Beck's Hydro-Electric Power, with all its labor-saving devices, had a great effect in freeing women from the drudgery of household tasks which had occupied so much time. Independence of spirit was evident in other ways. Skirts grew shorter and ceased to drag in the mud, and new fashions appeared—the hobble skirt was first noted in London in 1910, though this may have been more of an impediment to movement than anything else. London ladies were now beginning to operate their own cars and Judge Elliott's daughter was driving around in a new electric auto.

Edwardian society was shattered with the onset of the war: life was never to be the same again, leisure somehow departed, and inflation increased. Housing too was in short supply and some of the comforts of life took long to restore. Boom and bust usually alternated in wide swings, and wartime stringencies were thus followed by the Roaring Twenties as the world hastened to build up the supplies and luxuries which had been reduced by the war effort. As the Reverend Orlo Miller has pointed out, London of the period was a typical Canadian small town, with no great love for foreigners, a category which sometimes included anyone whose origins lay outside the city. Like other small Ontario and Canadian towns, London did not much like the rising centre of Toronto; however, the city had close ties with Montreal, to which it looked for many of its cultural and business connections.

London also was typical of most North American cities of the period in its almost strident boosterism,

or joy in pointing out its own great characteristics. As longtime City Clerk Samuel Baker, who held office from 1904 to 1933, stated, London was beautiful and well named the "Forest City." Some of the attitudes which were expressed appear strange to us today; for instance, the 1926 centennial publication emphasized London's charity and its "lavish generosity where the need is shown." In addition, the centennial publication once again stressed labor reliability: "London's workers are keen, intelligent, productive, and contented." Writing on the history of modern London in 1927, Fred Landon summed up the situation with a quotation from Dominion Statistician R. H. Coats in the Census of 1921, which stated:

London is a microcosm of Canadian life, one of the most typical of Canadian cities, a community backed and surrounded by a prosperous agriculture to which it sells and for which it manufactures, at the same time reaching out to the markets of the world. London is the commercial centre of Southwestern Ontario, as rich an agricultural country as exists in Canada—or anywhere else.

CITY GOVERNMENT AND POLITICS

The period was characterized by a constant chopping and changing of the City Council's structure in attempts to improve efficiency and reduce costs. The 1914 creation of a Board of Control, with four elected controllers, was followed by a return to a ward system, with the aldermen elected by wards, in 1916. The Board of Control was abolished in 1918 and wards again abolished in 1924. Eight aldermen were then elected for two-year terms with four coming up for reelection each year. In 1930 the City Council returned yet again to a ward system. All aside from the Board of Control experiment, London had tried five different methods of electing aldermen and structuring wards in less than thirty years.

Municipal politics were more stable than the structure of municipal government. The City Council tended to be dominated by the same type of conservative business leaders as in the past. During the years before World War I there was a surge of labor activity. This was further stimulated by the economic stagnation which was followed by a large number of layoffs in business. Before wartime economy came to the rescue in 1914-1915, London's unemployed had increased to between 700 and 1,000. Union membership increased too and several labor aldermen were elected, but generally they were not very radical. Mayors, such as Charles R. Somerville in 1918-1919, Edgar Sydney Little in 1920-1921, or John MacKenzie Moore in 1926-1927, were frequently members of well established and affluent business families.

The most remarkable political event of the period was probably the election of 1916. Dr. Hugh A. Stevenson, who was running for his third annual term as mayor, lost to Colonel William M. Gartshore of McClary stoves in a very tight election. Gartshore accordingly became mayor, but Stevenson demanded a recount and it was discovered that both had 3,887 votes. This unique occurrence threw the decision to the city clerk, and Sam Baker voted for the return of Dr. Stevenson. Unseated after only fifteen days in office, Colonel Gartshore holds the record for London's shortest tenure in the mayor's chair. London's most colorful twentieth-century mayor also made his first appearance in the period: George Wenige, who was elected mayor for nine annual terms spread over five different periods between 1923 and 1950. No one else was to be elected mayor of London so many times, or to be remotely so enduring in city politics.

THE ENFRANCHISEMENT OF WOMEN

The last years of the century's second decade saw the

The Ontario Hydro-Electric Commission and its participating municipalities, including London, encouraged Ontarians to use hydro. Advertisements promoted electric irons and toasters, vacuum cleaners, stoves, and refrigerators. In the Labor Day Parade of September 1913, the old way—a horse-pulled delivery wagon—was contrasted with the new way—a battery-powered truck. Courtesy, UWO

franchise extended to women and the entrance of women's groups into political activity. In London, one of the first women's triumphs came at St. Paul's Cathedral when they were allowed to attend a vestry meeting in September 1917. In December an inaugural meeting was held for the Women's Political Club at the YWCA, and a women's Liberal organization was set up. The next year women received full federal franchise and in 1919 they voted in the provincial Ontario election which defeated the Tories, unseating Sir Adam Beck in London and carrying the United Farmers party to a surprise victory in Ontario. Also in 1919, with the support of the London Council of Women and the Board of Trade, the women's groups ran candidates in the Board of Education election. Three women headed the polls. In 1923, with another provincial election impending, the Conservative party organized a women's group and the Liberals ran London's first female candidate, Isabel C. Armstrong. The results, however, were not too satisfactory; Sir Adam Beck was returned in a Conservative landslide for his last term in office before his death in 1925, and the official Labor candidate, former mayor Dr. Hugh A. Stevenson, received more votes than Miss Armstrong. The United Farmers were slaughtered af-

HARRIET ANNE BOOMER

An early champion of women's issues in London, Harriet A. Boomer served as president of the London Local Council of Women, organized in 1893, and as Ontario vice president of the National Council of Women. Courtesy, UWO

To say that the Victorian era was completely dominated by the male sex overlooks the fact that, while there were only a few suffragettes and anti-tavern activists, there was a great number of energetic ladies who in a quiet way not only devoted a good deal of their time to building up charitable works, but also probably were the dominant figure in their family groupings. Harriet Anne Boomer was a leader among the group of women who founded a good number of still-surviving women's organizations in turn-of-the-century London, which helped make the city a much healthier and more pleasant place in which to live.

Harriet Anne Mills was born in 1835, in either Taunton or Bishop's Hall, Somerset, England (the sources differ), the daughter of a solicitor, Thomas Milliken Mills and his wife Anne Benton. There is little known of her early life. She was obviously well educated, possibly by her mother who was a schoolmistress of some note. By 1851 Mr. Mills was dead and his wife was asked to take charge of a children's school at the Red River near Winnipeg. At the time the access to the area was via the north and Mrs. Mills and her two daughters, May Louisa and Harriet, sailed to York Factory on James Bay and then were canoed southwestward by Indians to their destination—a taxing trip for two Victorian ladies.

At the Red River, May Louisa married a future chief justice of Quebec and in 1856 Harriet and her mother returned to England, where Mrs. Mills had been appointed principal of Queen's College, Harley Street, London. Harriet was enrolled in some classes there, but she could only have attended for a fairly short time as two years later she married Alfred R. Roche, who had connections with the Hudson's Bay Company and also an interest in South African mines. He and Harriet later sailed to Africa to inspect his interests and travel, but he died on December 4, 1876, on the voyage home and was buried at sea. Harriet was later to write two books on their adventures, an account of the voyage titled *On Trek in the Transvaal,* and later, to aid Huron College, *Notes on Our Log in South Africa* (London, Ont., 1880).

In November 1878 she married the Reverend Michael Boomer and, as her obituary stated, "since then has spent most of her life and energies in London." Boomer, a widower who had been rector of Trinity Church, Guelph, for more than thirty years, was appointed dean of the Anglican Diocese of Huron and principal of Huron College by Bishop Isaac Hellmuth. In 1877 Boomer presided over the organizational meeting of the University of Western Ontario at Christ Church and the next year, with the grant of the charter, became in effect the first president of the university until 1885, when ill health forced him to retire from both Western and Huron College. He died in 1888.

In her thirty-three years of widowhood Harriet played a remarkable role in establishing and administering a wide variety of women's societies, many of them associated with medical services. Her main activity seems to have centred around the London Local Council of Women, founded in 1893 as an umbrella group for all the women's guilds. Mrs. Boomer probably assisted Mrs. E.N. English, the first president, in establishing the council and was president herself for some twenty years around the turn of the century. During her term of office the women's groups raised funds to construct the children's wing of Victoria Hospital. By 1903 she was also vice president for Ontario for the National Council of Women. Lady Aberdeen, that most formidable wife of a governor-general, described her as a "delightful speaker with a great gift of humor."

Harriet was also a member of the Imperial Order of the Daughters of the Empire, and though she was never the London regent of that body, a Harriet Boomer Chapter was named in her honor. Her medically related activities began with the establishment of the first Red Cross Society in London to aid soldiers fighting in the Boer War. It was allowed to lapse afterward, but was revived in September 1914 with Lady Beck as president and Harriet Boomer, then almost eighty, as the honorary president. Their campaigns helped raise almost one million dollars for war work. She was also the first president of the Victorian Order of Nurses in London from 1906 to 1912. As well, she had connections with the Board of Education, the Canadian Club, the Mother's Union, the St. John's Ambulance Association, the Women's Christian Association, and, of course, the various Church of England bodies.

In 1921 her funeral, conducted by Bishop David Williams at Bishop Cronyn Memorial Church, brought out the establishment of London. The pallbearers included County Judge Thomas Talbot Macbeth; City Solicitor Thomas G. Meredith; Fred P. Betts, K.C., of Cronyn, Betts and Coleridge; Harvey Skey, manager of the Bank of Montreal; and the Honorable Charles S. Hyman. Practical to the last, she had insisted that memorial tributes be limited to one or two flowers per person and, except for a few large organizations, all obeyed her. The *London Free Press* praised her as "perhaps London's most philanthropic and patriotic worker."

ter one of the most confused administrations in the history of Ontario.

By 1910 the City Hall was obviously outdated and plans were discussed to build a more appropriate hall on a more impressive site. The idea of a Federal Square was pushed by some of the Conservative politicians after their party returned to power in Ottawa in 1911, and General Sam Hughes apparently promised federal government support. As with the downtown renewal promised by the Liberal government many years later, assistance failed to materialize. In anticipation, however, the old City Hall was sold for $100,000 in 1911 and a block at Dundas and Wellington streets was purchased for $75,000 as a temporary headquarters. The old City Hall became a bank and was finally demolished in 1969. After 1911 there were various plans for a municipal structure, some of which combined the city and county buildings into a single municipal centre. None of these schemes came to anything. Finally, in 1928-1929, a new, lacklustre City Hall was ereted adjacent to the new Public Utilities Commission building at Dundas and Wellington streets. It was a far cry from the magnificent plans originally envisaged.

While plans were being made for a new City Hall, the Public Utilities Commission was assuming its modern form. The origin of the commission goes back to the Board of Water Commissioners in 1878. The board was gradually extending and improving the facilities of the waterworks and in 1909, at the suggestion of Adam Beck, it was given the power to distribute electricity. In 1912 it took over the authority for parks management in the city, a logical extension of its work at Springbank Park. Finally, in 1914, the Public Utilities Commission was created by provincial legislation, although there was some argument that city committees should be established to handle its duties instead. The distribution of heat in the downtown area was left to private enterprise and in 1914 the Greene-Swift Company was franchised to distribute heat in a restricted downtown area; later it was allowed to continue its operations after the franchise expired. In 1918 the Public Utilities Commission Building was opened at the northeast corner of Dundas and Wellington streets. Originally a three-storey structure, it was increased to four stories in 1928 at the time the new City Hall was erected adjacent to it. The total cost for the PUC Building was $190,000.

The commission continued to expand its services. In 1909 an artesian well system planned by Beck was completed and reservoirs were built at Springbank in

Above left: *World War I volunteers and conscripts were mobilized and trained in warfare at the Carling Heights camp, adjacent to Wolseley Hall on Oxford Street East. Within an enclosed, roofless facility, soldiers washed up with hot and cold water piped in from Wolseley Hall. In the distance are the bell tents for sleeping and the long mess tents for eating and lectures. Courtesy, Alan Noon*

Above right: *During World War I, industry throughout Canada retooled for conversion to the military production of shells, weapons, and materiel for the Western Front. In this interior view of London's E. Leonard & Sons foundry and boiler works, shells were piled on skids, ready for packing in boxes seen stacked to the rear. Courtesy, UWO*

1921 and London East in 1935. In 1912 the commission had assumed control over Queen's Park, or the Fairgrounds, and Victoria Park. The commission was also authorized to establish a playground department and by 1923 there were nine supervised city playgrounds with 1,200 children on an average day. Tennis was available at three locations and three swimming pools were constructed. In 1924 the commission also opened up the Thames bank across from Springbank Park as the Thames Valley Golf Course.

LONDON AND WORLD WAR I

The decades preceding the outbreak of World War I had been marked by so many international crises that the actual outbreak of war in 1914 came as something of a surprise. In London, the old regiments were ready to march as a Canadian contingent to any Imperial battles, but the war was to require new means of recruiting and a vastly stepped-up volunteer force. London was the headquarters of the 1st Divisional Area—later Military District No. 1. In 1914 Wolseley Barracks was quickly remodelled for the headquarters staff, which settled there in close proximity to the troops, who were soon being trained on Carling Heights. London became one of the most important recruiting centres in Canada; a large, frame barracks was erected on the heights and the buildings of the Western Fair were taken over to house troops in training except at fair time. In all, 45,000 troops were raised in the military district and many of them received at least part of their training in London. By 1916 there were 16,000 troops in training on Carling Heights and it was then necessary for the government to open Camp Borden to provide adequate space. When these troops reached Europe many were redivided among units that had shortages as a result of the incredibly high casualty rate.

The back-up for recruiting and the support measures for the troop training occupied much of London's attention. In 1915 the school cadets were organized and the Canadian Officers' Training Corps at Western University was set up; it prepared 450 men for overseas. The university also provided a complete field hospital and staff for overseas services. The various women's organizations were active, the Imperial Order of the Daughters of the Empire running a service club on Dundas Street with a recreation room and hot lunches at all hours.

With total organization for war, the change-over to peace was a difficult one. On November 11, 1918, London marked the Armistice with a parade through

the streets and celebrations for 20,000 people at Victoria Park with the Kaiser burnt in effigy. But the Armistice was only the beginning of a new phase in the reorganization of the city. Immediately provision had to be made for the invalid Canadian soldiers, as many of them suffered from tuberculosis or lung infections often caused by the deadly poison gases that were used. Other Londoners died in the successive waves of Spanish influenza that appeared in the city in October 1918 and swept around the world for the next year. Churches, schools, theatres, and all places of public assembly were shut to contain the spread of the disease. In October 1919 the visit of the Prince of Wales on his Canadian tour symbolized the opening of the reconstruction era. The Imperial Order of the Daughters of the Empire organized collections to help build the War Memorial Children's Hospital as a practical monument to the men who went overseas, and then in 1925 began another collection for an appropriate cenotaph at the southeast corner of Victoria Park. Designed by Sir Edward Luytens as a replica of the Imperial Cenotaph on Whitehall in old London, it was duly unveiled in November 1934.

The changes wrought by the war with its shortages and disruption of normal building are well shown by the housing crisis. With construction stopped during the war, by 1919 there was an acute shortage of dwellings. A London Housing Commission was established and as an emergency measure it erected sixty-eight houses, sold forty of them, and rented the balance. In addition, the commission provided individual loans for the erection of 103 houses but had to report "the adventure has not been an unqualified success." The commission continued its efforts until it was abolished in 1940; but keeping an adequate supply of subsidized housing available was always a race against the increasing numbers of those who required it.

Despite these problems, City Clerk Baker in his 1925 survey of London could truthfully report that "London is pre-eminently a city of broad, well-shaded avenues and beautiful residences." Most people owned their homes and fine residential areas were expanding southward along Ridout Street in South London and north along Richmond Street toward Huron Street. London East remained a district of workingmen's homes and some of the new subsidized houses were in that area.

For the rich, life in large mansions was becoming a problem with increasing costs and the difficulty of obtaining servants. When John Labatt II died in December 1916, his Queens Avenue mansion was sold to the Sisters of the Precious Blood for institutional use, pointing the way to the future of many of these spacious homes. Others were demolished, such as the mansions of Colonel John W. Little and Sir George Gibbons on the south side of Victoria Park, which were replaced by the London Life Insurance Company's new head offices in the mid-1920s. Some Londoners, of course, continued to live in their huge houses, such as the Smallmans at "Waverley" on Grand Avenue, which remains a showplace of the city. Something new was also appearing in London residential life with the building of apartments at Queens Avenue and Wellington Street by John Hayman & Sons. Whatever the size of their homes, Londoners generally were finding life more comfortable. The 1926 centennial publication was able to report that of the 17,000 homes and apartments in the city, 80 percent were occupied by their owners. Further, 98 percent of the households were electrified and more than one-third were cooking with electricity.

SERVICES AND DEPARTMENTS

The city market remained a centre of urban life and by the mid-1920s had an annual business turnover of $1.2 million. On market days, no fewer than 815 rigs were to be found parked there. In 1922, under the impetus of Colonel Ibbotson Leonard, a town planning commission was established. London was fortunate enough to arrange to have the Geodetic Survey of Canada prepare a complete survey map of the city showing every building. This was done at a cost of $20,000, half paid by the federal government. The maps became available in 1927. The city also retained the services of well-known British planner Thomas Adams to prepare a town development report in 1922. A zoning bylaw was drafted, but unfortunately

Above: *Lieutenant-Colonel Ibbotson Leonard (1880-1974) continued the family association with E. Leonard & Sons into the third generation. The eldest son of Frank E. Leonard, he entered the firm in 1899 and became president on his father's death in 1923. He was chairman of London's Town Planning Commission and a founder of the London Health Association. Courtesy, UWO*

Opposite page, top: *Services at the Cenotaph are held in remembrance of "The Glorious Dead" who sacrificed their lives in war to preserve our freedom. Located at the southeast corner of Victoria Park, the Cenotaph was erected in 1934 through the efforts of the Imperial Order of the Daughters of the Empire. Designed by Sir Edward Luytens, R.A., it is an exact replica of the cenotaph at Whitehall, London, England. Courtesy, London Historical Museums*

Opposite page, bottom: *"Waverley" at 10 Grand Avenue remains one of the largest residences in London. It was built in 1883 for barrister Charles F. Goodhue, son of pioneer merchant George Jervis Goodhue, and was later occupied by Thomas H. Smallman, a wealthy oil refiner. In recent decades it has housed the Shute Institute, famous for its Vitamin E research. Courtesy, UWO*

very little came of any of the planning efforts. However, considerable progress was made on the more mundane aspects of the city's life. Street paving and the sewer system were greatly extended, the storm sewer system completed, and an East End sewage disposal plant built in 1916. Regular garbage collection began in 1913 and an improved type of municipal incinerator was built. By 1925 the garbage collection system had been expanded to take in the entire city.

The court systems also were improved, with a juvenile court begun in 1923 and a new police station built on King Street in 1928-1930. One of the greatest law enforcement problems facing the police was the inauguration of Prohibition in September 1916. For nearly eighteen years until Prohibition was abolished in July 1934, there was an unending battle: the prohibitionists attempted to maintain the legislation, the police attempted to enforce it, and from all the accounts, a large portion of the citizenry tried to get around it. For London, with two major breweries located within its limits, the legislation was not only unpopular but also bad for the economy and employment. Tests for the automation of the Fire Department were begun in June 1911 and on the first three occasions the horses started more quickly than the fire engines. Finally, a new self-starting motor put the mechanical engines ahead, and the last horses were retired some years later. There were some bad fires, particularly the destruction of the Perrin Biscuit Company on Dundas Street in 1911 with a loss of $150,000.

Municipal health services were greatly expanded and improved. In 1916 the Board of Health began employing TB nurses. A nurse for communicable diseases was added in 1917, and three years later a venereal disease nurse was hired. School dental clinics began in 1917 and a day nursery followed a few years later, as did a committee on children's welfare. The provincial government built an Institute of Public Health in 1911, which was run by the university. Hospital services expanded too. Women's associations were successful in raising $125,000 of the $300,000 total cost for the eighty-bed War Memorial Children's Hospital, opened in 1923. The federal government built Westminster Hospital as a psychiatric unit for 500 military patients. The London Red Cross was revived in 1914 with Lady Beck as president and Women's Auxilaries were founded at Victoria Hospital in 1924 and St. Joseph's Hospital in 1934.

EDUCATIONAL DEVELOPMENT

In spite of the interruption of the war, the decade after 1912 saw more than half a dozen schools either built or reconstructed. In 1921 London became the first city on the continent to provide education without any fees from kindergarten to university level. In April 1920 London Collegiate was destroyed by fire. The city rebuilt it, and Sir Adam Beck Collegiate Institute in East London and South Collegiate were constructed for students who could not reach downtown easily. Under the leadership of H. B. Beal, after whom it was later named, the technical school expanded and began to develop evening classes. The

Above: *The Faculty of Medicine of the University of Western Ontario was organized in 1881. Opened in 1921, its new building on South Street, opposite Victoria Hospital, possessed all the facilities needed for an effective medical school. Students are pictured in one of the labs. Courtesy, UWO*

Opposite page: *By 1913 annexations had added considerably to London's area, thereby augmenting police patrolling responsibilities. As walking was the police officer's principal means of transit, mechanization became a necessity. The first motorized patrol, or "paddy" wagon, here pictured in 1923, was introduced in 1913 to replace a horse-pulled prisoners' wagon. Courtesy, UWO*

public library system was also decentralized with branches being opened in the East End in 1915 and in South London in 1917.

With secularization and its modern structure of government established in 1908, plus the development of government financing, the university underwent one of the greatest periods of expansion in its history. With its name changed from Western University to the University of Western Ontario, it moved from the Old Huron College location at St. George Street and College Avenue to the present expansive campus, then located well beyond the built-up urban fringe. The expansion was directed by two of the most powerful figures in Western's history: Arthur T. Little and W. Sherwood Fox. Little, a son of Mayor John W. Little in whose memory the 1929 university stadium was named, provided both continuity and leadership as chairman of the Board of Governors from 1919 until 1954; his formidable portrait by Clare Bice, a masterpiece of London art, hangs in the Great Hall. The expansion was accomplished without a president as the Reverend E.E. Braithwaite was dismissed in the frequently mysterious manner of university presidents in 1919. The triumvirate who took over the leadership for eight

Above: *The new London Township campus of the University of Western Ontario was not unlike a farmer's field—indeed, it was one! "Bellevue Farm" had been purchased by the Board of Governors in 1916. Here, framed by the posts of University Bridge, the newly completed Arts Building of 1924 perches majestically atop University Hill. Courtesy, UWO*

Opposite page: *Brescia College became affiliated with the University of Western Ontario in 1919. Founded as a Roman Catholic girls' college in Chatham, Ontario, Brescia was reestablished in London in 1920, initially occupying a house on Wellington Street facing Victoria Park. In 1925 the present building, situated on a height of land southwest of the main campus, was opened to admit its first forty students. Courtesy, UWO*

years included the other dominant figure of Western's middle years, W. Sherwood Fox, who became president in 1927 and held that office for twenty years. A recognized classical scholar and a well-known naturalist who wrote charming books on the Bruce Peninsula, Fox was also a millionaire with excellent connections who was well able to stand up for the university as both dean and later as president.

Plans for moving to the new campus began with the purchase of one of the Kingsmill properties, "Bellevue Farm," in 1916. The 260 acres were later extended by purchasing adjacent lands. Then, with $800,000 from the province, $200,000 from the City of London, and $100,000 from the County of Middlesex, the construction of the new university began. The plans called for two buildings: an arts building, today University College, at the head of the hill, with a natural science building (now the Physics Building) which would house the various natural science departments and a cafeteria. Collegiate Gothic was chosen for the architectural style under Fox's impetus because of its connection with the universities of the old world. Thanks to contributions from the County of Middlesex for a memorial to the troops, Middlesex Tower was added to the plans for University College; it is still the focal point of the campus. From the first, particular attention was given to landscaping the grounds and planting trees. "The People's University," as one member of the administration rather overenthusiastically called it, was opened in October 1924.

With a donation of $200,000 from the provincial government in 1919, the university built the new Medical School at the corner of Waterloo and South streets, which is today the Victoria Hospital Services Building. There the faculty developed rather remotely from the university. Dr. Frederick Banting was briefly associated in 1920 before he went on to Toronto and his discovery of insulin. Four years later Kathleen Braithwaite Sanborn was the first female medical graduate. At the main campus the foundations of the library were soundly laid by Fred Landon, who was university chief librarian from 1923 to 1947. Like his successor, James J. Talman, Landon had a true genius for acquiring collections. Even before Landon came to Western, he persuaded John Davis Barnett of Stratford to donate to the university his huge library of more than 40,000 volumes, including many rarities and an impressive Shakespeare collection. His donation marks the real start of the Western library of today. Women's activities were also growing up in connection with the university. In 1919 a Women's Faculty Club was organized by Mrs. W. Sherwood Fox and a year later the University Women's Club was formed.

During the same years Western developed a system of affiliated colleges in London and in the surrounding counties. Huron College, which did not move to the new campus immediately, retained its affiliate status. Several of the new affiliates were institutions connected with the Catholic Church. In 1919 Brescia Hall, operated by the Ursuline Sisters, affiliated as Ursuline College, now Brescia College. The $400,000 Brescia Hall was erected in 1924. St. Peter's Seminary also became associated with the university at this time. Originally, its classes were held at the old Bishop's Palace next to St. Peter's Cathedral. Thanks to the generosity of Sir Philip Pocock, who received a papal knighthood for his many charities, the fifty-acre Sunshine Park was purchased in North London in 1919 for $20,000. Funds were then raised for the $500,000 St. Peter's Seminary, erected in 1926. Outside London, Assumption College at Sandwich, now the University of Windsor, affiliated in 1919, and Waterloo Lutheran College, now Wilfrid Laurier University, affiliated in 1925.

Like other Canadian cities, London was shaken by the controversy over the union of the Methodists, Presbyterians, and Congregationalists which formed United Church in 1925. The dozen Methodist churches went into union automatically on the resolution of their General Assembly and two Congregationalist congregations also came in, although other Congregationalists remained out. The Presbyterian Church split wide open over the issue; in the end each congregation was allowed to vote on its fate. The controversy dragged on for months and the subsequent voting was reported in all the newspapers. In London, six churches of the Presbyterian belief joined the United Church, including St. Andrews and First Presbyterian churches. Five Presbyterian congregations led by New Saint James and Chalmers remained outside the union. As in other Canadian cities, the union

THE MEREDITH FAMILY

While most of London's leading families have played an important role in the history of the city over several generations, the Merediths are remarkable for their rapid rise to prominence in London, Toronto, and Montreal and their equally rapid disappearance from the scene. The patriarch of the family, John Walshingham Cooke Meredith (1819-1881), and his wife, Sarah Pegler, had eight sons and six daughters; but four daughters and two sons never married and several others had no children, a pattern which repeated itself in the next generation.

When Meredith came to British North America in 1834 after graduating from Trinity College, Dublin and studying some law, he had already been preceded by three cousins who achieved prominent places in other cities; one of them was Sir William Collis Meredith (1812-1894), later chief justice of the Superior Court of Quebec. Arriving in London about 1844, John picked up a variety of minor appointments: market clerk, clerk of the division court, and justice of the peace. He sat on the Town Council in 1852-1853, and was a founder of the Board of Trade in 1857. Meredith successfully expanded the funds he had brought over by lending money. In the 1870s he built a large house on the corner of Talbot and Albert streets, and when he drowned in 1881, the oldest victim of the *Victoria* disaster, he left a fortune estimated at $150,000.

Of the eight sons, four went into law and four into business. Their relative success is difficult to estimate, as most tended to leave their fortunes to each other and their sisters. The eldest son was Sir William Ralph (1840-1923), who graduated from the University of Toronto and studied law with and became a partner of Thomas Scatcherd in London. When Scatcherd died in 1876 William succeeded him as city solicitor, and was one of the defence lawyers in the Donnelly trial.

Sir William Ralph Meredith succeeded John Carling in the Ontario Legislature in 1872. He was Conservative opposition leader from 1878 to 1894, when he was appointed chief justice of Ontario. Courtesy, London Historical Museums

In 1872 William was elected to the provincial legislature as a Conservative and from 1878 to 1894 was the leader of the party and of the opposition in the Legislative Assembly. He was chief justice of the Court of Common Pleas of Ontario until his death in 1923. Knighted in 1896, Sir William sat on two commissions to revise the Ontario statutes, and drafted the 1915 Workmen's Compensation Act. He was chancellor of the University of Toronto from 1900, and a member of the Royal Commission which restructured its government in 1905-1906. Sir William left an estate of $133,877 to his children.

Edmund (1845-1921) specialized in criminal law and advised the Donnelly family in the trial, though he did not appear in court. He was mayor of London in 1882-1883. Richard Martin (1847-1934) studied law with Edmund and then became his partner, specializing in chancery law. He was appointed a judge of the Chancery Division of the High Court of Ontario in 1890. In 1905 he became a judge of the Court of Appeal, in 1912 chief justice of the Common Pleas, and finally from 1922 until he retired in 1930 president of the High Court. He was also chancellor of Western University from 1912 to 1916. Richard never married, and he died in 1930, leaving an estate of $235,598.

Thomas Graves (1853-1945), the last brother to enter the legal profession, studied law with Scatcherd & Meredith and joined the firm in 1878. In 1894, when Sir William became a judge, Thomas took over as city solicitor of London and retained the post until his death fifty-one years later. He was president of the Huron & Erie (and the Canada Trust) from 1907 to 1926, chairman until 1933, and finally both president and chairman until 1943. His estate, partly inherited, was $445,047. He married Jessie, daughter of Sir John Carling, and they had two sons.

The dominant figure among those brothers who went into business was Henry Vincent (1850-1929), who married a daughter of Andrew Allan of the Allan Line of steamships. Joining the Bank of Montreal in 1867, he rose to general manag-

Brother of Sir William Ralph Meredith, Thomas Graves Meredith was president of the Huron & Erie Loan and Savings Company (1926-1933) and city solicitor (1907-1945). Courtesy, UWO

er of the bank by 1911, was president from 1913 to 1927, and then chairman. He was also president of the Royal Trust Company and the Royal Victoria Hospital. He received a baronetcy in 1916, becoming Sir Vincent. He left an estate of well over a half-million dollars.

John Stanley (1844-1926) worked for the Merchant's Bank, largely in Montreal, and retired to London in 1898. His career must have been successful; though the first brother to die, he left $420,429. Charles (1855-1928) also went to Montreal and married a daughter of Richard B. Angus, the president of the Bank of Montreal before his brother Sir Vincent. In 1887 he purchased a seat on the Montreal Stock Exchange, of which he was president from 1902 to 1905, and retired because of ill health in 1924. Llewellyn (1861-1933) was a London real estate agent. Of the next generation, Stanley (1888-1966), a son of Thomas Graves, was a patron of the London Little Theatre and other drama groups. His estate came to $492,671.

Though the Merediths obviously made judicious marriages, and assisted each other through their positions in the Tory party and in finance, their collective careers demonstrate a great deal of ability. Connections may have helped start some of their careers, but working up through so many offices as they did shows their aptitude in handling a wide variety of responsibilities.

caused a certain church redundancy. First and St. Andrews United churches joined to form the present First St. Andrews congregation in 1938. First was sold to London Life for a parking lot.

CLUBS, ASSOCIATIONS, AND ENTERTAINMENT

As the city expanded and new problems arose, more associations made their appearance. The London Humane Society was established in 1912 and six years later the London Child Welfare Association was organized. Many of the new associations were founded by women's groups. The London Women's Canadian Club was formed in 1910 with Lady Gibbons as first president; it brought in many leading Canadian figures as speakers. The London Local Council of Women was reorganized in 1914 and Lady Beck became the president through the war years. The Jewish women of the city formed the Rose Caplan Hadassah Chapter of London in 1918.

The men too were forming organizations, particularly ones with a business or fraternal orientation. For instance, the East London Businessmen and Property Owners' Association was formed in 1910 and five years later the London Rotary Club was organized. In 1916 came the London Advertising Club and then in 1918 the Board of Trade became the Chamber of Commerce. The active fraternal orders and service clubs included the Foresters, Orangemen, Kiwanis, Lions, and Masons. The last group built a new Masonic Hall on Queens Avenue in 1912. One order that has been forgotten was the Ku Klux Klan, which held a funeral in full regalia at Woodland Cemetery in 1926.

Londoners' opportunities for entertainment expanded in the second decade of the century with the rise of vaudeville, and movies began to appear regularly. At least five new theatres opened, of which Lowes was the most famous. They presented a wide variety of entertainment. The outstanding musical was probably *Chu Chin Chou* with fourteen scenes, eighteen musical numbers, and four ballets performed by an enormous cast in 1920. Native son Guy Lombardo performed with his brothers at London and Port Stanley before moving on to the wider world of the United States in 1928. Movies that achieved great popularity in the city included David W. Griffith's "Birth of a Nation" in 1915 and Charlie Chaplin's six-reel photoplay "The Kid" in 1921. Movie stars appeared in the city; Tom Mix, the cowboy film star, and Tony, his wonder horse, performed at the Sell-Floto circus to the joy of the young.

Livestock judging and farm machinery displays have always been important features of the annual Western Fair. In these two early 1920s views, proud breeders parade their prize livestock in front of the grandstand before judges (top), while discerning farmers examine tractors and combines (above). Courtesy, London Historical Museums

Jack L. Warner, one of the four legendary Canadian brothers who pioneered talking pictures, was born in the city in 1892. With movies and vaudeville flourishing the professional theatre went into a decline, opening the way for various amateur dramatic groups. The London Drama League was established about 1927 and lasted for thirteen years under the patronage of Grace Blackburn and Stanley Meredith.

One unplanned entertainment was the mysterious disappearance of impresario Ambrose Small in Toronto on December 2, 1919. Small, who had originally been associated with Colonel Whitney of Detroit, had built up a large Ontario chain of theatres, called Grand Operas. He decided to take the opportunity of selling out while the going was still good and disposed of his theatres for $1.75 million. He then deposited the cheque, lunched with his wife, and after purchasing a paper from his usual newsboy, vanished. As Small was carrying no money his disappearance was hard to understand, although his churlish, tight-fisted personality had certainly made him many enemies. Offers of reward, international police searches, and clues in many directions all failed to find either the reason or the body. The Small disappearance remains a mystery today.

The most likely course of events would seem to be that he was murdered at his Toronto Grand Opera House and the body incinerated in the furnace. Nat-

Before the domination of the large automobile makers, small manufacturers existed to supply the local market. A London example was Barton & Rumble Truck Manufacturers. Never employing more than ten workers, the Hamilton Road shop assembled approximately forty B & R trucks between 1916 and 1923. Standing before the garage, this vehicle was destined for the Lucan Milling Company. Courtesy, Alan Noon

urally, legends quickly sprung up in his other opera houses that they had been the real scene of his final disposal. For London's Grand Opera House, now the Grand Theatre, it has been suggested that Small's body was somehow transported across Southern Ontario's horrendous roads and either cremated in its furnace or otherwise disposed of. The logistics here seem pretty impossible, but the incident does make a nice legend. When the Grand Theatre was practically rebuilt in the late 1970s, many waited for a skeleton to come tumbling out of a wall. No skeleton appeared, but Small's ghost is still seen lurking around the scenes of his lifetime activities—as is only appropriate for a theatrical wraith.

Londoners had another new source of entertainment in the radio. Station CFPL made its initial broadcast as station CJGC on November 30, 1922, when Sir Adam Beck delivered a dedication address over the air. London had its own amateur radio Marconi Club on Dundas Street in 1935. In sports the city's reputation was led by C. Ross "Sandy" Somerville, who won many amateur golf championships in the 1920s and 1930s.

The Western Fair continued as a main city attraction. The Crystal Palace burned down but was replaced in 1927 by the Confederation Building. The next year a new arena was built, and fairgoers were entertained at an expanded midway operated for many years by Paddy Conklin of Conklin Shows. Among the midway performers was Prince "Nicholi," a "Russian Prince" who was exhibited as the smallest man in the world at sixteen and a half pounds and a height of twenty-seven inches. He died at the Grand Trunk Station in September 1911. By this time the large number of visitors from outside the city were also entertained by special movie weeks put on by the theatres.

BUSINESS AND TRANSPORTATION

Postwar business in London underwent drastic changes. As elsewhere, the increased production required to catch up on shortages caused by the war set off a boom which lasted through the 1920s. For London specifically there was a major shift in the industrial picture. As City Clerk Baker expressed it, "in less than a score of years, industries like brewing, cigar-making, and carriage building were scrapped." The cigar factories closed down or moved out of London, as the oil industry had done years before, and the decentralized carriage industries, which had flourished in most cities, were replaced by centralized automobile manufacturing at a few points. Yet, the demise of these local industries represents only a

Above: *By the 1920s London's principal hotel, the Tecumseh House, was clearly outdated. The Hotel London opened its register for its first guest in July 1927 and closed in February 1972. The location of London's major conventions, the 350-room facility had every modern convenience—bars and lounges, a barber shop, flower and gift shop, a ladies' hat shop, and other stores. Courtesy, UWO*

Opposite page: *The new Smallman & Ingram building of 1907-1908 allowed an increase in merchandise lines, making the business a true department store. A mail order catalogue, first published in 1911, appeared twice yearly. As in this 1922 spring and summer issue, it displayed a wide variety of goods, ranging from dresses and coats of the latest fashion to aluminum kitchen wear and baby buggies. Courtesy, UWO*

part of the change that was underway.

In the past London manufactories had developed from local firms set up by Londoners; now, new industries tended to be branches of firms with headquarters in other places—such as the Kellogg Company from Battle Creek, Michigan. Still another trend was the move of industry away from the downtown to East London, a change which, as noted, was encouraged by the City Council. The McCormick biscuit factory was transferred there in 1914. There was little new industry downtown. In 1926-1927 McCormick's site was taken over by the new million-dollar, fireproof Hotel London, which was advertised as being ideal for tourists, conventions, and transients. The hotel, which remained in operation until 1972, opened in July 1927, and rapidly took business away from the old Tecumseh House which closed two years later, partly the victim of rivalry, partly of depression.

With the boom of the 1920s following close on the heels of wartime inflation, the cost of living was rising rapidly. While there had been periods of high inflation alternating with severe depressions between 1815 when the Napoleonic Wars ended and the outbreak of World War I in 1914, the cost of living had not greatly changed. By the 1920s, however, it was moving up quite rapidly although the prices and

wages still seem extremely low today. In 1920 the London Hod Carriers, Local 492 of the Hod Carriers and Laborers, struck when offered fifty-five cents per hour, not the seventy cents they demanded. Even the fifty-five cents was rather a high wage. In 1916 the City Hotel at the southwest corner of Dundas and Talbot streets was offering $1.50 per day for first class waitresses and kitchen help during the busy fair week. The waitress earning her $1.50 per day would have found that she could not get her hair bobbed at Smallman and Ingram's elegant fifth floor salon for less than thirty-five cents. For the Hod Carrier wishing to purchase tires, the Tiger Tire & Rubber Company of Dundas Street was selling cord tires for only $11.55. Obviously there were much higher wages in London and obviously also much cheaper shops.

Financially, London was undergoing changes as well. New bank branches were being opened in the city and even more trust companies were making their appearance, such as the Premier Trust and Consolidated Trust, which opened in 1915. In 1925 the Northern Life Insurance Company ran into difficulties and was taken over by a local group, "The Northern Life Syndicate," composed basically of C.R. Somerville of the paper box company, Ray Lawson of the printing firm, and solicitor R. G. Ivey. Somerville and then Ivey were the presidents of the company until 1960 and the syndicate continued in their families' control until 1974.

Wages and prices were also affecting the London Street Railway which, inevitably, was always running into complaints with regard to services. In 1913 the LSR adopted the labor-saving device of pay as you enter streetcars and were soon rebuilding all their older cars along these lines. In 1914, after a ten-year battle, London finally saw the advent of the Sunday streetcar which was allowed to start running at 10 a.m. in order to get churchgoers to their destination. Like other innovations which liberalized the strict sabbath laws, Sunday streetcars proved immensely popular. Oakley Smith was the first of 22,249 revenue-paying passengers to ride on the streetcars the day Sunday service became available.

Increased fares were a recurring innovation which was decidedly unpopular. A 1919 increase meant that for twenty-five cents adults received only six tickets instead of seven, and children only eight tickets instead of nine. The increase was squashed in court but reinstated on appeal. The LSR not only had to put up with irate customers, but also with a strike for higher wages, which led to the Ontario Railway and Municipal Board taking over management in May 1920 and running the system for a year. Later, in 1924, legislation which authorized higher fares was first repealed and later reinstated. These changes naturally were accompanied by increasing public demands that the LSR be taken over by the city, following the recent example of the Toronto Transportation Commission established in 1923.

Unlike the tale of the LSR, the London & Port Stanley Railway had one of its most successful periods during the World War and the following decade. In 1912 Beck began urging electrification of the railway and his idea was approved by the voters in a 1913 plebiscite. The city then took over the operation of the railway and electrification was completed in 1915. London continued to operate the railway, under a commission which was first chaired by Adam Beck, until it was turned over to the PUC in 1936. During the period wide passenger connections were retained, with the railway having interchange agreements with the Michigan Central Railway and the New York Central Railway, as well as the Pere Marquette and Wabash systems. Further, the opera-

Above: *Possibly more than any other twentieth-century Londoner, Guy Lombardo (1902-1977) brought fame to the city. With his three brothers, he formed a band, the Royal Canadians, which played at London and Port Stanley before going to the United States in 1923. There they quickly became popular and by 1929 won a permanent place at New York's Hotel Roosevelt and, later, at the Waldorf-Astoria, where their rendition of "Auld Lange Syne" became synonymous with New Year's Eve. Courtesy,* London Free Press

Opposite page: *"There's an old home town in Canada, Where the old folks welcome you home, Back to London in Ontario." So go the words to the chorus of the song "Come On Home," composed by Wilfred Traher for the London Old Boys' Reunion of 1926. Twelve years later, in July-August 1938, the last of these celebrations was held. Nicholas Wilson, a veteran London teacher, originated the idea in 1897 and Old Boys chapters were founded by former Londoners in many Canadian and American cities. Courtesy, UWO*

tion of the railway was profitable. Baker, an expert on London and Port Stanley problems, advised that while from 1853 to 1914 the railway had lost $520,453 from the city takeover, from 1915 to 1922 it made a profit of $479,200. The wartime effort and efficient management would have been a great help in building up this profit; nevertheless, the very existence of the profit also showed that the L&PS could be a viable enterprise in the years before the automobile.

The convenience of travel on the electric railway, coupled by the belief of Beck and many other Londoners that the railway should broaden into related enterprises to make a profit, meant that Port Stanley was virtually a summer suburb of London until World War II. In 1915 Thomas H. Purdom, whose politics were the opposite of Beck's, noted proudly that the city-owned road to London's harbor was "a Public Utility owned and operated by the people." And the London centennial publication in 1926 praised the railway and its enterprise in building up Port Stanley, which developed into "The Coney Island of Western Ontario" with two million visitors per annum in the mid-1920s. The original Casino, the largest ballroom in Canada when it was built in 1908, continued in use until it burned in 1932. It was supplemented by a pavilion built by the Railway Commission in 1926, which was in its turn the largest ballroom; advertisements proclaimed that it could hold 3,000 dancers and spectators. The Pavilion had the best bands from across the continent: Benny

His Worship the Mayor
JOHN M. MOORE
Aldermen and Old Boys
of the
CITY of LONDON, ONTARIO, CANADA
Request you to
Come On Home
for the
Grand Centennial Celebration
of the City of London
and
Home Coming of Former Londoners
TO BE HELD IN
LONDON, CANADA, JULY 31st TO AUGUST 7th 1926
A MUSICAL INVITATION
COMPOSED BY
WILFRED TRAHER
PUBLISHED BY
W. C. TRAHER
LONDON, CANADA.

Goodman, Count Basie, Glenn Miller, Louis Armstrong, and of course London natives Guy Lombardo and his brothers. Until it burned in 1979 it had a great sentimental attachment for many Londoners. Other attractions were a boardwalk with the usual games and rides and a bath house with 1,000 steel lockers, sterilized swimming suits and towels for rent, showers, and even electric hair dryers. For those who did not like swimming or just wanted to sit around, there was the cafeteria with its most delicious foods, well selected by skilled chefs, and scrupulously clean conditions which "provided a gourmet treat to highlight a day at the beach."

The demise of the L&PS was already on the horizon, however, with the increasing auto registrations in the city. In 1920 London had more than 3,000 cars registered; by 1930 the number had increased to nearly 13,000. This was reflected in the number of passengers and the amount of freight carried on the railway. In 1923 there were 914,808 passengers; twelve years later in 1935, despite the Great Depression, this had dropped to 389,215. During the same period the freight carried by the railway dropped from 564,472 tons to 206,281 tons. The truck as well as the car was playing its part in undermining railroad usage. Simultaneously, the provincial government was providing financial support for highway construction. In 1931 the road from St. Thomas to Port Stanley was paved, providing a good surface all the way from London. City traffic control presented increasing problems. In 1929 a manually operated traffic signal tower was erected at Richmond and Dundas streets, but only five years later it was replaced by London's first fully automated traffic lights.

London was also growing as a centre for air travel. In 1912 Beckwith Havens conducted the first airplane flight to take place over London and a couple of months later Miss Dora Labatt became the first London lady to take a plane ride. In 1919 A.B. Jones, a former RAF pilot, became the first Londoner to purchase an airplane. A municipal airport was a necessity and in 1927 London's first airport was established at Lambeth. On September 1 of that year Captain Terry Tully and Lieutenant James Medcalf left from a field at the opposite end of the city aboard their Stinson Monoplane, the *Sir John Carling,* in an ill-fated attempt to win the $25,000 prize offered for the first plane to reach London, England. They were lost in the fog off Newfoundland.

In 1928 the first directional arrow appeared on the roof of the Imperial Oil Company's Dundas Street East building to point the way to Lambeth Airfield. August 1928 was a great time in London's air history. The Goodyear dirigible *Puritan* became the first aircraft of its kind to pass over London en route from Akron, Ohio to the Canadian National Exhibition in Toronto on the 21st. At the same time London airport was officially opened with a hangar provided by the Kiwanis Club and the Chamber of Commerce. The final coup came with the inauguration of airmail service on a flight that proceeded from Toronto to Hamilton to London to Windsor over a period of several days. As the first mail plane taxied in across a sea of mud at Lambeth, the city entered yet another transportation era.

Two years earlier London had celebrated the centennial of its founding with a series of events lasting from July 31 to August 7, 1926. These included yet another "Old Home Celebration" and London put out a special publication to commemorate its prosperity and beauty. That London was certainly prosperous, beautiful, and had a good industrial and financial base went almost without saying; these factors were to carry it safely through the troubled years which soon succeeded the Roaring Twenties.

Welcomed by cheering crowds of 300,000 people who lined city streets, Their Majesties King George VI and Queen Elizabeth visited London on June 7, 1939. Having received a twenty-one-gun salute, the King inspects an honor guard of the Royal Canadian Regiment, standing at attention in front of the Canadian National Railway station. Three months later, Canada would enter World War II. Courtesy, UWO

CHAPTER VII

Depression, War, and Recovery, 1929-1961

T

HE GREAT DEPRESSION, 1929-1939

The decade before World War II was marked by wild economic swings, as the 1920s boom ended with the crash of the stock market in October 1929 and deepening recession until 1932. In 1936 and 1937 there was an upturn in the economy; but in 1938 it turned down again and was only revived by the outbreak of war. For London the Great Depression was marked by much less hardship than in most Ontario industrial cities; the population increased by slightly more than 6,000 and there was no need for the Ontario government to step in and regulate the city's finances. During the first few years of the Depression the Conservative government at Queen's Park was loath to take alleviative action, as was the Conservative government at Ottawa. Municipalities to a large extent were left to handle their own problems of welfare, with disastrous results for both the poor and the municipal finances. After the election of the Liberal party provincially in 1934 and federally in 1935 more action was taken, particularly at the provincial level.

In London, employers were often able to retain most of their staffs by cutting costs through wage reductions, retirements, and deferrals of promotion. By 1932 the number on relief in London was only 8 percent, far lower than any of the neighboring cities of Hamilton, Windsor, or Toronto. A year later unem-

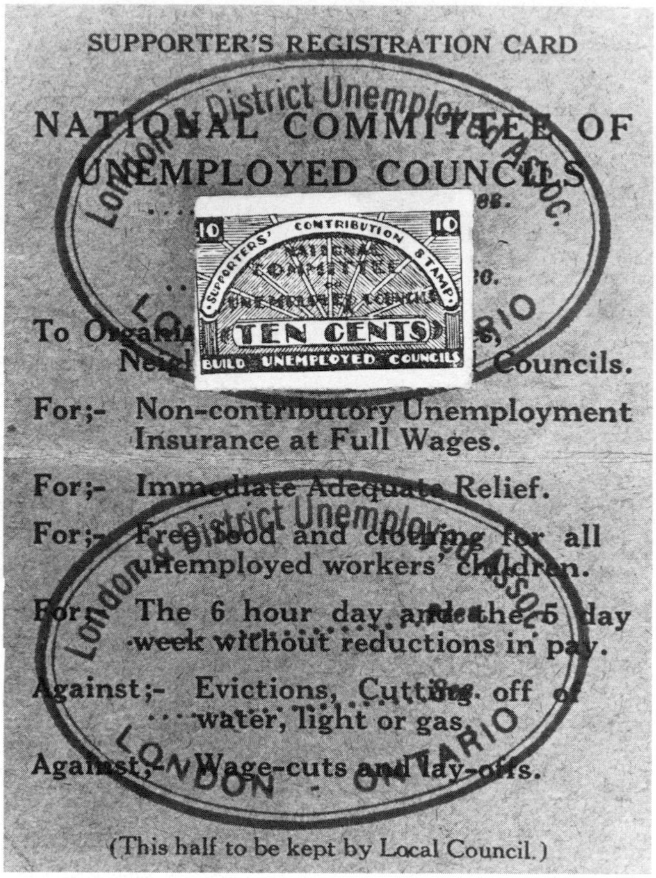
SUPPORTER'S REGISTRATION CARD

NATIONAL COMMITTEE OF UNEMPLOYED COUNCILS

To Organize ... Councils.

For;- Non-contributory Unemployment Insurance at Full Wages.

For;- Immediate Adequate Relief.

For;- Free food and clothing for all unemployed workers' children.

For;- The 6 hour day and the 5 day week without reductions in pay.

Against;- Evictions, Cutting off of water, light or gas.

Against;- Wage-cuts and lay-offs.

(This half to be kept by Local Council.)

London & District Unemployed Assoc.
LONDON - ONTARIO

10 SUPPORTERS' CONTRIBUTION STAMP 10
NATIONAL COMMITTEE
TEN CENTS
BUILD UNEMPLOYED COUNCILS

During the Great Depression, national groups such as the National Committee of Unemployed Councils were formed to promote issues of importance to the unemployed. Reproduced is a supporter's registration card for its London affiliate, the London District Unemployed Association, issued in 1932. Pasted on the card is a dues stamp for the amount of ten cents. Courtesy, UWO

ployment in Canada was to reach an unprecedented 32 percent, far above London's figures. However, the city was still short of funds and on March 8, 1933, it decided to cut single men off the relief rolls. As a result, of course, the men were sustained by soup kitchens and any other charitable help they could find. By 1934 unemployed single men were being sent to a work camp near Lakefield, Ontario, and 300 went from London. Later in 1934, under a new plan for a cash-for-work relief system, nearly 135 men were employed in the city. Despite these problems political activity did not swing far from the traditional parties, although London's first CCF candidate, Everett O. Hall, ran unsuccessfully in the 1935 federal election.

Since the provincial governments regulate cities under Canadian law, the province was inevitably involved in providing depression aid, particularly as so many cities were soon in financial difficulties. The machinery for doing this was already available through the Ontario Railway and Municipal Board, which had been created in 1906 to oversee financial problems and then expanded in 1917 to also look into public utility difficulties. It was in this latter capacity that it had taken control of the London Street Railway in 1920-1921. In 1932 the name of the board was changed to the Bureau of Municipal Affairs and supervision of the depression problems was placed in its hands. Three years later it began a general overview of municipal problems. In 1936 the municipal income tax, except for corporate income, was taken over by the provincial government and a year later the province began a municipal subsidy equal to one mill on the tax rate. The province also began assuming certain welfare payments that had formerly been handled by the cities, particularly mothers' allowances and old age pensions. From 1937 these were paid by the provincial and federal governments in a joint agreement.

Private organizations provided a wide variety of assistance. The May Court Club, which had started as a hospital committee to help raise money for the Children's Hospital, established Goodwill Industries in 1935 as a shop and workroom for the "less fortunate." By 1937 there were more than forty women's organizations in the city, many involved with different types of charity. Assistance was also provided on special occasions, such as the 1939 Christmas dinner arranged primarily through the efforts of the Reverend Dr. William Beattie for 300 London homeless, single, and jobless men. In 1940 the various charitable organizations came together in the First Community Chest Drive which developed into the United

Left: *Pictured shortly after its completion in 1936, the Dominion Public Building on Richmond Street, which replaced the Post Office of 1858-1860, remains one of the finest examples of Art Deco architecture in Canada. Built at the height of the Great Depression, its construction provided work for many unemployed laborers. Courtesy, UWO*

Above: *Obviously, not everyone suffered during the Depression. Thanksgiving Day was always a significant event for the London Hunt and Country Club, marked by a popular hunt and a traditional dinner. The remarkable table centrepiece for the 1931 dinner re-created the hunt in miniature, with jumps, horses and riders, dogs, and, presumably, the fox. Courtesy, UWO*

Appeal. The London objective in the first year was $50,000.

LIFE IN A DEPRESSION-ERA CITY

Public works, though hardly extensive in a depression, could still be used to provide municipal employment, such as the construction of the magnificent 1936 Federal Building which still stands on Richmond Street. The subways under the Canadian National Railways tracks at Wellington and Richmond streets were opened in 1931 and the Richmond Street Bridge into South London was completed three years later in 1934. At the same time work began on the construction of a new Canadian National Railways Station to replace the 1853 structure. It was opened in 1936. Municipally, the garbage department was motorized in that year, but few other improvements were possible. In 1935 the City Gas Company switched over to natural gas.

The development of air transportation continued to provide some much-needed diversions during the Depression. In 1930 Florence Spencer, the London Flying Club secretary, became the first woman pilot in Southwestern Ontario; later the same year, at a two-day air show which was the first held in London, Colonel William A. "Billy" Bishop, the Canadian war hero, was the banquet speaker. Events a year later were less satisfactory, though no less spectacular, when in June Canada's first successful aerial bandit escaped by airplane after robbing the Richmond and John streets branch of the Bank of Toronto. In 1934 London was a stopping point for Clyde Pangborn and Hugh Herndon, the first men to cross the Pacific Ocean by air. The greatest development of the decade was the construction of a proper airport at the hamlet of Crumlin, the London Airport of today. The land was purchased in 1939 and in June 1940 Clarence Decatur Howe, Mackenzie King's minister of munitions and supply, officially opened the airport. Scheduled airline passenger service to London began on August 1, 1940.

With the Depression the expansion of educational and medical facilities was minimal; however, St. Joseph's Hospital was able to build a wing in 1931. The University of Western Ontario added a few new buildings and faculties. The Lawson Memorial Library was opened in 1934 and the Hume Cronyn

ELSIE PERRIN WILLIAMS

The daughter of a wealthy biscuit manufacturer, Elsie Perrin Williams is pictured in the 1920s with her husband, Dr. Hadley Williams, who, like her, was an avid golfer. Courtesy, UWO

Elsie Perrin Williams is not a name readily familiar to most Londoners, even though it is engraved along the facade of the central library. Although she was wealthy, she was not active in civic organizations and basically was a shy and retiring woman. Also, she died more than fifty years ago. Yet, she bequeathed to her city that which she loved best: "Windermere," her sixty-eight-acre estate north of the city. This wonderful gift, a legacy to be shared by all, is just one means by which she should be remembered and endeared, for she also left virtually her entire fortune to London.

Born December 15, 1880, Elsie Perrin was the only child of Daniel S. Perrin, of the London-based Perrin Biscuit Company. He had inherited and greatly expanded his father's bakery, established in 1855, so that by the time Elsie was born the family was financially secure and comfortable. Although Perrin and his family lived in a fine home at 469 Park Avenue (now Clarence Street), he looked for a summer retreat away from the bustle of the city and purchased "Windermere" from the heirs of William Glass, who had died in 1893. The fine old Victorian farmhouse with its secluded acres soon became the Perrins' beloved home away from home. There the family spent many leisurely hours boating on the Medway River, horseback riding, playing tennis, and just relaxing in a hammock in front of the ivy-covered farmhouse. Before long they began laying out their own park on the estate. In 1895 fifteen-year-old Elsie designed the Victorian gatehouse at the eastern end of the property. Two pavilions and several log bridges were also built.

Years later, in 1903, Elsie married Dr. Hadley T. Williams, a successful young physician who was born in Devonshire, England, February 14, 1868. While still a youth his family immigrated to Canada and lived in Clandeboye. In 1883, after receiving his medical degree from the University of Western Ontario, he went back to England where he later qualified as a surgeon—the first person from this city to do so. After returning to London, in 1900 he began instructing in surgery and anatomy at Western's Medical School where he was instrumental in the further development of medical studies. In addition, he served as chief of surgery at Victoria Hospital. To celebrate the occasion of his daughter's wedding, Perrin presented the newlyweds with "Windermere," which they made their permanent home.

The couple devoted much of their spare time to golf and extended trips—once even to Japan. But with the outbreak of the First World War their affluent lifestyles changed drastically. Hadley served in the Canadian Medical Corps as a lieutenant-colonel, stationed at the Ontario Military Hospital in Orpington, Kent, England. Elsie followed her husband and on at least one occasion she was caught up in the war, when during a German air raid on a London suburb she assisted in the evacuation of a group of shoppers. During their absence the old "Windermere" house was torn down and replaced with a California-style Spanish mansion. The old coach house survived until 1985, when it threatened to slide down the hill and had to be removed. The new house, with its orange-clay roof tiles and white stucco siding, was and still is a refreshing change to the "old north."

Later, in 1929, the Williamses added the Great Hall, featuring a traditional English beamed ceiling, Gothic windows, and stonework, thus adding to the already unorthodox style of the house, reflecting the individualism of its owners. Other examples of this are not difficult to uncover. After Hadley's death in 1932, Elsie arranged to have him buried in the garden, where she was also laid to rest. They are surrounded by many of their pet dogs. After her own death, in 1934, she left "Windermere" to the city to be used as a museum and a park. Along with it she bequeathed her fortune, stipulating that the family housekeeper, Harriet Corbett, be given the use of the house and an annual income for the rest of her life. The city did not completely honor Elsie's last wishes and by an act of the Ontario legislature in 1938 managed to break the will in order to build the present central library and also to add a wing on to Victoria Hospital. After Miss Corbett's death in 1979 the estate reverted to the city and is now used as a conference centre and reception hall. The surrounding land is open to the public, for all to enjoy, just as Elsie wanted.

Memorial Observatory in 1940. A year later the McIntosh Memorial Art Gallery was begun and finished in 1942. The names of these buildings indicate the continuing support of London's old families for the construction of educational and medical facilities in the city. Without the Cronyns and the Lawsons, as well as other families such as the Harrises, Iveys, Spencers, and Weldons, London would lack a good number of its institutions and amenities.

Another benefactor to the city, whose estate settlement was to cause a great deal of controversy, was Elsie Perrin Williams, the heiress to the Perrin Biscuit fortune. On her death in 1934 she left the city both her money and her estate north of London, subject to the life residence of her housekeeper. After the will was changed by court action, much of the money was used to build the new Elsie Perrin Williams Memorial Library and Art Museum on Queens Avenue in 1939-1940, a structure which has since been expanded and still serves as a central library of the city. With an art gallery in the Williams Library and another at the McIntosh Gallery at the university, London's role as an art centre was greatly enhanced. In 1936 its sports facilities were also improved when the Labatt family purchased what is now Labatt Park and provided an additional donation of $10,000 for its improvement. With tight economic times any state funding for the arts or the theatre was virtually non-existent; nevertheless, with the support from some of the old families, London theatre was able to continue through the Depression. In 1934 the London Little Theatre was formed by amalgamating several different groups, and in October it began its first season at the Grand Theatre. Thanks to the generosity of Famous Players, who turned down a higher bid, the London Little Theatre was able to purchase the Grand Theatre in 1945 for $35,000, thus saving it from becoming a parking lot. In 1937 the London Promenade Orchestra was formed under the management of Ruth Bricklin.

Thanks to sound federal legislation, Canada, unlike the United States, had no bank failures during the Depression. However, Londoners did lose a few of their old companies. In 1936 the *London Advertiser* finally disappeared from the scene after some years of difficulties, leaving the *Free Press* with a monopoly on the newspaper scene in the city. In the same year one of London's oldest corporations, Carling Breweries, which had already been suffering under Prohibition and had been sold, was transferred to Toronto.

Another change witnessed by Londoners was the

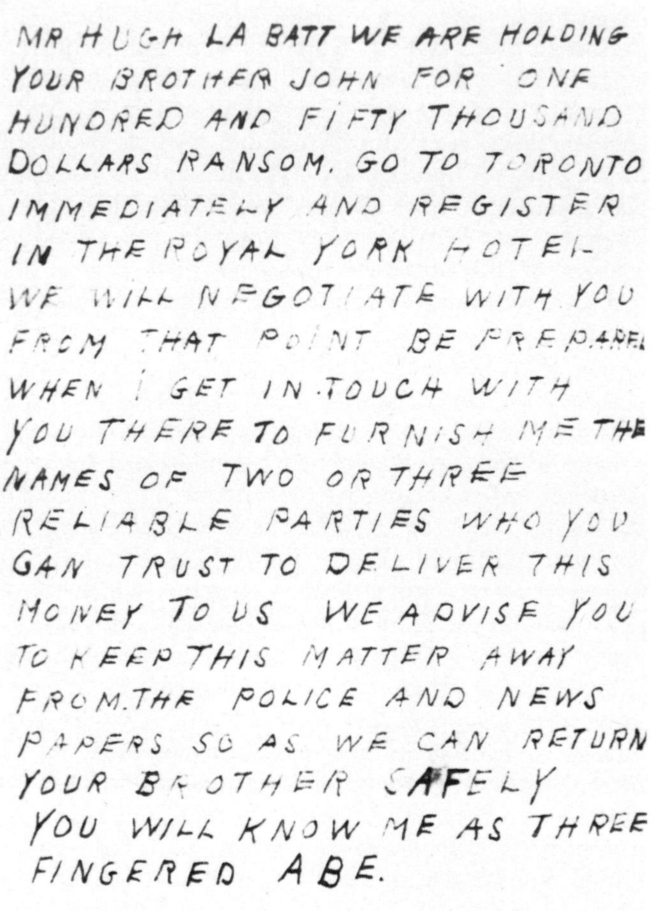
MR HUGH LA BATT WE ARE HOLDING YOUR BROTHER JOHN FOR ONE HUNDRED AND FIFTY THOUSAND DOLLARS RANSOM. GO TO TORONTO IMMEDIATELY AND REGISTER IN THE ROYAL YORK HOTEL WE WILL NEGOTIATE WITH YOU FROM THAT POINT BE PREPARED WHEN I GET IN TOUCH WITH YOU THERE TO FURNISH ME THE NAMES OF TWO OR THREE RELIABLE PARTIES WHO YOU CAN TRUST TO DELIVER THIS MONEY TO US WE ADVISE YOU TO KEEP THIS MATTER AWAY FROM THE POLICE AND NEWS PAPERS SO AS WE CAN RETURN YOUR BROTHER SAFELY YOU WILL KNOW ME AS THREE FINGERED ABE.

Above: *One of the most sensational London events of the 1930s was the kidnapping of John Labatt, president of Labatt's Breweries. Taken from his car, Labatt was bundled off to a Muskoka cottage by kidnappers Michael McCardell and two others on August 14, 1934. They later panicked and released him. Reproduced is the ransom note demanding $150,000 from Hugh Labatt, John's brother, signed by "Three-Fingered Abe," alias McCardell. Courtesy, UWO*

Opposite page: *Dikes were erected after the terrible flood of 1883 and strengthened after a 1905 freshet. They lulled Londoners into a false sense of security and left the city unprepared for the great inundation of April 26-27, 1937. A mild winter and very wet spring combined to raise the Thames River water level twenty-three feet above normal and force a mass evacuation of the flooded areas. In this photograph, water flows in a torrent over a portion of London West. Courtesy, UWO*

spread of the chain store replacing the old family groceries, which gradually joined chains or, except for a few cases, went out of business. London's first neighborhood A & P grocery store appeared at the corner of Waterloo and Grosvenor streets in 1936. For those Londoners who had jobs, prices were not too bad because the Depression had largely wiped out the inflation of the war years and the 1920s. For instance, in January 1917 Craven "A" Virginia Cigarettes sold at ten cents for a package of ten; in January 1938 Phillip Morris Cigarettes sold in packages of twenty for twenty cents or ten for ten cents. The Londoner going to a downtown grocery store in 1934 would have found sirloin steak at seventeen cents a pound, tender wing steaks at eighteen cents a pound, and shoulder roast beef at ten cents a pound.

Like other cities in Ontario, London looked to a happier past in bad times. In 1938 the last Old Boys Reunion was held with a week of celebrations in July and August. London also evidenced very definite signs of the strict Victorian morality, sometimes with what seemed rather extreme reactions. In 1932, for instance, one Austin McLellan of Sydenham Street, aged thirty-seven, was fined seven dollars and costs after pleading guilty to the charge of acting in a disorderly manner at Gibbons' Park; he had been swimming in the river in his underwear. In 1938 sixteen Londoners were fined and twenty-two slot machines ordered smashed in an effort to strike a death blow to pinball and slot machine gambling in the city.

In 1934 Londoners were diverted from the Depression by the kidnapping of John Labatt III. Labatt disappeared on August 14 while driving from Sarnia to London and a ransom note left in his abandoned car demanded $150,000. After three days of confusion he was released in Toronto. Although there were arrests, convictions, and some releases, the whole matter was never clarified completely. Public speculation was rampant. During Prohibition it had been possible to manufacture alcoholic beverages in Ontario but not to sell them in the province, whereas in the United States manufacturing was prohibited but sales were not impossible by one means or another. There were rumors that Labatt's and the Hiram Walker Distilleries at Windsor were cooperating in a smuggling venture across the Detroit River. Allegedly, barges loaded to the gunnels would take off at twilight for "Havana" and return empty in the morning with a dispatch that would put the Concorde to shame. Naturally there were questions as to whether or not the kidnapping was Mafia-related. Like the disappearance of Ambrose Small, the Labatt kidnapping

remains a subject of discussion to this day.

The 1937 flood was a very different kind of diversion. During the years after the 1883 flood London had suffered on various occasions, but never too badly. Attempts had been made to improve the breakwater in West London, as well as the Springbank Dam. After a heavy rainfall on April 26, both branches of the river flooded and for four days 500 acres, largely in West London, were inundated. Some 1,000 houses were damaged in the area. Total losses were estimated at $800,000 for private owners and $94,000 for city property by the time the floods went down on April 30. Fortunately, the flood had resulted from the waters rising gradually, not suddenly bursting through the area as in 1883, so there was only one fatality when a rescue worker's boat was swamped. After the flood the embankments protecting West London were again improved and increased in height and strength, but still no program was undertaken to provide a general system of flood control for the Thames River.

By this time the clouds of war were spreading over Europe and in 1939, just a few months before the war broke out, Canada received its first visit from a reigning monarch with the arrival of King George VI and Queen Elizabeth. The Royal Cavalcade reached London on June 7, 1939, and was viewed by an estimated 300,000 citizens and visitors. It was the last great event for the city before the Depression was replaced by wartime conditions.

LONDON IN WORLD WAR II

On September 1, 1939, when Poland was invaded by Germany, the British ambassador delivered an ultimatum to Hitler. Two days later, on Sunday the 3rd of September, many a clergyman in the city mounted the steps to his pulpit and announced that the ultimatum had now expired and the British Empire and Germany were at war. Prayers for peace and victory followed. Canada declared war a week later. London's First Hussars and the Royal Canadian Regiment, which had celebrated its Golden Jubilee in 1933, were immediately mobilized. The Western Fairgrounds were taken over and the buildings remodelled for use by the soldiers. There were to be no more fairs until after peace came in 1945. In 1941 Mayor J. Allan Johnston departed for active service and in February 1942 the Canadian Fusiliers were mobilized. Not surprisingly, when the plebiscite on military service came two months later, Londoners voted

Above: *At the Depot No. 1 Army Reception Centre, a captain hears the oath of allegiance as pledged by four new recruits in 1941. Framed pictures of Their Majesties King George VI and Queen Elizabeth, draped by the Red Ensign, attest to the official nature of the proceedings. Courtesy,* London Free Press

Opposite page: *As in the First World War, militia received basic training at Carling Heights during World War II. Two soldiers from the 4th Division Petrol Company, Royal Canadian Army Service Corps, wear respirators and anti-gas clothing while receiving instruction in gas attack survival. Courtesy,* London Free Press

for conscription with a majority of 24,050. By the end of the war more than 30,000 men had been recruited from London's Military District No. 1, with 525 fatalities.

Although Londoners, like other Canadians, did not suffer badly during the wartime period, there were shortages and some foods were rationed. Basically the grey life of the Depression continued on into the new era, although economic prosperity was booming again with wartime spending. In London the first blackout test was held on May 31, 1943. In the same year the first individual who refused to work under the National Selective Service orders was taken to court, not surprising in a town where recruiting was so successful. There were many rallies and concerts held to support the causes of Britain and its allies. In January 1942 Lowes Theatre on Dundas Street was packed for a concert that raised money to send medical supplies to the Soviet Union.

The victory loans were, needless to say, very successful and the total purchase in London in the nine sales was $273,383,050. In 1944 HMCS *Middlesex* was dedicated at Port Stanley and adopted by the city and county. Unfortunately, it foundered in the Bay of Fundy in December 1946. Even with the end

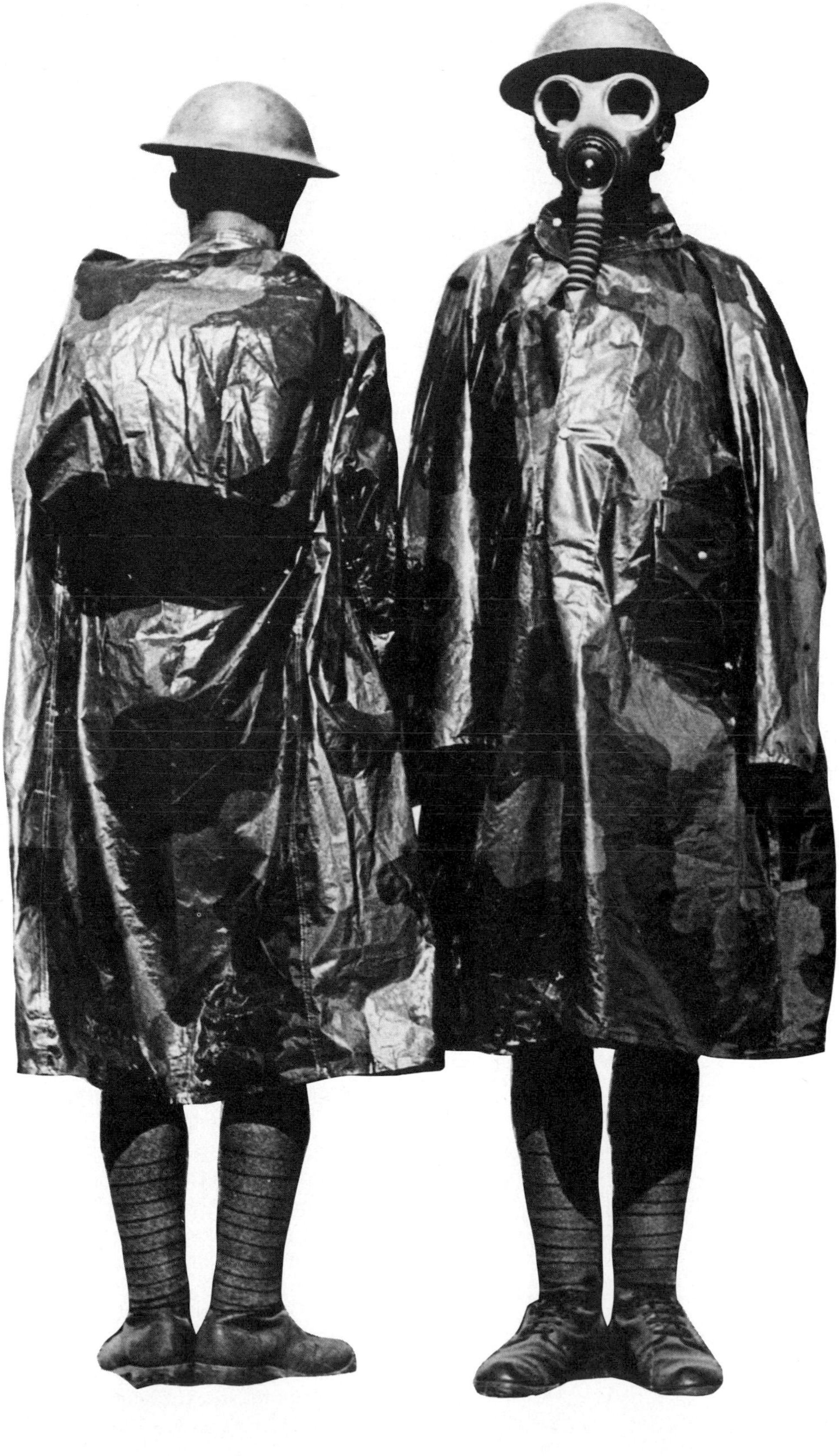

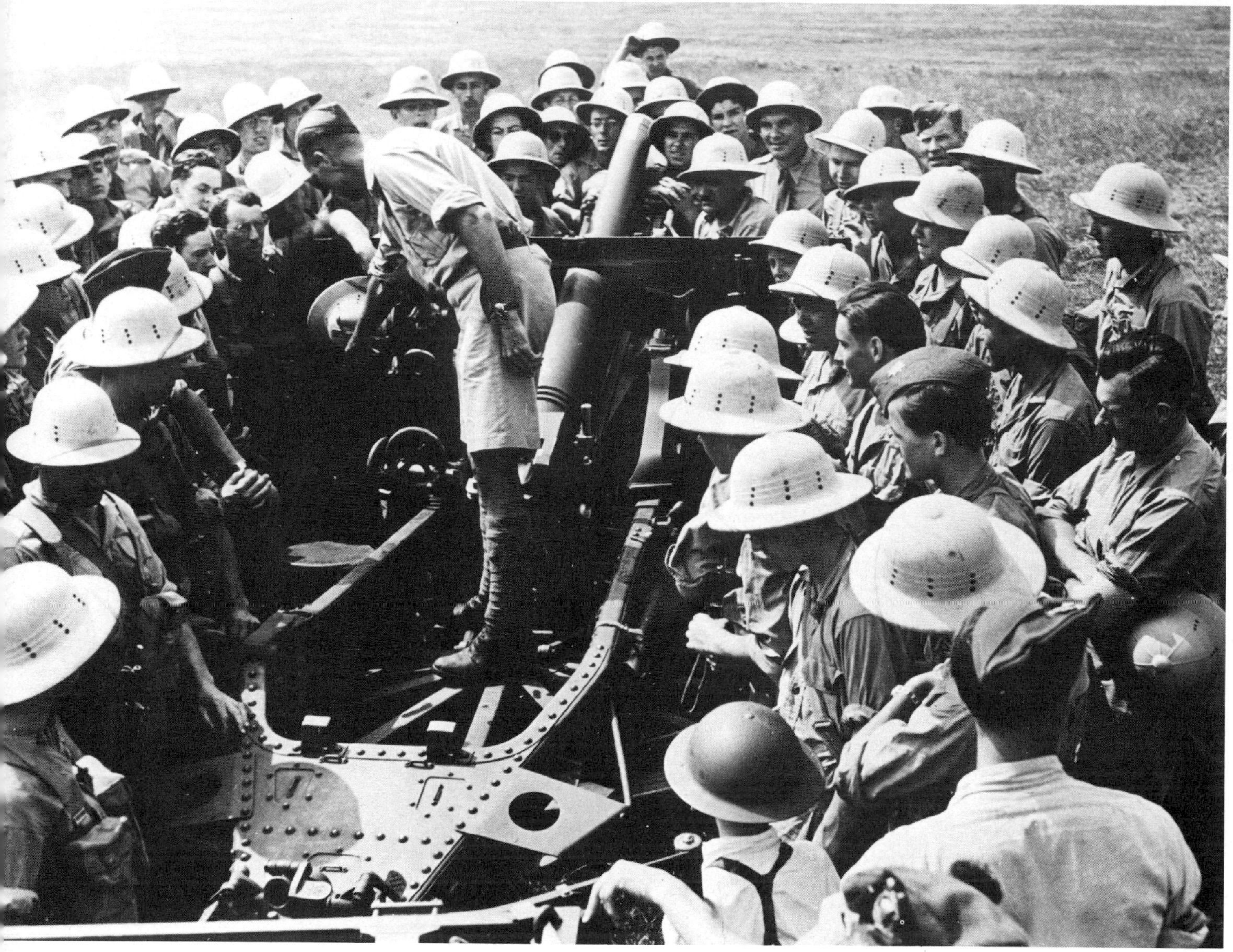

Above: *Members of the Middlesex and Huron Regiment take a close look at the 25-pounder gun, which was demonstrated in June 1943 for Reserve Army troops at the Thames Valley Reserve Army Camp, near London. Courtesy,* London Free Press

Opposite page: *With many of Canada's men overseas in the armed forces, manufacturers turned to women to produce the guns, ammunition, and vehicles necessary to conduct the war effort. These women produced military parts at the converted McClary Manufacturing Company plant. Courtesy, London Historical Museums*

of war in 1945 London was still involved with various military measures. From 1945 to 1947 the Crumlin Airport was taken over as a military hospital. There were also the problems of setting up a Civil Defence System. In 1952 a practice alert was held with a siren blaring on top of the Hotel London. Unfortunately, it was estimated that at least four more would be needed to properly warn the city of an emergency should there be an air attack.

POSTWAR CITY GOVERNMENT AND SERVICES

In 1940 the City Council had been reduced to nine members: the mayor and eight aldermen representing four wards. After the war there were changes in the

ward boundaries but the citizens in plebiscites showed themselves unwilling to either create further wards, or to elect the City Council by a general vote, or to elect it for a two-year term. The last of these proposed changes, which was of course much sought after by the councillors, did come into effect in 1953. Five years later, in 1958, the vote was extended to all persons over the age of twenty-one.

As long as the one-year term was still in force, the mayors tended to change fairly rapidly and almost rotated the office among themselves. George Wenige came back for his fourth and fifth sessions as head of the government, Ray A. Dennis was mayor on two separate occasions, and J. Allan Johnston, who had left the job to go to the war, was elected for a second period. In 1955 there were three mayors: Allan J. Rush, who was appointed superintendent of the Dearness Home in March; George E. Beedle, who followed Rush both as mayor and then after Johnston's death in August as Dearness superintendent; and Ray A. Dennis, who served his last term in the final part of that year. Beedle, who was chosen as mayor by the council, was the first to proclaim himself a Labor mayor, although Dr. H.A. Stevenson had Labor ties. In 1948 the council instituted a general civic pension plan for future service only; but four years later this was extended to cover past service pensions for all civic employees.

After the war, as after World War I, emergency housing was an immediate necessity. In 1946 housing projects were undertaken by a new organization, Housing Enterprises Limited, which built 186 units at Bellwood Park and another forty-eight apartments at Comfort Place. An emergency shelter committee was also appointed. In 1947, when a major flood threatened, the corporation shelters in St. Julien Park were closed and the residences transferred to Crumlin, where some buildings were leased from the dominion government, at a dollar per annum each, as emergency shelters. The city soon set up a temporary school at the airport for children. Other emergency shelters at Queen's Park were closed, as the fair was

GEORGE WENIGE

Although London has not lacked colorful city fathers in the twentieth century, only one mayor can be said to have added a certain blaze of color worthy of nineteenth-century mayors Thomas Dixon or Frank Cornish: George Wenige, who lasted for more terms than any other mayor of the city. From his first election as alderman in 1921, until his last unsuccessful candidacy for mayor in 1952, he was always at the centre of municipal affairs. Twenty times a candidate for mayor, he won on nine occasions, holding the office at five different periods of time: 1923-1925, 1928, 1934-1935, 1947-1948, and 1950.

Born in Detroit in 1874, Wenige first moved to Toronto in 1895 and then to London in 1899. His original work was as a brush salesman; however, he soon moved into the bicycle trade and not only ran a successful business, but also became a trick rider. It was in the last capacity that he first came to London to perform at the Western Fair. Once settled in the city, he became the foremost bicycle salesman and was at one time reported to have the largest bicycle agency in Canada. In 1929 he went into the real estate business, but the bicycle continued to be his trademark and many of the later *Free Press* Ting cartoons picture him riding a bike.

His political style is best described as flamboyant. Wenige himself said that his hobby was "meeting people" and he loved to entertain friends, members of civic groups, veterans, and fraternal organizations at a New Year's Open House, somewhat along the lines of a less-dignified lieutenant-governor's levee. He had views on every subject and liked to say that he represented the working people and their interests. Certainly, he used his "native" Ward 3—the southeast quadrant—as a power base. He also loved slogans, which he manufactured with alacrity. As a bicycle salesman he struck gold with "Wenige, the man who makes walking expensive," and as a politician he came up with such mottos as the "Candidate of All the People." He had a natural aptitude to attract publicity, which he thoroughly enjoyed, through a variety of activities such as giving civics lessons to Grade VIII pupils—possibly the only interesting civics lessons ever taught in Ontario. Other flashy demonstrations were less appreciated, such as his wearing a jaunty straw hat at Sir Adam Beck's funeral. Some said that he was in essence a "wheeler-dealer."

Naturally, his political activities matched his personal style. He loved referendums, originally running as alderman with a call for a vote on the purchase of the London Street Railway. Efficiency drives were another favorite, from streamlining the city committees, or the Fire Department (a favored theme), to firing the department heads, to providing incentive pay for good workers, to cutting costs at Victoria Hospital. Of course, he wanted to attract industry, and advocated "pay as you go" programs. These cost-saving ideas ran starkly counter to some of his finest flights of imagination. In 1924, when the LSR was in trouble over its fares, he advocated that

the city found a rival bus system at an estimated cost of $8 million! He also recommended purchasing the London Street Railway for $1.4 million after proclaiming shortly before that it was worth only $600,000. In 1947 he promised to reestablish civic bingo games, ignoring the minor problem that they were illegal. When reelected he went ahead and did so.

On the other hand, Wenige backed a great number of projects that came to fruition—though in how far through his efforts might be argued. He had a hand in improving the Western Fair, getting a new Canadian National Railway Station, and expanding Parkwood Hospital and the Hotel London. He also advocated a new City Hall at the present Victoria Park site and was in favor of building a covered market with parking, though he did not live to see either underway. In the broader picture, in his first year as mayor, 1923, he was responsible for founding the Ontario Association of Mayors and Reeves as a pressure group at both Queen's Park and Ottawa. He was also instrumental in founding the Canadian Federation of Mayors and Municipalities, in which he was given a life membership in 1951. As he summed up his contributions in that year: "This is my city and there is not a thing since 1923 that was promoted and was worthwhile that I did not support in or out of office." In his later years, when not running for office, he was active in the Moose Lodge and the Maccabees and enjoyed spectator sports. He died of a heart attack on December 31, 1952.

Wenige was a dynamic individual, a somewhat inconsistent and dictatorial mayor, and something of a big-time spender despite his economy compaigns. His 1924 expense account, to the joy of his opponents, was $3,400. Yet, as the *London Free Press* said in 1951: "So much has London been involved with his activities, his plans, and theories, that London is as much a part of him as he is inseparably a part of it." Not far from his own estimate. His frequent description of himself as "ballot scarred" in a way sums up his career. The 1963 Wenige Expressway, although one of the shortest ever built, provides the type of active memorial that he would have enjoyed.

Above: *George Wenige came to London in 1899 and turned his bicycle racing talents into a successful sales and repair business. Wenige posed in front of his Wellington Street store in the 1920s with many of his customers. Courtesy, UWO*

Opposite page: *George Wenige held the office of London mayor a record nine times. Courtesy,* London Free Press

coming back. In 1951 all the emergency shelters were closed; but there were difficulties involved owing to the large numbers of evictions that were necessary. In the general picture, a London and Suburban Planning Board was established in 1946 and three years later the first official plan and zoning bylaw were prepared.

In 1941 the Police Department had acquired a radio system for its cars, and with the increasing number of automobiles in the city, in 1948 it became necessary to install parking meters in the downtown. The first radar speed testing unit was purchased in 1957 and breathalyzer testing devices arrived the next year. The drivers, however, received one bonus when King Street and Queens Avenue became one-way streets in 1950 in an attempt to relieve traffic problems. A family court system was begun in London in 1955 to supplement the existing courts. In 1951 Walter George Rowe of Detroit was the last person to be hanged in the city.

The Fire Department received a new $210,000 central fire hall at the corner of York and Waterloo in 1955; the next year a County Mutual Aid Fire System was approved on a reciprocal basis for London and Middlesex. London's highway connections outside the city were also improving with the opening of Highway 401, sweeping around the south of the city from London to Woodstock in 1957, and then on to

Toronto in 1960. By 1963 there was a clear 515-mile, four-lane highway stretching from Windsor to Montreal. Again, as with the railways 110 years earlier, London was firmly located on the mainstream of traffic. The new highway was to have a considerable effect on the direction of city growth, drawing industry and then housing developments to its area. Dundas Street ceased to be a main highway, reducing traffic and business at its motels, while Wellington Street South leading to Highway 401 built up rapidly as the axis of the new southern expansion.

With the coming of peace, the various city boards and commissions had expanded their operations. The Western Fair resumed in 1948 and opened the new livestock coliseum two years later. In the following years its heated buildings made winter displays possible. The Public Utilities Commission in 1950 began one of its most extensive projects, the conversion of the London area from twenty-five-cycle electricity to sixty-cycle, and had the work completed two years later. The commission also built new structures, including the swimming pool at Gibbons' Park in 1950, and Storybrook Gardens children's zoo, which opened in 1958. In 1950 the Kiwanis dedicated the Memorial Band Shell in Victoria Park. There were also many discussions over the type of arena which should be built in the city.

In April 1947 London suffered a third major flood which was fortunately contained by the breakwalls, and as a result an Upper Thames Conservation Authority was finally set up to control the river. The area under the jurisdiction of the Authority covered the entire Thames basin above Dingman Creek,

Above: *Fishermen cast their lines before the Fanshawe Dam, erected across the North Branch of the Thames River in 1950-1953 by the Upper Thames River Conservation Authority. As London's major flood control structure, it brought relief to a city that had long suffered from the rising waters of the Thames River. Photo by Alan Noon*

Opposite page: *From the inception of the London Police Force in 1855, officer communications had progressed from briefing sessions, written messages, and curbside call boxes to car radios, introduced in 1941. The last innovation was probably the most important: for the first time, officers were placed in continuous and instantaneous reach of each other. Courtesy, UWO*

which joins the Thames River ten miles southwest of London. It encompasses 1,325 square miles, including most of Middlesex, Oxford, and Perth counties and a small part of Huron County. In 1950 the Authority began construction on the $4.89 million dam at Fanshawe Park. Completed in 1953, the dam has a crest length of 2,100 feet and a height of 77 feet. Behind it the four-mile-long, recreational Lake Fanshawe was developed, along with park and boating facilities. Completion of the dam, which has successfully defended London from floods, was followed by a 1955 clean-up program for the Thames River. In 1956, thanks to the efforts of Dr. Wilfrid Jury, the Pioneer Museum was established at Fanshawe Park. Finally, in 1965, additional flood protection was provided by the Wildwood Dam near St. Marys, which is 2,100 feet long in the crest by 71 feet high. It developed another recreational reservoir five and three quarter miles long, along Trout Creek.

Education and medical services began a rapid expansion in the years after the war. In 1950 Catholic Central High School was opened at Queens Avenue and Colborne Street, amalgamating earlier schools. H.B. Beal Secondary School produced several prominent artists including Jack Chambers. In 1958 a new Teacher's College replaced the 1898 Normal School, which became the Education Centre for the city. The Teacher's College was to join the University of Western Ontario Faculty of Education in 1973 and was renamed Elborn College. The university was beginning its postwar expansion by the end of the 1940s. The Faculty of Nursing opened in 1947 and the School of Business Administration in 1949.

The picture also was changing greatly for the affiliated colleges. Huron College moved to new buildings adjacent to the university campus in the same year and in 1951 the university's original buildings on College Avenue were demolished. The Catholic Church opened Christ the King College, now King's College, as a men's college in 1955. The university began its Faculty of Law in 1959 and at the same time opened its new Engineering Building. Between 1953 and 1960 the affiliation agreements with the out-of-town colleges were terminated. In 1939-1941 Victoria Hospital had been expanded and in 1955 the new Y wing was opened. Dearness Home was built as a senior citizen's home in 1954. The Sisters of St. Joseph opened Fontbonne Hall as a children's hostel in 1953 and the Marian wing of St. Joseph's Hospital opened in 1954. The Salvation Army began its village and the Canadian National Institute for the Blind Centre on Ridout Street was constructed in 1952.

TRANSPORTATION AND COMMUNICATIONS

The revival of the automotive industry after the war meant the end of the London and Port Stanley Rail-

way. From 1934 to 1958 the line had had an operating deficit in one year only. In 1943, at the height of the wartime boom, there had been twenty-one trains daily, carrying 1,705,233 passengers. By 1953 the number of passengers had declined to 162,171 as car ownership increased and the Blue Bird Bus Line's services expanded. Some reorganization and action to cut down the impeding losses was obviously needed. In 1955 the control of the railway was turned back to the corporation and two years later, in February 1957, passenger service was discontinued. Although the L&PS had purchased new diesel engines after the city took over, in 1965 it was decided to sell the system to the Canadian National Railways, which took control on January 1, 1966, thus ending London's long excursion into the railway business.

Above: *Dr. John Dearness (1852-1954) was a noted educator and botanist. Previous to his appointment as the first vice principal of the London District Normal School in 1899, he was for twenty-five years the public school inspector for Middlesex East. Courtesy, Bell Canada*

Opposite page: *Lake Fanshawe's recreational facilities include swimming beaches, large picnic areas, and a modern campground. Courtesy, Visitors and Convention Bureau*

Opened in 1953, the Dearness Home for Senior Citizens on Southdale Road was named in honor of centenarian Dr. John Dearness, botanist and educator. Owned by the City of London and situated on fifty-seven acres of parkland, it offers a comfortable retirement residence for men and women over sixty who, through ill-health, advancing age, or other factors, find it difficult to maintain their own home. Photo by Alan Noon

Changes were also taking place on the other railway lines. The Canadian National and the Canadian Pacific both introduced new piggy-back rail service in 1955. In 1966 the Canadian National finally closed the carshops in London East, but it built two successive utilitarian passenger depots for the city on York Street.

The London Street Railway replaced the last streetcars with buses in 1940, and the following year the streetcar tracks were removed from Dundas, Richmond, and Oxford streets. In a 1949 plebiscite the voters supported the city's takeover of the London Street Railway by 7,670 to 5,983. Accordingly, one million dollars in debentures was issued to purchase the company's stock and on January 1, 1951, the London Transit Commission came into being. The Greyhound Bus Lines Terminal, located on the Tecumseh House site at the southeast corner of York and Richmond streets, was opened in 1952 to provide central service.

Communications in London also underwent revolutionary changes. In 1950 the first domestic dial telephone was installed in the city and by 1951 the

In 1923 the London Street Railway, today's London Transportation Commission, began to gradually replace its electrical streetcars with gasoline-powered buses. Phased out on all other routes, the last of the streetcars continued along Dundas Street until a November 27, 1940, blizzard damaged the lines. Buses then took over the entire system. A Ford bus stands beside a stranded streetcar, abandoned the day of the storm, at the corner of Eleanor and Dundas streets. Courtesy, London Free Press

majority of phones had been converted to the dial system. Direct long-distance dialing was introduced nine years later in 1960. Radio station CKSL started broadcasting about 1956. Joe McManus' radio CJOE began as a Canadian centennial project in 1967 and became CJBK after his death in 1976. Television too made its appearance. In 1949 the Benson-Wilcox Electric Company demonstrated the new Marconi TV sets at the Western Fair. In November 1953 the Blackburn interests began the regular CFPL-TV broadcasting over Channel 10 from their new eighty-three-acre site on Commissioners Road. London Cablecast was not established until 1969, when MacLean Hunter TV and London Cable TV made an agreement on the division of the city.

THE CHANGING CITY

By 1955, when London celebrated the centennial of its incorporation with a birthday party at Hotel Lon-

don followed by the usual week's celebrations, the city was very obviously expanding rapidly and pushing against its boundaries in all directions. In the year of the centennial the city began to take preliminary steps to lay out redevelopment areas in the downtown and surrounding area. Parking, which was presenting an increasing problem, was partially solved by the development of the Covent Garden Market Parking Properties. In 1953 the voters supported leasing the market square to a private corporation for the construction of a market and parking building, and three years later a thirty-year lease was granted to Covent Gardens. The 1953 market was then demolished and the new Covent Garden Market, which has remained one of the most popular spots in the downtown area, was opened in its place. The first city-owned and -operated parking lot, on the site of the old King Street firehall, was opened in 1959. While the market parking was being discussed, attention was also turning to a downtown mall for the city. In 1954 the voters had refused to purchase the old General Steelware (McClary) property on York Street and five years later this was taken over by Webb, Knapp (Canada) Limited. The $11 million enclosed downtown Wellington Mall shopping centre was formally opened by William Zeckendorf of Webb, Knapp in August 1960.

Outside the downtown area, the city subsidized housing projects at Chelsea Heights and Glen Cairn Woods in 1959. But the great problem for the city fathers lay just beyond their jurisdiction in the townships of London and Westminster. To the northwest in particular, new subdivisions were going up outside the city's boundaries, often without the overall planning or the complete services that would be demanded within the city limits. Also, the industrial parks were growing up beyond the limits of city taxation. Oxford Street East was developing with the 1949 $5 million General Motors Diesel plant. To the south, as noted, other industrial areas were opening up along Highway 401. The situation resembled the oil boom of the 1870s, and the solution was the same. It was obvious that the city, in order to plan properly for the future, would have to control overall expansion by taking in large parts of the neighboring townships. Consequently, a series of small annexations took place in the 1950s, followed by the great annexation of 1961, which created modern London.

Opposite page: *CFPL-TV went on the air for the first time on November 28, 1953. Here cast and crew ready themselves for the inaugural broadcast at 6 p.m. Walter Blackburn, publisher of the* London Free Press, *was responsible for the establishment of the television station. Courtesy, CFPL-TV*

Looking through a window of City Hall, three children view a five-layer cake, baked in celebration of the centennial of London's incorporation as a city in 1855. City Hall is depicted in icing on the bottom layer, with Victoria Park in the layer above. The trees and leaves on the other layers were indicative of London's reputation as the "Forest City." Courtesy, London Free Press

The bright afternoon sun lights modern London's central core. Bridges direct traffic over the Thames River into downtown, and lofty towers command the skyline. Beyond, the city's residential areas spread their forested avenues eastward toward the horizon. Courtesy, Visitors and Convention Bureau

CHAPTER VIII

The Modern City: London Since 1961

GOVERNMENT AND POLITICS IN LONDON
In the 1950s, after nearly a half-century's pause, London again began annexing land around the city. At first only small areas were brought in, generally in the southeast, because of the need to develop subsidized housing under municipal control. The developers who were building more expensive housing were working well beyond the city limits and generally in the northwest. The first annexation took place in 1950 when 120 acres in the Hale-Trafalgar area of London Township were acquired for housing development. In 1954 the city added a 350-acre section of Chelsea Heights from Westminster Township, and in 1959 another 160-acre section of Westminster known as the McClure Subdivision. This was extended southward in 1959.

By then it was obvious that some comprehensive form of expansion was necessary; after a survey of the surrounding area the city applied for annexation of a total of 42,550 acres from Westminster and London townships. Hearings were held before the Ontario Municipal Board in 1959, a favorable decision was obtained the next year, and the area was annexed on January 1, 1961, increasing the population of London to 165,815.

With annexation the number of wards in the city was increased to seven, each electing two aldermen. A four-member Board of Control was established as

Above: *London's Mayor F. Gordon Stronach was undeniably one of the city's most colorful political figures. Stronach served as London's mayor for more than seven years, during which time he was often embroiled in various heated controversies. Courtesy,* London Free Press

Opposite page: *With Mayor Herbert J. McClure presiding, the London City Council held its first meeting in the chambers of the new City Hall on April 5, 1971. Built at a cost of $5.22 million, the lofty, marble-clad Dufferin Avenue building replaced the long inadequate Municipal Offices. Courtesy,* London Free Press

an executive committee, and in 1969 the new post of deputy mayor was created. In April 1978 the council approved the televising of its meetings. With the two-year term, coupled with the fact that Ontario voters often seem willing to reelect a mayor two or possibly three times, there was much less changeover in the headship of city government. Mayor F. Gordon Stronach held office from 1961 until his death on January 1, 1968. The City Council then elected Herb J. McClure, who remained in office until 1972 when Fred Gosnell was elected. Gosnell resigned on March 6 after a heart attack—the third shortest mayoralty in London's history—and council, after some discussion, elected Jane E. Bigelow as London's first woman mayor. Bigelow, who was also London's first NDP mayor, led council for six years before being replaced by Al Gleeson, London's first Roman Catholic mayor since Frank (later Senator Sir Frank) Smith in 1867. In the 1985 elections Tom Gosnell, a son of former mayor Fred Gosnell, emerged as the new incumbent.

There have been some rather stormy scenes in the council. In 1960 an alderman was unseated under a fiat of the Supreme Court of Ontario, as he was an employee of the London Transit Commission and the position represented a conflict of interest. When he resigned from the commission three months later he was reinstated as a councillor. In 1973 there was a somewhat parallel case when the County Court unseated three aldermen, all of whom were school teachers, for voting on a matter with financial implications for the Board of Education. In this case only a two-week disqualification was handed down.

The growing size of the city and the increasing complexity of municipal administration have resulted in many structural changes over the last quarter-century, some of which have limited municipal powers. In 1968 the province took over the administration of justice and a year later assumed control of assessment. The city itself set up a wide variety of new departments and commissions in the 1960s. The new Planning Board was created in 1961, a city Legal Department established in 1962, and an Industrial Development Department in 1964. The Visitors and Convention Services of Greater London followed in 1971 and the Community Services Department in 1975. With this increasing complexity in departmental structure, the post of chief administrative officer was established in 1971. During the last ten years fewer changes have been made in municipal structure, although a new Planning and Development Department combining various services was formed in

1981. The biggest shakeup in city hall history came in 1980 when the chief administrative officer resigned and two other senior officials were stripped of their responsibilities. That London has done well financially was demonstrated in 1977 when Wall Street gave it the first Canadian A.A.A. municipal credit rating.

The federal and provincial governments have increasingly been using London as a centre of regional administration for the Southwestern Peninsula, although at times federal relations with the city have been rather stormy. In 1976 it appeared that London would lose its historic military base and the Royal Canadian Regiment would be transferred to Camp Borden. After considerable local pressure London was able to retain Wolseley Barracks. In 1978 there was a great deal of controversy over federal government plans for a medium-security prison in the London area. In the elections of that year some council members who had supported the project were unseated and the proposal was then dropped because of "spending restraints."

Provincially, London's F. Ray Lawson was the first lieutenant-governor of Ontario from the city, holding office from 1946 to 1952, and London members have played a key role at Queen's Park. As premier of Ontario from 1961 to 1971, London North member John P. Robarts presided during a period of great expansion in the province and watched over the interests of his old university and city. John H. White of London South was for some years treasurer of Ontario and more recently chairman of the Ontario Heritage Foundation. Most recently, in 1984, David Peterson became Ontario's premier after the fall of the Tory dynasty. Thus London has had three of its members—Draper, Robarts, and Peterson—at the head of provincial government. In 1976 one of the most colorful contretemps in provincial politics occurred when Marvin Shore, Robarts' successor in London North, left the Liberal party and joined the Progressive Conservatives. In the general election the next year, as so often happens to members who leave their party, he was defeated by the Liberals.

COMMISSIONS AND SERVICES

The great problem facing the Public Utilities Com-

JOHN P. ROBARTS

London's most distinguished citizen of modern times was, indisputably, John Parmenter Robarts. At the zenith of his political power he ruled Ontario with the shrewdness of a gifted businessman, yet, almost paradoxically, he was a compassionate, caring person. Evident throughout his career were many acts of kindness and public worth. He was also a man of vision who foresaw the needs of the modern province and acted strenuously to update and adapt his government to better serve Ontario.

Robarts was born in 1917 in Banff, Alberta, where his father was employed as a bank manager. With the mobility typical of banking families, the Robarts moved first to Winnipeg, then to Galt, and finally London. Here young John graduated from Central Collegiate and then enrolled in the University of Western Ontario's business administration program, having chosen it in preparation for law. He enrolled at Osgoode Hall, Toronto, in the autumn of 1939. The outbreak of war, however, interrupted his education and the next spring saw Robarts in the Royal Canadian Navy. He served throughout the war in the North and South Atlantic, the Mediterranean, and also the South Pacific. After his discharge in October 1945 as a lieutenant, he resumed his law studies and was called to the bar in 1947. After practicing in Hamilton for a year, he returned to London and in 1954 was appointed a Queen's Counsel.

His political career began moderately enough on the London City Council in 1950 as alderman in Ward 2. In 1952 he entered the provincial arena and there he excelled. As the Conservative candidate for London North he won a major victory against his Liberal opponent. For the next six years he sat as a back-bencher in the Ontario legislature; but in 1958 he became a minister without portfolio, having been appointed to the Ontario Water Resources Commission. In 1959 Robarts was appointed minister of education, a position he held until 1961 when he succeeded Leslie Frost as leader of the Conservative party and premier of Ontario, an office which he held until 1971 when he resigned and was succeeded by William Davis.

The first post-Confederation Ontario premier to represent a London riding, John Robarts was elected by the voters of London North in 1951. Appointed to the cabinet in 1958, he served as premier from 1961 to 1971. Courtesy, London Free Press

Resigned, but far from retired, he continued to represent North London provincially and was a member of two law firms, one in London and the other in Toronto. In addition, he was named a director of Midland-Olser Securities Limited, the Canadian Imperial Bank of Commerce, and Metropolitan Life of New York. He held positions with the London Health

Association and the Pension Committee of the Anglican Church of Canada. In 1972 he was named chancellor of the University of Western Ontario and later of York University. His last government project came in 1977, when Prime Minister Trudeau selected him to co-chair the task force on Canadian Unity.

Although Robarts continued his contributions to government and to corporate projects, his personal life was tragic. In 1977 he divorced his first wife, the former Norah McCormick, who died in May 1981. He remarried, but lost his only son, Timothy, in the same period. Robarts continued working at a hectic pace, but in 1981 and 1982 suffered a series of strokes which left their effects in depression and some incapacity of speech. On October 18, 1982, he committed suicide. At his lying in state at the legislature and funeral service at St. Paul's Anglican Church on Bloor Street, Toronto, nearly 4,000 mourners paid their respects.

Although it is too early to attempt an evaluation of his work, the tragedy of his last years should not be allowed to obscure the successes of his premiership in which he has rather aptly been compared to the chairman of a large and flourishing corporation. His premiership of Ontario was marked by vast strides in adapting to increasing urbanization, and educational advance, to note just two major changes. His moderate brand of "red Toryism" gave a balanced government to Ontario, and he passed on his province and party to his successor as strong as he received them from his predecessor. It is appropriate that his memory be perpetuated in his city and university by the $10 million John P. Robarts Institute for heart and stroke research.

On July 1, 1967, all of Canada joined together to observe the country's 100th birthday. More than 3,000 participants marched in London's Centennial Parade, including this youth delegation celebrating Canada's ongoing dynamic spirit as the country begins its second century. Courtesy, London Free Press

mission was providing an adequate supply of unpolluted water. By the 1950s the expanding number of artesian wells was lowering the water table under Hyde Park and around London generally, and farmers were filing damage suits against the commission. Some new source was needed. Plans were first considered for obtaining water from Lake Fanshawe, but this ran up against the problem of filtration plant costs to ensure safe water. In 1958 City Council attention shifted to obtaining water from either Lake Erie or Lake Huron by a pipeline; however, the Public Utilities Commission still favored drilling more wells. By 1962-1963 the Ontario Water Resources Commission was brought in to examine financing plans and engineering surveys. It came out strongly for a Lake Huron pipeline, something for which Londoners can be immensely grateful, as pollution problems have mounted in the St. Clair River-Lake Erie system.

Then in 1964 John Robarts came to the rescue and announced that Ontario was willing to build a pipeline from Lake Huron for an estimated $14 million and municipalities would be allowed to connect with it. Their exact costs would be decided later. The Lake Huron pipeline to the Grand Bend area was completed by 1967 at a cost of $18.7 million and London's pumps soon began bringing in the new water. The artesian wells were closed down, but the

Dr. J.A. Vance of the Ontario Water Resources Commission oversees the dedication ceremonies at the opening of the Lake Huron pipeline on September 27, 1968. The completion of the $20 million pipeline vastly improved the availability of water to the entire Southwestern Ontario region. Courtesy, London Free Press

equipment was kept in working shape for possible emergencies, and a much larger reservoir was constructed at Commissioners Road. Shortly after the pipeline was completed, and after an equally long and probably more acrimonious battle, London water was finally fluoridated.

The Public Utilities Commission was active in other fields. In the early 1960s the Dutch elm disease reached London, destroying many of the trees in the city's parks and along the streets, including the Governor Simcoe elm in Gibbons' Park, probably the most magnificent tree in the area. This caused a great deal of extra expense for tree replacement. The PUC and the Upper Thames River Conservation Authority have also been engaged in developing the banks of both branches of the Thames River as parkland. Now Londoners can walk or bicycle along magnificent stretches of riverside parkland which will eventually connect many of the major parks of the city. Between 1958 and 1966 the Conservation Authority acquired the seventy-acre Byron Bog through a series of purchases and gifts, including a gift of several acres from Sifton Properties.

As London's all-season entertainment centre, the Western Fair with its excellent parking lots has become a center for racing, bazaars, Sunday flea markets, and travel shows. Today it has achieved a happy position as a regional fair, much larger than

In 1975 London played host to the Ontario Summer Games. Although most of the events had to be rescheduled because of foul weather, Bob Secord, director of the Sports and Recreation Bureau, noted the cooperation and spirit that prevailed and called the games "a definite success." Courtesy, London Free Press

the town fairs of the surrounding municipalities, although not of the size of the Canadian National Exhibition. Considerable expansion has taken place in the grounds since the early 1950s; the Western Fair property has been extended along King Street and in 1972 the old CNR carshops were purchased. New buildings also have been constructed, the most recent being the large Progress Building in 1967.

TRANSPORTATION PROBLEMS

With the increasing number of cars, London has had to face continuous problems in the rebuilding and expansion of its streets. Most of these changes have been generally accepted without controversy. In 1979 the last important brick street, Talbot Street south of York Street, was replaced with asphalt pavement. Cement pavement still exists in some sections of the city, such as in Old South London. Bridges were constructed over the CNR tracks on Adelaide Street and at Highbury Avenue and over the CPR tracks at Quebec Avenue. Several major road improvements have also been made: the Ontario Department of Highways widened Richmond Street to four lanes

Above: *London's new airport at Crumlin, a former hamlet in London Township, was opened in 1965 at a cost of $1.56 million. Today, the airport is one of the busiest in Canada in terms of transborder traffic with the United States, and accommodates more than 300,000 passengers each year. Courtesy, Alan Noon*

Opposite page: *A recent recreational innovation has been the annual Hot Air Balloon Fiesta, held each August in Harris Park. All eyes lift heavenward as the wicker gondola, suspended beneath a multihued nylon envelope, slips all earthly bounds to gracefully drift into the cloud-streaked sky. Courtesy, Visitors and Convention Bureau*

from Huron Street north to Arva, and Dundas Street was widened to four lanes from Highbury Avenue to Clarke Road in 1963. Similarly, in 1973 Queens Avenue was extended westward, a new bridge over the Thames opened, and the Dundas Street extension carried across Wharncliffe Road in 1976. Connecting Wonderland Road and Hutton Road by the Guy Lombardo Bridge to create a new north-south throughway west of the central city was another great improvement and one which, with great foresight, included bicycle paths. A very controversial development was the Horton Street extension, which called for demolition of some dwellings. It is still under construction to create a new east-west corridor across the city.

In the wider scene, the plans to connect Highway 401 with a new Highway 402 from London to Sarnia caused many arguments in the city and its environs, and for years there was disagreement over the route it should take. In 1960 the city retained A.D.

Since 1975 the city has hosted the London International Air Show. Held over two days in early June, the event features piloting tricks by precision aerobatic teams, daredevil acrobatics by wing walkers, skydiving parachutists, and vintage aircraft, such as this restored World War II American Mitchell B-25 bomber. Courtesy, Visitors and Convention Bureau

Margison & Associates of Toronto, which had designed that city's Don Valley Expressway, to look at both the problems of traffic inside the city and the best Sarnia highway connection. The two projects were not exactly compatible. Margison first suggested a $5.1 million plan which would have included expressways carrying 1,500 vehicles per hour through the centre of the city along the river valleys. Strong objections were raised to freeways passing under Victoria Hospital and the disruption of the farming area north of the city by a four-lane highway. A second commission to Margison in 1963 resulted in another report, which still stressed throughway construction along sections of both branches of the Thames River. Fortunately for the beauty and quality of life in London, this was never implemented. In the end Highway 402 was joined to 401 just west of the city, and the river banks were saved from development.

For the railways the period was not one of expansion, with the London and Port Stanley sold in 1966 and passenger service discontinued on the CPR in 1971. However, VIA Rail has taken over the passenger transport and London still has good connections both eastward and westward. Air transport was improved greatly, as a new terminal was completed in 1965 at a cost of $1.56 million. However, London's air connections with other cities are limited, presenting difficulties in attracting new businesses to the city. Since 1975 London Airport has been the scene of the London International Air Show. The airport had already demonstrated its capacity for handling large planes when the first 747 Wardair jumbo jet landed in 1974, and in June 1979 the world's largest aircraft, the United States Air Force Lockheed C-5A Galaxy, landed during the airshow. In a very different field of air travel, in recent years Harris Park has been the scene of the Hot Air Balloon Fiesta.

While speaking of transportation and its problems, something should be recorded about the periodically dismal weather that affects London. The sleet storm of March 1922 has been noted in connection with the havoc it wreaked on the wires of the new hydroelectric system. Yet that storm is only one in a long

Rising over the frozen banks of the Thames River, London's modern office towers penetrate the crisp blue winter sky. Photo by Alan Noon

Above: *A sculler practices on the Thames River. Photo by John Bliss*

Left: *Students play a pick-up game of hockey at a rink on the University of Western Ontario campus. Courtesy, Ross Breadner*

Above: *A spinning cup ride creates a swirl of color at London's Western Fair. Photo by John Bliss*

Right: *A "teaser" provokes a dancing dragon at the Chinese Cultural Association's summer festival at Springbank Park. The festival features Chinese foods, crafts, and entertainment. Courtesy, Ross Breadner*

Left: *The band from Mocha Temple, a London chapter of the Shriners charity organization, marches through the city. Courtesy, Ross Breadner*

Below: *Members of the London International Folk Dance Experience perform an Israeli folk dance at the "Gathering on the Green" in South London. Courtesy, Ross Breadner*

Right: *A child prepares his descent on a slide at Storybook Gardens in Springbank Park. Courtesy, Ross Breadner*

Below: *Fall colors highlight Springbank Park and the Thames River. Courtesy, Ross Breadner*

Above: *London is the capital of a very productive agricultural region—rich farmland lies only a few miles from the downtown core. Photo by John Bliss*

Left: *Wildflowers bloom in London's hinterland. Photo by Hans Blohm. Courtesy, Public Archives of Canada, S19*

Opposite page: *Fall colors blaze east of London. Photo by Hans Blohm. Courtesy, Public Archives of Canada, S21*

Blue skies shine on a blanket of snow in a London suburb. Courtesy, Ross Breadner

On January 26, 1978, London was assaulted by one of the worst winter blizzards in memory. With gusts reaching near 80 mph and snow accumulations of twelve inches, the storm claimed eight lives. Many Londoners were stranded in their homes and places of work and schools were closed. Hotels and gas stations served as refugee camps for stranded motorists; in the storm's aftermath, abandoned cars littered the streets. Courtesy, London Free Press

and fairly regular series which has continued to cause power breakdowns in the older parts of London, as no steps have been taken to gradually bury all wires underground. What may have been the worst ice storm in London's history began in the evening of January 13, 1968; when it ended the next morning it had coated the city in one and a quarter inches of ice. It was four days before all the hydro was back in operation. In January 1971 a blizzard stopped the buses and stranded some 7,000 students at country schools. Finally, what has been called the "super storm" of January 26, 1978, dropped some twelve inches (32 cm.) of snow on the city, blew down signs, blew out windows in the downtown area, and left eight people dead in the London area.

For long there seemed to be something of a legend, rather supported by the weather office, but certainly not supported by historical evidence, that as far as Ontario was concerned hurricanes and tornadoes stopped at the American border. London fortunately

missed out on Hurricane Hazel in 1954 when it devastated Toronto, but in recent years there have been several tornadoes in the area. In June 1979 one touched a couple of areas in the city, felling trees and carrying off lawn furniture. Then about two months later there was major damage in the Woodstock area with two criss-crossing tornadoes. London was hit directly on September 2, 1984, when a tornado tore through the south part of the city, causing very considerable property damage but fortunately no fatalities.

SERVICES AND DEPARTMENTS

Annexing the suburbs led to problems because some of the new areas lacked full services and these had to be provided before attention could be paid to the old city's needs. Building sewers was a particular problem; in 1964 it was necessary to put in a proper storm and sanitary sewer system in part of the Byron area and in 1968 sanitary sewers had to be built in Oakridge Acres. The London Transit Commission also had problems of extending service to the many new areas and from 1972 has had to receive financial assistance from the city. Fire services were reorganized with new fire halls opened, as at Byron in 1961. One of the worst fires in recent years came in August 1973 following a series of gas explosions in the Oxford-Wharncliffe-Mount Pleasant section, which led to the destruction or damage of twenty-four homes.

The Police Department started hiring policewomen in 1962 and the next year its members began training at the Ontario Police College at Aylmer. In 1974 personal police radios came into regular operation, as did an emergency communication centre; computerized record entry and retrievals began a year later. The new Police Administration Building at the corner of Dundas and Adelaide streets was authorized in 1973 and opened two years later. At the same time justice facilities were being expanded with the new courthouse and registry office at Queens Avenue and Ridout streets opened in 1974. The huge, monolothic structure forms one of the focal points of the London horizon. In 1977 a new Elgin-Middlesex Detention Centre was opened in South London to replace the old jails of London, St. Thomas, and Woodstock.

One would expect that, in an old city like London, new crimes were unlikely to turn up. Nevertheless, new ground was broken in December 1978 when two Londoners were given four years in the penitentiary for running what is regarded as the city's first counterfeiting operation. They were making United States

Above: *Looming above the southernmost building of the Ridout (or Labatt) Restoration, the Middlesex County Courthouse presents a dramatic new addition to London's skyline. Erected in 1974, it replaced the old County Courthouse of 1827-1829. Photo by Alan Noon*

Opposite page, top: *On September 2, 1984, a tornado ripped through London's White Oaks area, causing severe damage to both residential and industrial property. Though many people were injured, there were no deaths reported in what remains one of London's worst natural disasters. Courtesy,* London Free Press

Opposite page, bottom: *Ten houses were completely destroyed and more than twenty others seriously damaged on August 7, 1973, when a ruptured natural gas line set off a series of violent explosions and fires in London's Oxford Park. Although twenty-seven people were injured, no one was killed. Courtesy,* London Free Press

Above: *After fifteen years as Bishop of London, the Most Reverend G. Emmett Carter was appointed Archbishop of Toronto by Pope John Paul II in 1978. Reluctant to leave London, Carter, who was soon elevated to the College of Cardinals, stated, "the bigger the city, the bigger the problems." Courtesy,* London Free Press

Opposite page, top: *After retiring as premier of Ontario in 1971, John Robarts was appointed chancellor of the University of Western Ontario, presiding until 1976. Dressed in university regalia, he addressed the Spring Convocation on May 30, 1972, on the occasion of his installation. Courtesy, UWO*

Opposite page, bottom: *Completed in 1971, the D.B. Weldon Library was the first University of Western Ontario building to break with the Collegiate Gothic tradition. Designed by London architects John Andrews and Ronald Murphy to accommodate one million volumes, it was named in honor of Lieutenant-Colonel D.B. Weldon, chairman of the Board of Governors, 1958-1967. Photo by Alan Noon*

twenty-dollar bills at their printing business on Bessemer Road. The fact that they did not waste their time or expensive paper counterfeiting depreciated Canadian dollars is possibly yet a further indication of the astuteness of London businessmen.

EDUCATION AND MEDICINE

London's expansion as a centre of education and medical research during the last twenty-five years has been one of the most important aspects of the city's growth. In the 1960s the Board of Education began to catch up with wartime delays and increasing population by building eight new high schools and twenty-two public schools. The names of some of these schools honored former Londoners, or possibly neglected former Londoners, such as Sir Frederick Banting; other names evidenced London's first steps toward biculturalism, such as Montcalm. The schools embodied the latest technology and the vast Saunders Secondary School was described as "the most modern secondary school in Ontario," although theories on huge, windowless schools have somewhat changed since that time. Some schools were built for special purposes, such as the 1974 Robarts School, a regional centre for the hearing handicapped. There were some labor problems: the first teachers' strike occurred in 1975 when the London and Middlesex County Roman Catholic Separate School teachers withdrew their services. In 1980 more than 1,500 secondary school students left their classes to demonstrate in support of the striking school secretaries and teaching assistants.

One of the major changes in Ontario education came in the 1960s with the creation of some twenty community colleges across the province. In London Fanshawe College opened in 1966, and was extended at different times in the following years. Fanshawe's Radio Station CXFM started broadcasting in 1976. The great expansion at the University of Western Ontario continued through the 1960s and 1970s when many new buildings were erected. The earliest of these, such as Middlesex College and Talbot College, continued to be built in the Collegiate Gothic style of architecture, but increasing costs of cut stone meant that changes had to be made. Alumni Hall, opened in 1967 by Premier Robarts, marked the beginning of a change to a more modern style. The new D.B. Weldon Library, University Community Centre, and the Social Science Centre built along Western Road in 1970-1972 swung completely away from the traditional style to modern concrete construction. The library demonstrated that it was quite possible to build a

striking building in a modern style. The university greatly extended its residence facilities during these years in styles varying from the Gothic of Delaware Hall women's residence, to the brick, utilitarian apartment blocks on the far side of Western Road, to the strange, striped structure which is just being completed at the university gates. Although cutbacks were obvious by the late 1970s, in 1978 Western was able to celebrate its centennial as the second largest university in the province and London's largest employer.

The changes in the city's medical facilities have been equally remarkable. Some of these have been connected directly with the municipal services and others with the growth of the hospitals. The Middlesex-London District Health Unit for the city and region was opened in 1969, a Children's Psychiatric Institute was settled at the old Beck Memorial (Queen Alexandra) Sanitorium in 1961, and the Scatcherd Children's Centre for the mentally retarded was opened in 1975. One of the most striking developments was the transfer of the Medical Faculty from the Victoria Hospital area to the campus of the University of Western Ontario with the construction of new Medical and then Dental buildings. In 1964 the Robarts Ministry approved a $30 million Univer-

Above: *In 1985, the Westminster Campus phase of Victoria Hospital's ongoing expansion was finally opened after thirty months of construction. The new $73 million facility, with its vast surgical and treatment network, stands as a significant advance for London's already excellent health care community. Photo by Alan Noon*

Opposite page: *The clock chimes of Middlesex College are a familiar sound to all who have attended the University of Western Ontario since the building's opening in 1960. It was constructed during the presidency of G. Edward Hall (1947-1967), a time of rapid expansion for the university. Building funds for Middlesex College came through the generosity of Major General A.C. Spencer and his sister, Mrs. Josephine Spencer Niblett. Photo by Alan Noon*

sity Hospital on twenty-six acres of land adjacent to the university campus. Opened in 1972, it is now being expanded by the addition of the John P. Robarts Heart and Brain Research Institute, which has partly been financed by a donation of $10 million from the Ontario government.

In South London hospital construction has been equally important. In 1962 the Federal Department of Veterans Affairs rebuilt Westminster Hospital. Then in 1977 the entire 342-acre facility was transferred to Victoria Hospital. That institution, which had severed its connection with the city corporation in 1973, began a two-phase development of a Westminster campus in 1982. In September 1985 the $76 million first phase was completed. When the work is finished, Victoria will have a new 900-bed hospital complete with children's wards at the Westminster location, as well as its old South Street Campus. Parkwood Hospital joined Victoria in the move to the Westminster Campus and its new building for geriatric and veterans' care opened there in 1984. In North London, St. Joseph's Hospital has announced plans for a $70 million reconstruction and renovation

program over the next few years.

SUBURBAN DEVELOPMENT

Over the last thirty years London's suburbs have grown to form a complete ring around the old city. Although many of the earlier subdivisions spread to the northwest, Highway 401 has increasingly acted as a magnet in pulling development toward the southern part of the city. As the great estates of some of the old families, such as the Kingsmills and the Labatts, are now being subdivided, northward expansion will also increase. Much of this development has been in private houses; however, a fair number of highrise apartments have appeared and increasing numbers of townhouses are being built in some areas.

Beyond the city, suburban towns and villages have increased in size, partially because of commuters living there and working in London, and partially because of industrial development. The opening of the Ford Motor Company plant at Talbotville in 1967 naturally drew people to southwestern London. The new industrial park in the Highway 401 area has led to other plants opening there, such as Northern Telecom in 1960. As in other North American centres, automation and cheap labor in other countries are adversly affecting London's labor force. However, the city has a diversified industrial base with more than 40 percent being in machinery, transportation equipment, electric products, and manufacturing, and another 20 percent in food, beverage, and tobacco products.

One of the most striking features of London's suburban growth has been the construction of shopping centres and malls throughout the city, with the strong support of the City Council. Today there are twenty-eight malls which have helped to create a series of distinct neighborhoods forming a circle around the older core. This process was underway in the

Above: *This contemporary view of Richmond Street, looking south from Queens Avenue in London's downtown business district, presents an interesting contrast in urban scale through time. The multi-storied, steel-framed towers of the late twentieth century present a sharp contrast to the three-storied blocks of nineteenth-century brick buildings characterized by symmetry and uniform height. Photo by Alan Noon*

Left: *On July 26, 1982, more than 600 million people around the world watched London's Karen Baldwin win the Miss Universe pageant in Lima, Peru. She was chosen over contestants from seventy-seven countries, becoming the first Canadian to win the title of Miss Universe. Courtesy,* London Free Press

Opposite page: *"In terms of architectural design and features," a contemporary prospectus states, "Wellington Square is without peer in North America." Officially opened on August 11, 1960, it was the first example of an enclosed suburban shopping centre built in a central business district. Eatons of Canada functions as the principal commercial tenant. The air-conditioned shopping mall leads the shopper by open-front stores. Photo by Alan Noon*

mid-1950s with the development of such shopping centres as that at Adelaide and Huron streets in 1955. Larger malls appeared a decade later; for instance, the 1966 Argyle Mall at Clarke Road and Dundas streets and the Northland Mall at Highbury Avenue and Huron Street. White Oaks Mall on Wellington Road South was briefly the largest mall in the city; however, this was a difficult title to maintain for very long. Westmount Mall, then the largest mall outside of Toronto, opened in 1973 as an $8 million shopping centre with an Eaton's store and some sixty other shops employing 1,000 people. The process has continued in more recent years with the multi-level Masonville Place, opened in August 1985. Containing 129 stores including both Sears and Eaton's, it is now London's largest mall, serving both the city and the surrounding community to the north.

THE CENTRAL CITY

The population shift to the suburbs, with the accompanying construction of a ring of shopping centres and malls around the old central city, now means that many Londoners and a good portion of the visitors from outside the city never enter the downtown area. As in other North American cities the malls, with their all-weather enclosed shopping areas and convenient, free parking, have come to present a major challenge to the survival of downtown. The revival of the central city represents one of the most immediate problems facing the municipal planners and council.

At the same time that the central business district has been assuming a much less important role in the life of London, it has been the subject of a variety of crucial and often acrimonious plans for urban renewal, cultural renewal, park development, and government offices. Although the discussions on these topics were frequently intertwined, they may be divided into several main themes for the purpose of a brief examination. These would include new construction in the central business district, the city hall square, the rehabilitation of the Forks with the accompanying historical restoration, and the new cultural institutions evolving in the city.

Although downtown problems have been regularly discussed over the last quarter of a century, a cohesive, overall strategy has yet to emerge. The City Centre lacks any real focus. Spot development has been allowed to proceed, planned density is extraordinarily high, and the sprawling length of Dundas Street from the Forks to the City Centre presents a formidable problem for the advocates of the type of mall found in Ottawa or Calgary. True, some major structures have been erected. The *London Free Press* built its new plant at the extreme southeast end of the central city in 1965, the Royal Bank added the first fifteen-story highrise in 1968-1969, and the City Centre complex was built with its Canada Trust, Northern Life, and Holiday Inn towers in 1974-1975. A second enclosed, large-scale downtown shopping mall, the London Centre Arcade, was opened in 1977, supplementing the Wellington Mall. In addition, some downtown highrise accommodation has been

Toronto's acclaimed architect, Raymond Moriyama, designed the new London Regional Art Gallery to "integrate with its historical surroundings at the Forks of the Thames." The finished exterior steel cladding is painted metallic blue and edged with silver. Courtesy, Visitors and Convention Bureau

THE BLACKBURN FAMILY

Without question, one of Canada's most enduring journalistic dynasties can be found in London's Blackburn family. The ongoing history of the Canadian Blackburns began when Josiah Blackburn, born in London, England on March 6, 1823, emigrated to Canada in 1850. Josiah's enthusiasm for literature and politics quickly led him into the newspaper field, first with the Paris *Star.* In 1852 he bought the *Canadian Free Press* which, after three years under his guidance, changed from a weekly to a daily publication and took the title the *London Free Press and Daily Western Advertiser.*

Though Josiah's main interests undeniably centred on the *Free Press,* in 1858 he ran for the Reform party in the general election, but was defeated by Marcus Talbot. In the next couple of years he quarreled with George Brown and his Toronto *Globe* and by 1865 had swung to support Conservative John A. Macdonald and become a close friend of John Carling. In the years that followed, Josiah aided in the establishment of the Conservative *Toronto Mail,* which opposed the *Globe.* In 1884 he participated in a Canadian government commission studying public printing methods in Washington, D.C.; the investigation resulted in the establishment of the Federal Department of Public Printing. Josiah always strove to ensure that his newspapers kept up with the latest advances in printing techniques while, at the same time, providing the reader with a clear, unbiased chronicle of the day's events.

The next generation of Blackburns followed in the path that Josiah had cleared when Walter J. Blackburn became president and general manager of the *Free Press* after his father's death on November 11, 1890. He had served with the Canadian militia in 1885 as a member of the Seventh Regiment in the Northwest Rebellion campaign. Each of the Blackburns held a primary concern in the newspaper world, yet each also maintained a secondary interest outside of journalism. For Josiah, it was politics; for Walter, it was sports. He was president of the Tecumseh Baseball Association and held a life membership in the Ontario Hockey League, as well as the honorary presidency of the Western Ontario Colts' League. The main focus of his attention outside of the *Free Press* was the state of Canadian journalism as a whole. Walter served on the first board of directors of the Canadian Press Limited, an organization which was greatly responsible for bringing the quality of Canada's newspapers up to world standards.

After Walter's death in 1920, Josiah's other son, Arthur, was elected president and managing director of the *London Free Press.* Like the rest of the Blackburns, he was also attracted to pursuits outside of journalism, particularly science and invention. Arthur was fascinated by photography, was one of London's first residents to own a wireless radio set, and took the *Free Press* into broadcasting.

Arthur's sister, Victoria Grace Blackburn, served as the literary and dramatic critic of the *Free Press* while Walter was president, and continued to make frequent contributions (under the pen name of "Fan Fan") after Arthur had assumed leadership of the newspaper. While Victoria eventually turned most of her attentions to her "secondary interest," poetry and literature, before her death in 1928, Arthur remained devoted to the publication of his family's newspaper until his death in 1935.

About a month after Arthur's death, his son, Walter Juxon Blackburn II, joined the *Free Press* while still a student at the University of Western Ontario. He would go on to become publisher of the newspaper, as well as chairman of the board. Again widening the family communications system, he established CFPL-TV in 1953. Walter's "secondary interest" stems from his years at the University of Western Ontario. For almost half a century Walter maintained close ties with that institution, helping *Free Press* editor Arthur R. Ford establish the journalism department. He was also a member of the governing bodies of Huron College and the university.

Walter shared his father's enthusiasm for science and devoted much of his energy to the establishment of first-rate medical, research, and health care facilities on the university campus. He was chairman of the Planning and Building Committee overseeing the construction of University Hospital, which opened in September 1972. With Walter's death on December 16, 1984, the presidency of the *Free Press* passed to his son-in-law, so that, though the name Blackburn has disappeared from London, the family retains its influential position.

In 1852 Josiah Blackburn (1823-1890) purchased a small London weekly, The Canadian Free Press. *His keen business sense quickly made it a success and Blackburn became one of the era's most politically influential newspapermen. In 1855 he began a daily, the* London Free Press, *a newspaper that remains the most important newspaper in Southwestern Ontario. Courtesy, London Historical Museums*

Above: *The opening of Centennial Hall on June 21, 1967, marked the completion of one of London's most ambitious projects. Ontario Premier John P. Robarts oversaw the ceremonies, after which he and more than 450 others attended the London Symphony Orchestra performance of Beethoven's Ninth Symphony. Courtesy,* London Free Press

Opposite page: *Another legacy of Elsie Perrin Williams' estate was her home, "Windermere," a pleasantly wooded and landscaped park of sixty-eight acres in northwest London. The Spanish-style mansion of white stucco and red clay tile was built in 1916. After the death of her housekeeper, Miss Harriett Corbett, in 1979, the property passed to the city. Today the grounds and house serve as a reception and conference centre. Courtesy, UWO*

constructed around Colborne Street. Still, a pattern is not developing, and the continuing popularity of the market remains one of the main attractions of the core area.

Major projects on the downtown fringe have not been complete successes. The city hall plaza, which developed to the east of Victoria Park from 1957 to 1971 with a new City Hall on the south, an apartment building on the east, and Centennial Hall on the north, has aroused considerable controversy. The buildings fail to form a unified group in style or coloring, there is an incomplete arcade on the park side, and the addition of an apartment house has meant that the square cannot be used for public gatherings because the noise will disturb the tenants. Centennial Hall, planned as a facility equally suitable for the symphony, concerts, conventions, flea markets, or wrestling matches, proved to be most unsuitable. It is

hoped that the recent remodelling will improve the situation.

In the western part of the core, the urban renewal project at Talbot Square failed to evolve as planned when the federal government backed off from its commitments, and possibly fortunately, the developer failed to produce a project of incredible density. In addition to the new provincial courthouse, London acquired a federal building, possibly the most faceless federal structure ever built, and a new Bell Telephone regional headquarters, a boon to the city's economy. The new, rather unidentifiable sculpture surrounding these structures appears to include a large segment of dinosaur intestine.

The opening up of the Forks, despite many contretemps, has been the most successful of all the new projects in the city. In the early 1970s, Labatt Brewing Company restored several of London's oldest buildings on Ridout Street as its new corporate headquarters, the city's first major example of historic preservation. After a great deal of contentious discussion over the use of the Forks itself, which culminated in an Ontario Municipal Board hearing, the County Council restored the old courthouse as its administrative headquarters, and the new London Regional Art Gallery was erected on the Forks beside it. While the architecture of the new gallery will remain controversial, both from the point of aesthetic appeal and as to whether or not London acquired a copy of a Texas gallery for its money, the gallery's large display area provides a potential site for the joint operation of the LRGA and the London Historical Museums. Elsewhere in the downtown, the restoration of the 1901 Grand Theatre in 1977-1978, preserving the historically important features and adding modern facilities for both players and audi-

Sponsored by the London Folk Arts Multicultural Council, Kavalkade is a popular three-day festival held in London every September since 1980, offering the best in music, art, culture, and cuisine from London's ethnic communities. Here the London Holy Trinity Greek School dancers entertain at the Greek Hellenic Community Centre on Southdale Road. Courtesy, London Free Press

ences, has been an unquestioned success. Like the Labatt's restoration and other historical preservation projects in the city, it represents a realization that in London, as elsewhere, a city is enriched by a combination of the old and the new. The restoration of many of the old houses north of the downtown core area as apartments, and the new apartments designed in compatible style to the surrounding homes by the Ivey's Alcor Investments Ltd., are good examples of how a pleasing atmosphere can be retained.

Outside the centre of the city London has again been fortunate through the generosity of the Lawson family, who in 1981 backed the restoration of "Grosvenor Lodge" as a historical museum of London, and the construction of the Lawson-Jury Museum of Indian Archaeology. The Children's Museum, established in 1976, provides another focus of interest, as does Elsie Perrin Williams' "Windermere" Estate, now a conference-reception centre.

Just as it expanded medical and educational facilities in the past, London is now broadening its cultural activities. Beyond the new art gallery, the reconstructed Grand Theatre, and new musuems, the London Symphony Orchestra has been reorganized, and since 1974 the Home County Folk Festival has been held each July in Victoria Park. The annual Kavalkade ethnic festival, begun in 1980, started with three ethnic clubs and has increased to twenty-eight. It has added diversity to the city's culture, as have the growing number of ethnic restaurants.

CONCLUSION: PROBLEMS AND PROSPECTS

As it approaches the 1993 bicentennial of the arrival of Lieutenant-Governor Simcoe and Lieutenant Thomas Talbot, London's situation is, in essence, an enviable one that would be a joy to most cities. "The Fat Cat City," as even its own leaders sometimes call it, is financially sound in an expanding area of the nation's most prosperous and diversified province, with no internal tensions, crime waves, or ethnic clashes. It is unquestionably a major centre of education, although Ontario funding for education was not the best for some years, and it has evolved into a world-class centre for medical treatment and research. In addition, the city is attracting regional administrative offices of both government and corporations.

There are problems, however: automation is creating unemployment; persuading new industries to locate in any city is difficult in a competitive climate; and London has only a limited tourist trade. Also,

On February 15, 1965, London joined all of Canada in ceremonies nationwide raising the country's new flag. Here, Staff Sergeant William Buckle hoists the flag from atop City Hall after prayers and dedications by various London dignitaries. Courtesy, London Free Press

there is another, potentially serious problem: London has witnessed the control of almost all of its largest business and financial institutions pass from the hands of the old families during the last few years. However, the very fact that most of the head offices of these corporations have stayed here says something not only about the size of their investment in physical plants or the ease of modern communications, but also about the quality of life in the city.

These problems raise a serious question for those who must decide on the future directions of development. London may do well to concentrate on the improvement of its river valley parks system and cultural institutions, and the enhancing of the general quality of its life, as part of its programs. Such activities may bring in and retain more businesses than anything else. In an era when the pace of life is becoming progressively more stressful, is the image of the "Forest City" a healthy one rather than a liability? The answer, of course, will be highly individualistic; but from the record London has a good number of citizens who may well prefer the forest theme. Dreams of expansion and endless growth, even if realistic, do not necessarily mean an endlessly improving way of life. London has a lot going for it—it must now plan how to best hold what it has, as well as expand into new fields.

During the oil fever stimulated by the discovery of oil in Lambton County in 1857, an oil well was drilled in London at the Forks of the Thames about 1865. Instead of oil, up gushed sulphur water! Undaunted, Charles Dunnett, an enterprising promoter, opened a health spa ("Ontario White Sulphur Springs"), the tower-like derrick its symbol. Until 1906 its salubrious waters—good both internally and externally—attracted visitors from as far away as the southern United States. Courtesy, UWO

CHAPTER IX

Partners in Progress

The arbored avenues, emerald expanses of parkland, and winding waterway form a stunning backdrop for the vibrant City of London, the principal urban centre of Southwestern Ontario.

In conformation, performance, and promise, the Forest City is richly endowed. From the ranks of pioneering settlers early in the nineteenth century, and then the waves of upwardly mobile newcomers drawn to the bustling town on the Thames, a resilient and resource-laden community has emerged.

London today—home for 276,000 residents, a world-renowned medical centre, and a commercial-industrial entity of national import—is far advanced from the frontier assembly of 12,000 residents that barely qualified for city status in 1855. And, consistent with generations of determined civic leadership over the intervening years, the proponents of progress are again sighting on new targets.

Solidly emplaced for the next ascent are incomparable hospitals and institutions of learning, a flourishing and diverse manufacturing sector, complete financial services, and a growing array of retail enterprises. This base of assets will effectively support the incumbent municipal and business leaders in their pursuit of downtown renewal, a research and development park, incentives for small business development, sites for industry, and aggressive promotion of tourism.

In fact, several major developers have recently evinced positive interest in core building projects and the city is already the third-largest convention centre in Ontario. The municipality is currently addressing the need for extended service from the under-utilized London Airport to improve a transportation network that has been influential in attracting new commercial and industrial establishments. Internally, local authorities are engaged in a program of upgrading roads, sewage, and water systems to accommodate a larger population.

Investment in every area of the economy has flowed to London in this century—and at an increasing rate since World War II—as the direct result of a favorable living and working environment. Significantly, a host of national corporations have opted to locate, or retain, their head offices in the Forest City. As well, hundreds of companies have been attracted for reasons of access to markets and a healthy business climate. The overall scenario lends credibility to the contention of the London Economic Development Department: "We're Fit for Business!"

The organizations whose stories are detailed on the following pages have chosen to support this important literary and civic project. They illustrate the variety of ways in which individuals and their businesses have contributed to the growth and development of London.

THE LONDON CHAMBER OF COMMERCE

One of the oldest nongovernment business organizations in the nation, The London Chamber of Commerce has made a lasting and positive contribution to virtually every phase of advancement in the Forest City over a period of 130 years.

The founding session was convened in April 1857, 10 years prior to Confederation, by 42 pioneer businessmen "to promote the betterment of the London area as a place to work and a place to live." They paid an annual fee of one pound for membership in the original London Board of Trade. Today the chamber (the name was changed in 1918) is comprised of more than 2,000 business and professional people who remain committed to enhancing the city's appeal to business and industry and preserving the high standard of living conditions.

The first president of the association was Adam Hope, a former town magistrate who would later attain prominence as the first president of the Huron and Erie Savings and Loan Society, the forerunner of Canada Trust. He was followed by equally dedicated community leaders who spearheaded industrial and commercial development and tourist promotion in the early years.

Other areas of concern in the last century were law reform, consumer protection, fair taxation, improvements to municipal and transportation facilities, a broader educational opportunity, and support of the agricultural sector. The latter lent encouragement to the establishment of the Western Fair and Queens Park in 1888 which today hosts over one million people each year.

The chamber emerged from a restructuring in 1918 to tackle a greater diversity of functions relating to cultural concerns, city beautification, airline service (the London Airport was a chamber-inspired asset), and extensions of educational and hospital services at all levels.

Consistent with this involvement was support for the construction of the University of Western Ontario, the library and art museum, and a community college of applied arts.

Programme of London Chamber of Commerce

Board of Directors and Officers of London Chamber of Commerce

Geo. M. Reid, President

Extensive program and leaders in 1918, a year of restructuring and the adoption of the name, The London Chamber of Commerce.

The chamber has had a long-term commitment to creating a spirit of cooperation between the city and surrounding farm community. Backing up that commitment has been the promotion of Middlesex County and the Covent Garden Market, the establishment of the Farmer of the Year Award, and 70 years of involvement with the 4H program.

By providing an information service to its members and the public, The London Chamber of Commerce continues to communicate business concerns to all levels of government. It provides a forum for the business community to develop opinions and programs that contribute to the social, economic, and physical betterment of the area.

Mechanic's Institute & Museum was one of the early meeting places for The London Board of Trade.

WESTINGHOUSE CANADA INC.

Distribution apparatus serving the electrical power requirements of private and public industry has been the primary function of the London plant of Westinghouse Canada Inc. since its inception almost 30 years ago.

Today the facility fulfills that general objective and more. Staff has increased threefold; sales have increased more than fifteenfold; and product mix and design have adapted to meet the requirements of utility, industrial, government, commercial, and construction markets reaching to the far corners of the globe.

The 120,000-square-foot manufacturing and office building opened in April 1957 on a 40-acre site in northeast London and was a relative newcomer to the nation's Westinghouse operations. The firm had been distributing in Canada since 1886 and making air brakes for railroads at Hamilton, Ontario, since 1896. In the first half of the twentieth century, Westinghouse contributed significantly to industrial growth in southern Ontario, the national interest in two world wars, and consumer convenience in the form of household appliances. All the while, a strong presence was maintained in the provision of equipment for the large power and transit commissions. In recent years company expertise in research and development has been applied to the nuclear, high-technology, and computer fields.

A final check of the thyristor controllers for electrostatic precipitators before shipment to Indonesia.

At London a staff of highly qualified technical and professional people and skilled employees—numbering 500 in all and working under rigid quality-control standards—have achieved distinction in the manufacture of transformers and other distribution products for utilities, commercial/industrial uses, and a variety of specialized power applications. Their competence earned a world mandate from the parent organization in 1984 for the production of transformer rectifiers and controls for the electrostatic precipitation industry. This equipment affords effective pollution control to vitally important installations such as generating plants and paper mills.

In co-operation with the city, Westinghouse of London also won recognition for leadership in the conversion from overhead to underground electrical distribution in residential developments, a trend that has spread across North America. The London Public Utilities Commission was in the forefront of committing all future residential growth to underground systems, and the local Westinghouse plant responded by developing the necessary electrical equipment.

Over the years Westinghouse personnel have participated in the advancement of the city by serving on boards of service clubs, community associations, and professional societies. Plant manager Glenn K. Irvine was president of The London Chamber of Commerce in 1984-1985.

An aerial view of the Westinghouse factory and office in London.

Pole-mounted distribution transformers ready for shipment must meet rigid quality-control standards.

STIHL LIMITED

Andreas Stihl founded his company in Stuttgart, Germany, in 1926. Sympathetic to the woodcutters of the day who worked long hours with their manual crosscut saws, or "misery whips" as they called them, he was convinced he could invent a portable "tree-felling machine." He had already developed an electric chain saw for sawmill use.

By 1927 Stihl's first gasoline chain saw was ready. It was a portable, two-man unit with a 7.5-horsepower engine. It weighed all of 141 pounds! But development was swift and by 1930, sustained by trips to Canada and Eastern Europe by Stihl, export orders flowed into his factory. The first Stihl saws were sold in Canada about 1936. Through the 1930s and 1940s, constant research had brought lighter and more powerful saws, the invention of the centrifugal clutch, and automatic chain oiling.

By 1950 the first one-man Stihl chain saw was produced, and in 1954 the Stihl BLK 4.5 horsepower, weighing 31 pounds, became the first practical, lightweight chain saw.

But loggers really rejoiced with the introduction of the 26.5-pound Stihl "Lightning" in 1959. This unique and revolutionary saw, producing six horsepower, was years ahead of its time in dependability, ease of handling, and power. Thousands of "Lightnings" are still in use, and spare parts are still widely available.

According to London Stihl dealer Don McFarlan, even in those days (circa 1959) "you had to be special—you had to be good" if you wanted to sell Stihl chain saws. There were strict standards for dealers: "Not just anyone could sell them. They were great saws and still are!"

In 1961 Ontario distribution was assumed by Oneida Power Equipment of Ontario. The 1960s were a time of phenomenal growth, both in manufacturing output and new product lines. During this period Stihl developed its antivibration system (which has since been adopted by nearly all chain saw manufacturers), a completely encapsulated electronic ignition, and the Stihl Oilomatic system (which forces oil onto the chain rivets, permitting superior lubrication).

By the mid-1970s Stihl products included hedge trimmers, brushcutters, sprayers, Cutquik cut-off saws, as well as a wide variety of chain saws designed for specific markets. This product diversification meant expansion of manufacturing plants in Germany and construction of new manufacturing and assembly plants in Switzerland, Brazil, the United States, and Australia.

Distribution had grown too complex and large to be handled by independent Canadian importers. In 1981 Stihl moved to assume its Ontario and British Columbia

Past and present Stihl saws. In 1927 the gas-powered tree-felling machine, weighing 141 pounds, was introduced. In 1986 Stihl's new-generation 034 hit the market, weighing in at 13 pounds.

Stihl Limited's brand new Canadian corporate head office and warehouse facility, constructed in 1986.

product distribution network and regroup the existing dealers under a new Canadian subsidiary, "Stihl Limited."

Simultaneously, Stihl examined several possibilities for its Canadian corporate and warehouse headquarters. London became the obvious choice for several reasons, including a stable work force, an ideal central Canadian corridor location; major highway, air, and rail connections; and an abundance of choice, serviced industrial land. But equally important was, and is, the quality of life to be found in London.

The decision to move to Canada and locate in London has certainly proved beneficial to Stihl. In Stihl Limited's first four years of operation, it had become the number one power equipment supplier in Canada by expanding its dealer network from 126 to over 700 and by quadrupling the company's market share.

Stihl Limited has a number of future plans, many of which will also be beneficial to London. These include construction of a new 30,000-square-foot office and warehouse complex. Groundbreaking ceremonies were held in June 1986.

"The history of Stihl Limited in London is comparatively short," states president Fred Whyte, "but we've only just begun!"

LONDON LIFE INSURANCE COMPANY

A pillar of the insurance industry, nurtured in the fledgling city of London more than a century ago and elevated by innovative, aggressive management to the forefront of the Canadian business establishment, London Life Insurance Company occupies a special niche in the annals of the Forest City as a historic, truly homegrown enterprise—a civic asset prized by the community, shareholders, and several generations of employees.

London Life is the nation's largest provider of life insurance and seventh-ranked in terms of assets, out-manning competitors with a sales force of 2,660 representatives and managers serving clients in all provinces and the territories north to the Beaufort Sea. The head office complex takes up a city block south of Victoria Park, where 1,600 staffers comprise the core of personnel operating out of 165 regional offices across Canada. Yet through all the decades of growth and change, the underlying philosophy embraced by five visionary businessmen who secured the charter on March 24, 1874, has remained intact. London Life, under family control for most of its life and a new corporate alliance recently, counts service to customers as the principal strength for holding and attracting a policy owner complement that now exceeds 1.5 million.

London was small (area population about 20,000) but flourishing as the financial and distribution capital of western Ontario when five local businessmen met on April 4, 1874, to launch London Life with a seed capital subscription of $112,500. Three of the founders—William Woodruff, M.D., industrialist John Walker, and banker Joseph Jeffery—were subsequently elected to the first board of directors, while lawyers Edward Harris and James Magee were appointed solicitors. As charter president, Jeffery was the forerunner of an unbroken line of family control that would last until the early 1980s when the Jefferys joined with Brascan in founding Trilon Financial Corporation. In 1985 Lonvest Corporation—the insurance arm of Trilon—assumed a 97.6-percent ownership of London Life. The Trilon connection, associating London Life with Royal Trustco, Wellington Insurance, Royal-LePage, and CVL Inc. (Canada's largest vehicle leasing firm), has created a comprehensive approach to the financial planning needs of Canadians.

The head office of London Life Insurance Company at 255 Dufferin Avenue.

The London Life building on the present site was opened in 1927, enlarged in 1951 and 1964, then modernized in 1982 at a cost of $18 million to create a model office complex, complete with new computer technology and instant electronic communication from coast to coast. All the while, intensive training of staff, new product development, and marketing expertise contributed to substantial gains in volume until today London Life enrolment stands at one of every five insured Canadian families and 13,000 businesses with 700,00 employees under group insurance plans.

The London Life Queens Avenue entrance presents this modern exterior.

O-PEE-CHEE COMPANY LIMITED

O-Pee-Chee gum being delivered in Brandon, Manitoba, July 25, 1913.

A leading Canadian confectionary manufacturer, the O-Pee-Chee Company Limited recently observed the 75th anniversary of its founding in London—a period distinguished by growth from a small chewing gum maker to national stature as a supplier of candy, chewing gum, and picture-card products targeted to the young Canadian market.

Family-owned from inception, the firm actually dates to 1897 when brothers John "J.K." McKinnon and Duncan Hugh McDermid joined the C.R. Sommerville Company, a local manufacturer of boxes, popcorn, candy novelties, and chewing gum. After the gum operation was sold to American Chicle and moved to Toronto in 1908, the McDermids acquired the box division (Sommerville Paper Box Limited). In February 1911 they reentered the gum business with the formation of O-Pee-Chee, an Indian word meaning "the Robin" and coincidentally the name of the family's summer cottage. Featuring Gipsy Gum, the venture was an immediate success. A decade later—with added lines of mints and popcorn, notably Krackley Nut—a staff of 30 was handling close to $200,000 in annual sales.

The parent manufacturing facility at 430 Adelaide Street was built in 1928, primarily to meet increased production for export to the United Kingdom. O-Pee-Chee remained relatively static through the Depression, then survived the imposition of sugar rationing during World War II by converting to the provision of dried egg powder for beleaguered Europe. Meanwhile, John Gordon McDermid (the son of J.K.) and Frank P. Leahy had joined the firm in the early 1930s, the latter as sales manager. The younger McDermid served as president from 1946 until his death in 1953. Leahy then succeeded to the office and proceeded to carve out a broader market by negotiating licensing agreements with two American corporations whereby O-Pee-Chee commenced the manufacture and sale of their products in Canada. Subsequently, Leahy purchased the company from the McDermid estate in 1961.

Two phenomena of the 1960s—Beatlemania and gum-card collecting—contributed significantly to O-Pee-Chee volume. Acquiring the rights to make and sell Beatle Bubble Gum Cards in Canada, Leahy took the organization into a succession of popular movie and television "spin-off" cards such as "Batman," "Happy Days," "Charlie's Angels," and "Superman." More recently, *Star Wars, The Empire Strikes Back, Return of the Jedi,* and *E.T.* have been top-selling themes. The company also markets major league hockey and baseball cards, supplementing the core production of gums, candies, sunflower seeds, Thrills, Bazooka, SweeTARTS, and Nerds.

After Frank Leahy died in 1980, his son-in-law, Gary E. Koreen, became president and owner in charge of a staff of 200 employed locally or in the national sales force.

The main plant of O-Pee-Chee Company Limited was built in 1928 at 430 Adelaide Street, London, Ontario.

CLARKSON GORDON

The high-profile accounting firm of Clarkson Gordon was already a formidable national company of considerable stature in the profession when the London office was opened by a skeleton staff on August 3, 1948. In the ensuing 38 years the elements of strong leadership, client service, and competency within the practice have been successfully applied to build by far the largest accountancy firm in southwestern Ontario as well as a market share surpassing all other offices of the worldwide Arthur Young International accounting federation with which Clarkson Gordon is associated.

No small measure of credit belongs to Ken Lemon, who headed the original London staff of six professionals and two office workers operating out of an old downtown warehouse. Lemon established policies cultivating personnel development, client priority, and community involvement that prevail today among 165 professional and 45 administrative people who occupy two and one-half floors of a downtown office tower. Only three managing partners have followed Lemon: John Robinson, one of the original group who moved from Toronto; John Cronin, a member of the office since 1952; and in 1984, Bruce Beckett.

The clientele of Clarkson Gordon in London spans the whole spectrum of business, commercial, institutional, industrial, and government enterprise, and it reaches out to the United States, Europe, and other areas where companies with roots in London have expanded their operations. Longtime clients include John Labatt Limited, Avco Financial Services, Commonwealth Holiday Inns, Charterways, *London Life,* and *The London Free Press,* but the main area of service is the small and medium-size business market in recognition of its importance to the city's economy.

Ken Lemon, founding partner of the London Office.

Innovation and adaptation to changing business needs have enabled Clarkson Gordon to evolve from a basic accounting, auditing, and tax advisory role to a full-scale financial services organization. Management and consulting work has grown enormously under the Woods Gordon division to the point where an operations management group formulates productivity improvement plans, recruits executives, and employs engineers to design plant layouts. An agri-services division was opened five years ago, complete with staff agrologists, to deal with all phases of an increasingly complex farm industry.

The London office has earned distinction, too, as a training ground not only for some 25 partners who graduated to other Clarkson Gordon locations but also as the source of financial officers for a large number of companies. As the firm approaches four decades of service to the Forest City, the aspirations and objectives of its founders have been more than fulfilled.

TOUCHE ROSS

From a local accountancy practice launched nearly 40 years ago, Touche Ross has progressed through growth and merger to a diversified public accounting practice with a clientele representing a wide spectrum of the business community in London and surrounding areas.

The founder of the London office was the late Ralph Cowle, who opened his own practice in the city in 1947 after qualifying as a chartered accountant with George A. Touche & Company. In 1951 Cowle merged with the Touche firm. That same year Ted Johnston—who is presently the partner in charge of the London office—joined the practice. Today Touche Ross in London is represented by seven partners as well as 36 professionals, student accountants, and technicians, and 10 secretarial support staff members.

As auditor for the public sector—the City of London since 1951, the County of Middlesex and the Towns of Strathroy and Seaforth—Touche Ross has remained in close touch with the development of the area. Over the past 35 years it has built up a client base ranging from agribusiness to owner-managed enterprises to multinational corporations.

In the course of expanding activity, a leading role has been achieved in the provision of financial and special services. Task forces may be deployed to deal with matters of litigation, mergers and acquisitions, business evaluations, insolvencies, and other financial problems. Services to clients embrace auditing, accounting, and tax and estate planning, in addition to advice on management and information systems. In recognition of the importance of agriculture to southwestern Ontario, Touche Ross advises on strategies to assist farmers in coping with their complex and rapidly changing economic environment.

Touche Ross Canada—with offices in 40 cities across the country—is a part of Touche Ross International, which has operations in 89 countries. The present Canadian firm derives from accounting practices established in Montreal in 1858 by Philip S. Ross and in London, England, in 1899 by Sir George A. Touche. Mutual interests, notably the advantage of national coverage, led to a merger in 1958. In 1983 the London, Ontario, firm of Atkinson Leach & Neill merged with Touche Ross at its new office complex in the Victoria Park Executive Centre on Dufferin Avenue.

Partners in the London office of Touche Ross are (front row, left to right) Bob Earley; Ted Johnston, partner in charge; and Bill Hill. In the back row (left to right) are George Shaw, Bill Neill, Dave Atkinson, and Archie Leach.

VICTORIA HOSPITAL

Victoria Hospital has just published the history of its first century of saving lives and restoring health in a book entitled *Growing To Serve,* which was compiled by the institution's Archives Committee. The volume documents a rich legacy of health care advances, professional dedication, and community involvement—as well as setting the stage for massive redevelopment on a new site that offers unlimited potential for improved health services to western Ontario residents.

In 1848 London's first medical facility had an inauspicious beginning in a former military barracks, a log building constructed in 1838. In 1858 a wood-framed structure was relocated to the site of Victoria Park and became known as the London General Hospital.

As was the case with many early hospitals, its patients were chronically ill paupers. Respectable citizens were born and died in their own homes.

The institution became an entity in 1875, when the city erected a two-storey brick building with a slate roof on the south side of what is now South Street, beside the Thames River. It housed 56 patients' beds, apartments for stewards and assistants, and offices for the medical staff. Provincial inspection in that first year rated the facility as "excellent, both in respect to order and cleanliness." The logical sequence of a medical school to complement the hospital was soon pursued by London's small group of doctors, who resisted affiliation with the University of Toronto and instead persuaded the fledgling University of Western Ontario to establish a faculty of medicine—which they joined in 1882. Shortly after, they constructed a small medical school facing St. James Street between Wellington and Waterloo streets. The hospital expanded its teaching role in 1883 when, with enlarged quarters, the medical staff established a training program for nurses.

In 1899, then occupying a full city block and accommodating 100 patients, the facility was renamed Victoria Hospital to honor the Diamond Jubilee of the reigning monarch.

Its concern for the young led, in 1900, to the opening of a Children's Pavilion, subsequently renamed the War Memorial Children's Hospital in 1922 and then the Children's Hospital of Western Ontario in 1985, in recognition of its status as a designated regional pediatric centre. Since those early days children's medical and surgical programs have achieved a national reputation.

A medical research program grew with Victoria Hospital and was formalized in 1921, when the UWO established its new medical school and faculty of medicine at Victoria. Although in 1965 the medical school moved to the university campus, Victoria continues as a major university teaching unit and research centre, as well as a large community hospital.

A continuing commitment to excellence has attracted a succession of medical leaders whose accomplishments have conferred international distinction on Victoria Hospital. Notable among these are the first artificial kidney machine in Canada; and the early work by Dr. Ivan H. Smith in cancer radiation for patients from far outside the London area, which led to establishment of the Ontario Cancer Treatment and Research Foundation in Victoria Hospital in 1954 (this clinic was the first in the world to use cobalt-60 radiation treatment). Victoria also founded

the first neurological sciences centre in a Canadian teaching hospital, led by Dr. Charles Drake, whose pioneering operations brought him and the institution international acclaim. Its specialists conducted the first open-heart surgery in the region. Victoria Hospital is the main referral centre in southwestern Ontario for the treatment of eye diseases and the acknowledged Canadian leader in the management of cataracts by extracapsular extraction and intraocular lens implantation.

Victoria Hospital serves the city of London and surrounding counties. Since it is a public facility, patients are accepted from any accredited medical practitioner—with the result that its services are widely available and increasingly in demand. An 850-bed capacity is only one measure of its service to

The new Victoria Hospital on the spacious Westminster Campus is presently in the final stages of development. When finished, it will be the largest health care facility on one site in Canada.

the greatest number of all patients treated in London and acceptance of referrals throughout Ontario. In fact, ambulatory and outpatient visits constituted by far the largest segment of Victoria Hospital's 238,000 patient visits in 1985, reflecting not only changing needs in the community but greater ability by medical staff to conduct more complicated diagnosis and treatment without requiring patients to remain in hospital.

Aside from its reputation for services in general medicine, Victoria has served patients particularly in all aspects of cancer surgery, thoracic and vascular surgery, cancer treatment, trauma and critical care, orthopaedics, and other associated and specialized care. As well, it provides active treatment for Canadian Armed Services veterans living in southwestern Ontario.

And despite the numbers of patients needing active care, and the increasing complexity of treatment, the average length of stay has declined over the years as a result of improved procedures.

Victoria entered its second century in 1975 with the opportunity to begin relocating from the original, restricted site on South Street to the spacious Westminster Campus. Planning commenced for a major regional medical centre, powered by a unique, economical "Energy From Waste" installation. Construction of the first half of the redevelopment began in 1982 and was completed in 1985, within one percent of budget. The first patients were admitted in October 1985 to the "new Vic" hospital, Phase I, comprising two seven-storey patient-care towers and five surrounding two-level pods housing stores, kitchens, and outpatient facilities.

Until the second half is complete, Victoria Hospital will function at two locations: South Street and Westminster Campus. The new hospital has a licensed helipad and is one of four Ontario centres for the transport of critically ill patients.

With a staff of about 4,000 persons, Victoria Hospital is one of London's largest employers. When the Westminster project is completed, it will comprise the largest health care facility on one site in Canada.

COPP BUILDERS' SUPPLY COMPANY LIMITED

The full-range home centre and construction supply business known to Londoners as Copp's Buildall has played a prominent role in city building activity for more than a century—from the provision of stone and lime in the late 1800s to a complete line of materials and products required by the contractors and do-it-yourself trade of the 1980s. For most of that period, the company has been controlled by a succession of three generations of the Copp family, who have widened its interests through internal expansion, acquisition, and refinements to merchandising and marketing.

The forerunner of the enterprise was a stone quarry and lime kiln on Brick Street (now Commissioners Road), with an office outlet at 95 York Street, opened in 1877 by Barnabus Skuse as a source of building blocks for a then-growing city of some 20,000 persons. In 1908 William and Thomas Copp, two of five brothers from Devonshire, England, who were all active in London building trades, purchased the business. They operated as Copp Bros. until 1924 when the firm was incorporated as Copp Builders' Supply Company Limited, the present designation. That same year Stanley F. Copp, son of Thomas, entered the company; within four years he had acquired the interest of his uncle, William, and was appointed manager.

T. Brayl Copp, owner and president.

Over the years the business has shifted westward along York Street to progressively larger quarters dictated by rising volume and inventory. A turning point was the addition of lumber in 1932. This was followed by several property acquisitions for storage and vehicles that led to the construction of a new showroom at 85 York in 1951, as the company moved toward a total home centre concept. The site of the present downtown location at 45 York Street, acquired in the early 1960s, was occupied in 1966 and enlarged 10 years later to a warehouse-showroom-office complex of 65,000 square feet.

In 1965 the first step toward multibranch operation was taken with the opening of the Nor'West home centre on Highway 22 near the Hyde Park corner. Subsequent expansionary moves included the purchase of London Lumber Ltd. assets in 1971, the acquisition of Kitchener Lumber Company in 1972, the purchase of Kernohan Lumber in 1979, and the buy-out of Hunt Lumber in Lambeth in 1981. (The Nor'West centre, destroyed by fire in September 1981, was rebuilt and reopened five years later as the NorWest Do-it Center.)

The major growth of the Copp's Buildall organization has occurred under the leadership of T. Brayl Copp, who joined the firm in 1952 and succeeded his father, Stanley, now honorary chairman of the board, as president and owner in 1964. Together the four London and one Kitchener divisions employ 180 persons and transact gross sales exceeding $25 million annually.

Copp Builders' Supply Company Limited's head office and showroom on York Street.

SIFTON PROPERTIES LIMITED

In an era of scarce housing and rising demand, Harry L. Sifton hastily abandoned a real estate venture in favor of residential construction—exercising the judgment, perception, integrity, and initiative credited with the escalation of Sifton Properties Limited to the forefront of property development and building in southwestern Ontario.

The elder Sifton had moved to London from the family farm near Ridgetown in August 1921 and purchased John Anderson Real Estate. In early 1923 he sold the firm to Carling Real Estate and Insurance, turned his talents to home building, and sold six Sifton houses by year's end. He built widely across the city while establishing a reputation for quality, and picked up momentum with the completion of 200 new residences between 1940 and 1948. The addition of his son, Mowbray, to the company in 1946, postwar demand for housing, and the assembly of large tracts of raw land commencing around 1951 positioned the organization for a full-scale foray into land development and diversified construction.

Since incorporation in 1951, Sifton Properties has successfully undertaken three major London developments—Oakridge, Berkshire Village, and Westmount—and completed a fourth, Whitehills. It has also designed, built, and activated income-producing properties elsewhere in the city as London's largest and most influential developer for the past three and one-half decades. Among high-profile Sifton holdings are seven of the 15 major downtown office buildings in London, Westmount Mall, shopping centres in Guelph and Tillsonburg, and 2,636 units of rental town houses and apartments in southwestern Ontario. Over the years the company has been involved in commercial and housing projects in several Ontario cities and in Florida.

Chairman W. Mowbray Sifton (left) and president Glen R. Sifton (right), son and grandson, respectively, carry on the traditions of founder Harry L. Sifton (seated), who began building homes in the London area in 1923.

As leader of the early 1950s' "flight to the suburbs," Sifton Properties earned distinction for innovations in design and amenity. It was the first developer to install all utility services underground and the first to finish subdivisions with paved streets, curbs, and gutters. A multifamily housing mix was introduced with town houses, row houses, and apartments in close proximity to retail and recreational facilities. For years the firm set aside nearly twice the amount of public open space required by provincial statute.

Sifton Properties strongly believes in Canada and will focus on substantial acreage held on the west side of the city for future housing development throughout the 1980s. The firm intends to strengthen its income properties, purchase and build new ones, and diversify when the opportunity exists.

A third generation of the family now heads the company in the person of Glen R. Sifton, president. His father is chairman, and his grandfather, the organization's founder, serves as honorary chairman. Other officers are D.M. Dalton, executive vice-president, K.R. Morris, vice-president/finance and administration and treasurer, L.R. Broadley, vice-president/shopping centres, D.A. Lester, vice-president/office industrial, B.R. Parker, vice-president/residential rental, and W.R. Wolfenden, vice-president/housing and land.

UNIVERSITY HOSPITAL

The anatomy of London's newest full-service hospital is multifaceted—a functional blend of bold ground-breaking medical procedures performed in harmony with traditional modes of patient care and management.

The concept, design, and support system at all levels of the University Hospital organization form an ideal working environment for talented physicians and researchers and professional support staff assailing human affliction on many fronts. Enthusiasm, idealism, and unrelenting determination are fundamental in a facility deeply committed to exemplary treatment and excellence in teaching and research.

London's University Hospital, dedicated to excellence in patient care, teaching, and research.

The doors of University Hospital were officially opened in the fall of 1972, but the seed that ultimately grew to become this university teaching institution was planted many years earlier by a group of caring and concerned citizens, led by Ontario's hydroelectric pioneer, Sir Adam Beck. In 1909, under Beck's leadership, the London Health Association was formed to combat one of the principal health concerns of the day—tuberculosis.

The organization built and administered the Queen Alexandra Sanitorium, which became the Sir Adam Beck Memorial Sanatorium in Byron, after Beck's death. It served patients from across southwestern Ontario. By the early 1960s it was apparent that advances in the treatment and prevention of this once-dreaded disease would soon render the sanatorium obsolete. Not content to abdicate their community health role, London Health Association members took up the challenge to plan and build a university teaching hospital to complete the Health Sciences Complex of the University of Western Ontario.

In June 1962 the association established a planning committee, chaired by London newspaper publisher Walter J. Blackburn, to thoroughly examine all aspects of such a facility. The high standards and international recognition attained by University Hospital from its inception are in large measure attributable to the vision of its founding organization.

Neurosurgery at the hospital includes surgical treatment of epilepsy.

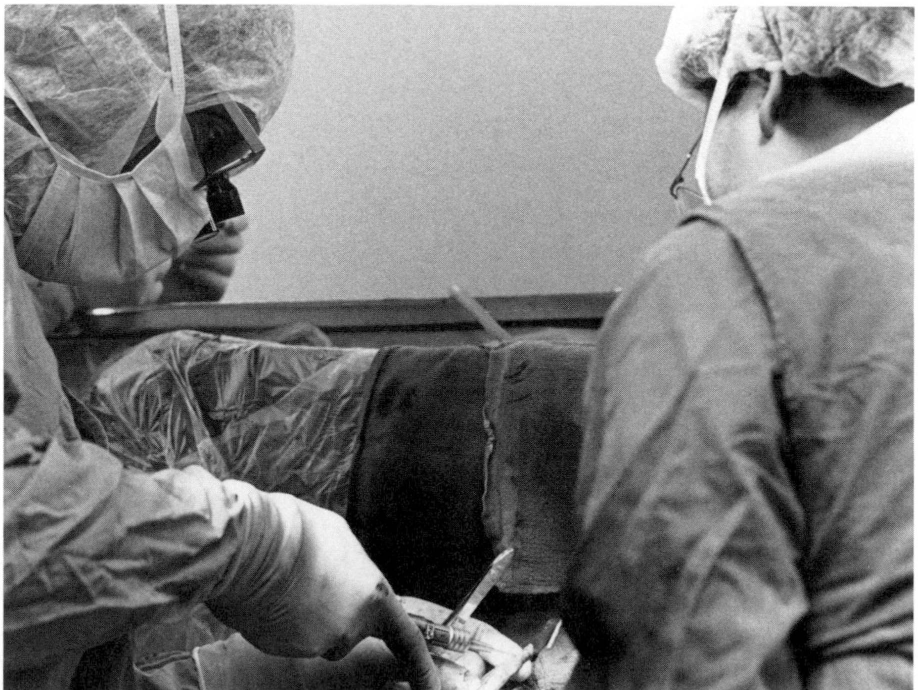

In retrospect, too, the words of the late Dr. Wilder Graves Penfield, who opened the hospital in September 1972, were prophetic. He remarked: "May this hospital serve the purposes of human compassion and of academic medicine, and in the years to come, may it be said in all truth that here humanism is joined with medical science in the art of the practice of medicine."

In the ensuing years University Hospital has fulfilled the mandate set down by the founding organization and by Dr. Penfield, and in fact has ventured beyond the original objectives to a host of achievements in the health care field. Today this teaching and research facility plays a leadership role in the health system while continuing to provide the highest quality of health care to its patients, top-level education to health care personnel (and future practitioners) and ongoing research in a broad spectrum of medical disciplines. In addition, the institution's leadership maintains a close liaison with the community in areas of public information and funding, preventive medicine, and public education, all of which contributes to understanding and support in the extension of technology and facilities.

Lab technologist Rob Coles counting cells to monitor organ rejection, part of a successful transplant program.

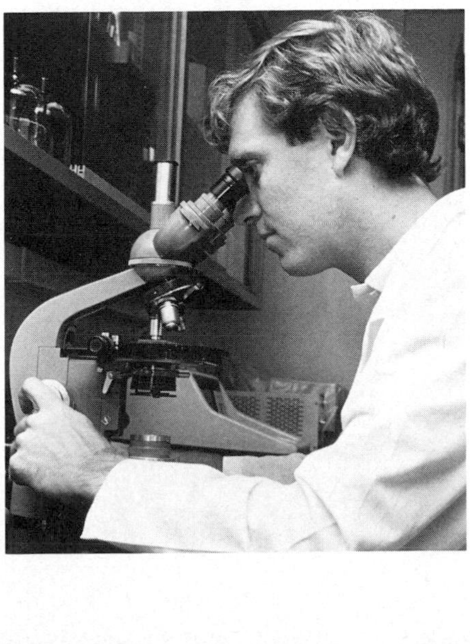

Owned and operated by the London Health Association, University Hospital is a 463-bed active treatment teaching facility that contains all the clinical and service departments found in large general hospitals, with the exception of obstetrics and family practice. All medical staff appointees hold university academic rank, and each has a teaching and research responsibility.

In its prime function as a regional centre and referral institution serving western Ontario, University Hospital cares for patients requiring specialized treatment. Patients are referred to the institution by family physicians and other doctors who select the University Hospital specialist best qualified to treat the patient's particular illness. The referring doctor is kept fully informed of care, treatment, and progress. When the patient is discharged, all pertinent information is communicated to the referring doctor for subsequent patient care and records.

Since 1972, when University Hospital was established, rapid advances in technology have resulted in a continuous upgrading of plant and equipment and have led to stunning breakthroughs in the medical field. However, the institution has kept in perspective its primary consideration—the well-being of the patient, expressed in respect for the dignity and rights of the individual.

The hospital's practical and convenient layout and decentralized management system allows health care providers to spend the maximum time possible with their patients. Doctors are able to see inpatients and outpatients, to teach students, and to conduct research without having to leave the floor on which their offices are located. Nurses and other health care workers are relieved of many of the traditional administrative duties. An active in-house training program ensures that hospital personnel are well schooled in the latest techniques, both in patient care and management.

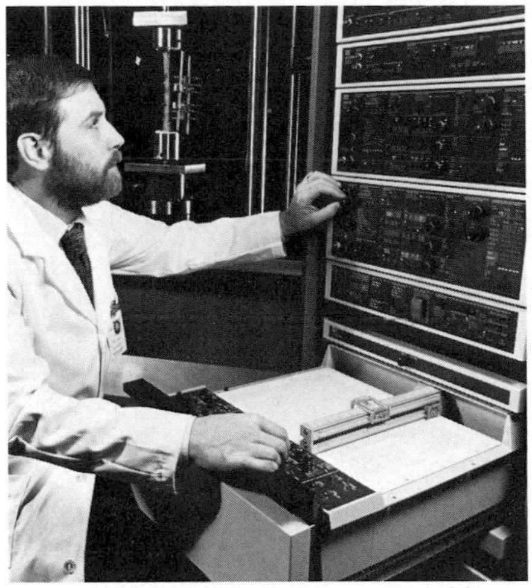

Peter Andrae conducts orthopaedic research at University Hospital.

With a $100-million operating budget and more than 2,400 employees, University Hospital is a

Carrie Bradley, another transplant team member, in the tissue-typing laboratory.

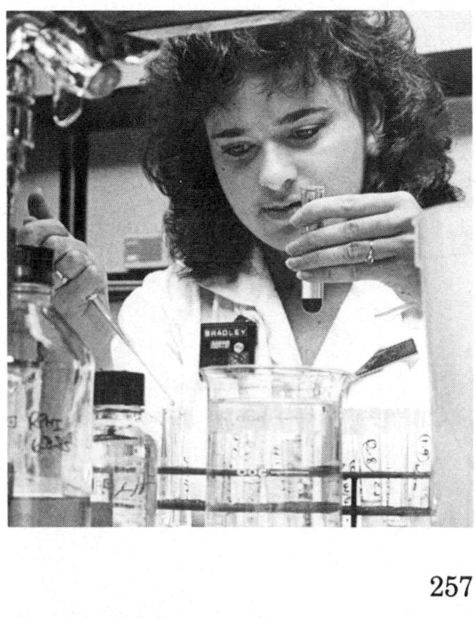

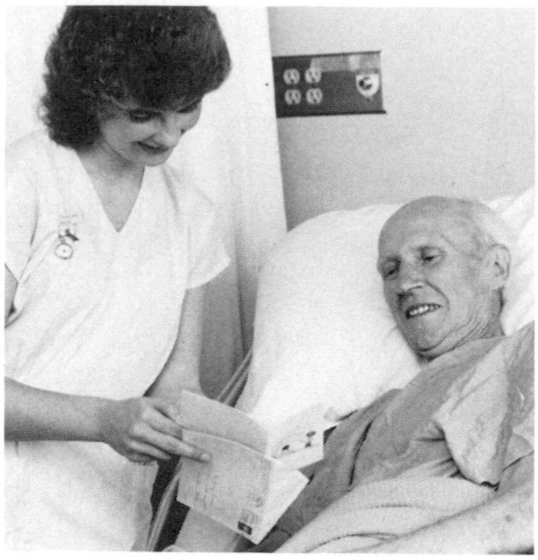

Exemplary patient care is a primary goal of University Hospital.

valued component of the London-area economy. In terms of service, the profile is even higher, touching the lives of 1.5 million residents of western Ontario and accepting patients from all of Canada's provinces and territories and indeed, from all corners of the globe. In addition, the competency and scope of the institution is in a constant state of enhancement as a medical centre of excellence in Canada.

University Hospital is the nation's leading organ transplant centre, having recently developed a comprehensive Multi-Organ Transplant Unit. It is a world-renowned facility for the surgical treatment of brain aneurysms under the guidance of Dr. Charles Drake, and also is famous for the treatment of electrical disturbances of the heart. The institution also is one of the leaders in the field of in-vitro fertilization.

In 1986 a four-bed Epilepsy Unit was opened to monitor patients being treated for epilepsy in a safer environment with greater diagnostic efficiency. In addition, the development of a strategic plan to help the hospital establish priorities in terms of programs, staffing, facilities and equipment was undertaken.

An addition to the complement of medical research resources is the John P. Robarts Research Institute, named in honor of the former Premier of Ontario and London resident who was a stroke victim. Under the guidance of scientific director Dr. Henry Barnett, a neurologist who shares international acclaim with Dr. Drake in the neuroscience field, the John P. Robarts Research Institute is focussing on the study and treatment of strokes and aging, heart disease, and disturbed immunological systems. Among specialized areas of investigation are juvenile diabetes, multiple sclerosis, and the control of organ rejection.

The institute is operated as an autonomous medical research organization, having been funded by public monies, notably a $10-million seed grant from the Province of Ontario, and private subscription for a combined total of $24 million. It is jointly sponsored by University Hospital and the University of Western Ontario. Located between the hospital and the university's Health Sciences Complex, the John P. Robarts Research Institute will ultimately engage 200 researchers in basic and clinical science and effectively unites the laboratory scientist and practising physician in the pursuit of better health care.

As 1986 draws to a close University Hospital is well positioned to launch major new medical procedures and innovations from the traditional triad of patient care, teaching, and research. In the view of Dr. Barnett and his senior associates, the teamwork approach applied so successfully to past accomplishments will continue to serve the public interest. Their confidence is underpinned by an evaluation of tremendous depth in all departments of the institution.

Executive director Pat Blewett and associate executive director Diane Stewart, both with University Hospital from the beginning, also live by the institution's motto, "Finding a Better Way," which includes cost effectiveness and fiscal responsibility compatible with overall philosophy. A progressive board, composed of experts in their fields from the community, contributes guidance and consultation while the newly formed University Hospital Foundation helps to ensure adequate financing.

Neurologist Henry Barnett, M.D. (left), and neurosurgeon Charles Drake, M.D., who share international honors for the development of surgical techniques in their specialty, exemplify the commitment and achievement of University Hospital in many areas of medical advancement.

MORPHY CONTAINERS LTD.

Refinements to manufacturing capability, customer service, and employee communications have secured Morphy Containers Ltd. on the leading edge of a highly specialized field serving a diversity of industry in southwestern Ontario.

Although only 16 years old, the company founded by Donald Morphy is one of the better-known container sheet plants in the province, a status accruing from the assembly of experienced personnel, modern equipment, and a flair for flexibility and versatility. With particular expertise in the supply of small quantities, Morphy has built a strong market within a 100-kilometre radius of London for a variety of products, including standard and custom-designed shipping cartons, point-of-purchase displays, and an extensive line of corrugated paper products—anything from a plain regular carton to a litho-laminated display.

In 1986 the firm added a second plant with the acquisition of Z-H Paper Products in Brantford, a corrugated box business similar to the London operation. The purchase increased Morphy's market to cover the area from Mississauga west to Sarnia, and made available a second line of machinery for more efficient production.

President and sole owner Donald Morphy brought some 15 years' experience in the corrugated box and paper industry to the start-up of his new venture in November 1970. Within five years the original industrial mall area of 7,500 square feet at 94 Bessemer Court grew to 20,000 square feet as new presses, tapers, and die-cutters were added, in step with rapid expansion through the 1970s. In the fall of 1980, commemorating the 10th anniversary of the company, a free-standing 36,000-square-foot plant was opened on a four-acre site at 1001 Green Valley Road in London. The following summer, installation of an Italian-built flexo-folder gluer costing $450,000 greatly increased plant capacity.

The modern plant of Morphy Containers Ltd. manufactures specialized corrugated products for a large industrial clientele.

A flexo-folder gluer contributes to versatility and efficiency in filling orders.

In the course of developing from three employees to 50 and attracting a large volume of custom work for the luggage, furniture, automotive, and a host of other industry clients, Morphy has moved in several directions to ensure continuity and quality. Internally, a profit-sharing plan has functioned since 1981; an employee communications committee meets regularly with the president; and a combined group of management and floor personnel addresses quality concerns. A design department—rare in the corrugated sheet plant industry—responds to customer needs as well as creating original configurations with a high rate of acceptance.

Morphy and 10 other independents formed Tencorr Packaging Ltd. in 1983 to produce their own raw material. Don Morphy is immediate past president of the Washington-based Association of Independent Corrugated Converters, with 600 members worldwide.

ROBERT HUNT CORPORATION

The home office for the Canadian and U.S. operations of Robert Hunt Corporation is located on Wilton Grove Road.

An accurate and timely assessment of rising demand for quality exterior openings—windows, doors, sunrooms, and, more recently, skylights—has been validated many times over by the massive growth and increasing share of the residential market achieved by the Robert Hunt Corporation.

From a single sales outlet on Princess Street in 1962, a manufacturing, assembly, and sales network spanning Canada and reaching into the southern United States has emerged to claim a leading role in the industry. Total employment in the seasonally sensitive business ranges from 800 to 1,000 men and women, of whom 400 to 500 are based in London, the centre of production and administration.

The fledgling enterprise launched by Robert Alan Hunt, a young entrepreneur from nearby Brantford, was on an expansionary course almost from the beginning, with construction of a new building on Highway 135 in the southwest section of the city by late 1962. Since then, an unending series of additions to manufacturing and display facilities in the major urban centres of Canada, and latterly in Florida, accompanied by product development and aggressive promotion, have propelled the Hunt Corporation to a high profile in the home-building field.

Characteristically, founder Robert Hunt downplays his role in the success of the company that he took from obscurity to the forefront of a fiercely competitive industry. Instead, he credits a good product fashioned by skilled personnel whose workmanship is matched by executive excellence in the management and marketing divisions of the corporation. In particular, he cites the contributions of George Fleming, vice-president and product specialist, and president Bill Costello, whose efforts have paced the organization to record volumes year after year.

The first substantial phase of national growth occurred in the late 1960s, when sales locations were established in Toronto, Sudbury, Kitchener, and Winnipeg, all served from the combined head office, production, and delivery complex on Highway 135. By then, in addition to the Hunt window line, the firm had begun selling the well-known Pella product, which was imported from the United States under an exclusive distribution arrangement. The two trade names prevail today in a proliferation of advanced designs keyed to a more sophisticated home owner demand.

The build-up of a Canadian branch network continued over the next decade, commencing with a plant-warehouse in Dartmouth, Nova Scotia, and light assembly installations in Calgary, Alberta, and Ottawa in 1973, followed by a small branch in St. John's, Newfoundland, in 1974. Hunt Corpora-

Robert Hunt, of London, chairman and founder of the Robert Hunt Corporation, shown with his son, Daniel, who is vice-president of the company.

Hunt Corporation's 400,000-square-foot manufacturing plant and head office is situated on 30 acres in south London.

tion moved into Quebec in 1976 with the acquisition of Pella Quebec Limitee, and built a new plant in Edmonton the following year. A large number of affiliated sales offices were opened in conjunction with the new branches, including outlets in Windsor, Regina, and Saskatoon.

Formation of the Robert Hunt Corporation U.S.A. dates to the purchase of a subsidiary company in Florida in 1979 for the distribution of Hunt and Pella products south of Jacksonville. During the next five years sales offices were opened in Tampa, Boca Raton, Sarasota, Fort Myers, South Miami, and Vero Beach, as well as a main branch plant-showroom of 60,000 square feet in Orlando. With an additional 60,000 square feet brought on stream by 1984, the Orlando operation now employs 75 people.

Meanwhile in Canada, the parent company pursued a relocation program initiated in 1976 whereby all future manufacturing capacity would be consolidated on a 30-acre tract of land along Wilton Grove, south of Highway 401. Significantly, 1976 was a boom year with a record 275,000 housing starts in Canada, so the time was ripe for constructing 170,000 square feet of warehouse and assembly space around the original lumber mill established on the property in 1968. With the transfer of the head office to new quarters at Wilton Grove in 1979, the Highway 135 structure was converted to a customer service centre.

Extensions to the Wilton Grove plant in 1983 and 1986 have resulted in a grand total of 376,000 square feet of operational area at the site, where all basic manufacturing is carried out. Essential, too, is adequate storage for a heavy inventory of low-value/high-cube product held in readiness for seasonal peaks.

Of the total Hunt Corporation output, approximately 95 percent is sold directly to the industry, the balance being distributed through dealers in outlying areas. Although the bulk of sales are to the new residential sector, the company has developed a position recently in home and commercial renovations, new commercial building, and hospital, school, and nursing home construction. The combination of broader markets with a solid track record of initiative and performance augurs well for the future viability of the organization.

The shipping area of the bustling south London plant.

STEVENSON & HUNT INSURANCE BROKERS LIMITED

President George W. Ley (seated) and vice-president Paul V. Sabourin have added agencies and specialty coverages to Stevenson & Hunt Insurance Brokers Limited, one of Canada's larger private insurance brokerages.

The solid foundations put down by the partnership of C. Clifford Hunt and Wilfred D. Stevenson more than half a century ago are very much in evidence at one of Canada's largest private insurance brokers in downtown London.

From the opening of business on July 2, 1935, Hunt and Stevenson embraced principles of service, stability, and the provision of a broad range of coverage to meet client needs. Today the greatly expanded and modernized form of Stevenson & Hunt Insurance Brokers Limited values highly the reputation built on those early tenets of sound management.

The original partners brought a wealth of business and insurance experience, and not a little energy and ambition, to the small office at 294 Dundas Street. There, the lone employee was Freda Johnson, who would remain for 33 years and thereby set a pattern for long service followed by many staff members. The first agent was a woman, Ruth Florence, who with the founders was the nucleus of an eventual force of insurance representatives and real estate sales people throughout southwestern Ontario.

Announcement of the new agency in *The London Free Press* hinted at an aggressive approach, offering complete insurance coverage of the city and nine counties as agents for two leading insurance companies. Customer surveys, diversity of coverage, and efficient, prompt, and courteous dealings were further inducements by which Hunt and Stevenson proceeded to carve out a large share of the area's insurance market.

In the mid-1950s the firm divested itself of the real estate division and Phillip Stevenson, son of the founder, took over along with Frank Wrong, former general manager of the Halifax Insurance Company. In 1967 George Andrews joined Stevenson & Hunt, eventually becoming president and serving until his death in 1977.

Several relocations were necessary as the company grew, and offices were established at 267 Dundas Street in 1973, the year the present owners, George Ley and Paul Sabourin, merged their agency with Stevenson & Hunt. In 1978 they became sole owners of the company. Since that time five additional agencies have been folded into the brokerage, widening specialty coverages.

The firm embarked on a program of automation and product innovation that has more than tripled its size, while fine tuning the access to records of some 14,000 policy holders. This rapid growth precipitated another move in 1981 to house the staff of 40 brokers and support people in larger quarters at 200 Queens Avenue.

Today Stevenson & Hunt proudly comprises a one-stop shopping place for the full range of insurance requirements such as property/casualty and life insurance, group benefits, annuities, and actuarial services.

Stevenson & Hunt has long outgrown the original premises on Dundas Street next to the old city hall.

CBS EQUIPMENT LIMITED

By every standard of measurement—physical expansion, sales volume, and modernization—CBS Equipment Limited is an outstanding success in a select field supplying power components and ancillary equipment for all kinds of industrial applications.

The company's head office and main stockroom at 145 Adelaide Street South in London, a fully computerized operation co-ordinating an inventory of 27,000 parts, is the hub of a network reaching into a large area of southwestern Ontario. With branches in St. Thomas and Simcoe, a 60-mile radius of service is maintained from each location.

Basically a distributor of power transmission parts—bridging the gap from power source to machine—CBS Equipment transacts a substantial business in bearings, v-belts, chain, couplings, clutches and brakes, gears, motors, and reducers, as well as conveyor components and material-handling equipment. In addition to a core clientele of industries, the firm caters to a growing roster of customers in the construction and agriculture sectors.

Established in a small building on York Street by Morley Wilkins of London in 1959, CBS Equipment was acquired on July 1, 1968, by the present owner-partners, Bill Cruden; Lloyd Boughner; and Bill Clinton, who retired as president in 1983. After five extensions of the Hamilton Road premises, they moved to the Adelaide Street building in 1979, more than doubling capacity to 8,000 square feet. The Simcoe division was opened in 1976 and St. Thomas in 1982.

Over the past 18 years sales volume has multiplied almost 20 times to four million dollars annually, while inventory has increased tenfold to a value of $500,000. Personnel has grown from a staff of six to 27 full-time employees, of whom four are engaged in sales—two in London and one in each branch.

A number of factors have contributed to the emergence of CBS Equipment as a leading distributor, and incidentally the only home-grown London business in its specialty. A principal asset is the provision of lines from major manufacturers in Canada, the United States, Europe, and Japan, coupled with intensive training of CBS employees in the composition and adaptation of the units. In order to improve purchasing power, the firm joined with 11 Ontario and two Quebec companies to form Independent Distributors Inc. (IDI) in 1984; and the London organization is also a member of the Power Transmission Distributors Association of America.

Rounding out the system for total control and expeditious handling of the flow of stock, CBS Equipment has achieved full computerization of all departments in a carefully phased-in program dating from mid-1983. With the installation of instantaneous order processing via photo facsimile last year, the company is well positioned for further advancement in the marketplace.

CBS Equipment Limited, a distributor of power transmission parts, has its head office and main stockroom at 145 Adelaide Street South in London, with branches in St. Thomas and Simcoe.

KELCOATINGS LIMITED/OAKSIDE CHEMICALS LIMITED

Awareness of a potential market in the paint coating field, coupled with a background in the paint industry and a desire to establish an independent business to which his growing sons might succeed, led Edwin Kelly into the development of a highly successful venture on the southwestern outskirts of London.

KelCoatings Limited at 97 White Oak Road has more than fulfilled the founder's expectations, expanding on four occasions to meet an ever-increasing demand for custom-made paint coatings for metal applications. As well, two sons have joined the firm: Sharon Kelly, a bachelor of science graduate in chemistry from the University of Western Ontario, is general manager after 10 years with the company; and Ted Kelly, a graduate in engineering technology from Fanshawe Community College, came on staff recently.

A graduate in chemistry from the UWO, the founder had spent 20 years with a major paint manufacturer prior to launching KelCoatings in 1968 on the present site. At the outset the 40- by 40-foot plant was surrounded by farmland, the only industry in a remote area served by a dirt road. Total staff was four, including the owner.

The office and plant of KelCoatings Limited and Oakside Chemicals Limited on White Oak Road in southwest London. Oakside was established in 1975 to reprocess dirty solvents.

The concept of blending, testing, and producing paint coatings on request from a wide spectrum of industrial users proved right for the times. KelCoatings' plant today comprises 50,000 square feet of office, laboratory, manufacturing, and warehousing space, the latest addition in 1986 being a 10,000-square-foot warehouse extension to make way for a new development laboratory. Coatings are formulated for a variety of applications—including a large volume of coil coatings, appliances, office furniture, food jar caps, automobile engines, and metal decorating finishes for pails and cans. Quality control, of paramount importance to the operation, is carried out in two self-contained laboratories.

The computer age has also arrived at KelCoatings in the form of a state-of-the-art color computer capable of critical definition with savings in time and effort, and total computerization of the office procedure.

Current staff of the company is 30, including five sales representatives covering London, Toronto, Hamilton, and Montreal, where an additional warehouse is maintained. Two active employees—vice-president Hugh Eaton and plant manager Alex Poczik—and retired office manager Peter Dekoter date their service to the inception of the business.

A native of Lambeth, Edwin Kelly served as a village trustee from 1967 to 1981, a period distinguished by population growth from 300 to 3,000. KelCoatings sponsored the London Majors baseball team for three years, and currently sponsors the Lambeth Flyers hockey club.

Family management of two companies is represented by Sharon Kelly (left), general manager of KelCoatings, Edwin R. Kelly, president and founder of KelCoatings and Oakside, and E.R. "Ted" Kelly, general manager of Oakside.

FIRESTONE STEEL PRODUCTS OF CANADA

A decision taken by the parent American company in the fall of 1966 to establish a Canadian facility for the manufacture of truck wheels and rims has more than fulfilled early expectations, tapping a huge North American market and triggering successive expansions and increased employment at the west-end London site.

Firestone Steel Products of Canada—a division of Firestone Canada Inc., and thereby wholly owned by Firestone Tire and Rubber Company of Akron, Ohio—is the nation's leading producer of rims and wheels for the truck industry. It supplies all the major truck and trailer companies on the continent, with some 80 percent of output being exported to the United States. Continual updating of assembly lines and technology—combined with precision tooling, rigid testing, and quality-control standards—has developed the plant at 31 Firestone Boulevard, off Clarke Side Road, into the most modern and efficient installation of its kind in the country.

The Firestone presence in London actually dates to 1949—in association with The London and Petrolia Barrel Company Limited, which functioned as a Canadian licensee for the production of Firestone Steel Products until June 1, 1968. By that time Firestone had erected the first building on the present 65-acre property—a 152,000-square-foot structure housing eight rim and ring production lines, as well as press and paint shops—where 237 employees under president Alan G. Brown commenced operations in the summer. Brown remained at the helm until 1984, overseeing several expansions of plant, equipment, and product line, and earning recognition as the key person responsible for the exceptional growth of the company.

The foresight, planning, and subsequent efforts of management and staff are highly visible in 1986 at a sprawling industrial complex covering 615,075 square feet of usable space. Slightly more than half is production area, while the office occupies 46,680 square feet; raw material storage, 43,400 square feet; and outside concrete storage pad, 222,000 square feet. The manufacturing space includes the recent addition of 50,000 square feet to accommodate a high-speed rim line and wheel assembly. In fact, the company's records reveal extensions to plant and equipment in virtually every year since its inception, including a $20.1-million building program that doubled the size of the operation in 1979.

Modernization and growth has been accompanied, too, by a steady increase in staff to 922—704 hourly and 218 salaried—all of whom are well trained in the particular skills and expertise essential to the multimillion unit flow from Firestone Steel Products to the transportation industry each year.

A major London industry, Firestone Steel Products of Canada supplies a large segment of rims and wheels to North American truck and trailer manufacturers.

JOHN LABATT LIMITED IN LONDON

The history of John Labatt Limited has always been closely bound to the city of London. Although it is today a major Canadian corporation with facilities across North America and ownership spread among thousands of shareholders, its large brewery on the banks of the Thames River dates continuously from the 1830s when London was little more than a settlement of a few hundred people.

For more than a century this site functioned as both the sole operation of the company and the base for its national expansion. In the past 30 years, while that expansion has steadily embraced food and beverage industries in various regions of the North American continent, the head office of Labatt's has remained in London—located at the forks of the Thames River in a complex of Victorian houses, professionally restored at company expense, just downstream from the historic site of the brewery.

The small enterprise founded as London Brewery had existed for perhaps a decade when John Kinder Labatt in 1847 bought into the business, first in partnership with a friend from St. Thomas and then in 1855 as sole proprietor. Its ownership remained in his family for nearly a century.

Of Irish Huguenot parentage, Labatt had emigrated from England to Upper Canada with his wife, Eliza Kell, in 1833. They had settled on land in Westminster Township, which together they gradually transformed into a 200-acre farm, beginning at the same time a family that eventually numbered 14 children.

The farm was sold in 1846 in order to raise capital for investment that would enable his growing family to move from agriculture and the country into the town and commercial enterprise. Brewing presented some continuity from cultivation of the fields; and if the entrepreneur lacked experience, he entered upon his new career with certain very real advantages.

John Labatt, president and owner of the company from 1872 until his death in 1915.

Like Thomas Carling—another English immigrant, who founded his City Brewery in the 1840s—Labatt found London a good place to develop the market for English types of ale. There were British troops stationed at Victoria Barracks, and London's growth as a judicial and financial centre was attracting a number of professional people. From seven licensed taverns in 1835, the figure grew to more than 20 when the community became a city in 1855.

Beyond London were the inns on roads that connected with nearby villages; and the railways beginning in the 1850s expanded the potential market for fermented beverages to include more distant towns, such as Sarnia and Windsor to the west and Hamilton and Toronto to the east. A network of transportation was developing that would enhance opportunities for Labatt products when the second John Labatt succeeded to the venture in 1866.

His dedication to the brewing and malting industry, combined with his willingness to take risks, made John Labatt one of the more successful entrepreneurs among London's business leaders during the next half-century. By the 1880s the company was producing 22,000 barrels a year, at least six times its capacity when he took over the enterprise two decades earlier.

Within these quantities there was not a great variety of brands, certainly not on the scale that exists today. John Labatt accepted and continued the Stock Ale of his father, but added to it his own innovation in the form of India Pale Ale. Modelled on an English recipe and first produced in the 1870s, it soon became the firm's most distinctive brand, bringing to John Labatt himself an association with quality that seems to have influenced all areas of his business activity.

In addition to buying the best of local barley as an expert maltster, often through seed merchants in Chatham, then selling his malt as far away as Halifax, it was important for him to display his fermented beverages and to compete internationally as well as locally. He entered his India Pale Ale and Stock Ale into competitions at such expositions as Philadelphia, in 1876; Paris, 1878; London, England, 1886; and at the Chicago World's Fair, 1892. It was then possible to incorporate the prizes and medals into his labels. About the same time, in the 1890s, he adopted the new medium of advertising in the form of the colorful

The first Labatt's trucks about 1923, decorated for a Labour Day Parade.

lithographic poster.

By the turn of the twentieth century, John Labatt was indeed the head of an established brewing and malting company. He had a family of nine children; a large house on Queens Avenue; travelled to England frequently, living as a gentleman on the great ocean liners; and spent his summers at Newport, Rhode Island, or at Virginia Beach. Yet his roots were in London. It was there that he worked and supervised his family, sending his daughters to private schools elsewhere but being approving and encouraging when they married into other business and professional families of London.

The daughters are a part of the story of the organization because they shared equally in the inheritance of ownership when John Labatt died in 1915. Incorporation in 1911 had created a limited number of shares that were distributed equally among the seven daughters and two sons, John S. and Hugh Labatt. Shareholder meetings were entirely family affairs, with no one figure emerging to dominate—a feature of ownership that influenced the firm during the years of Prohibition that began in 1916.

The ban on the sale of full-strength beer in Ontario had a crippling effect, which might have led to the end of the company had it not been for a decision agreed to within the large Labatt family. Although not participating personally in sales or distribution, they appointed a manager who directed a twofold operation: brewing and selling full-strength beer for export to the United States; and making smaller amounts of weak and legitimate beer for sale in Ontario. The combination enabled the firm to survive in a strengthened position when Prohibition ended for Ontario in 1927.

The image of a corporation that had made profits out of beer and liquor sales lay behind the kidnapping of John S. Labatt in the summer of 1934. It was an event that captured national headlines. For the people of London it brought attention and notoriety that seemed not to accord with the mild-mannered, diffident, and domestic character of the man who had been kidnapped. After his release, though unharmed, he returned to the fold of his family and his home

One of Labatt's innovative streamlined trucks, dating from the 1940s.

on Princess Avenue, which faced Victoria Park. Avoiding publicity, he came to rely on a new manager, Hugh M. Mackenzie, whose drive transformed the marketing area and eventually the size of the Labatt brewing enterprise.

Mackenzie accepted the challenge of competition from Canadian Breweries Limited—which had purchased the Carling Brewing Company in London and closed it down, moving the operations of that firm to Toronto. Labatt's would remain in London and compete from there for the large Ontario market, including Toronto and Hamilton. The operation required both enlarged production and a well-maintained fleet of tractor-trailers. These colorful trucks travelled the new two-lane highways on a regular timetable, carrying cases and kegs of I.P.A. and Crystal Lager while displaying the Labatt name to a more mobile public. By the end of World War II, the organization was associated with quality fermented beverages well beyond the London area.

With the postwar boom and a growing Canadian population, Labatt's was poised for further expansion—this time in the number of plants that would produce as well as distribute its products. The family decided to make it a public company in 1945, for the first time issuing treasury shares that could be purchased and traded on the Toronto and Montreal stock exchanges. New opportunities were now available for the borrowing and raising of capital.

Advertisement for I.P.A., Labatt's most popular brand from the 1890s to the 1940s.

N.E."Peter" Hardy, chairman of the board.

P.N.T. Widdrington, president and chief executive officer.

An existing brewery was purchased in Toronto, but, if expansion was to extend beyond Ontario, given the character of the Canadian federal system, provincial licenses would have to be arranged for each province in which the firm wished to operate. Its strong capital base enabled Labatt's in the 1950s either to purchase existing facilities or to build new ones in Quebec, Manitoba, and British Columbia. During the 1960s J.H. "Jake" Moore, whose family roots were in London, led the company in a continuing policy of building and acquisitions, until by 1971 Labatt's owned and operated breweries in every province of Canada with the exception of Prince Edward Island.

On the way to this achievement, certain social obligations were remembered. In London the company donated to the University of Western Ontario, and bought Tecumseh Park, sponsoring renovations and donating it as Labatt Park for the playing of amateur baseball. Subsequently, as breweries were acquired or built in other provinces and a corporate national structure evolved, local traditions were maintained to keep intact a base of respect for regional loyalties that grew out of the corporation's experience in the London community. One of the central figures, whose astute counsel has helped to shape this balance between regional and national operations, was N.E. "Peter" Hardy, who has served since 1980 as chairman of the board.

By the 1970s, however, management grew increasingly aware that opportunities were limited for further brewing expansion. Labatt's had doubled its share of the national market from 17 percent in the 1950s to 35 percent in the 1970s; new brands such as Blue and 50 had been launched from London to attain a national appeal, but this market leadership in brewing had now to be combined with expansion in other directions.

The challenge has been exciting; it has led to decisions that have transformed the company. Under the leadership of Peter Widdrington, who became president in 1973, a dynamic quality has entered into planning and growth. His executive direction over the past 13 years has been driven by the expansive goal of turning John Labatt into a major North American food and beverage company.

Today John Labatt Limited has 70 manufacturing and processing facilities in Canada and the United States. The company employs 13,000 people who generate sales of close to four billion dollars. Of this total, while 35 percent comes from brewing, and Labatt is still Canada's largest brewer, 65 percent of sales are now identified with non-brewing operations.

Milk processing includes such prominent names as Ault, Silverwood, and Sealtest in Canada, and Johanna Farms in the United States. Flour is milled from Canadian grain by Ogilvie Flour Mills; grocery products are made by Catelli; frozen foods by Chef Francisco in the United States and Omstead Foods in Canada; fruit juices by Holiday Juice; with wines from Chateau-Gai in Canada and La-Mont winery in California.

This expansion of product and plant has in fact led the company to become North American in the scope of its total operations; 30 percent of gross sales are now derived from businesses in the United States.

Innovation in sports and the media has accompanied this continental growth. Labatt in 1976 took the initiative in founding the Toronto Blue Jay baseball team in the American League, and the company maintains a 45-percent ownership in one of North America's most colorful sports franchises.

Wide public interest in the broadcasting of sports has carried over to investment in cable television. Since 1984 Labatt has owned and operated The Sports Network (TSN), a specialty service that broadcasts professional and amateur sporting events as well as sports news and magazine shows from all over the world.

These many varied interests have transformed John Labatt Limited into a multiproduct, multiplant company with annual profits that now exceed $100 million, ranking it among the top 50 of the largest Canadian corporations. The firm's senior executives continue to live in or near London, and they take a vital interest in the affairs of the local community.

Head office of John Labatt Limited in restored nineteenth-century bank buildings on Ridout Street.

LONDON WINERY LIMITED

The seventh-largest winery in Canada is a many-faceted enterprise—a landmark in its home city, a historic link to the very beginning of the nation's wine making, and a gold medallist in international competitions. The development of London Winery Limited is also distinguished by an unbroken line of family ownership and management, spanning three generations, at the same site atop Winery Hill on Wharncliffe Road South where brothers A.N. and J.C. Knowles founded the business in 1925.

Historically, London Winery can trace its roots back to 1871 when Canada's first such operation, the Hamilton Dunlop Winery, was established in Brantford, Ontario, by Major J.S. Hamilton, the dean of Canadian wine producers. In 1888 he and Thaddeus Smith of Vin Villa vineyards (established in 1860 on Pelee Island) merged their firms into the Pelee Island Wine and Vineyard Company, which was purchased by London Winery in 1945. One of the original Hamilton Winery products, St. Augustine red Communion wine, remains on the market today as probably the oldest brand in Canada.

The colorful background of London Winery, including antique bottles and wine-making equipment, is featured in the new Tourist Centre. It will open this year—complete with theatre, wine store and museum, and boutique—to inform the public about the industry.

The operation has expanded greatly since the arrival of the brothers Knowles: A.N., an electrical engineer who also set up the largest electrical contracting business in the area while serving as president of the winery; and J.C., a trained wine maker. From the first few hundred gallons of sherries and ports then in vogue, output branched into table, sparkling, dessert, honey, cooler, and flavored wines and chablis. Fermenting and aging cellars were extended underground, and bottling facilities were increased to four lines, which produce more than four million bottles annually. A six-week period each fall sees more than 100 tons of grapes from Niagara Peninsula growers crushed each day in the London plant.

The company is also preparing for the future by planting 48 acres of research vineyards with several varieties of vinefera and hybrid grapes at its Cedar Springs, Ontario, property. The first harvest in 1988 is expected to provide vital information in the quest to meet maturing tastes and the demand for more sophisticated wines.

Family administration of London Winery continues today under the direction of A.N. "Peter" Knowles (named for his father), executive vice-president, and his four children: Neville, director of sales; Peter, quality control; Jim, vineyard manager; and Lisa, accounting.

The original London Winery building on Wharncliffe Road South is depicted in this architect's sketch, circa 1925.

ANGLO-GIBRALTAR INSURANCE GROUP

A special property and casualty insurer, holding a pre-eminent position in the tobacco insurance industry while building a balanced portfolio of general farm, personal, and commercial property clientele, the Anglo-Gibraltar Insurance Group is far advanced in size and scope from a modest beginning some 60 years ago in Western Canada. Founder Robert H. Cook was no doubt more concerned with the fortunes of the wheat crop than with flue-cured tobacco (then in its infancy in Ontario) when he launched a farm mutual insurance company in Saskatchewan in the 1920s.

All that began to change in the early 1930s when Cook—with his sons, R.E. "Bob" and J.W. "Jack," moved to Toronto and opened Anglo Canadian Underwriters Limited, a managing general agency for organizations such as Lloyd's of London. In fact, it was an arrangement made by the senior Cook with a syndicate of Lloyd's that led Anglo into the selective field of tobacco crop insurance, servicing a group of Port Hope-area growers. Acquiring their father's interest in 1947, the Cook brothers operated the underwriting firm until the early 1950s when it was discontinued in favor of a new approach.

The postwar era had seen a trend to wholly owned, self-contained insurance companies with branch offices, encouraging R.E. Cook to incorporate the Anglo Canada Fire and General Insurance Company on January 18, 1949. Within five months a branch was opened in Tillsonburg, central to tobacco production in southwestern Ontario. Under the direction of E.O. Shieck, who would later succeed R.E. Cook as general manager and president, the operation prospered from the outset. Anglo Canada assumed leadership in the tobacco insurance field, and in 1960 erected a two-storey office building in Tillsonburg.

Anglo's head office was maintained at various locations in Toronto for more than 20 years. Family control of the organization ended in 1957 when La Nationale Reinsurance Company (now known as SCOR) of Paris, France, purchased a majority shareholding. Subsequently, SCOR also acquired Gibraltar General Insurance Company, which had been incorporated by R.E. Cook in 1958. On January 1, 1984, the two operations were purchased from SCOR by Mutuelles Unies/Drouot of France and are currently held by AXA Canada (70 percent) and Provinces Unies Canada (30 percent).

The head office was transferred to London in 1972, first to 200 Queens Avenue and in 1981 to the handsome new Anglo-Gibraltar building at 171 Queens Avenue. There a staff of 85 functions in conjunction with fully automated processing of all insurance requirements. Additional staff comprises 20 personnel in each of the Tillsonburg and Toronto facilities.

To diversify and increase volume, the company has recently moved Anglo into the general agricultural business. The Gibraltar division is poised to augment the current strong presence in Western Ontario by expanding its base of personal automobile, personal property, and retail commercial business across the province.

The head office building of Anglo-Gibraltar Insurance Group at 171 Queens Avenue in London.

THE UNIVERSITY OF WESTERN ONTARIO

"A great university of diverse faculties and professional schools, a graduate school, and affiliated colleges. . . ."

This assessment by Professor J.R.W. Gwynne-Timothy in *Western's First Century,* published in 1978 to commemorate the centennial of The University of Western Ontario, succinctly summarizes a long and arduous ascent to maturity. In his exhaustive, thoroughly researched account, the author records the unwavering determination of the founders and succeeding generations of leadership to build an educational entity that would ultimately attain world-class status and recognition.

And in the 1980s the institution described by Gwynne-Timothy again has broadened its base of learning and inquiry on the slopes of the River Thames in north London with the recent completion of a National Centre for Management Research and Development in association with the Business School; the John P. Robarts Institute for medical research in co-operation with University Hospital; and the construction of Alumni House to accommodate student residents. These projects followed expansion of the science and engineering buildings in 1984 as part of an ongoing improvement program.

Founder Bishop Isaac Hellmuth of the Anglican Diocese of Huron could hardly have contemplated the present immensity of the city's second-largest employer (3,840 full-time and 680 part-time with an annual payroll of more than $141 million) or the current enrolment of more than 20,000. But Hellmuth had no reservations about the practicability and need for higher learning in southwestern Ontario and he undertook the mission with zeal, energy, and resourcefulness. First, in alliance with Bishop Benjamin Cronyn, whom he served as archdeacon, he was instrumental in establishing the diocesan college of Huron in 1863 on a site between St. James and Grosvenor streets and St. George Street and the River Thames. Subsequently, Bishop Hellmuth secured provincial assent to the incorporation of The Western University of London, Ontario, on March 7, 1878. (The present name was assigned by an Act of Provincial Parliament in 1923.) A year later the university moved from the old Huron College site to spacious farmlands assembled over the years in the vicinity of Western

Middlesex College on The University of Western Ontario campus and Huron College (inset) in 1930.

University College is representative of the magnificent Gothic architecture that is seen among the 68 buildings on campus.

Road.

Almost from the inception of Western, the Medical School has served as an armature of the institution, virtually sustaining the university while the Arts and Law faculties faltered in the early years. Established in 1882, the Medical Department moved to a new building at the northeast corner of York and Waterloo streets in 1888 to be closer to London General Hospital. A new medical college at South and Waterloo streets was occupied in 1921, opposite Victoria Hospital and the Institute of Public Health. Only in the years following World War II did the staged transfer of nursing and medicine to the new main campus take place in concert with the development of the health sciences complex.

When Western moved to the existing campus in 1924, accommodations consisted of University College and the Physics Building. Now there are 68 buildings housing 14 faculties (Applied Health Sciences, Arts, Dentistry, Education, Engineering Science, Graduate Studies, Law, Medicine, Music, Nursing, Continuing Education, Physical Education, Science, and Social Sciences) and three schools (Business Administration, Journalism, and Library and Information Science). A close relationship is maintained with three affiliated colleges—Brescia, Huron, and King's—and the neighboring Westminster Institute for Ethics and Human Values.

Research is an integral part of the activity of all faculties, and external support of research projects in the university exceeds $35 million a year. Special research resources include the Cancer Research Laboratory; Centre for Radio Science; Centre for Interdisciplinary Studies in Chemical Physics; Photochemistry laboratory; Boundary Layer Wind Tunnel; Systems Analysis, Control, and Design Activity; Surface Science Western; Health Care Research Unit; University Observatories; Computing Centre; and Social Science Computing Laboratory.

A valued asset is the extensive University Library System, comprising seven libraries, which were recently co-ordinated by an on-line catalogue system following a 10-year conversion program. The university reaches into the community through continuing education programs centred on professional and language learning for adults and also co-operates with local cultural and arts organizations.

Finally, as part of one of the broadest university curriculums in the nation, the purple and white school colors have adorned many a championship football and basketball team over the years. In 1984-1985 more than 80 percent of Western teams placed in the top three positions in Ontario men's and women's intercollegiate athletic competition, a feat unrivalled by member universities.

On-campus athletic facilities are unexcelled. J.W. Little Memorial Stadium offers one of the finest natural-turf surfaces for football in the country, while Thames Hall contains a large gymnasium, weightlifting area, and swimming pool. Alumni Hall, a multipurpose auditorium, can seat 1,800 for basketball and other events. The University Community Centre has a complete range of fitness, games, recreational, and personal service installations. The J. Gordon Thompson Arena, with four curling sheets, a hockey/skating rink, and 200-metre indoor tartan track, is used for community as well as university activities in keeping with Western policy.

The River Thames Bridge, an idyllic setting at the University of Western Ontario.

AVCO FINANCIAL SERVICES CANADA LIMITED

The creation of a local sales finance company by two London businessmen more than three decades ago was, in retrospect, not only a bold but an inspired decision. The enterprise that Reginald A. Palmer, an appliance store proprietor, and Ninian T. Sanderson, a commercial market gardener, originated with a few thousand dollars is today one of the outstanding success stories in Canadian business history: Avco Financial Services Canada Limited.

An agreement signed December 4, 1954, set the venture in motion with a total allocation of $25,000, primarily to finance receivables at Palmer's Appliances Limited on Dundas Street East. However, even in the first phase, the founders looked ahead to incorporation with a capital base of perhaps $100,000.

In 1986 those early objectives have been exceeded many times over by a greatly expanded organization administered from a modern head office building at 201 Queens Avenue. There a staff of 250 coordinates a Canada-wide network of 239 branches transacting approximately $624 million in receivables. In a broader context Avco Canada contributes roughly one-fifth of the volume handled by the parent Avco Financial Services Inc. group, a corporation spanning three continents.

The original partners were participants in a rising tide of consumer credit expansion triggered by postwar demand for durable goods and serviced by sales finance companies whose share of the new market rose from 2 percent to 27 percent in the period from 1945 to 1956. Within weeks Palmer and Sanderson were in the process of securing additional bank credit and incorporating Delta Acceptance Corporation Limited, which superseded the partnership agreement on March 26, 1954. Shortly thereafter, London restaurateur Freeman J. Talbot joined Delta as an investor-shareholder, and by summer 1954 another future source of equity capital—the Paul Revere Life Insurance Company of Worcester, Massachusetts—was expressing interest. The upshot of meetings in London was an infusion of new capital, a 48-percent position by Paul Revere, plans to raise equity to one million dollars through share and debenture issues, and the opening of a full-time office on King Street with Palmer in charge. By fall 1954 Delta had attracted a large clientele of small retailers and opened its first branch offices in St. Catharines and Sarnia.

This house on King Street in London served as Delta Acceptance Corporation's first office.

The inception of long-range corporate development of Delta dates to 1956, when the Worcester group of investors purchased control from Palmer and installed Richard W. Yantis as president. Under his direction the company diversified operations, built a coast-to-coast branch network, and established lines of credit with the major institutional lenders. From new offices in the Ontario Motor League building on Dundas Street, Yantis commenced the assembly of a strong management team and an expansion program.

A trip west in early 1957 led to two important acquisitions: the Crescent Finance Corporation Limited, a small consumer loan finance firm based in Regina; and Credit Acceptance Corporation Limited of Vancouver, with branches in Edmonton and Calgary. During this period Delta also achieved a considerable entry into the Canadian automobile acceptance industry. The company was successful, too, in attracting top-flight personnel such as H.S. Tennant, a leading executive with Household Finance, who came aboard in 1958 to head Crescent Finance. By 1964 he had increased the branches from five to 150 and multiplied receivables from one million dollars to $100 million. Another experienced executive whose expertise in management and capital markets contributed significantly to long-term growth was Henry P. Paterno, who joined the firm in 1959 and rose to the presidency of the international Avco Financial group.

Meanwhile, Delta strengthened its western position with the acquisition of Consolidated Finance Corporation in British Columbia late in 1958. An insurance division to cover the captive market emanating from Delta and the subsidiaries was chartered as the Adanac Insurance Company of Canada in May 1960. Then in July 1962 the London and Midland General Insurance Company was acquired through an exchange of common shares. Later that year Delta moved into the United States with purchases of the Colorado Industrial Bank and Security Acceptance Corporation, the latter a home-improvement-loan specialist on the Eastern Seaboard.

In the year immediately preceding the 1964 merger with Avco Corporation, Delta Acceptance experienced a rapid rate of growth—reflected by a rise in assets from $75 million to $266 million during 1961-1964. Three divisions were flourishing in Canada: Acceptance, 33 branches in eight provinces; Loans, 150 offices in all provinces; and Insurance, six branches in five provinces. In the United States, the industrial bank had five outlets, while the home-improvement division operated 18 offices in 10 states. Long-range problems inherent in the very size of Delta, combined with the advice of a leading investment broker, persuaded Delta directors to conclude the merger with Avco Corporation on December 7, 1964. (Mutual benefit flowed from the alliance, reducing Avco's dependency on defense contracts and releasing new cash reserves to Delta.)

Since the merger the finance company has undergone a third stage of development to attain truly international status. The initial step toward new horizons was taken in 1966 with construction of the international headquarters in Shaker Heights, Ohio, and the present Canadian head office in London. This was followed by the acquisition, by Avco Corporation, of Seaboard Finance Corporation in 1969. Seaboard, with operations in the United States, Canada, and Australia, was headquartered in Los Angeles. At that point Avco Delta and Seaboard were merged to form Avco Financial Services Inc. A United Kingdom division was opened in 1973. Avco Financial Services Canada Limited is currently under the direction of William A. Barrett, president, and Donald A. Morrison, senior vice-president.

In March 1985 the entire Avco Corporation was acquired by Textron Inc., a conglomerate with balanced operations in financial services, aerospace, and manufactured products, similar in size and stature to Avco. Combined revenue of the two companies exceeds $6.2 billion, with total employment of more than 69,000 persons.

The present head office building of Avco Financial Services Canada Limited (formerly Delta) on Queens Avenue in downtown London.

PATTON'S PLACE

The gleaming white facade along Wharncliffe Road South is a modern-day retail landmark in London, an attractive, inviting entranceway to the furniture store of the future.

Patton's Place reflects an upbeat approach to merchandising that has transformed a small appliance sales outlet into one of Canada's most successful privately held vendors of household and kitchen furnishings. And in 1986 owner-partners Gord Patton and Ron Logan commissioned a complete in-store restyling designed to meet sophisticated consumer needs well into the 1990s.

In addition to the enhancement of the sales premises, the firm also extended its program of benefits to its 83 employees, introducing pension and dental plans in addition to paid hospitalization. Company president Gord Patton says implementation of the new plans for staff members represents the completion of a long-range objective and recognizes the value of many employees who have contributed to a low turnover rate in relation to the industry.

The Patton-Logan association is long standing, dating from boyhood friendship through careers with the Frigidaire Division of General Motors in the 1950s. Patton was in sales and marketing for nine years, while Logan advanced through accounting, personnel, and human relations into sales. By 1958 both were on the road as divisional managers. It was at that juncture that Patton, impressed by the success of a retail client, laid the foundation for what would emerge as the largest single furniture and appliance retailer in southwestern Ontario.

Then 29 years old, Patton invested $10,000 of his personal savings and used a $50,000 line of credit from the bank and General Motors Acceptance Corporation to launch his fledgling business in 4,000 square feet of leased space on the site of the present Wharncliffe Road store. Logan, then 27 years old, helped in the store at night after his regular sales job, joining the firm four months later as an equal partner. Stocking only refrigerators, the pair put in long days on the floor, then delivered goods in a pickup truck until midnight. At first they didn't even have a cash register and just kept the money in their pockets.

Gord Patton (left), president, and Ron Logan, vice-president, boyhood friends, formed the household furnishings business and partnership in 1958.

Then as now, Patton recalls, the partners enjoyed hard work, thrived on challenge, and thought big, developing qualities that would prove invaluable as the venture ascended to volume buying, risk taking, and costly mass advertising in occasionally perilous economic times. Today newspaper and broadcast advertising commands some 5 percent of gross sales; even in the worst days of the 1981 recession, Patton's Place maintained a high volume of regular advertising.

In the course of expanding and diversifying into a full line of appliances and furniture, the partners made a second major decision of great importance to the viability of the business by establishing a large warehouse at Highway 135 and White Oak Road in 1964. Part

The attractive front entrance to Patton's Place, a major Canadian furniture and appliance retailer.

of the structure and $2.5 million worth of merchandise were destroyed by fire in February 1979. Today the rebuilt 90,000-square-foot warehouse is crammed with $3.5 million worth of white goods, furniture, and carpet. A discount carpet outlet under the direction of Jack Lawrence was constructed in 1984 at the warehouse location. This outlet serves the retail and construction trades with a full line of carpet and vinyl products. In all, coordination of the warehouse facility with the retail store is maintained under the direction of the warehouse manager, Bob Shadbolt.

The general offices of Patton's Place are located on Wharncliffe Road under the supervision of the controller, Denton Miller. All functions of the Company are computerized in keeping with industry trends.

Head office, warehouse, and fleet of distinctively marked trucks at Exeter and White Oak roads.

The showplace of the enterprise, the Wharncliffe Road store, has multiplied in size 15 times over to 65,000 square feet on two levels and features individual rooms displaying complete settings of furniture, bedding, and accessories. Although a total restyling had been carried out in 1979, Patton and Logan determined that a new interior was in order in 1986. They hired the world-famous store designer, Jim MacDonald of Los Angeles, to execute the attractive decor presently drawing accolades from the public and the trade.

Patton's Place was honored as Retailer of the Year by the London Advertising and Sales Club in 1980. Its proprietors have also earned distinction through community service activity. Patton was charter president of the London West Rotary Club and serves on the board of governors of the University of Western Ontario. Logan is president of the University Hospital Foundation and a former chairman of the hospital's finance committee.

CAMPBELL BROS. MOVERS LTD.

Today Campbell Bros. Movers Ltd. has 26 tractor-trailers and a licence to operate across Canada and in all the United States.

A blend of 40 years' experience and acquired capability in the highly competitive moving business has propelled a London company to the front lines of the industry as a large-volume conveyor of residential and commercial loads with a flair for tackling formidable assignments.

From a two-van, St. Thomas-based operation, Campbell Bros. Movers Ltd. has expanded to a 75-vehicle fleet offering service anywhere in the world from a modern head office on a 2.5-acre site in the Ponds Mill Industrial Park of south London. Although local and long-distance household moving comprise the bulk of activity, the firm has recently excelled in challenging new areas such as the relocation of hospitals and industries and the transport of a major league baseball team and a national theatre company.

The Campbell enterprise has been family owned and operated from its inception on October 8, 1945, when Alex Campbell—now chairman of the board—purchased the rolling stock of his father-in-law, George H. Target, of St. Thomas; his brother, Dougald, joined as a partner the next year. The two men erected a warehouse-repair shop on Talbot Street in St. Thomas in 1948, followed by the purchase of new trucks and then their first tractor-trailer in 1950.

As business increased in western Ontario, the original office was expanded in 1961; a second warehouse was secured in London in 1963; and licences were obtained to operate across Canada and into all the United States. By 1966 Campbell Bros. had 17 vehicles and were renting two additional warehouses. A move to larger quarters at Highbury and Oxford the following year preceded construction of the Ponds Mill building on Midpark in 1973.

Alex and Dougald Campbell headed the company until 1983, when Alex's son, Donald, was appointed president. Dougald is currently vice-president; and his son, Neil, is vice president of operations. Alex's daughter, Vickie, is president of Campbell Moving Systems Inc., a wholly owned subsidiary established in Mississauga five years ago.

It was she who won a contract to move the Toronto Blue Jays to spring training camp in 1984, an arrangement renewed for the past two years. Other endeavors of the firm include the transfers of Parkwood and Victoria hospitals to new sites—as well as the 10,000-mile U.S. tour of the Stratford Festival Company, and major moves for several large corporations.

To handle these special projects, plus an increasing flow of corporate household shipments, the firm employs a permanent staff of 80 (doubled at peak periods) and maintains 26 tractor-trailer units along with straight trucks, lift trucks, and ancillary equipment.

The International truck with a homemade box was part of the rolling stock purchased by Alex Campbell from his father-in-law, George H. Target, in 1945.

HAY STATIONERY INCORPORATED

An office-products professional well advanced in computer-age design and technology, Hay Stationery Incorporated took a giant step of its own earlier this year with the opening of a spacious office-showroom-warehouse complex in London.

Occupancy of the 50,000-square-foot building on an eight-and-a-half-acre site at 1950 Oxford Street East, near Clarke Side Road, capped 72 years of growth—during which the company emerged as a downtown landmark while supplying the increasingly sophisticated needs of a burgeoning business, educational, and institutional market in the city and western Ontario. And in conjunction with the move, the firm retained ties with the business core by leasing back one-third of its former York Street premises for retail purposes.

Hay Stationery was founded in 1914 by J. Bevan Hay, a native of Morpeth, Ontario, with roots in the business through exposure to bookstores operated by his father, Morice, in Ridgetown and St. Thomas. The first outlet, on Dundas Street just east of Richmond, was primarily a stationery store with a small office-equipment division on the side. The venture prospered immediately, necessitating larger quarters in 1919 at Richmond and York streets. A civic and business leader for many years, "Bev" Hay was joined by son J.B. "Jack" Hay in 1934; and together they fostered steady expansion, leading to plans for relocation in a building of their own design. The project culminated in Canada's most modern retail and wholesale office equipment and stationery headquarters at 151 York Street, which opened on April 13, 1955. The founder had died three months earlier, and was succeeded by his son.

Family ownership of the company ended on February 1, 1980, with the retirement of Jack Hay and purchase of Hay Stationery by three longtime employees: Noreen De Shane, president; Tom Mather, secretary/treasurer; and Bob Ryall, vice-president. Just as the first generations of proprietors had been confronted by inadequate facilities, the new owners were soon embarked on major redevelopment. With input from management, four full-time staff designers, and other personnel, a two-year period of intensive planning preceded the opening in March of Hay Stationery's latest home. Within the attractive steel and brick-faced structure is the ultimate in office supply display, storage, and administrative alignment.

With a clientele ranging from small commercial offices to large users such as hospitals, Hay Stationery serves a large area of southwestern Ontario from Sarnia and Chatham on the west to Cambridge and Burlington on the east, including a branch office in Brantford. From a staff of four under Bev Hay, the employee roster has increased to 80. The sales force, under the direction of sales manager Don Clark, comprises eight for general lines and two exclusively for office furniture.

Hay Stationery was founded in 1914 and by 1919 a move to larger quarters, at Richmond and York streets, was necessitated. The firm remained there for 36 years.

In 1986 Hay Stationery celebrated 72 years of growth by opening this 50,000-square-foot office-showroom-warehouse complex at 1950 Oxford Street East, London.

This building at 151 York Street was home to Hay Stationery Incorporated from 1955 to 1986.

PRICE WATERHOUSE

A comprehensive accounting service emphasizing personal contact and specialized counsel for a diverse clientele has resulted in significant growth for the London office of Price Waterhouse over a brief span of 18 years.

The city office of the internationally known accounting firm was opened in 1968 in the old Royal Bank building at Richmond and King by Bill Redrupp from the Toronto office, assisted by Bill Stewart, a student at the time. The London venture advanced to new, larger quarters in the Canada Trust building at 275 Dundas Street in 1975 and has grown to a staff complement of five partners, 10 managers, and a total of 55 personnel at the present time.

Managing partner of the London office is Phil Bowman, who succeeded Redrupp last year and is also responsible for the tax practice. The other partners are Stewart, who has remained in London from the inception and deals mainly with owner-managed businesses; David Chalmers and Rhico Hove, audit partners; and Steve Wilson, trustee partner.

In addition to auditing and accounting, Price Waterhouse offers a full range of taxation and business valuation, management consulting, insolvency, business advisory, and litigation support services. Clients range from small and medium-size owner-operated businesses to national corporations, representing financial, manufacturing, professional, and agricultural sectors. The London staff has developed a high degree of expertise in servicing the important local medical establishment, including nursing homes and medical partnerships, as well as farming and agribusinesses in southwestern Ontario. In all, the firm acts as a financial advisor in the broadest sense, with access to the Canada-wide resources of 22 Price Waterhouse offices employing 1,500 professionals.

Senior London staff members are actively involved in civic, charitable, service, and health organizations in the community. Phil Bowman is chairman of the Finance Committee at University Hospital; Bill Stewart is vice-president of Orchestra London; and David Chalmers is president of Madame Vanier Children's Services.

Price Waterhouse in Canada originated as a single office opened in Montreal in 1907 and is owned and controlled by 210 resident partners, while retaining an association with the World Firm operating in 95 countries.

Senior members of Price Waterhouse in London are (from left) Phil Bowman, managing partner; David Chalmers, audit partner; Steve Wilson, trustee partner; and Bill Stewart, owner-managed business partner.

ROMANUK DESIGN-BUILD INC.

The total-concept approach developed by Ken Romanuk from an extensive career background in the construction field has earned widespread acceptance in the execution of a diversity of building projects in London and surrounding areas.

Romanuk Design-Build Inc. offers single-source responsibility, unparalleled creativity, budget control, and completion on time for jobs ranging from multimillion-dollar complexes to residential renovation. Since 1977 the firm has successfully undertaken hundreds of projects spanning the industrial, commercial, retail, and land development sectors. Recently, Romanuk expertise was applied to the new Hay Stationery head office and showroom on Oxford Street East and the NorWest Do-it Center on Highway 22 near Hyde Park corner.

A graduate in civil technology from Ryerson Institute of Technology, Ken Romanuk came to London with the Engineering Department of the Canadian National Railway in 1963. General contracting work for W.A. MacDougall was followed by a seven-year stint with Sifton Properties Ltd. as construction manager. Then, in 1977, he formed Romanuk Design-Build, assembling an experienced staff that includes key personnel Bill Legg, project manager, with the firm for seven years; Henry Lariviere, a versatile builder for Romanuk from the beginning; and Bill Vanzanten, general superintendent. The founder's wife, Barbara, has served as treasurer from the outset. A staff of 14 permanent employees and up to 70 at peak periods is maintained.

The Romanuk process starts on the drawing board with basic input of space, costs, and objectives from the client. From that point, the company attends to the myriad details of site selection, permits and inspections, design details, and subcontract supervision—even the intricacies of financing a proposed project. The ultimate goal is an optimum building within budget.

In the course of developing, constructing, and renovating commercial malls, plazas, restaurants, industrial warehouses, and financial institutions, Romanuk attracted an exceptionally high volume of 80-percent repeat and referral business. Acquisition of the rights to Butler Building systems in 1980 provided cost-efficient solutions to a wide range of needs, including the capacity to retrofit old buildings and make them more energy efficient.

President Ken Romanuk is active in the London community, serving as a director of the London and District Construction Association and chairman of the Planning and Development Committee of The London Chamber of Commerce.

Veteran employees and principals in Romanuk Design-Build Inc. (from left): Henry Lariviere, Bill Vanzanten, Barbara and Ken Romanuk, and Bill Legg.

The office building project handled by the Romanuk firm for Hatherell, O'Hagan & Co., Chartered Accountants, and designed by Brevick, Scorgie, Wasylko, Architects.

KELLOGG SALADA CANADA INC.

The white concrete and glass facade rising to a height of nine storeys and dominating the skyline of east-end London represents not only a computer-age "factory of the future" but also the ultimate realization of an American revolution in breakfast food manufacturing with a long-standing Canadian connection.

Project 2000 is the culmination of a six-year modernization and expansion program carried out by Kellogg Salada Canada Inc. at a cost of $140 million to fully equip the Eva Street facility for low-cost production of its popular name-brand cereals well into the next century. Blending the latest in technology with human expertise and a co-operative, informed relationship with employees, the massive plant will serve as a test bed for the far-flung empire of the parent Kellogg Company of Battle Creek, Michigan.

The early beginnings of the U.S. company were tentative, disappointing, and successful in turn as Dr. John Kellogg experimented with nutritional foods in the interest of patients in the Battle Creek Sanitorium. He was joined by brother Will K. Kellogg, whose business acumen led to incorporation of the company in 1906 on the heels of limited advances in the production of granola crackers, wheat biscuits, and then the first wheat and corn flakes cereals around 1900.

London's role in the Kellogg enterprise actually predates the American formation of the company, linking to the establishment of the Battle Creek Health Food Company here in March 1905. Kellogg historical records attribute the London venture to Dr. John Kellogg, but a master's thesis by Benjamin S. Scott, a student at the University of Western Ontario in 1930, credits Toronto doctors S. Powell and Van Nostrand with founding the city branch. Scott pinpoints a small building on Grey Street at William Street as the original site in London, and also notes an interest by Powell and Van Nostrand in the work of Dr. Kellogg. It would be logical to regard the fledgling Canadian division as a joint venture.

In any event, the small Grey Street concern was not a financial success and in January 1906 a group of London businessmen bought out the recipes, name,

This 1924 advertisement proclaimed the familiar red, white, and green package the "GENUINE-ORIGINAL" Kellogg's Toasted Corn Flakes, which have been produced in London since 1906.

goodwill, and assets. President of the new firm, called the Battle Creek Toasted Corn Flake Company Limited, was Colonel A.A. Campbell, with Colonel Spitall as secretary and J.M. Moore, Robert Wallace, and Dr. W.F. Roome as shareholders. The Scott thesis relates that they shortly concentrated on the manufacture of corn flakes, for which they paid $75,000 to Dr. Kellogg for the sole rights in Canada. A ready market resulted in several expansions to the Grey Street property, leading to construction of a new facility on Dundas Street East near the McCormick factory in 1915.

The installation of hydroelectric power, new equipment and building extensions, including a new corn mill in 1919, saw the entire manufacturing process consolidated in London. As well, by-products such as hominy feed and grits were marketed under a subsidiary, the Corn Products Company.

Meanwhile, the American company of W.K. Kellogg had established a branch in Toronto in August 1916 for the manufacture of Corn Flakes similar in content and packaging to the London product. Litigation ensued for several years, culminating in a 1923 settlement whereby the U.S. firm bought out the interests of the Battle Creek Toasted Corn Flakes Company Limited. In March 1924 W.K. Kellogg transferred the Toronto operation to London and proceeded to enlarge and re-equip the plant with automatic machinery. Products that would contribute greatly to corporate fortunes—Bran Flakes, All Bran, Pep, and Rice Krispies—were introduced over the next five years. As the decade closed, the facility was running up to 24 hours a day at peak periods with a staff of 170.

With a dominant position commanding 48 percent of the Canadian cereal market today, Kellogg's influence locally and nationally is reflected by a work force exceeding 500 and a product line of 24 cereals. In addition, upwards of 125 million pounds of southwestern Ontario corn is purchased annually, principally from the fields of Kent County under special contract.

Kellogg Salada Canada Inc. is deeply rooted in Canadian business history, with the various components of Salada Foods Ltd. tracing back over 100 years. In 1883 F.A. Shirriff founded the Imperial Extract Company in Toronto to manufacture flavoring essences, jelly powders, and marmalade. Later on, fruit jellies, pie fillings, and puddings were added and the company name was changed to Shirriff's Limited, which eventually merged with Horsey Corporation, a Canadian business active in the Florida citrus industry, to form Shirriff-Horsey Ltd. in late 1955.

Subsequent corporate changes included the acquisitions of the Salada Tea Company of Canada Ltd. in 1957, adoption of the name Salada Foods Ltd. in 1962, and a complete merger with the Kellogg Company of Canada Ltd. in 1975. Kellogg Salada Canada Inc. currently employs 1,500 and operates other manufacturing facilities in Rexdale, Ontario, and Montreal, Quebec.

As part of Kellogg Salada Canada Inc.'s Project 2000 program, this "factory of the future" was completed in 1986 at a cost of $140 million.

CHARTERWAYS TRANSPORTATION LIMITED

The modern school buses and motor coaches of Charterways Transportation Limited have provided vital public conveyance to the London area for close to 30 years.

Charterways today, however, far exceeds local and regional boundaries with far-flung physical and contractual assets traversing Ontario and a large area of the United States. From a small school bus operation founded by John Skinner of nearby Thorndale in 1958, the company has expanded to an employer of 4,800 people with more than 4,350 vehicles under administration.

Through successive plateaus of growth, Charterways has concentrated on bus transportation, commencing with buyouts of small operators in western Ontario between 1958 and 1965. In the same period, the firm secured charter rights out of London and St. Thomas and purchased its first highway coaches. The fleet has since multiplied to 18 superbly designed and engineered coaches on scheduled routes connecting to Greyhound and Gray Coach to the east, north, and west.

Charterways has also maintained corporate headquarters in London over the years, despite heavy involvement in markets elsewhere. A significant early move into the Toronto area saw the company acquire Air Terminal Transport—an express bus and limousine service based at Toronto Airport—which was sold off in 1985. School bus operations were added between 1965 and 1973 in the Toronto area and a dozen communities of southern Ontario, as well as Sault Ste. Marie and Sudbury.

Late-model luxury motor coaches (top) and sturdy school buses (above) ply Charterways routes across Ontario and several American states.

The acquisition of Charterways by Commonwealth Holiday Inns of Canada Limited in June 1975 was followed by the purchase of school bus concerns in Dundalk, Kitchener, and North York, and a diversification into Motor Express Terminals, a freight warehousing and distribution centre in Toronto. In 1979 Commonwealth Holiday Inns (including Charterways) was acquired by Scotts Restaurants, subsequently reconstituted as Scotts Hospitality Incorporated.

Ventures south of the border in the 1980s brought into the Charterways fold some 20 school bus systems in the states of Massachusetts, New York, New Jersey, Illinois, Wisconsin, Maine, New Hampshire, Michigan, and Missouri. The current school bus complement is 4,250 including 1,250 in Canada and 2,500 in the United States which are owned outright, plus 500 under management. A total of 95 trucks—18 motor coaches and 20 dust control vehicles, the latter from a new business bought in 1984—are operated by Charterways.

The London operations base was greatly improved in January 1984 with the opening of a new terminal, comprising a six-bay garage and office building at 135 Towerline Place facing Highway 401. Personnel in London number 140 at the present time. Chairman of Charterways is Bruce Dodds, who is a member of the board of governors of the University of Western Ontario. President is Geoff Davies, who is a past president of both the Ontario Motor Coach Association and the Ontario School Bus Operators' Association.

The new terminal and office of Charterways at 132 Towerline Place in London.

TECUMSEH PRODUCTS OF CANADA, LTD.

Depth of experience at the management level and a burgeoning market for air conditioning and cooling equipment has elevated a small London company to a leadership position in its field. Today Tecumseh Products of Canada, Ltd., has domestic and export sales approaching $60 million annually.

Tecumseh Products of Canada manufactures refrigeration compressors and condensing units at a rate of 2,200 per day under stringent parameters of quality control in a 70,000-square-foot plant at 185 Ashland Avenue. The facility is larger, the equipment updated, and the product completely restyled, but five of the original executives who began business with a staff of 12 in 1960 remain in key positions today. The quintet includes Bill Shadwick, vice-president and general manager; Ted Warren, sales manager; Bill Middaugh, materials control manager; Jack Smith, wholesale, sales, and service manager; and Ross Chamberlain, shipping supervisor.

Now a subsidiary of Tecumseh Products of Tecumseh, Michigan, the company developed from roots in Kelvinator of Canada, which in the early 1950s built its own compressors and also Tecumseh compressors under a licence agreement. Kelvinator marketed the Tecumseh compressors through a subsidiary called Resco (Refrigeration Supplies Company) until 1960, when the licencing arrangement ended.

Five of the original group who are still on staff with Tecumseh Products: Ted Warren and Bill Shadwick (left to right, seated), Ross Chamberlain, Bill Middaugh, and Jack Smith (left to right, standing).

At that point Tecumseh opened its Canadian division in the former General Electric building on Ashland, employing most of the Resco staff. From an early concentration on servicing units, the firm gradually built up manufacturing capacity to sales of four million dollars in 1961 and then $13 million in 1968. Two additions in the mid-1970s brought the plant to its present size; its current staff numbers 140, although peak periods of production have required up to 250 employees.

The market for compressors comprises manufacturers of refrigerators, freezers, dehumidifiers, room air conditioners, and beverage coolers. Condensing units are sold to manufacturers of display cases for food stores and a host of other commercial applications.

Bill Shadwick credits quality and dependability—which is typified by such products as the compact and efficient Hermetic compressor—for the company's success in attracting a solid customer base over the past 26 years. Community activity by Tecumseh Products of Canada, Ltd., in London is exemplified by the award of an annual $4,000 scholarship to an engineering student entering the University of Western Ontario.

J.A. Cowan, vice-president and general manager, September 1, 1960, to December 31, 1968.

C.R. Partridge, vice-president and general manager, January 1, 1969, to August 31, 1979.

W.E. Shadwick, vice-president and general manager since September 1, 1979.

HURON STEEL FABRICATORS (LONDON) LIMITED

The strength and durability of a multitude of private and public buildings bear the imprint of a flourishing structural steel company based in southwest London.

Huron Steel Fabricators (London) Limited at 332 Exeter Road specializes in the custom design and production of steel members for institutional and commercial edifices. At the commodious office-drafting-assembly, where Herman Fratschko started from scratch with a single small building in 1962, the latest advances in computerization and technology are applied to precise configurations for the construction industry. And the entire process is anchored by president Fratschko, whose experience in the intricacies of the steel business dates to postwar Europe.

A mechanical engineer with the Austrian Iron and Steel Works in the late 1940s, Fratschko immigrated to Canada in 1951 and commenced an 11-year association with London Steel as a draftsman, designer, estimator, and salesman. In 1962 he formed Huron Steel with a group of associates whose interests he bought out in 1965.

President and founder Herman Fratschko with son Erich, vice-president.

Solid demand for Huron Steel products locally and nationally led to several expansions of the plant on the present site, culminating in a new office addition in 1975.

With a portfolio of some 3,000 building contracts over the past quarter-century, Huron Steel has furnished components for manufacturing and resource industries across Canada and parts of the United States. In London, involvement has included all of the hospitals, numerous schools, city and provincial buildings, and a large cross-section of industries and warehouses. Herman Fratschko expresses particular pride in his company's role in several challenging church projects as well as structures at the University of Western Ontario. Recently, Huron Steel completed contracts at the Sears store in the Masonville Shopping Centre and the National Centre for Management Research at Western. Earlier undertakings were Westmount Mall, Saunders High School, and the first building at Huron College on the UWO campus in 1963.

The tradition of family ownership is continuing at Huron Steel with Erich Fratschko, son of the founder, serving as vice-president. A permanent staff of 35 with competence in all aspects of structural steel fabrication is maintained by the firm.

The head office and assembly plant of Huron Steel Fabricators (London) Limited.

W.G. YOUNG COMPANY LTD.

W.G. Young Company Ltd. consists of many associated companies: Highland Investments; Young's Jewellers, a family of fine stores; H.R. English & Company Ltd., a jewellery-manufacturing division; George A. Young & Company Ltd., a contract sales division; and Robert Young Interiors Ltd. In all, more than 250 people are employed, including some with 40 years' service. In the past the organization was involved in other manufacturing, such as Hentschel clocks and world-famous Baetz furniture.

William G. Young, founder, 1894-1939.

George A. Young, president, 1939-1974.

Founder William G. Young, a master engraver and jeweller in his own right, opened the first store in London on April 1, 1894. Succeeding generations of "Young" presidents—George A. Young, who piloted the firm through the Depression years; and William B. Young, current president and chief executive officer, and also a graduate jeweller—have fostered steady growth through expansion and modernization programs blended with traditional business philosophies.

After operating out of one of the stores for 50 years, Young's established its first head office at 361 Richmond Street in London. In 1965 the present head office and distribution centre was built at 277 Adelaide Street South. The initial expansion out of London to Kitchener in 1933, has led to a 29-store retail network located in most major cities throughout Ontario.

The downtown London store at 214 Dundas Street, circa 1905-1908.

Young's has always encouraged involvement in the community and the jewellery industry by management and staff. George A. Young was president of the Canadian Jewellers' Association and president of the Canadian Jewellers' 24K Club. When William B. Young subsequently headed the 24K Club, he completed the first father and son occupancy of that office. A fourth generation of the Young family is represented in the business by the president's two daughters, Debbie Breivik and Barbara Mitchell, son, Bill Jr., and son-in-law, Chris Grover. Top-ranking executives of the company are vice-presidents T. Alan Dickinson, president of the Canadian Jewellers' Association in 1985-1986, Michael P. Johns, and Terry Mizzen, all of whom are active in a wide spectrum of civic service, church, and athletic endeavors.

William B. Young, president.

Robert Young, eldest son of George A. Young, has been singularly responsible for the interior design and merchandise presentation in the stores. He is the founder of Robert Young Interiors, a successful interior decorating venture for residential and commercial projects.

DIESEL DIVISION GENERAL MOTORS OF CANADA LIMITED

World power.

To most people, the term conjures an image of international politics. In London, "world power" means Diesel Division, General Motors of Canada Limited.

The company is widely recognized as Canada's leading manufacturer and marketer of power products ranging from highway truck engines to high-tech military vehicles. Furthermore, Diesel Division is one of the world's largest exporters of locomotives.

The 204-acre site has been a mainstay of London's industrial east end since 1950. Originally built to produce locomotives for Canadian railways, the plant has been expanded and refurbished many times over to support its drive into diverse markets: transit buses, off-road mining haulers, export locomotives, amphibious armored vehicles, and a myriad of power components for transportation and resource industries.

Over the years Diesel Division has emerged as a specialist in very-large-scale weldments and assemblies. Barely a handful of North American companies can approach the scope and dimension of facilities that now occupy the 37.5 acres of plant and operations buildings. In addition to its massive production machinery, the complex houses a pool of expertise in design, engineering, and parts and service. At the heart of its competitive capability is a corps of 2,000 highly trained employees providing a full spectrum of skills in all disciplines.

Its founding was prompted by a turning point in Canadian transportation history. Railway power was converting from steam to diesel, and Canada urgently needed these new locomotives. GM answered the call by forming Diesel Division in 1949. The plant was completed in time to deliver its first unit the following year. An engineering building was added soon after and, in 1953, an expansion readied the plant for its entry into export markets. In 1956 additions totaling 18,000 square feet introduced much-needed warehousing and test facilities.

Since the delivery of that first unit, the company has produced more than 3,300 diesel-electric locomotives for Canadian customers and another 1,200 for foreign buyers. Models have ranged from small yard switchers to huge 3,800-horsepower mainline freight locomotives. Recently, the plant delivered Canada's first all-electric heavy-freight 6,000-horsepower locomotive.

Diversification came in 1961, when the firm began assembling GM buses in London. A second plant was opened in Ville Ste. Laurent, Quebec, in 1974. While transit service and engineering are still based in London, manufacturing was consolidated in a new facility

The Diesel Division manufacturing complex now covers over 200 acres.

The first SD6OF, 16-cylinder, 710-engine microprocessor.

Heading for the main line. Locomotive model FP7A, 1950.

Engineering drawings being prepared for production in the early 1950s.

near Montreal in 1979. With a capacity of five buses per day, Diesel Division has delivered more than 10,000 units for service in cities from Alaska to Florida and from British Columbia to Newfoundland. This product line marked a major milestone in 1982 with the launch of the "Classic" bus, the first GM bus wholly designed, built, and tested by the Canadian company.

A much earlier addition to the London operation was Canadian marketing responsibility for Detroit Diesel engines. Established here since 1952, the distribution and service network gives the organization a valuable window into the power requirements of Canada's trucking, mining, construction, forestry, marine, and petroleum industries. In 1984 the division also took on the responsibility for the sale of Allison transmissions to original-equipment manufacturers, bringing the complete Detroit Diesel Allison line under one Canadian source.

In 1965 Diesel Division acquired Canadian responsibility for producing GM earth-moving equipment. Six years later the 33-15 hauler was unveiled—a "locomotive on rubber wheels" designed and built in Canada to handle 175-ton payloads for the open-pit mines of the world. Then, in 1974, the 33-15's big brother—the 350-ton-capacity Titan, still listed in the *Guiness Book of World Records* as the biggest off-road truck ever built—was unveiled.

The division can point to several more all-Canadian products developed by its London staff. A series of locomotives produced for the 42-inch-gauge railway lines of Newfoundland were the first narrow-gauge units produced by any GM plant. The Model G locomotive, designed in collaboration with GM's Electro-Motive Division in the United States, was the forerunner of today's successful export models.

Every new GM locomotive in the world, in fact, incorporates certain specialized components for which the London plant is the sole source.

In recent years Diesel Division has become the lead player in an international GM team developing, marketing, and supporting armored military vehicles. The defence sales group earned its first contract in 1977, calling for a fleet of 350 six-wheeled vehicles for the Canadian Forces. This order was later increased to 491 units. Since then, orders from Canadian and U.S. forces have led to the creation of one of the most technologically advanced vehicle production, test, and support facilities in North America.

To win certification under the world's most demanding military standards, the division has fine tuned its exhaustive quality-assurance systems, cost-control plans, and computerized parts management programs.

Commitment to "customer satisfaction" has evolved into a rigorous quality discipline uniting every aspect of the company's products and field services. Now, with satisfied customers in more than 20 nations, Diesel Division has firmly staked its claim as a leader in world power.

Welder confirming design details on locomotive model FP7A, 1950.

Robotic welding: robots at work within the General Motors' system ensuring quality every time.

Cad/Cam office: the world of the twenty-first century.

Indonesian locomotive model G26MC-2, 1986, the lowest-profile unit General Motors has ever built.

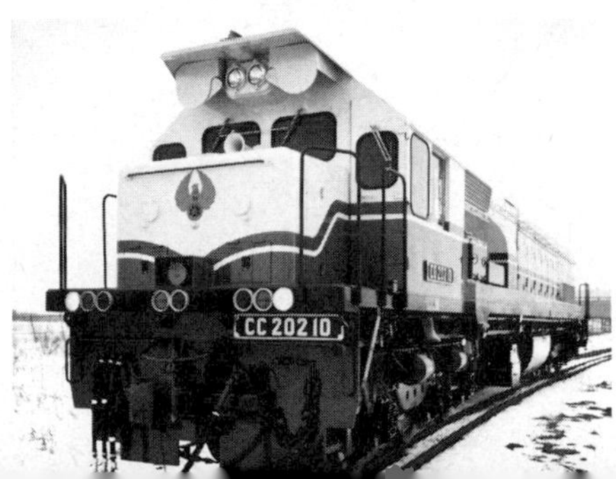

PARKWOOD HOSPITAL

An abiding concern for the plight of the elderly, the infirm, and the less fortunate in the community has served as the guiding inspiration of the Women's Christian Association of London for well over a century. Today the spirit of dedication and determination responsible for a solid record of accomplishment in the city is abundantly present in the organization's crowning achievement—Parkwood Hospital—a model facility specializing in long-term care and rehabilitation.

From the first informal alliance of caring members who recognized the need for aid to the sick and the deprived in 1874, the association moved swiftly to rectify areas of neglect. A Women's Refuge and Infants' Home was followed by the McCormick Home for aged men and women and a Home for Incurables by the time of the 25th anniversary.

In 1921 the WCA expanded its horizons with the acquisition of a stately Victorian house at 81 Grand Avenue, which would be developed as the first Parkwood Hospital. With additions and alterations, the residence sufficed until January 1985 when the new Parkwood Hospital on the Westminster Campus was occupied.

Like earlier projects of the WCA, the realization of Parkwood was fraught with degrees of delay, frustration, and revision from the time in 1968 when a master plan for a new facility was drawn. Although enjoying high government priority, the 475-bed hospital on 25 acres south of Commissioners Road and east of Wellington had to await health care studies and survive funding shortages before the first sod was turned on November 26, 1982. By that time Parkwood had accepted responsibility for the chronic care of veterans from the Veterans Care Centre and Western Counties Wing on the Westminster Campus.

From the moment the hospital plan was activated, input combining sensitivity, insight, research, and care flowed into the design of the $43.3-million structure. Architects, engineers, and other experts in hospital construction worked as a team to attain comfort and efficiency in an attractive, humanized environment. Consultation with staff and patients, experiments with mock-up rooms and mechanical systems, layout, landscaping, and color selection resulted in a functional, yet noninstitution-

The hydrotherapy pool is a popular feature of the rehabilitation centre.

Most patients' rooms face south, overlooking beautifully landscaped grounds.

An unusually quiet moment in the lobby. Courtesy, Media Centre Ontario Hospital Association

like structure—literally "a home with a view."

From the front, the building has a low, residential profile of four storeys; from the back, making full use of gently sloping land, five storeys open on to landscaped gardens, including many paths for wheelchairs.

The two pods of the hospital are connected at each level by a link. On the two lower levels, the cafeteria and main lobby form the link. On Level 3, the first patient floor, the link is a spacious lounge, with a panoramic window overlooking the grounds and space for recreational activities. On Level 4 is located another lounge and the Volunteer Services Department, while on Level 5 the Chapel connects pods A and B.

To the greatest possible extent, patient accommodation affords a view of the rolling landscape with the woods surrounding the Westminster Ponds. Nestling close to the building is a garden specially designed for people who use wheelchairs, with moderately sloped pathways, benches, and large planters for gardening accessible to the disabled. On the other side of the building is a scenic view of the city.

While bed capacity essentially replaced two existing facilities, the new hospital offers substantially more care to the community through new and expanded programs, including the Day Hospital, which operated at the previous site for six years and is equipped to treat more patients who continue to live in their own homes; the Palliative Care Unit, expanded from 5 to 14 beds, with an outreach program; the Regional Rehabilitation Centre, with 40 inpatient beds and outpatient services, to assist the rehabilitation of people who have been severely injured (this is the first such centre in western Ontario); and the Geriatric Teaching Unit, a 40-bed facility based on the philosophy that age itself is not a disease and that elderly people are capable of much independence, given the right treatment and support.

The openness and spaciousness of Parkwood is accentuated throughout the structure by such features as the large auditorium, which seats 400 with a stage accessible by wheelchair as well as an amplification system for the hard-of-hearing, and the main lobby with a downtown atmosphere created by street names, shops, and stores.

Advanced therapy and rehabilitation are an integral part of the hospital program, supported by the latest equipment and specialized teams of professionals. In physiotherapy a therapeutic pool, easily accessible to people in wheelchairs, and a Hubbard tank, or whirlpool, are used for hydrotherapy treatments. In speech pathology, a sound chamber provides audiology testing. A well-equipped "Daily Living" room helps to retrain patients for life outside the hospital.

Overall, Parkwood is a marvel of medical science and technology joined in an enlightened approach to the handicapped of all ages. From another perspective, the hospital is as much an accolade to the principle of community service fostered by the Women's Christian Association over a period of 112 years.

The cafeteria is a solarium for year-round use by patients and staff. Courtesy, Media Centre Ontario Hospital Association

R.C. DAWSON COMPANY LIMITED

Since its inception 16 years ago, a London design consultant specializing in office interiors and space planning has attracted an increasingly large commercial clientele across Canada.

R.C. Dawson Company Limited is a team operation offering professional advice on all phases of office environment, together with competent service and supervision—in all a total-concept approach. Additionally, the firm has access to more than 300 lines of furnishings and accessories from leading manufacturers.

The new head office facility, opened in June 1985 at 544 Egerton Street, is itself a showcase of design and decor that bears little resemblance to the one-van furniture dealership started by president Ron C. Dawson in a rented building at Ashland and Dundas in 1970. The ensuing years have also seen the development of a fleet of nine vehicles and a highly trained staff of approximately 36 people, including six graduate designers, with access to consulting engineers and architects.

The founder brought a wealth of experience to the fledgling business, having owned and operated Towne and Country Furniture Limited—a manufacturer of custom upholstered furniture at 825 Central Avenue—from 1955 to 1968, at which time the company was sold. Towne and Country was widely recognized for craftsmanship in the supply of furniture to Ontario House in London, England; the Canadian Embassy in Hong Kong; the Dallas Airport lounge; and the Queen's Park office of then-Premier John Robarts.

Management positions are held by family members David R. Dawson, systems coordinator; Ronald C. Dawson, president; Laurie H. Pomeroy, customer relations; and Craig A. Dawson, vice-president, operations.

By 1973 Dawson's new enterprise required more space, and the present site was acquired as well as an adjacent car sales lot for warehousing. Subsequent purchases of property on the north and east sides resulted in an area spanning 250 by 250 feet. With office, design, and storage facilities bursting at the seams, the organization embarked on a major building program in 1984. Construction work included a second storey on the office, steel siding, extensive interior renovation, and a new 50- by 80-foot warehouse.

R.C. Dawson concentrates on a full-service market within 150 miles of London, but undertakes jobs from Western Canada to the Maritimes. The founder's sons, Craig and David, and daughter, Laurie Pomeroy, hold executive positions with the firm. Treasurer Russell Pennington, C.A., is a valued longtime employee.

Active in the community, Ron Dawson is currently president of The London Chamber of Commerce and chairman of the Small Business Committee of the Canadian Chamber of Commerce.

The expanded, modernized head office and warehouse building of R.C. Dawson Company Limited on Egerton Street.

McKERLIE-MILLEN INC.

The far-flung automobile parts supply business operated by McKerlie-Millen Inc. in Ontario and Quebec has called London home base for close to four decades. Through eras of expansion, merger, and corporate change, company headquarters has remained at the original Horton Street site where L.F. "Lou" McKerlie, S.A. McKay, T.G. Byway, and J.A. McMillan set up shop in a tiny cement block building in the summer of 1948.

That winter, McKerlie and associates erected a new 5,000-square-foot building, and by spring 1949 they embarked on a branch network (the first outlet was in Owen Sound) that would eventually extend the breadth of the province. As dramatic growth ensued in the 1950s and 1960s, the company built a solid foundation on parts supply, machine shop service, and efficient distribution. The formation of Automotive Warehousing Limited, staged additions to London headquarters, and the installation of data-processing equipment further strengthened the organization.

McKerlie-Millen's Ontario management team.

The present name McKerlie-Millen derives in part from a similar business in Quebec, John Millen and Sons Limited, which prospered from an early 1900s perception of demand for car replacement parts. By 1967 McKerlie Automotive and Millen had developed their own central warehousing systems supplying a network of jobbing stores—both company-owned and independent—and both had created enviable reputations in the industry. In 1967 both firms became part of Steego Corporation, which controls automotive parts stores throughout the eastern United States, from Florida to New England, in a transaction described by Lou McKerlie as essential to the continued viability of the organization. Subsequently, the merger to form McKerlie-Millen Inc. was effected in 1974.

In the meantime, McKerlie and Millen had launched their Associate store programs simultaneously in 1972 with the goal of achieving further market penetration by inviting independents to affiliate. Today 170 Associate stores are serviced by McKerlie-Millen in Ontario and Quebec, representing what president Greg Stone regards as a "rock solid" alliance. The Associates and the 72 stores owned outright by the company benefit from year-round marketing and sales promotion emanating from head office. Additional properties of McKerlie-Millen include seven warehouses and 42 co-owned machine shops in the two provinces.

Buttressed by well-trained staff, modern equipment, and quality service and products, McKerlie-Millen Inc. is geared to serve a widening market not only in the automobile field but also in the industrial, agricultural, and do-it-yourself sectors.

The firm's outlets carry a complete range of automotive supplies, accessories, and service items.

THE LONDON METAL SERVICE LIMITED

An accurate assessment of rising demand for sheet metal for heating and ventilating applications more than 50 years ago set in motion the development and expansion of The London Metal Service Limited, a major distributor and wholesaler serving southern Ontario.

Alfred Barnett—the man who perceived the potential of the company and who still serves as chairman of the board—was in fact the first customer of the founder, Bill Clifton, who established London Metal Service in 1933. At the time, Barnett was a sheet metal contractor buying sheet metal for his shop in the old McClary Building on the present site of the Wellington Square Mall. By 1942 Barnett was in partnership with Clifton, and by 1950 he had acquired full ownership. In the early years the firm set up warehouses in the old Perin Building and then in the Baldwin Building, both on Carling Street. (During World War II Barnett earned respect and goodwill among tradesmen by distributing steel rations on an equitable basis, thereby keeping many in business.)

Purchase of the present site at 675 York Street and construction of the original warehouse in 1950 formed the nucleus of a one-stop shop of supplies for the sheet metal, heating, ventilating and air-conditioning trades. From 1959 to 1980 no fewer than five plant expansions and additions were carried out, including the purchase in 1968 of the adjoining Imperial Oil property and late-1800s warehouse—which is still in use. In all, the company has 35,000 square feet under roof on a 4.5-acre site.

The London Metal Service Limited is far advanced not only in size but in the technology that has evolved from wood- and coal-fired units to energy-efficient furnaces, bi-metal thermostats to programmable, computer-driven energy management systems, and hot-dipped steel to electroplated, galvanized, and special coatings. As a flat-rolled steel service centre and HVAC supply house, the company stocks more than 11,000 items from over 250 leading manufacturers and also offers complete semi-finishing steel-processing services.

Three generations of the Barnett family involvement in the company are pictured here. They are (front, from left) chairman Alfred Barnett and president W.L. "Bill" Barnett. Standing (from left) are Thomas Barnett; Robert Barnett, vice-president and secretary; W.J. "Bill" Barnett; and John Barnett.

Alfred Barnett's sons, Bill and Bob, assumed ownership in 1971 and are president and vice-president, respectively, and a third generation is already on staff in the persons of John, Bill, and Thom Barnett. A roster of 26 full-time employees represents a high level of stability with 15 years' average service.

In recent years the president and vice-president have been especially active in national and international trade associations, reflecting their commitment to the continual upgrading of their business and the industry they serve.

The office, plant, and warehouse of The London Metal Service Limited.

LOEB INC.

The London Distribution Centre of Loeb Inc. is approaching 25 years of service as a major wholesaler of food products and a growing line of confectioneries, tobacco, and other merchandise to southwestern Ontario.

Within the 190,649-square-foot office and warehouse building on Clarke Side Road, a finely tuned team effort dispatches more than three million items annually to an area bounded by Toronto and St. Catharines on the east, Barrie/Owen Sound to the north, and Windsor on the west. Some 265 employees are involved in various phases of administration, marketing, consumer analysis, and produce management, while transportation requirements are served by a fleet of 44 tractors, trailers, and straight trucks, logging one million miles annually.

A forerunner of the Loeb operation in London was the T.B. Escott Company, the original IGA franchise holder in southwestern Ontario, which was purchased by Foodway Distributors in 1959 and then acquired by Loeb three years later. The company bears the name of its founder, Moses Loeb, who started a small wholesale confectionery house in Ottawa in 1912 and expanded into western Quebec and eastern and northern Ontario in the 1950s. Subsequently, Provigo Inc. of Montreal, a national wholesaler with current sales exceeding four billion dollars, acquired Loeb in 1979.

Part of Loeb's fleet of vehicles serving southwestern Ontario.

Today Loeb Inc. consists of six operating divisions, of which four, including the London organization, are IGA franchise divisions providing support systems to a total of 113 IGA stores. The London franchise encompasses 14 counties—Grey, Bruce, Wellington, Waterloo, Brant, Middlesex, Lambton, Norfolk, Huron, Perth, Oxford, Elgin, Kent, and Essex—and supplies 21 IGA stores, 10 Cash and Carrys, Cash and Carrys in the Ottawa area (with institutional products), and a number of unaffilliated independents.

An extensive inventory is maintained at the London Distribution Centre, comprising a full line of groceries, health and beauty aids, dairy products, frozen food, store supplies, and tobacco and confectioneries. The divison also carries a wide variety of institutional merchandise to service London and Sudbury division Cash and Carrys, and co-ordinates with the Capital City Transport Terminal in Toronto for the movement of merchandise around the province.

Support systems available to retailers through Loeb Inc. entail specialized advertising, accounting, human resource, design, and engineering services. In addition, the firm develops new store sites and assists new franchisees with financing.

From the firm's London base, Loeb Inc. general manager Ken Stashick and his staff are committed to aggressive merchandising, improved operations and productivity, and a mandate for expansion in southwestern Ontario over the next three years.

The headquarters, warehouse, and transportation terminal of the London Distribution Centre of Loeb Inc.

PRA INTERNATIONAL INC.

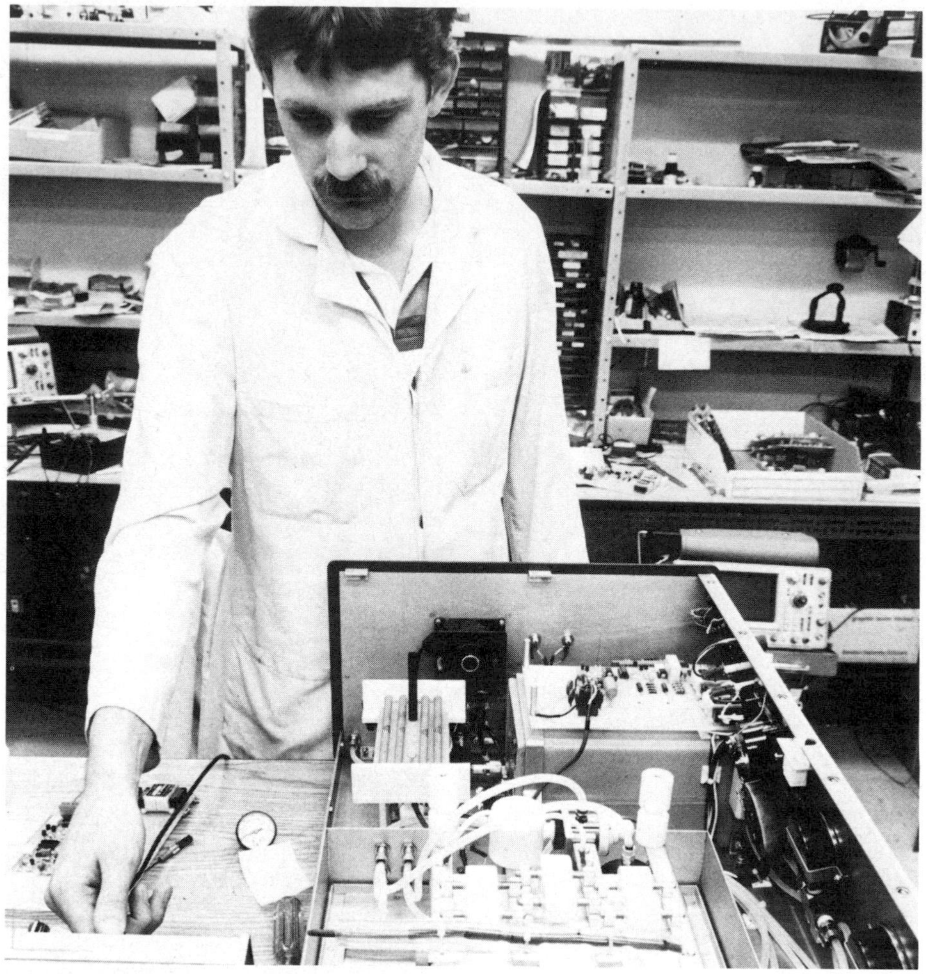

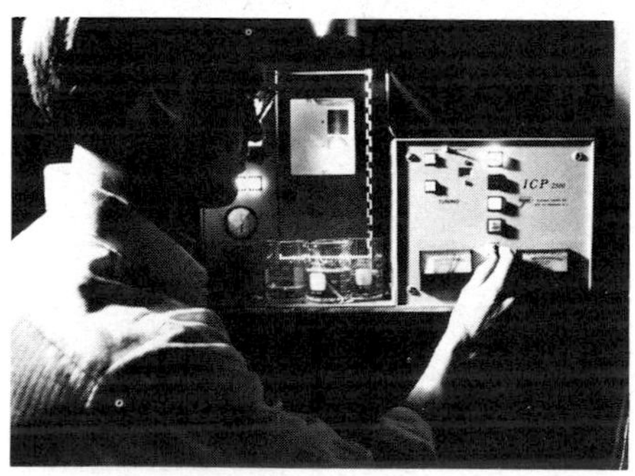

Fine instruments, assembled and tested in the laboratories of PRA International Inc., are reaching a broad market in the world scientific community.

An emphasis on high-technology products with a focussed marketing approach has secured a bright future for PRA International Inc. as a worldwide supplier of equipment for research.

The company, located at 45 Meg Drive in south London, is a manufacturer of electro-optical instrumentation, more specifically, instruments used for light generation, detection, and analysis. PRA products service a variety of scientific markets in the academic, industrial, and government sectors, and recent additions to its high-technology line have found acceptance in the areas of medical and industrial quality assurance.

The development of precision instruments, such as fluorescence lifetime instruments capable of measuring light emission from samples to the billionth of a second, has earned PRA an international reputation as well as support from all levels of government in keeping with national interest in the high-tech field.

With a large commitment to inhouse research and development and proven expertise in optical, electronic, and mechanical design, the firm is a strong contender for contract research and development as well as prototype manufacture.

The corporation also supplies a complete range of dye laser systems, including the Megaplus 2MW, the most powerful nitrogen laser commercially available. Laser Raman spectrometers, of interest to industrial polymer and fibre chemists, and more recently plasma emission spectrometers, representing a breakthrough in measuring trace concentrations of elements, are part of a growing product line marketed principally in the United States, Europe, Asia, and some Third World countries.

PRA International Inc. was established in 1976 to commercialize products originally developed by the Photochemistry Unit of the Department of Chemistry at the University of Western Ontario. The unit was one of the first of its kind in North America—an assemblage of renowned researchers occupied exclusively with the study of photochemistry and photophysics.

In 1979 a small group of private investors acquired a controlling interest in PRA from the university and relocated the operation to its present site. There its staff of 57 is based in 25,000 square feet of office, production, research, and development space.

From inception, more than 50 unique electro-optical products have been developed by PRA International Inc. at the London facility, where the opportunity is afforded customers to "test drive" working instruments in applications laboratories.

RAY CULLEN CHEVROLET LTD.

The transition from professional hockey to automobile sales was a predictable, perhaps inevitable, career choice for Ray Cullen, the president and owner of a high-volume General Motors Chevrolet dealership at 730 Wharncliffe Road South.

The youngest of three St. Catharines brothers whose names were emblazoned across North American sports pages for a couple of decades, he duplicated first the timing and then the success that accompanied the earlier passage of Brian and Barry from one fast lane to another. In a remarkable progression of decision making, the trio elected retirement from the National Hockey League at age 29 and subsequent entry into southern Ontario GM agencies (Brian is based in St. Catharines and Barry in Guelph). Today each is well established in the automobile business and a familiar figure to television and newspaper audiences in their respective markets.

A member of the Memorial Cup champion St. Catharines Tee Pees in 1959-1960, Ray Cullen played with the Minnesota North Stars for three seasons and also saw service with the New York Rangers, Detroit Red Wings, and Vancouver Canucks in the NHL. Joining Brian in 1970 he rose to general manager before accepting the challenge of launching a GM dealership in London in 1977. Although faced with constructing a showroom and garage, and assembling a staff from scratch, he assessed London as an ideal business and family location.

Ray Cullen, president and owner, traded a career with the National Hockey League for the Chevrolet dealership at 730 Wharncliffe Road South that bears his well-known name.

From an original staff of 14, Ray Cullen Chevrolet Ltd. now employs a staff of 70, including two of the proprietor's five sons: Gary, who is assistant sales manager; and Jeff, serving in sales operations. In 1985 sales volume was $22 million from 900 new and 450 used vehicles. That year also saw a $125,000 expansion program, adding six service and three body-shop bays on the 3.2-acre site. A two-acre property was recently acquired a mile north of the present site as a compound for new cars. Currently one of the stars in the Chevrolet lineup is the subcompact Nova, being manufactured by the GM-Toyota joint venture in California.

Ray Cullen is active in the community as president of the Highland Physiotherapy Clinic, a nonprofit treatment centre for accident victims. A past president of the London Franchised Automobile Dealers' Association, he is presently a director of the Ontario Automobile Dealers' Association.

EMCO LIMITED

A multinational corporation headquartered in London from its inception 80 years ago, Emco Limited is an outstanding Canadian business success with manufacturing operations in seven countries from the Pacific Rim to Europe and marketing activity in more than 100 nations. The company's history, dating back to a modest nineteenth-century plumbing shop on Richmond Street, is a fascinating account of vision and unwavering determination on the part of founder Thomas Allin Stevens and successive generations of leadership who guided the enterprise through periods of economic crisis and adversity to status as a very large and visible global supplier to home and industry.

Just as Stevens and partners William Turner and James Burns staked their fortunes on the rising expectations of a growing community—they built the first city waterworks in 1878—Emco has adjusted and expanded over the years to meet consumer and industrial requirements in the new age of technology. From a broad base of plumbing supplies, the firm has moved strongly into such areas as fluid-handling equipment for the petroleum industry and custom forgings. In that respect, Emco is a big player in the world market, having rung up a record sales volume of $506 million in 1985; but the underlying principles of integrity, quality, and initiative instilled by Tom Stevens remain very much in place.

New food preparation centre featuring integrated accessories by Waltec Sinkware.

By the turn of the century, the entrepreneur's foundry had failed after a fling at producing steam engines for farm machinery; and a second venture, The Stevens Manufacturing Company, had folded after a few unprofitable years devoted to household fixtures. In 1903 he joined with J.R. Minhinnick and George Trudell to incorporate The Empire Manufacturing Company—first located in a foundry at 443 Talbot Street, then moving two years later to a factory and warehouse on Governor's Road (now Dundas Street). This was the beginning of Emco and the involvement of the Ivey family through Charles Henry Ivey, a London lawyer who accepted shares for legal services. In 1911 his son of the same name joined the firm as an electrical engineer, setting the stage for a working alliance with J.H. "Jack" Stevens, a grandson of the founder, which would lead to some of the organization's greatest advancements.

Empire Manufacturing prospered in the early 1900s, converting to munitions production during World War I and promptly moving on in 1918 to implement Tom Stevens' plan for a company-owned sales network anchored by National Plumbing Supplies Company of Toronto, which had been acquired in 1916. Valves, faucets, and other items for the plumbing

Emco's head office and factory as it looked during the early days on Governor's Road (Dundas Street East). Incorporated in 1906 as Empire Mfg. Co. Limited, the company subsequently became Empire Brass Manufacturing Company Limited, and now operates under its updated corporate name, Emco Limited.

and heating trade met ready acceptance in the peacetime market, and the firm expanded westward to Manitoba and British Columbia. In 1927 Jack Stevens perceived an opportunity to participate in the national automobile boom through an arrangement with the A.W. Wheaton Company of Union, New Jersey, to sell valves, nozzles, and fittings to service stations in Canada. Securing a licence to sell Wheaton products in the British Empire, Empire Brass (the name had been changed in 1920) ventured overseas for the first time.

Sales and profits continued on an upward course through the 1920s—until the crash of 1929, a calamity compounded by the death of Tom Stevens on January 6, 1930. His youngest son, Chester, became president and managed to preserve the company by imposing rigid economies. When a turnaround finally commenced in 1938, Empire Brass was trim, fit, and hungry. With Chester Stevens coordinating, the operating team of Charlie Ivey and Jack Stevens swung into action.

A second wartime transition to military work was followed in 1946 by the purchase of control by Charlie Ivey and his brother, Richard, from the Stevens family. Empire Brass moved to leadership in the industry, built a strong sales force, and capped the spurt in growth by acquiring in 1953 The Thomas Robertson Company of Montreal—a major plumbing and metal supply house. As further acquisitions and branch extensions occurred over the next two decades, the range of products from plants and through licensing agreements was broadened. Notable additions were the single-handle "Delta" water faucet in 1960, and a venture into plastics with a Toronto factory in 1966.

Ivey family control of Emco (the corporate name adopted in 1957) ended in 1973 when the Masco Corporation of Michigan purchased 49 percent of the company. During 1977 new marketing skills and products were introduced for the growing "do-it-yourself" trend in North America—a major factor in the replacement market for faucets. Meanwhile, expansion outside of Canada had proceeded apace with the manufacture of petroleum-handling equipment in Britain in 1949, then Germany (1957), Australia (1962), and France (1966). Emco established operations in Japan and acquired the Wheaton firm in 1967, prior to opening a plant in Brazil in 1973. Under the umbrella of Emco Wheaton International, a number of fluid-handling subsidiaries were added to the corporation between 1979 and 1981. Yet three-quarters of profits continued to derive from the traditional plumbing and industrial group.

En route to its overall record volume in 1985, Emco reached $100 million in sales in 1971, $200 million in 1978, and $300 million in 1980. The latest operating improvement is partly attributable to the 1984 purchase of Waltec Inc., a multidivision North American manufacturer of a broad range of plumbing products, stainless steel sinks, custom plastic components, and nonferrous forgings in brass, copper, and aluminum. Walker Steel Corporation manufactures wellhead control equipment, down-hole pumping systems, and high-pressure valves for producing oil and gas wells. During 1985 Emco acquired several small companies and a new product line that strengthened its ability to service various markets. Starkman's Plumbing and Heating Limited (Almar), leading supplier of hand showers to the retail trade in Canada, was purchased by Delta Faucet of Canada Limited. The acquisition of the custom forgings division of the Canada Metal Company makes Waltec Components the major supplier of nonferrous forgings to the Canadian market.

An important event in April 1986 was the purchase of Western Supplies Limited, a wholesale distributor of plumbing, heating, and piping products. The addition of Western Supplies creates a truly national network, and provides Emco with a coast-to-coast distribution system of 75 branches.

Emco management is committed to continued expansion and diversification in related fields, as well as internal growth, reflecting an entrepreneurial spirit in the mode of founder Tom Stevens.

European styling highlights Delta's "Epic" collection of faucets.

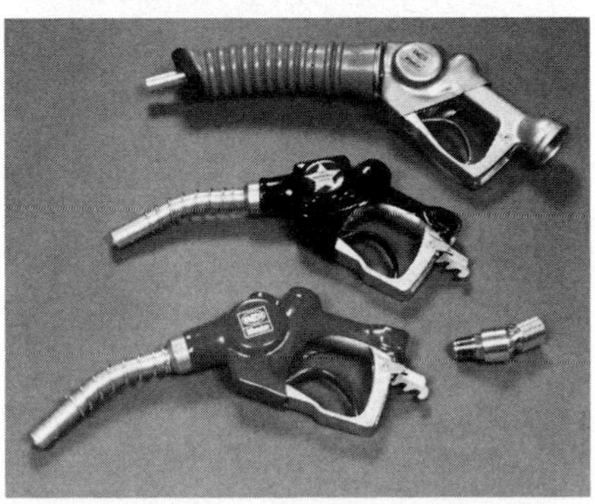

With more than 72 products, service station equipment is Emco Wheaton Inc.'s largest product group.

M.M. DILLON LIMITED

A distinguished military figure and professional engineer, Brigadier M. Murray Dillon was the founder of a company that has changed the face of London, while leaving an imprint on public and private projects across Canada and abroad.

Forty years have elapsed since Dillon returned to London from a World War II assignment supervising Canadian Army construction to reestablish his consulting structural engineering practice. Late in 1945 he formed M.M. Dillon and Company in partnerhip with Colonel George E. Humphries, and began operations in the basement of a house on Horton Street with one draftsman and a part-time secretary.

Geared to design and contract administration for the building industry, the firm soon added architectural service—a continuing component to this day—and branched into structural design for bridges in the city and surrounding area. Within a year the company required new quarters in the Toronto Dominion Bank building at Richmond and King streets. Four additional partners, R.M. Dillon, D.M. Gunn, I.D. Patterson, and G.M. Burns, came aboard in 1948, followed by Middlesex County engineer W. Ken Clawson three years later.

In 1953 the business was incorporated to form M.M. Dillon and Company Limited. Expansion to new areas began with the opening of a Toronto office in 1956. Today Dillon offices operate in 12 Canadian cities, from Halifax (Porter Dillon Ltd.) to Alberta and the Northwest Territories (GCG Dillon Consulting Ltd.). The firm's staff of 300 people provides a broad range of engineering, scientific, and planning services. Professional fees have escalated from $18,500 in 1946 to approximately $15 million in 1986.

Brigadier M. Murray Dillon, company founder.

Colonel George E. Humphries, founding partner.

Currently, the London office is located at 495 Richmond Street in a building designed by Dillon in 1972. There, 70 staff members provide administration and professional services in civil and environmental engineering and building design.

The London office building of M.M. Dillon Limited at 495 Richmond Street.

The company has designed and supervised many projects familiar to Londoners, including water reservoirs, water- and waste-treatment plants; Airport and Wonderland roads; the Guy Lombardo, Queens, Wharncliffe Road, and Adelaide Street bridges; Wolseley Barracks installations; and dams, bridges, subdivisions, and industrial plants throughout western Ontario.

Employees of M.M. Dillon Limited have contributed significantly to community and professional organizations. George Humphries served as president of the Engineering Institute of Canada and the Association of Consulting Engineers of Canada. Richard M. Dillon was appointed dean of the new Faculty of Engineering Science at the University of Western Ontario in 1960.

Under the guidance of President James H. Kearney, the firm continues to grow to serve the changing needs of private and government clients.

PHILLIPS TOOL & MOULD (LONDON) LIMITED

The closely co-ordinated production and development facilities of Phillips Tool & Mould (London) Limited deliver a total capability in the provision of interior components to the automobile industry. From a background of lengthy experience in the tool and die making trade, president Otto Phillips has taken the company all the way to finished armrests, dashboards and steering wheels, with an assured market for 90 percent of output among the major U.S. car manufacturers.

The newly enlarged Pulsar division on White Oaks Road, which produces interior fittings for the automobile industry.

Phillips Tool & Mould, presently the umbrella organization for the multi-unit operation at several south London locations, was the founder's original venture in the city. Previously the manager of a local tool firm, he went on his own in 1975 with a staff of four and 5,000 square feet of leased space at 1050 Hargrieve Road.

The new company was soon handling a rising volume of plastic-injection and compression moulds, die casting, and general machine work. As the business flourished, Phillips relocated at 25 Invicta Court in 1979, occupying 20,000 square feet while retaining (to the present time) the Hargrieve property. Subsequently, he purchased the Invicta Court building in 1984, enlarging it to 28,000 square feet with the completion of an engineering facility in 1986.

In the meantime Phillips had established Pulsar Plastics Limited in 1981 at Cobourg, Ontario, a step that soon vindicated his confidence by attracting an increasing flow of orders from General Motors of Canada. Exports to the United States commenced in 1983, along with expansion of the product line through development of a rotational moulding facility. The high point of the year occurred when Fisher Body USA selected Pulsar as a source for several interior-trim contracts.

The original plant of the Phillips companies at 25 Invicta Court in south London.

Shortly thereafter Phillips purchased a 35,000-square-foot plant on White Oaks Road in London to centralize the Pulsar enterprise, which by 1984 was totally targeted on U.S. customers. With a recent addition enhancing the frontage on White Oaks, Pulsar has been extended to more than 80,000 square feet and employs 180 people in the production of quality, precision-made trim for a variety of automotive applications. The Phillips organization employs another 80 persons at PT&M, 15 in its Pour Mould Division, 10 in the McAdams Model Shop, and 3 in Can-Am Electroforms Ltd., the latter an industrial plating specialist involved in experimental projects.

Key executives in the companies are Josef Phillips, Jr., and Brian Fenn, both directors and shareholders in PT&M; and Edward Harris, a partner in Can-Am.

CANADA TRUST COMPANY

When 25 businessmen gathered above MacFie's store in downtown London in 1864, they couldn't have dreamed that the tiny Huron and Erie Savings and Loan Society they were creating would someday become Canada Trust—the nation's biggest trust company by a wide margin and the seventh-largest financial institution.

The Huron and Erie was formed to offer an alternative source of funds to industrious individuals exploited by unconscionable money lenders. The founders recognized the vital relationship between the well-being of business and agriculture and the overall economic health of the community and set about to establish moderate interest rates. Response from area people was immediate. Within five years the company boasted assets exceeding one million dollars.

The growth had begun.

By August 1986 corporate and administered assets exceeded $51 billion and a staff of over 15,000 served several million Canadians from 301 financial, 152 real estate, and 21 trust services branches coast to coast.

Over the years more than 50 mortgage, loan, trust, and real estate companies have been brought together under the Canada Trust banner, with each adding geographic diversity and specific strengths. The most recent amalgamation was with the Canada Permanent Mortgage Corporation on January 1, 1986.

Mergers and growth brought several name changes through the years. In 1876 the original name was altered to the Huron and Erie Loan and Savings Company, and by 1915 the name was changed to the Huron and Erie Mortgage Corporation.

The Canada Trust name dates back to the turn of the century. In 1899 the Huron and Erie acquired the charter of The General Trust Company of Calgary. Three years later the firm opened for business in London as the Canada Trust Company, in a well-timed move to fill a growing need for trust services.

In 1961 the registered name became Canada Trust-Huron and Erie, though the two component companies continued to operate separately. In 1976 the firm dropped the Huron and Erie name in favor of a name that reflected the nationwide scope of the firm and became known legally as Canada Trustco Mortgage Company, and to the general public, simply as Canada Trust.

Through the years corporate headquarters has moved several times in the heart of London's business district. The first company office was in the Crystal Block at Dundas and Richmond streets. In 1864 the young firm moved to a building on Talbot Street, then in 1866 took up operations in leased premises at 37 Dundas. By 1872 the company felt confident enough to construct its own building, on Richmond Street at Queens.

In the depths of the Great Depression, a new nine-storey office

Today Canada Trust's twin towers at Dundas and Wellington boast the latest in technological innovation, electronically linking head office with over 470 financial services, real estate, and trust branches, coast to coast.

In the company's earliest days, letters were written by hand and copied in a letterbook by means of a hand press. By 1914 electric lighting, telephones, and typewriters had become integral to everyday operations at Huron and Erie's office.

structure was built on Dundas Street at Clarence.

Today's Canada Trust Tower at Dundas and Wellington streets was constructed in 1973 as part of a city block redevelopment project that provided much-needed space for the expanding organization.

Guiding the company through mergers, continuous growth, name changes, and technological advances that have seen the introduction of telephones, electric lighting, typewriters, and, more recently, computers, has been a dedicated group of presidents: 1864-1866, Adam Hope; 1867-1870, Ellis W. Hyman; 1871-1874, John Birrell; 1875-1878, Charles Stead; 1879-1886, William Saunders; 1887, W. P. Street; 1888-1908, John W. Little; 1909-1924 and 1933-1941, Thomas G. Meredith; 1925-1932, Major Hume B. Cronyn; 1942-1956, Morley Aylsworth; 1957-1972, J. Allyn Taylor; 1973-1978, Arthur H. Mingay; and 1978- , Mervyn L. Lahn.

With foresight, founding president Adam Hope and his associates determined to establish a firm committed to the principles of prudence, strict business morality, and the cultivation of trust. Time hasn't caused those tenets to waver. They continue to direct the day-to-day operations of today's Canada Trust—a leader in the financial services industry.

Staff of the predecessor Huron and Erie Loan and Savings Company, London, 1895.

3M CANADA INC.

Aerial view of the sprawling 3M Canada headquarters on a 100-acre site in east London.

3M Canada Inc. is a London-based company manufacturing and marketing some 50,000 innovative products for industry, the professions, business, government, and the consumer. Headquartered in London, 3M also has two plants in Perth, Ontario, making Scotch-Brite products and several types of tape; an industrial minerals operation in Havelock, Ontario; and an epoxy resin plant in Morden, Manitoba.

Although 3M Canada's formal existence only dates back to 1951, 3M products have been manufactured and sold in Canada since 1930. Canadian Durex Abrasives Limited was the Canadian arm of a consortium of U.S. companies headed by Minnesota Mining and Manufacturing (the 3M Company), which was based in Brantford, Ontario. When the Durex Corporation was dissolved, 3M created its first international division by acquiring the assets of Durex and forming Minnesota Mining and Manufacturing of Canada Limited, later to become 3M Canada Inc. The new Canadian company manufactured abrasives, pressure-sensitive tapes, adhesives, and coatings in a leased portion of an old aircraft hangar in Brantford, until a new plant facility was built in London.

The company was officially established on January 17, 1951, and on May 1 of that year the general administration office opened in London, to be followed the next day by sales offices in Halifax, Montreal, Toronto, Winnipeg, and Vancouver.

The manufacturing plant, covering 145,000 square feet and containing new tape-making, adhesive-mixing, and abrasive-converting equipment, came to life on August 2, 1952. Over 200 employees relocated in the move from Brantford and some 200 more were added that year. The first year of operation saw total sales reach $2.8 million.

At first, 3M Canada Inc., as it is now known, was an importer of 3M products; then it became a manufacturer; later, through exports to the United States and other countries it began to enter the international scene; and more recently it has become a nationalized manufacturer for the North American market for several of the company's products. Abrasives, tapes, specialized nonwoven products, and others are exported to upwards of 20 countries and represent anywhere from 40 percent to 85 percent of total Canadian manufacture of these products.

Sales growth over the years has been accompanied by physical changes in plant size and capability and growth in the number of divisions and businesses. In 3M typically, as businesses grow, new divisions are formed to serve the expanded customer base.

The acquisition of Irvington Varnish and Mica Insulator Com-

The old hangar at Brantford Airport where 3M Canada started operations in 1951.

pany in 1955 necessitated 3M Canada's first expansion of 60,000 square feet to accommodate the new varnish coating tower and varnish house.

Subsequent additions to the plant and office areas of the London complex over the 1950s, 1960s, and 1970s, have brought the covered floor area to some three-quarters of a million square feet as 3M reinvested its profits into improved and expanded production equipment and technology.

In 1979 two 3M centres were built, one in Montreal and one in Calgary. At the same time, to mark the 25th anniversary of the company, a recreation area and park were being built on the plant property for the employees. The 14-acre facility includes two baseball diamonds, a soccer pitch, four tennis courts, locker and shower rooms, and a playground and fitness area.

That same year a plant was announced for Perth, followed by the unveiling of a second plant for the Perth site in 1980. During this period a $2-million laboratory addition was made to bring all the technical and research and development operations into one modern facility in London.

Research and development in 3M Canada functions as an integral part of the flow of technology and new products in the worldwide $7-billion 3M organization, which employs over 85,000 people. While many products are conceived by the parent company, 3M Canada has a highly qualified staff of more than 100 scientists and technicians who custom tailor products to Canadian needs and contribute to the constant stream of new products. Consequently, the Canadian operation fulfils the historic 3M objective of generating 25 percent of sales in any given year from products that did not exist five years earlier.

While innovation, growth, and invention have underpinned the rising fortunes of 3M Canada throughout its history, the firm has always been an integral part of the community. Projects such as the Commute-A-Vans it operates for employee transportation save fuel and reduce pollution, as does its energy-from-waste facility at the London plant. The company also supports education with bursaries and scholarships to some 40 universities and colleges across the country. Company and employees alike contribute to and support with time and effort, a broad range of charitable, benevolent, and community organizations.

With some 2,000 employees from coast to coast, 1985 sales of $418 million, and eight operating divisions, 3M Canada is one of the major manufacturers in the country.

Letter announcing start-up of the new company in Canada.

CANADIAN MINNESOTA MINING
& MANUFACTURING COMPANY, LIMITED

POST OFFICE BOX 757 · LONDON, CANADA

TO ALL EMPLOYEES: April 30, 1951

On May 1st you and all of us are starting out as employees of a new company in Canada, and I am very pleased to have you with us in Canadian Minnesota Mining & Manufacturing Company Limited.

You have all heard of "3M". It is a progressive organization whose products - some of which you know - are to be found in every phase of industrial or commercial activity. Our company has been established to manufacture and sell these products in Canada, and we are proud to be associated with Minnesota Mining & Manufacturing Company, who look continually forward to expanding fields of activity.

As you are aware we have had to find a new home and cope with all the difficulties of moving. As a result there will be a period through which we will pass that will be attended by some inconveniences. Plans have been made to integrate our operation as closely as possible, but with our sales and general office in London, our conversion and shipping at the Brantford Airport, and the manufacturing operations at Canal Road, and all the attendant difficulties of intercommunication, our problem is not as simple as it might have been had we been housed under one roof, which of course we hope to do as soon as possible. We hope that you will bear with us during this unsettled period.

Details of any changes in your place of work, or any of your activities while at work, will be given you by your supervisors and we will endeavour to keep you informed through them or by bulletin, of any impending change.

Those of you who will be working at the Airport will for the time being travel to and from work on Canada Coach Lines buses, arranged for by the company and a time table is attached for your convenience. You will be provided with a pass which will entitle you to make the trips to and from work. This pass must be shown when boarding the bus and will also be required at your place of work.

I know there will be many questions in your mind but these your supervisors should be able to answer.

Finally, I look forward to a successful and pleasant relationship with you all.

Yours sincerely,

M. H. Patterson
General Manager.

"SCOTCH" BRAND PRESSURE-SENSITIVE ADHESIVE TAPES · "SCOTCH" BRAND SOUND RECORDING TAPE · "SCOTCHLITE" BRAND REFLECTIVE SHEETINGS · "3M" ABRASIVE PAPER AND CLOTH · "3M" ADHESIVES AND COATINGS · "UNDERSEAL" RUBBERIZED COATING FOR AUTOMOBILES · "3M" CHEMICALS

THE BLACKBURN GROUP INC.

Since the first day of 1853, when a resourceful and ambitious Josiah Blackburn assumed control of the weekly *Canadian Free Press* in downtown London, a dynamic interplay of innovation, determination, and sound management has prevailed to shape the fortunes of The Blackburn Group Inc.

Under the chairmanship today of Martha G. Blackburn, who represents the fourth generation of the Blackburn family, the company is a model of publishing and broadcasting excellence; a highly valued community asset; and, by independent assessment, one of the best employers in the land.

Over 133 years of development, from hand-set type and flatbed press to computerized newspaper production, and on to the frontiers of broadcasting technology, the city's largest locally owned enterprise has added several dimensions of activity.

Just as Josiah Blackburn took the newspaper to daily frequency in 1855, coincident with the attainment of city status by London (population 12,000), his sons, Walter J. and Arthur S., ventured into extensions of publication, news gathering, and plant improvement on a broad scale. Then grandson Walter Juxon Blackburn amplified and polished the newspaper-broadcasting entity during nearly half a century of stewardship. Today Martha Blackburn is bringing the corporation to the next level of maturity, consolidating the assembly of a nationwide shopper network and a market research company folded into the group in recent years.

Cameraman Peter Ousey is shown on location at Camp London, Ethiopia. A CFPL-TV-London news team spent two weeks at the camp gathering material for an award-winning news special "Time for Ethiopia." Victoria Hospital, with the aid of the television station, raised more than $200,000 to help improve facilities at the camp.

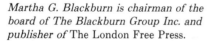

Martha G. Blackburn is chairman of the board of The Blackburn Group Inc. and publisher of The London Free Press.

The weekly *Canadian Free Press* was in fact founded in 1849 by William Sutherland, who increased circulation to 2,000 but courted financial ruin with an abortive attempt at a companion daily, *The London Daily Free Press,* in early 1852. Enter Josiah Blackburn, 29, an English-born printer by trade who was at the time working for his brother John at the *Paris* (Ontario) *Star.* A flair for business, writing, and politics served Josiah well after he took charge of the *Canadian Free Press* on January 1, 1853, in a plant on the east side of Talbot Street, a few doors north of Dundas. He accurately perceived a city on the move, already engulfed in real estate speculation and soon to be serviced by rail.

Josiah Blackburn promptly embarked on advance planning—a three-storey building on the north side of North Street (now Carling), midway between Talbot and Richmond; a Northrup power press; a newsroom capable of receiving telegraphic dispatches from New York; business office, and stockroom—all designed to produce a daily newspaper. On May 5, 1855, *The London Free Press and Daily Western Advertiser* made its debut. With the exception of one month in 1857, it has been continuously published daily ever since.

The building at 369 York Street in London houses the Blackburn Group head office, The London Free Press, *and FM-96 and CFPL Radio 98.*

The weekly *Canadian Free Press* was retained then and for another 40 years as the daily's financial anchor.

The new daily prospered from the outset, surviving in a period when many other pioneer papers foundered. In that first year Josiah cultivated readership with an "extra" containing the first local news of the fall of Sevastopol, turning point of the Crimean War. During his 38 years as editor, he established an enviable record of "firsts" in the newspaper business, among them the distinction of publishing a story from the paper's own war correspondent, Malcolm Brenner's account of the Fenian Raids near Fort Erie in 1866.

In 1868 the Blackburns (younger brother Stephen had joined the firm) transferred the company to a new three-storey building at 430 Richmond Street, where the newspaper remained until 1931. The structure was still in use for several departments until the modern plant on York Street was occupied in July 1965. (Stephen Blackburn sold his quarter-share in the *Free Press* in 1871 to William Southam, an employee of the Blackburns who later founded *The Hamilton Spectator.* The interest was repurchased from the Southam newspaper chain by *The London Free Press* Holdings Limited in 1975.)

By the time of his death in 1890, Josiah Blackburn had not only secured *The Free Press* a position of eminence in London and southwestern Ontario but had also contributed notably to civic improvement. The history of The University of Western Ontario *(Western's First Century* by J.R.W. Gwynne-Timothy, 1978) documents the publisher's editorial endorsation of a "Western University of London."

As circulation grew rapidly—from 1,000 in 1862 to 15,000 by 1868 and 34,000 in 1912 (including an evening edition launched on May 10, 1875)—*The Free Press* engaged in a fiercely competitive struggle for readership and revenue with *The London Evening Advertiser.* Early in the 1890s president Walter J. Blackburn and his younger brother Arthur S., who was secretary/treasurer, opted to concentrate on the newspaper property and spun off the job-printing division into a separate company called London Printing and Lithographing. Rivalry with the *Advertiser* ensued on a grand scale of political difference, as well as news and advertising sources, until *The Free Press* recorded the demise of its adversary in 1936.

Walter J. Blackburn died in 1920. He had, like his father, enthusiastically supported news gathering co-operation between the country's newspapers. While Josiah had been a founding father and member of the first executive of the Canadian Press Association, forerunner of the Canadian Daily Newspaper Publishers Association,

The composing room of The London Free Press *in 1922. Production of the newspaper was revolutionized in the early 1970s when the "hot metal" process of setting type was replaced by photo composition.*

Walter enrolled *The Free Press* as one of the first members in The Canadian Press wire service.

Arthur S. Blackburn, who succeeded Walter as company president, applied an abiding interest in mechanical and scientific developments to upgrade production processes at the newspaper. He took the first action picture ever published in *The Free Press*—a photograph of the 1906 King's Plate finish at Toronto. His interest in early wireless telegraphy led to the company's initial foray into broadcasting, radio station CJGC, in 1922.

With daily circulation at 38,850 by 1931, larger quarters were occupied in a building formerly the head office of Huron & Erie Mortgage Corporation and The Canada Trust Company at 442 Richmond Street. Arthur Blackburn opened radio station CFPL in the top floor of this building in 1933, but he died in a diabetic coma in 1935 before the full potential of the broadcasting arm was realized.

Walter J. Blackburn faced formidable odds when he succeeded his late father in 1936. At 21, fresh out of business administration at Western, he was the youngest publisher in Canada. What transpired over the next 47 years is legendary. From an aging newspaper plant and a radio station of limited range, there would emerge a media corporation of such integrity and strength as to deflect even the severest critics of press and monopolies unleashed by Ottawa.

In the tradition of his predecessors, the man familiarly known as "W.J." traversed the route of renovation, improvement, and expansion—all the way from an early insistence on adequate lighting in the composing room to high-speed color presses and an automated newsroom for the *Free Press.* Simultaneously, his energies, comprehension of airwave transmission, and business acumen were directed to filling out the basic AM radio station with modern studios housing CFPL-FM and CFPL-TV, the latter the area's first television station in 1953.

A stunning accomplishment during Walter Blackburn's tenure was the construction of the handsome London Free Press-CFPL Radio building at 369 York Street in 1965. Affording the most modern environment available to the industry, it also serves now as the headquarters of The Blackburn Group Inc., the management company that owns and advises all the operating subsidiaries.

Another side of W.J., who died on December 16, 1983, of cancer, was an unstinting devotion to improving the quality of life in his home city through leadership in the provision of education and health facilities. He was signally honored with a doctorate at Western in 1977 for service to the university board of governors and University Hospital, which he spearheaded as chairman of the London Health Association planning committee.

In addition to chairing The Blackburn Group, his daughter, Martha, succeeded as publisher of *The Free Press,* which enjoys a paid circulation of 128,321. The other divisions of the corporation are CFPL Broadcasting Limited; CKNX Broadcasting Limited of Wingham; Netmar Inc., the shopper and distribution business operating in 17 Canadian centres; and Compusearch Market and Social Research Limited of Toronto, which was acquired in 1984 and serves extensive clientele in Canada and the United States.

The Blackburn Group itself employs 103 persons who provide finance, accounting, data processing, human resources, personnel, and other services to the autonomous subsidiaries. In all, the Group and subsidiaries employ 1,700 and generate additional work for about 8,000 independent carriers.

A recent rating of the group as one of the 100 best companies to work for in Canada (compiled by *The Financial Post* in March 1986) was hardly surprising to the large complement of veteran staff members or to people familiar with the philosophy of the corporation. Long-standing practices of fair treatment and mutual trust initiated by W.J. in the late 1930s continue to command a high priority in what *The Post* depicted as a "happy, humane organization."

The London Free Press *building on Richmond Street in London in December 1929.*

PUMPS & SOFTENERS, LIMITED

A 1945 sketch of the head office of Pumps & Softeners, Limited.

A London company credited with manufacturing the country's first electrically powered piston pumps has survived depression and recession to emerge as a leader in its field.

Pumps & Softeners, Limited, has prospered from a series of engineering, design, and marketing refinements in the handling and treatment of water over the past 54 years.

Many thousands of Duro pumps have been manufactured and distributed by Pumps & Softeners since five of its shareholders launched the enterprise in a shed adjoining the Empire Brass Manufacturing Company (now Emco Limited) on June 20, 1932. Four of the founders—Chester and Jack Stevens, Charles Ivey, and Bert Smith, Sr.—were Emco personnel. The other was W.T. Hatmaker of the Duro Pumps Company of Dayton, Ohio. Their venture coincided with the introduction of electricity to Canada's farmlands.

The purchase of the former Ford building at 680 Waterloo Street in 1945 signalled the start of expansion and diversification for Pumps & Softeners. Before the decade was out additional production capacity and an Engineered Products Division were functioning in the stately four-storey structure.

Rapid growth carried on into the 1950s, when Ontario-wide conversion to 60-cycle power created a strong demand for the company's centrifugal pump. Sales and production teams were recruited and a new dimension added with the formation of AquaSoft Service Limited to retail domestic water-softening equipment. A quest for export markets commenced in 1962 with Pumps & Softeners (U.K.) Limited acting as distributor to several countries in Europe.

The product line was successively broadened with the important acquisitions of Darling Brothers Limited of Montreal (pumps and heat exchangers) in 1971 and the Shurz Corporation of California (control valves) in 1975. Four years later Trupar Incorporated joined the lineup, bringing to the London parent the top line of submersible well pumps and the original Duro Dayton pump rights for the United States.

A major move into the vital U.S. market was achieved in 1983 with the buyout of Ruth Berry Pumps of Houston, Texas, effectively tripling volume in the American water well pump market. In 1985 Ruth Berry was merged with Trupar Dayton in a single manufacturing operation. The company is now positioned for real growth in North America on both sides of the border.

Key figures in the company's development are (seated, left to right) John H. Dinsmore, Eng., LLD., C. Robert Ivey, Robert W. Stevens, QC., Peter J. Ivey, and Carl C. Morrison. Standing (left to right) are J. Donald Miller, P.Eng, H. Larry Wilson, John M. Stevens, Eng., George H. Stewart, MA, RIAP., and Norman W. Barton, RIAP.

CARDINAL KITCHENS LIMITED

Nearly two decades of continual adjustment, adaptation, and expansion in response to home owner demand for high-quality kitchens have elapsed since Howard Keast brought business acumen, but scant knowledge of the industry, to Cardinal Kitchens Limited.

In that time he has developed a flourishing market for custom-designed units of cabinets and vanities anchored by craftsmanship in the Exeter Road assembly plant and a dealer network across western Ontario. In 1985 he went to the drawing board once again for new showroom and storage additions to the existing building.

The company, which is now solely owned by Keast, was organized by Tom Nelson in 1962 as Cardinal Sales of London Limited, in his home on Garfield Avenue. At first, kitchens were purchased from Nordon Products of Toronto for sale in the area, but a shortage in 1964 prompted Nelson to commence manufacturing in rented quarters on Egerton Street. A year later he acquired the present site, operating the company there until his death in 1967.

At this juncture Keast accepted an offer to manage the firm. He stayed to become president and then acquire full ownership in 1975, by which time some 10,000 square feet had been added to the facility. With completion of the new brick-and-glass showroom and steel storage structure in 1986, Cardinal Kitchens occupies 31,000 square feet. An average staff of 32-34 is employed by the company; even during the recession of the early 1980s, the work force was 25.

A great deal of experience is prevalent in the production sector, under production manager Tony Dunt, who has been with the organization since 1967. The owner's wife, Ruth, is secretary/treasurer; their son-in-law, David Lucy, is sales and general manager.

Howard Keast has seen numerous changes in the industry, from a builder-dominant market at the outset to current sales primarily through 12 dealers in an area bounded by Windsor, Sarnia, Owen Sound, Kitchener, Tillsonburg, and St. Thomas. About one-third of the totally custom-made Cardinal output is sold to a few builders and to the public outside of the dealer perimeter. A complement of sophisticated woodworking equipment has been installed over the years to meet the rising expectations of Cardinal's middle- and high-income clientele.

Active in Rotary Club endeavors, Keast is also currently president of the Easter Seal Society of Ontario, an association of 235 service clubs providing assistance to crippled children. He is also a past president of the Canadian Kitchen Cabinet Association.

The attractive main entrance to the office and plant of Cardinal Kitchens Limited on Exeter Road, serving western Ontario with quality, custom-made cabinets.

FANSHAWE COLLEGE OF APPLIED ARTS & TECHNOLOGY

An artist's sketch of the Provincial Institute of Trades, which later became Ontario Vocational Centre and then Fanshawe College in 1967.

The proliferation of physical plant, staff, and enrolment has proceeded apace throughout the four-county area since the founding of Fanshawe College in London 20 years ago.

Acceptance by the private and public sectors of the unique combination of career education and skills training offered by Fanshawe—the sixth largest of Ontario community colleges—has far surpassed the expectations of local and provincial authorities.

The college arose from a perceived need in the early 1960s for an institution that would be an educational alternative to universities and would offer career-specific courses. This conclusion was reached by a London Chamber of Commerce task force coincidentally with the launching of a province-wide network of community colleges envisaged by the Ontario Government led by then-Premier William Davis.

Conveniently, the search for a site for Fanshawe (derived from words meaning "a temple in the woods," already in use as the name of a local park) led to the campus of the Ontario Vocational Centre on Oxford Street East, which was absorbed into the new institution with its opening in 1967. Principal of the O.V.C. at the time was Harry Rawson, who in 1979 succeeded original Fanshawe president James A. Colvin.

From a first-year student body of 720 postsecondary day students, the college has grown dramatically to an enrolment of over 6,600 postsecondary, approximately 1,500 apprentice, and 2,500 adult training students on a full-time basis each year. In addition, upwards of 40,000 registrations for continuing education are received annually. The annual operating budget has increased from $3.5 million to more than $60 million.

While the London campus remains the nerve centre, Fanshawe College has extended into 22 towns and cities in the counties of Elgin, Middlesex, and Oxford, and the region of Haldimand-Norfolk. Major campuses have been established in St. Thomas, Simcoe, and Woodstock, all of them involved in adult-training programs and continuing education. A two-year Farm Business Management Diploma program is unique to the Woodstock campus and consistent with college policy of tailoring curricula to community environment.

Fanshawe is a leading community college in co-operative education, a system integrating classroom study with related on-the-job work experience. More than 90 post secondary programs are offered in three major divisions: business and applied arts, health sciences and human services, and engineering technology.

Perhaps the most impressive achievement of Fanshawe has been the contribution to date of more than 26,000 highly skilled graduates to the work force.

The college in 1967 with Dr. James Colvin, the first president of Fanshawe College.

WICKES KAYSER-ROTH CANADA, LTD.

Changing times, fashions, and markets have been a way of life for Wickes Kayser-Roth Canada, Ltd., during 75 years of uninterrupted ladies' wear production in London.

The Canadian branch of the Holeproof Hosiery Company, an American concern dating to 1886, was established in the city in 1911 with 30 employees engaged in the manufacture of silk and cotton hosiery. Over the years the firm has successfully adapted to new product lines encompassing a wide range of ladies' apparel and accessories, while expanding into two local plants with a combined work force of 400 people.

The original factory on King Street was soon replaced by larger quarters on Dundas Street and then the occcupancy of four separate buildings in London by 1918. At this juncture a decision was made to build a new factory in anticipation of continued growth, culminating in a four-storey structure at the corner of Bathurst and Clarence streets. Here, on the site still occupied by the company, the entire manufacturing operation was consolidated in 1922. Four years later the first full-fashion hosiery machines were installed; in 1950 a one-floor addition was constructed to house offices and equipment.

World War II was accompanied by pressures on all clothing suppliers, resulting in a Holeproof factory in Goderich to manufacture men's socks (this operation was discontinued in the late 1950s). The return to peacetime saw an aggressive approach by Holeproof management with entry into high-quality lingerie (Luxite) in rented premises. The existing lingerie mill at Highbury and Brydges was opened in 1951. At Bathurst Street, a throwing operation for hosiery was installed; and tricot knitting, dyeing, and finishing machines were acquired to produce raw material for the lingerie plant.

A historic merger of the parent Holeproof and Julius Kayser textile companies of the United States in 1955 also fused the London operation with the large Kayser subsidiary in Sherbrooke, Quebec, under the new name of Julius Kayser Company of Canada Ltd., with head office at Bathhurst Street. In 1958 Chester H. Roth Company purchased the multi-brand concern, which became Kayser-Roth of Canada Ltd. until 1975 when the U.S. conglomerate Gulf & Western purchased the company. In 1985 Wickes Companies Inc. of Santa Monica, California, acquired control.

Wickes Kayser-Roth distributes a complete line of brand-name ladies' hose, lingerie, casual and exercise wear, accessories, and fabrics to major retailers and specialty shops from coast to coast.

Karen Baldwin paid a visit to Wickes Kayser-Roth Canada, Ltd., in her hometown of London during her reign as Miss Universe of 1982.

N-J SPIVAK LTD.

A native of the Ukraine whose first job in London was as a laborer on the Fanshawe Dam construction crew has since poured solid foundations for a large cross-section of residential and commercial projects in the city and surrounding area.

This original cement mixer, dating to the inception of the company, is preserved as a valued memento by owner Nick Spivak.

Nick Spivak, president and owner of N-J Spivak Ltd., had survived a German labor camp and qualified as a Master of Construction in France when he decided to immigrate to Canada in 1951. Stints at Fanshawe, then another dam in northern Ontario, and a return to London to work for Watson Construction in early 1953 led to formation of the Spivak company on a small scale on April 17, 1953. With a loan of $1,000 and basic equipment—two wheelbarrows, four shovels, a hose, pail, and 3.5-cubic-foot mixer (retained today as a memento)—he set up shop at 5 Webb Street with a four-man crew.

From pouring concrete for sidewalks, porches, and basements, the firm soon advanced to full-scale foundations and into home building by 1955 with a work force of 30. Between 1955 and 1962 the company constructed 157 houses and an apartment building in London while extending its sphere of operations into warehouse and industrial footings. Key moves in the growth of N-J Spivak were the acquisition of truck mixers and a batching plant on the present site at 1158 Wonderland Road South in 1960 and exodus from home building two years later in favor of concentration on the concrete business.

A complementary venture into gravel supply was undertaken in 1968 with the purchase of a pit at Base Line Road and North Street in Byron from HighCrest Properties (London) Ltd. Although the cost, including new equipment, exceeded one million dollars, the transaction ultimately proved advantageous to the company. Today N-J Spivak operates two pits in Byron, one in Dorchester, and one in Delaware.

Nick Spivak, president and owner of N-J Spivak Ltd.

The headquarters facility has also expanded greatly—from a small yard and basement office to a modern head office, two complete ready-mix plants, and all of the rolling stock necessary to service high-rise buildings, manufacturing plants, and shopping centres with structural concrete.

The peaks and valleys of construction have seen the Spivak work force vary from 250 in the 1970s down to a dozen during the recession of 1980-1981, and back to the current average of 140-160. Throughout his business career, Nick Spivak has been very active in Ukrainian community, business, and church organizations. Recently a son, Walter, joined the firm (another son, Jim, who was active in the business, was killed in an accident in 1983).

BALDWIN GARMENTS LIMITED

The search for a Canadian branch plant site by a rising young American manufacturer of work apparel more than 75 years ago led not only to the establishment of a new industry in London, but also to a permanent home and three generations of family business proprietorship.

Baldwin Garments Limited, a leader for many years in the design and supply of work clothes, originated with the formation of Baldwin Garment Company, Inc., of Holyoke, Massachusetts, in 1908. Founder W.C.P. "Will" Baldwin was a butcher-grocer in his early twenties who parlayed a flair for innovative garments—housedresses, duck goods, and butcher frocks—into popular lines attracting international recognition. Astute and expansion minded, he commenced to patent garments in many countries, a process that in Canada required a manufacturing facility for patent protection.

Baldwin's first location in the city was a small building at 589 Richmond Street, which opened in 1910. However, by 1913 he had sold the Holyoke business to American colleagues, moved to London, and established a manufacturing plant at 96-98-100 Carling Street. A city directory of the era dates the Canadian branch from 1911 and reports early acceptance of the Baldwin 4-in-1 housedress. The founder was also successful in launching a linen supply business in 1913 under the name London Coat and Apron Supply Limited, which flourished for many years as an important adjunct of the garment-making division until it was sold in 1959 to Canadian Linen Supply Company.

Baldwin Garments counted the McCormick Manufacturing Company as one of its first and one of its largest customers, having commenced the supply of rental garments to the new McCormick plant in 1914. At first Baldwin bought such items as coveralls for rental to industry. However, the firm soon developed its own lines of coveralls, pants, coats, and other work clothing as markets expanded in London and throughout western Ontario. In the early years many of the garments were fashioned from sugar bag material.

In the 1940s the volume of the linen supply business increased dramatically to the point where the company was renting goods to some 75 percent of the industrial and commercial firms in the area. A White Shirt rental program, developed in 1948 by Ben Baldwin, then sales manager of the renamed Baldwin Coat and Apron, was a spectacular success with a turnover that taxed the resources of the company to meet a demand exceeding 100 dozen new shirts per week.

Longtime president William Baldwin (left) and vice-president Ed Clark, both now retired, were key figures in the growth of the company.

Baldwin built a new plant in 1956 at 155 Adelaide Street South to replace the Carling Street operation. This was acquired by Canadian Linen Supply when it bought the linen supply business in 1959. Then Baldwin Garments top management—president William Baldwin, son of the founder; vice-president and general manager Ed Clark; and plant manager Bruce Lynch—proceeded to construct a modern plant and office at 200 Adelaide Street South, where the firm has operated continuously in garment manufacturing since early 1961. Additions to the building in 1969 and 1973 increased space for sewing, cutting, warehousing, and administrative use to 27,600 square feet, where 80 employees currently

are engaged in producing a wide variety of basic work clothing for sale across Canada.

In 1978 the active direction of Baldwin Garments Limited was passed into the hands of Bill Baldwin, who succeeded his father, William, as president after gaining experience on the staff of Canadian Linen for 20 years. The president's brothers and sisters—Beverly Bell, Betsy Casbourn, Ted Baldwin, and Bob Baldwin—are directors of the company along with Ed Clark.

The acquisition of J.B. Goodhue Inc. of Bromptonville, Quebec, in 1979 greatly extended the specialty garment offerings of the company. A major force in the Canadian work place since 1893, Goodhue's product line made available to Baldwin a full range of rugged workwear, including fire-retardant and chemically resistant clothing. The Quebec plant continues in operation under the Baldwin/Goodhue label.

Now retired, William Baldwin was a member of the board of governors of The University of Western Ontario from 1968 to 1977, serving as chairman in 1976-1977. He also is a past vice-president of the London Chamber of Commerce. The late Ben Baldwin was a City of London controller. Bill Baldwin has served with many community organizations over the past 20 years.

The manufacturing plant of Baldwin Garments Limited opened in 1961 and has since been expanded on two occasions.

In relating the development of their company over the years, Baldwin spokesmen credited first the vision of the founder, who took an instant liking to London and saw the potential of a new garment supply service. Quality fabrics and workmanship, custom design, innovation, and prompt service to an ever-changing marketplace were cited as principal factors in the long-term growth and prosperity of Baldwin Garments Limited.

IDEAL MONUMENT WORKS LONDON LIMITED

A half-century of craftsmanship in the design and creation of fine quality memorials is the foundation of Ideal Monument Works London Limited, a leader in its specialized field in western Ontario.

From its beginning in 1934 as a one-man shop, the company, founded by Thomas Rapson, has placed a premium on workmanship and materials to fashion works of art in the tradition of master masons. Since then the business has expanded in terms of physical assets, including showrooms, area branches, and production facilities, but its headquarters at 303 Springbank Drive has remained on the original site in what was the Village of Kensal Park in the 1930s.

Much of the early growth of Ideal Monument Works took place under the direction of Lloyd Rapson, a son of the founder, who, in the period from 1945 to 1977, rebuilt and enlarged the London works while establishing branches in Aylmer and Tillsonburg. The company was puchased by Allan Hutchinson, current president and general manager, and Murray Manson in 1977. They were partners until 1984 when current secretary/treasurer Bill Bethel bought Manson's interest.

Since Hutchinson purchased the firm branches have been opened in Alvinston, Thamesville, West Lorne, Simcoe, and Chatham. In addition, Ideal Monument Works acquired Lambton Memorials in Sarnia in 1980. Over the past 10 years the company's staff has doubled to 23 employees.

Recent improvements to the London property include the purchase of 299 and 301 Springbank Drive for office space and parking, and a complete remodelling of the main showroom. In the shop area, where granite and other materials capable of withstanding severe Canadian winters are used exclusively, a wide selection of predesigned monuments and custom-made personalized memorials are honed to perfection by experienced artisans. Exemplifying the high level of craftsmanship is Bill Bull, an expert in layout and design, who has served Ideal Monument Works London Limited continuously since 1945.

Hutchinson is active in trade associations, serving as a director of the Ontario Monument Builders Association and as a trustee of the Monument Builders of North America. He is also chairman of the Board of Compassion Canada, a London-based organization providing food for some 15,000 children and funds for research and development in Third World countries. In addition to its ongoing program, Compassion Canada responds to crisis situations such as famine in African countries.

A wide selection of predesigned monuments and custom-made personalized memorials are crafted to perfection by experienced artisans.

REED STENHOUSE LIMITED

The names of the founding businessmen have long since disappeared from the masthead, but the insurance agency they nurtured to national prominence retains a strong presence in London under the umbrella of one of the world's foremost brokerage organizations.

Known now as Reed Stenhouse Limited—an international broker of long standing and member of the Alexander & Alexander Group of the United States since 1985—the London Branch occupies the entire sixth floor of the City Centre Tower at 380 Wellington Street. With 60 employees, the latest office technology, and a much broader diversity of service, the facility is greatly advanced from the original insurance office opened 136 years ago. Over the intervening years the small firm established at 170 Princess Street by William B. Beddome in 1850 has expanded dramatically, at first through the efforts of astute local ownership and latterly in company with proficient contemporaries via the merger route.

In the early stages Beddome was joined by partner George T. Brown, and new quarters were secured in what was then known as the Prevost Building on Richmond Street. Later it was relocated above the old Boughner's store on Richmond. In 1919 Philip Pocock, a nephew of Brown, entered the business and subsequently acquired control for $45,000. V.P. Cronyn joined the firm in 1921, followed by partner G.W. Robinson in 1931—at which time the name was changed to Cronyn, Pocock and Robinson.

Through World War II, headquarters were maintained in the Dundas Building; in the late 1940s moves were made to modern offices on Queens Avenue and then to a colonial-style structure at 150 Fullarton Street in 1961. By this time partners G.P. McEvenue and G. Ernest Jackson had taken their seats on a board of well-known Londoners, with Cronyn as president.

A historic merger in 1968, creating one of the larger insurance brokerage firms in the world, cemented an all-Canadian alliance of the London company with Reed, Shaw & McNaught of Toronto (dating to 1872) and Osler Hammond and Nanton of Winnipeg (established in 1883). Ben Lowry was appointed branch manager of the combined group known as Reed Shaw Osler.

A further merger—the largest in the history of the insurance industry—was concluded in 1973 with the UK-based Stenhouse Holdings Limited, leading to the name Reed Stenhouse Companies Limited in 1978. Succeeding Lowry as branch manager in 1983 was Bertram Polgrain, who is presently chairman of the Victoria Hospital board—in the tradition of many of this firm's executives who have served the community.

Senior vice-president and branch manager Bertram R. Polgrain (seated) is flanked by key members of the operating team at Reed Stenhouse Ltd. From the left are Terry McCullough, senior vice-president/group; Jack T. Keogh, vice-president/institutional; and James E. Bryan, senior vice-president/sales and service.

CUDDY INTERNATIONAL CORPORATION

In the game of Trivial Pursuit, one question asks, "What is the turkey capital of Canada?" The answer is Strathroy, Ontario, and the reason is A.M. (Mac) Cuddy. How Strathroy, an unassuming hamlet on the fringe of London, became the turkey capital of Canada is a story of hard work, risk, and ambition in the pursuit of a dream.

What started as Mac Cuddy's Turkey Farms in 1950 has grown into Cuddy International Corporation, the largest turkey-breeding and -hatching company in the world. Cuddy divisions are involved at all levels of food production in Canada and the United States, selling turkey and chicken hatching eggs, day-old turkey poults, and chicks; processing turkey and chicken meat into roasts, cutlets, and nuggets and also operating as a world-class standardbred racing stable. And even though corporate offices have relocated to London, the original ingredients of the Cuddy philosophy —service and quality—are imbued into the Cuddy framework.

In his youth Mac Cuddy tended his mother's chickens. Not content with their egg production, he placed kerosene lamps in the henhouse to increase the hens' laying schedule. Years later he adapted the principle of photoperiod stimulation to produce turkey hatching eggs year-round. Young Mac found great satisfaction in exhibiting livestock at local fairs, demonstrating both stockmanship and a keen competitive nature at an early age.

He attended the Ontario Agricultural College, majoring in horticulture, and graduated on the Dean's Honor List. One of the trademarks of a Cuddy farm, hatchery, and processing plant is the immaculate grounds, a tribute to Mac Cuddy's fine sense of landscape architecture.

Before he could settle down to the business of farming Mac volunteered for overseas duty in the Canadian Army, retiring four years later with the rank of captain. For the next five years he worked for the Veteran's Land Act awaiting the opportunity to buy land and build his future. On June 15, 1950, Mac Cuddy and his young family moved 10 miles from the family homestead to the present headquarters of Cuddy Farms, just north of Strathroy.

This inauspicious 100-acre farm had the assets that a young entrepreneur could grow with: good soil, a century-old brick house, a set of turkey porches, and a traditional red-sided barn that soon boasted the name "Mac Cuddy's Turkey Farm."

Being discontent with the quality of turkey poults available, he purchased two used duck incubators in 1953, and kept his own breeding flock. That signaled the start of the turkey-breeding business. In the early years Cuddy and the firm's few dedicated employees worked long hours, hatching and rearing turkeys by day, and dressing turkeys by night for "next-day-delivery" to Toronto markets.

Early in his career Cuddy met California turkey-breeding pioneer George Nicholas. That meeting changed the lives of the two men. They developed a mutual admiration and unquestionable trust that lasted a lifetime. Nicholas convinced Cuddy to abandon his dream of becoming a primary breeder, and to concentrate instead on the hatching business. In 1984 George Nicholas died. In his memory, Mac Cuddy established the Nicholas Memorial Fellowship of industrial sabbaticals for agricultural scientists.

By the mid-1950s Mac began to amass land holdings whenever prime farmland became available and financing was possible. Business multiplied with new technology and new products, such as artificial insemination and white feathered turkeys. Mac foresaw turkey meat becoming a year-round food. That meant production and hatching every month of the year. So the time came to apply his boyhood lesson, control the breeding cycle of turkey hens by light stimulation. That led to total-confinement, environmentally controlled buildings with forced air ventilation and automatic feeding. At the other end of the food cycle was processing and marketing, so Mac Cuddy became a partner in two turkey abattoirs.

An architect's sketch of the new Cuddy Food Products Ltd. processing plant in east London.

A.M. "Mac" Cuddy (centre) and his five sons, all key players in Cuddy International.

In the meantime Cuddy saw opportunity for expansion south of the border. His decision to base his U.S. operations in the Carolinas was totally economic: abundant land, cheap labor, available facilities, and super highways to the industrial northeast.

He purchased hatcheries in South and North Carolina. Darkout houses were constructed on parcels of previously untouched land and range facilities for breeders were chiseled from enormous stands of pine. Transient Canadians and native Carolinians battled the heat and blackflies. Cuddy was convinced his was the right choice; North Carolina would someday boast being the largest poultry state in the union. With a growing reputation for year-round delivery of quality day-old poults, both Canadian and U.S. hatcheries were expanded. Cuddy is planning for the future of the industry, and the market demands of the twenty-first century; the firm recently constructed a broiler chick hatchery, capable of producing 36 million chicks annually, making this facility one of the largest in the world.

Cuddy has never been one to sit idly by when action and opportunity abound. Two recently acquired turkey-processing plants located in Marshville and Monroe, North Carolina, bear testimony to this bullish no-nonsense philosophy. Cuddy currently makes the list of the top 10 processors of turkey products in America.

In light of his success in the rearing and breeding of turkeys, it is not surprising that Cuddy became the first further processor of turkey products in Canada. Expanding from a line of basic rolls, roasts, and deli products, the company now offers a broad selection of breaded and portion-controlled items for both retail and food-service outlets. Cuddy Foods is constantly researching, testing, and changing products to keep pace with the explosive convenience food market. In 1980 Cuddy became the sole supplier of chicken products to the giant McDonald's Corporation. It now has a broad product line including not only turkey and chicken but also prepared foods and frozen vegetables. These products are marketed by the largest sales and marketing organization of its kind across Canada, to restaurants, institutions, delis, and supermarkets.

With an ever-expanding market share, Cuddy has begun construction of a new processing facility in London, projected for completion in 1987. It will be the largest and most technically advanced operation of its kind in Canada, and one of the largest processing facilities in North America.

Today Mac Cuddy is chairman and president of a company employing thousands of men and women in Canada and the United States. His diversified turkey business includes producing and marketing turkey hatching eggs, day-old poults, dressed roasting turkeys, and processed poultry meats, in addition to the McDonald's chicken contract. Cuddy International remains a family-owned and -operated business, with Cuddy's five sons involved in various aspects of the work.

Since boyhood, Mac has had an appreciation for fine horses. Through the years he has built Cuddy Stables into one of North America's foremost standard-bred breeding farms. His honours include the Governor General's Cup, winning the Hambletonian Stakes, and directorships on the Hambletonian Society, the Ontario Jockey Club, and the Lexington Breeder's Association.

Founder Mac Cuddy's commitment to check every turkey poult before delivery continues today, just as in this 1955 scene.

CINRAN PLASTICS INC. OF LONDON

By all the standards of corporate excellence—physical assets, product development, and market acceptance—Cinran Plastics Inc. of London is an unqualified success in a highly specialized field.

From sophisticated extrusion and imprinting equipment, millions of polyethylene bags and packaging materials flow annually from the manufacturing assembly at 22 Pegler Street to the counters of the nation's industry, supermarkets, and other retail chains.

With a solid foothold in the world of modern merchandising and plans on the drawing board for another major expansion in the late 1980s, Cinran has more than vindicated the judgement of founders G.A. Parsons—who is now president and sole owner—and R.M. Crawford. With separate, but complementary, backgrounds—Parsons was sales representative for the CIL plastics packaging division in London; and Crawford, of Victoria Paper Company, was a principal customer—they launched Cinran Plastics Company on September 1, 1967.

G.A. Parsons, founder and president of Cinran Plastics Inc.

Cinran's plant and offices cover 30,000 square feet.

The business commenced on a very limited scale with three employees, 1,000 square feet of manufacturing space at the rear of the Telequipment Ltd. building at 200 Adelaide Street South, and an office at 20 Craig Street, all centred on the production of plain polyethylene bags. By contrast, the operating area of the company has expanded to 45,000 square feet, the staff to 100 permanent employees, and the payroll from $16,000 in the first year to $2.25 million in 1986.

Several stages of growth in the early years of Cinran Plastics attest to timing of the venture in concert with rising demand for new, lightweight, consumer packaging. In November 1968 the firm moved into 5,000 square feet of rented space at 32 York Street, where it continued to flourish until purchasing the former Jackson's Bakery property on the present Pegler Street site in February 1972. (Interestingly, sections of the bake shop and head baker's quarters are identifiable in the central part of the building today; the stables are gone, and their occupants hauling bread wagons through city streets are but a fleeting memory to senior residents.)

At first the 20,000 square feet on Pegler Street was shared with associated companies. By 1976, in the wake of increasing profitability, the addition of printing equipment and the escalation of Cinran to status as a major supplier of polyethylene bags in Western Ontario, an additional 10,000 square feet of floor space was required. At the same time, the building was completely renovated, sprinklered, painted inside and out, fitted with level loading docks, and serviced by new offices. The company had also made a large expenditure the previous year on three extruders to manufacture polyethylene material in both low and high density, completing the move to full integration.

Between 1978 and 1980 Cinran experienced further growth and took over all of the facility on Pegler Street as the sharing companies moved to new locations. In 1979 the management team was strengthened in the areas of engineering and finance with the hiring of a general manager and a chartered accountant as controller. Shortly afterward the organization purchased its first computer and proceeded to build a software package unique to the industry.

In March 1980 a new company was formed, Cinran Holdings Inc., and the manufacturing operation was sold to Cinran Plastics (1980) Inc. Cinran Holdings retained the land and building, and has since purchased additional property to the east, facing on Hamilton Road.

The past six years have seen numerous additions to technology, increased sales, and improved profits from a wider product mix highlighted by the development at Cinran of its patented Deli-Close Pak. The popular "deli bag" is made from Cineclear film, which was also formulated at the London plant and is the only material of its kind in the world. Across Canada this product represents 90 percent of the plastic bags used at the delicatessen counters of major food and departmental chains.

Two other significant changes occurred at Cinran recently. In February 1984 Parsons purchased all the outstanding shares held by R.M. Crawford in Cinran Holdings Inc. to attain sole ownership. Then, in May 1985, a 15,000-square-foot warehouse was leased to release space for manufacturing in the existing building. Current plans reveal expenditures of one-half million dollars for new equipment.

Cinran Plastics is well positioned to augment a predominantly Canadian market (exports are five percent of sales) with a strong presence from coast to coast, including a warehouse in Vancouver to service western Canadian customers accounting for 15 percent of sales. The firm is also keying to selective segments—butcher, retail, and specialized small industrial manufacturers—with the expertise to meet special requirements.

Meanwhile, Parsons is contributing to the plastics industry as chairman of a committee, writing the first comprehensive safety manual for the Plastic Film Manufacturers Association, of which he is a director. He also has served as a director of Goodwill Industries of London for the past four years.

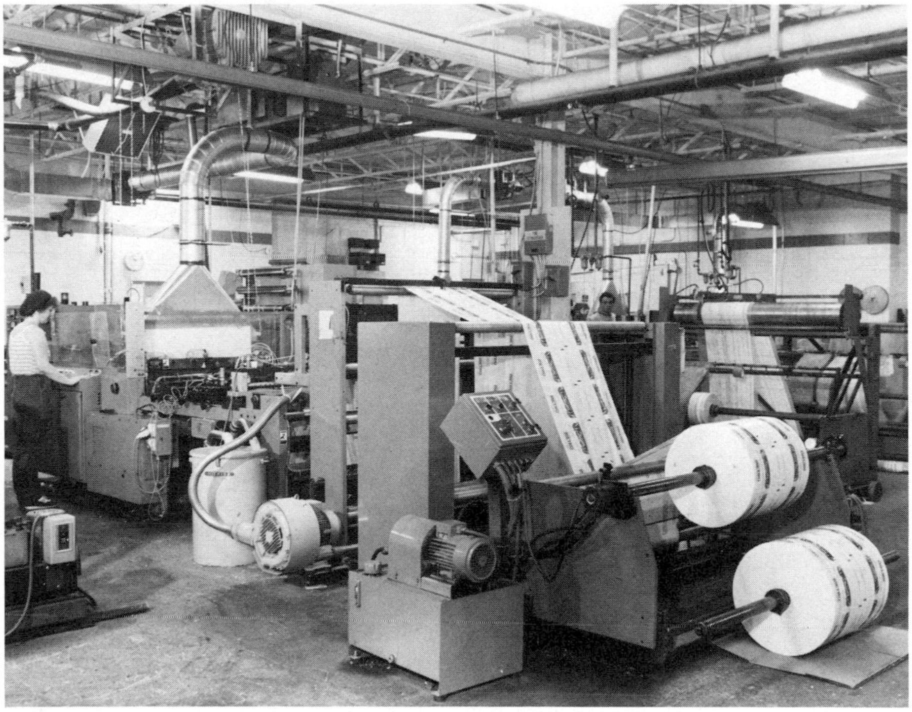

One of the most up-to-date bag machines in Canada.

Cinran's six-color, 50-inch web printing press.

GALLOWAY FROST INC.

A teamwork approach by experienced professionals, with a complete range of in-house resources, has attracted a widespread and diversified clientele to London's senior advertising and public relations agency.

Galloway Frost Inc. is approaching 20 years of service, with a growing roster of major Canadian, American, and European accounts. And, in an industry vulnerable to disaffection, the firm enjoys a record of stability, having held its principal accounts for an average of over seven years, with two exceeding 15 years.

The full-service stature of Galloway Frost Inc. reflects the backgrounds of president Tom Galloway in client service and graphic arts, and vice-president Steve Frost in the marketing and creative areas of the business. Galloway, who has worked in the print and advertising field in London since 1961, founded the agency with the acquisition of Group Graphics Ltd. in 1971. Frost joined him seven years later, and the name was changed in 1980, as the original name no longer reflected the matured agency service being offered.

T.S. Galloway, president.

"When I started in the graphic arts industry over 25 years ago, there were only two advertising agencies in London," Tom Galloway explains, "and both were branches of offices from Toronto. At that point, with the way London was growing, I knew the advertising industry needed an agency that was based in London, for London. After my purchase of Group Graphics I let it grow with the city and here we are today."

Galloway Frost Inc. functions with a staff of 17 in an 85-year-old residence at 847 Dundas Street, where restoration and renovation have fashioned a modern agency setting. In-house facilities include a complete creative, design, and finished art staff; photography studio; digital phototypesetting; production; public relations and marketing departments; copywriting; general administration; media department; and account services group.

A third member of the Galloway family, daughter Kim, a graduate in radio and television arts from Ryerson, became production co-ordination in the spring of 1986 to join her mother, Marlene, who is secretary/treasurer.

Offices of Galloway Frost Inc.

D.H. HOWDEN & CO. LIMITED

In the gun shop. At far right is founder David Hartford Howden, and from left to right are John Valentine Givins, a hardware dealer, and Lyle Johnson. (Inset) The new Pro Store in White Oaks Mall, London.

The national wholesaler D.H. Howden & Co. Limited is again tapping the keyboards of computer-based retail science in the London headquarters and testing ground where the firm has flourished since 1900.

In the spirit of founder David Hartford Howden, who with partners John V. Givins, James Brown, and Lyle Johnson, started a hardware supply centre on York Street and soon built up a large dealership across western Ontario, the modern-day enterprise is well launched toward new plateaus of growth.

This time the corporation is fine-tuning the electric communications and marketing support systems serving more than 300 franchised Pro Hardware outlets coast to coast, while branching into the building/home centre field with some 30 franchised "Do-it" stores in the fold by late 1986. The upgrading of the Pro division, through new logos, interior designs, and a raft of value-added services from Howden—along with the new presence in the retail lumber and building materials market—represents an overall strategy to improve company performance in the years ahead.

In fact, D.H. Howden & Co. has been on the move since its inception in what was then the Cruickshank building at York and Richmond streets. The business was relocated within six months to the present York Street premises of Raymond Tent & Awning, and in 1904 gained momentum by acquiring the inventory of the failed Bowman Hardware. In 1907 Howden attained limited company status and erected a new warehouse at 200 York Street.

Norman R. Howden succeeded his father as president in 1918 and embarked on an expansion program, first with the 1922 takeover of Kennedy Hardware of Toronto and then in 1930 with the purchase of H.S. Howland Sons & Company Limited, a sizable Ontario hardware distributor. After Norman Howden died in 1938, his wife, Lydia Howden, became president. J.J. Stewart, a Toronto bank manager and son-in-law of D.H. Howden, served as chairman of the company for many years, fulfilling a mandate to provide sound financial management. D.H. Stewart became vice-president and managing director in 1954.

Major additions to the Howden holdings were a new warehouse on Southdale Road in 1960 and the White Oaks distribution centre in the late 1970s, bringing approximately 400,000 square feet under roof in the city. The firm was already advanced into a new dimension of wholesale/retail service, having secured the Pro Hardware franchise for Canada in 1962. In 1969 the company went public on the T.S.E. and at that time David H. Stewart, grandson of Norman Howden, became president and chairman of the board, succeeding Lydia Howden.

Michael C. Tucker was appointed president in 1984, with Stewart continuing as chairman. Coincidentally, Tucker obtained the Canadian rights to the U.S.-based Do-it franchise in 1984. The current strength of D.H. Howden & Co. is reflected by annual sales exceeding $100 million of goods delivered by a fleet of 60 company transports to dealers from Newfoundland to British Columbia.

FURTNEY FUNERAL HOMES LTD.

A continuing program of renovation and improvement at the two London facilities of Furtney Funeral Homes Ltd. has added a large measure of comfort and convenience to a considerable depth of experience offered by the management of this vital community service.

Enhancement of the properties began shortly after president and owner George A. Furtney purchased the business from the sons of the late George E. Logan in 1962. Recognizing the importance of parking, the new proprietor acquired additional property at the Logan Chapel site at 371 Dundas Street in 1963 and 1965, then built a two-storey brick and glass addition in 1972 at the front, with a portico on the west side adjacent to the spacious parking lot. The new structure was designed to blend with the original building while affording an airy, brighter decor and providing a commodious receiving foyer and lounge.

In a similar vein, the Evans Chapel at 648 Hamilton Road, which was purchased by Furtney in 1976, was modernized in 1986. In order to better accommodate the public, all conveniences for the handicapped were installed along with the latest energy-conserving materials in heating and air-conditioning systems.

The Logan facility in 1986 is a spacious, convenient edifice on the east side of downtown London.

The Logan branch of the business was founded in 1892 on Dundas Street, within a block of the courthouse. Following relocation to the east side of Richmond Street, just north of Dundas, the present location was purchased—and early in 1922 one of the few buildings designed specifically for a funeral home in Ontario was opened there.

The Evans Chapel dates to 1924, when it was started by Clifford Evans as a community service to east London and the Hamilton Road area.

George Furtney commenced a lifelong vocation in the funeral-directing profession as an apprentice with Evans, followed by enrolment in the Canadian School of Embalming where, at 20 years of age, he was the youngest graduate in the history of the institution. Positions with Toronto and London funeral homes led to a partnership in a New Toronto firm, Arthur B. Ridley Funeral Home Limited, in 1957. He sold that interest in 1962, coincident with buying the Logan company.

Furtney has served as president of the London, Western Ontario, and Ontario Funeral Directors' associations and is a past director of the International Order of the Golden Rule. Associated with him in management are Stewart Rice, Jim Squires, and Peter McCabe—combining more than 75 years of funeral service experience.

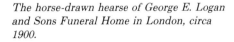

The horse-drawn hearse of George E. Logan and Sons Funeral Home in London, circa 1900.

Patrons

The following individuals, companies, and organizations have made a valuable commitment to the quality of this publication. Windsor Publications and The London Chamber of Commerce gratefully acknowledge their participation in *The Forest City: An Illustrated History of London, Canada.*

ABA Computer Centre
Anglo-Gibraltar Insurance Group*
Archibald, Gray & McKay Ltd.
Ault Foods Limited (Silverwood/ Sealtest)
Avco Financial Services Canada Limited*
Baldwin Garments Limited*
Bank of Montreal, Dundas & Wellington
Bell Cellular Inc.
The Blackburn Group Inc.*
Brandy Tree Shoppes Inc.
Campbell Bros. Movers Ltd.*
Canada Trust Company*
Cardinal Kitchens Limited*
CBS Equipment Limited*
Charterways Transportation Limited*
Cinran Plastics Inc. of London*
Clarkson Gordon*
Coopers & Lybrand
Copp Builders' Supply Company Limited*
John W. Cram
D.D. Crawford & Son Ltd.
Cuddy International Corporation*
Ray Cullen Chevrolet Ltd.*
Davies Wetstein & Co. Chartered Accountants
R.C. Dawson Company Limited*
Deloitte Haskins & Sells
Diesel Division, General Motors of Canada Limited*
M.M. Dillon Limited*
Dixon Van Lines Ltd.
Ellis-Don Limited
Emco Limited*
Fanshawe College of Applied Arts & Technology*
Firestone Steel Products of Canada*
Forest City Auto Leasing
Furtney Funeral Homes Ltd.*
Galloway Frost Inc.*
Hay Stationery Incorporated*
John Hayman and Sons Co. Ltd.
D.H. Howden & Co. Limited*
Robert Hunt Corporation*
Huron Steel Fabricators (London) Limited*
Ideal Monument Works London Limited*
Interior Trend Ltd.
Bruce B. Johnson
KelCoatings Limited/Oakside Chemicals Limited*
Kellogg Salada Canada Inc.*
John Labatt Limited in London*
Col. Tom Lawson, CM
Loeb Inc.*
The London Flower Boutique
The London Hunt and Country Club, Limited
London Life Insurance Company*
The London Metal Service Limited*
London Middlesex Roman Catholic School Board
London Vending Service Ltd.
London Winery Limited*
McKerlie-Millen Inc.*
James Magee Limited
May's Truck Rentals
Morphy Containers Ltd.*
N-J Spivak Ltd.*
O-Pee-Chee Company Limited*
Parkwood Hospital*
Patton's Place*
Phillips Tool & Mould (London) Limited*
Nancy Geddes Poole
PRA International Inc.*
Price Waterhouse*
Pumps & Softeners, Limited*
Reed Stenhouse Limited*
Romanuk Design-Build Inc.*
J.T. Rourke
Sifton Properties Limited*
Stevenson & Hunt Insurance Brokers Limited*
Stihl Limited*
Tecumseh Products of Canada, Ltd.*
That Graphics Place Ltd.
3M Canada Inc.*
Touche Ross*
University Hospital*
The University of Western Ontario*
Victoria Hospital*
Westinghouse Canada Inc.*
White Oaks Mall
Wickes Kayser-Roth Canada, Ltd.*
Wolverine Tube Limited
W.G. Young Company Ltd.*

*Partners in Progress of *The Forest City: An Illustrated History of London, Canada.* The histories of these companies and organizations appear in Chapter IX, beginning on page 243.

A P P E N D I X A

Mayors of London

+ = died in office
R = resigned
N = note at end of table

Presidents of the Board of Police
1840-1847

1840	George Jervis Goodhue
1841	James Givins
1842-43	Ed. Matthews
1844	James Farley
1845	John Balkwill
1846	Thomas W. Shepherd
1847	Hiram D. Lee + (to Oct. 29)

Town Mayors
1848-1854

1848	Simeon Morrill (1)
1849	Thos. C. Dixon
1850-51	Simeon Morrill (2)
1852-53	Edward Adams
1854	Marcus Holmes

City Mayors 1855-1986

1855	Murray Anderson
1856	William Barker
1857	Elijah Leonard, Jr.
1858	David Glass (1)
1859	William McBride
1860	James Moffat
1861-64	Francis Evans Cornish
1865	David Glass (2)
1867	Frank Smith
1868	William Simpson Smith
1869	John Christie (to Feb. 22)
1869-70	Simpson Hackett Graydon (from Feb. 22)
1871	James Mitchell Cousins
1872	John Campbell (1)
1873	Andrew McCormick
1874-75	Benjamin Cronyn, Jr.
1876	Duncan Cameron MacDonald
1877	Robert Pritchard
1878-79	Robert Lewis
1880-81	John Campbell (2)
1882-83	Edmund Allan Meredith
1884	Charles Smith Hyman
1885	Henry Becher
1886	Thomas Daniel Hodgens
1887-88	James Cowan
1889-91	George Taylor William
1892	Melville Spencer
1893-94	Emanuel Thomas Essery
1895-97	John William Little
1898-99	John Dolway Wilson
1900-01	Frederick George Rumball
1902-04	Adam Beck
1905	Clarence Thomas Campbell
1906-07	Joseph Coulson Judd
1908-09	Samuel Stevely
1910-11	John Henry Alfred Beattie
1912-14	Charles Milton Richardson Graham
1915	Hugh Allen Stevenson (1)
1916	William Moir Gartshore N1 (from Jan. 1-15)
1916-17	Hugh Allen Stevenson (2) N1 (from Jan. 15)
1918-19	Charles Ross Somerville
1920-21	Edgar Sydney Little
1921	John Cameron Wilson
1923-25	George Albert Wenige (1)
1926-27	John MacKenzie Moore
1928	George Albert Wenige (2)
1929-30	William John Kilpatrick
1931-32	Edwy George Hayman
1933	Ferrier Baker Kilbourne
1934-35	George Albert Wenige (3)
1936-38	Thomas F. Kingsmill
1939-40	Joseph Allan Johnston (1) N2
1941-45	William J. Heaman N2
1946	Frederick George McAlister
1947-48	George Albert Wenige (4)
1949	Ray Ameredith Dennis (1)
1950	George Albert Wenige (5)
1951-55	Allan Johnson Rush R (to Mar. 29)
1955	George Ernest Beedle R (Apr. 1-Aug. 8)

1955-57	Ray Ameredith Dennis (2) (from Aug. 8)
1958-60	Joseph Allan Johnston (2)
1961-68	Frank Gordon Stronach + (to Jan. 1)
1968-71	Herbert Joseph McClure (from Jan. 8)
1972	James Frederick Gosnell R (to Mar. 6)
1972-78	Jane Elizabeth Bigelow (from Mar. 15)
1979-85	Martin Alphonse Gleeson
1986	Thomas Charles Gosnell

(N1) 1915 — On a recount W.M. Gartshore and H.A. Stevenson were found to both have 3,887 votes. City Clerk Sam Baker then cast the deciding vote in favor of Stevenson, so Gartshore was unseated.

(N2) 1940 — W.J. Heaman was appointed presiding officer on September 8, 1940, as J.A. Johnston was on active service in World War II.

APPENDIX B

Population Statistics for London

As Part of London Township	
1827	133
1830	274
1833	603
1835	1,037
1837	1,090
1839	1,409
1840	1,716
First Town Incorporation	
1841	2,078
1847	3,942
Second Town Incorporation	
1848	4,668
1850	5,124
1852	7,035
1854	10,060
City	
1855	about 12,000
1860	11,200
1870	14,118
1875	18,413
1880	19,941
1885	26,254
1890	30,786
1895	34,429
1900	39,059
1905	43,154
1910	46,727
1915	58,055
1920	59,281
1925	64,274
1930	71,310
1935	75,484
1940	77,369
1945	82,633
1950	94,027
1955	101,855
1960	102,743
1965	185,562
1970	215,870
1975	243,928
1980	261,841
1985	276,000

The British military garrisons stationed in London from 1838 to 1853 and from 1861 to 1869 are not included in these totals.

The London Collegiate Institute, London's first modern high school, opened in 1878 in this High Victorian building on Dufferin Avenue at Waterloo Street. It burned in 1920. Courtesy, London Room

Suggestions for Further Reading

The following list of books has been divided into three sections for the convenience of the reader: bibliographic sources; general works on London; and special studies and journals with material on London. Few articles have been included, however, so reference should also be made to Olga Bishop's *Bibliography of Ontario History.* A great number of the theses on various aspects of London's development have been written in the geography and history departments at the University of Western Ontario.

The largest collections of both printed and manuscript material relating to London can be found at the London Room of the London Public Library, and the Regional Room at the D.B. Weldon Library of the University of Western Ontario.

1. BIBLIOGRAPHIES

Aitken, Barbara B. *Local Histories of Ontario Municipalities: A Bibliography: 1951-1977.* (Toronto, 1978)

Armstrong, Frederick H., Alan F.J. Artibise, and Melvin Baker. *Bibliography of Canadian Urban History.* Part IV: *Ontario* in Vance Bibliographies. (Monticello, Il., 1980)

Artibise, Alan F.J., and Gilbert A. Stelter. *Canada's Urban Past: A Bibliography to 1980 and a Guide to Canadian Urban Studies.* (Vancouver, 1981)

Bishop, Olga B. *Bibliography of Ontario History, 1867-1976.* (2 vols., Toronto, 1980)

Canadian Council on Urban and Regional Research. *Urban and Regional References, 1945-1969.* (Ottawa, 1970). Also supplements.

Morcom, Jean. *Annotated Bibliography of the History and Development of London, Ontario, to 1900.* (London, 1959)

Morley, William F.E. *Canadian Local Histories to 1950: Ontario and the Canadian North.* (Toronto, 1978)

Neary, Hilary Bates, and Robert Sherman. *Ontario Historical Society: Index to the Publications, 1899-1972.* (Toronto, 1974)

Toronto Public Library. *Early Canadian Companies.* (Toronto, 1967)

2. GENERAL WORKS

Armstrong, Frederick H., and Daniel J. Brock. *London, Ontario: A Case Study in Metropolitan Evolution.* (Ottawa, n.d.)

___________. "The Rise of London: A Study of Urban Evolution in Nineteenth-Century Southwestern Ontario," in F.H. Armstrong, *et al*, eds. *Aspects of Nineteenth Century Ontario: Papers Presented to James J. Talman.* (Toronto, 1974)

___________. *Reflections on London's Past.* (London, 1975)

Baker, Samuel. *The Rise and Progress of London.* (London, 1924)

Bremner, Archie. *Illustrated London Ontario Canada.* (London, 1897)

Brock, Daniel J. *Dan Brock's Historical Almanack of London.* 3 vols: *Spring, 1975; Summer, 1975; Autumn, 1975.* (London, 1975)

Campbell, Clarence T. *Pioneer Days in London.* (London, 1921)

___________. *1826-1926 Milestones, London, Canada.* (London, 1926)

___________. *History of the County of Middlesex, Canada* (also known as Goodspeed). (Toronto, 1889)

Landon, Fred. "London in Early Times" and "London in Later Times" in Jesse E. Middleton and Fred Landon, eds. *The Province of Ontario.* (Toronto, 1927)

Purdom, Thomas H. *London: And Its Men of Affairs.* (London, 1915)

Talman, James J. "London." *Encyclopedia Canadiana,* vol. 6. (Toronto, 1970)

Whebell, C.F.J. "London." *The Canadian Encyclopedia.* (Edmonton, 1985)

3. SPECIAL STUDIES

Addington, Charles. *A History of The London Police Force.* (London, 1980)

Buchanan, Edward V. *A History of Electrical Energy in London.* (London, 1966)

___________. *London's Water Supply.* (London, 1972)

__________. *The Professional Engineers of London.* (London, 1972)
Canadian Jewish Congress Centre Region, Research Committee. *The Jewish Community of London, Ontario: A Self Survey.* (Toronto, 1959)
Conron, Brandon, ed. *The London Hunt and Country Club.* (London, 1985)
Corfield, William E. *To Alleviate Suffering. The Story of the Red Cross in London Canada. 1900-1985.* (London, 1985)
Due, John F. *The Intercity Electric Railway Industry in Canada.* (Toronto, 1966)
Ford, Arthur R. *As the World Wags On.* (Toronto, 1950)
Fox, William Sherwood. *Sherwood Fox of Western: Reminiscences.* (Toronto, 1964)
Gray, Leslie Robb. *Proudfoot to Pepperbox to Posterity 1833-1983.* (London, 1983)
Gwynne-Timothy, J.W.R. *Western's First Century.* (London, 1978)
Hamil, Fred Coyne. *Lake Erie Baron: The Story of Colonel Thomas Talbot.* (Toronto, 1955)
History: London Fire Department. (London, n.d.)
Honey, Terrace W., ed. *London Heritage.* (London, 1972)
Hughes, David, and T.H. Purdom. *History of the Bar of the County of Middlesex.* (London, 1912)
Judd, William W. *Historical Account of Byron Bog (Sifton Botanical Bog) London, Ontario.* (London, 1985)
Landon, Fred. *Up the Proof Line.* (London, 1955)
The Local Council of Women London: Res Gestae Mulierum. 1893-1937. (London, 1937)
London, City Clerk's Department. *The Municipal Handbook.* (London: various issues, 1895-1985)
London and Middlesex Historical Society: Transactions. 1902-1937, 1966.
London Public Library and Art Museum. *Occasional Papers.*
Lutman, John H. *The Historic Heart of London.* (London, 1977)
__________, and Christopher L. Hives. *The North and the East of London.* (London, 1982)
__________. *The South and the West.* (London, 1979)
Miller, Orlo. *A Century of Western Ontario.* (Toronto, 1949)
__________. *Gargoyles and Gentlemen: A History of St. Paul's Cathedral, London, Ontario, 1834-1964.* (Toronto, 1966)
__________. *The London Club.* (London, 1954)
Morningstar, C.K. *From Dobbin to Diesel.* (London, 1973)
Plewman, W.R. *Adam Beck and the Ontario Hydro.* (Toronto, 1947)
Poole, Nancy G. *The Art of London, 1830-1980.* (London, 1984)
Read, Colin. *The Rising in Western Upper Canada: The Duncombe Revolt and After.* (Toronto, 1982)
St-Denis, Guy. *Byron: Pioneer Days in Westminster Township.* (Lambeth, Ont., 1985)
Shawyer, A.J. *Broughdale: Looking for Its Past.* (London, 1981)
Seaborn, Edwin. *The March of Medicine in Western Ontario.* (Toronto, 1944)
Stark, Foster. *A History of the First Hussars Regiment, 1856-1980.* (London, 1981)
Sullivan, John R., and Norman R. Ball. *Growing to Serve . . . A History of Victoria Hospital, London, Ontario.* (London, 1985)
Talman, James J. *Huron College, 1863-1963.* (London, 1963)
__________, and Ruth Davis Talman. *"Western" 1878-1953.* (London, 1953)
Upper Thames River Conservation Authority. *Twenty Years of Conservation on the Upper Thames Watershed, 1947-1967.* (Stratford, Ont., 1967)
University of Western Ontario Library. *History Nuggets.* (1943-1969)
__________. *History Notes.* (1942-1972)

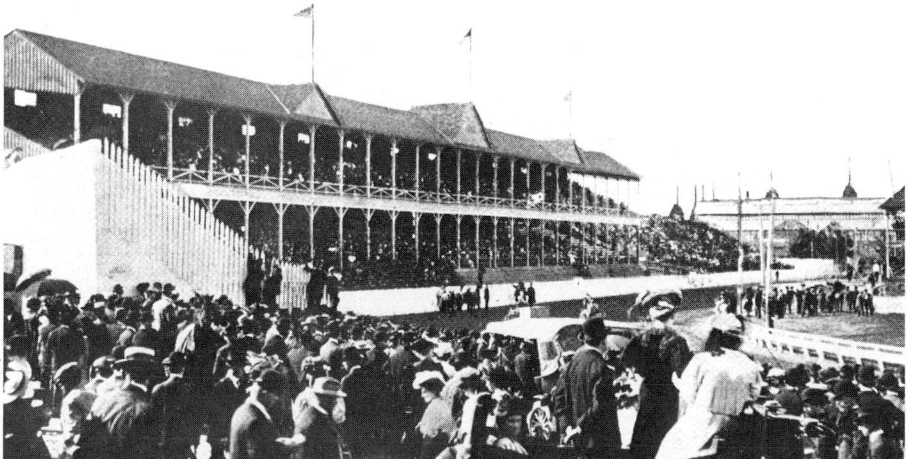

Even before the Western Fair relocated in Queens Park in 1887, a racetrack, today's Western Fair Raceway, was laid out in 1879 on the eastern edge of the grounds. Courtesy, London Historical Museums

Acknowledgments

AUTHOR'S ACKNOWLEDGMENTS

Many people have helped with the preparation of this work. I would particularly like to thank the three people who read the manuscript and made many helpful suggestions: Guy St-Denis; Les Bronson, who was also good enough to write a foreword for the work; and Dan Brock, my collaborator on many London projects, who also let me have access to his many chronological notes on London's history. Guy St-Denis and David R. Brooks assisted with the preparation of some of the biographical sections. For more than two decades Edward C.H. Phelps and James J. Talman have always been generous in sharing their knowledge of London's history, as was the late Fred Landon when I began my researches. Ed Phelps has also helped with numerous crises. Colin F. Read has given me the benefit of his vast knowledge of the Rebellion of 1837. Assisting in a variety of ways were Charles Addington, Margaret Banks, Olga B. Bishop, Glen Curnoe, Leslie R. Gray, William E. Hitchins, Margaret R. Martin, Orlo Miller, James Reaney, E. Madaline Roddick, L. Elizabeth Spicer, Wayne Paddon of St. Thomas, and Maurice Careless, Robin S. Harris, and John W. Holmes of Toronto. Colin E. Friesen and Desmond Neill of Massey College have gone out of their way during many summers' research to provide a perfect work setting at Massey College. Successive chairmen of the department of history have helped make my researches easier, including Jack Hyatt, Peter Neary, and most recently Robert Hohner, without whose expertise the London and Los Angeles word processors would never have achieved compatability. John H. Lutman has been a most cooperative photo researcher, and Jerry Mosher has been a more than patient editor. My secretaries, Melanie Wolfe, who typed the first half of the manuscript, Chris Speed, and especially Lori Morris, who saw the text through the even more chaotic than usual final stages, deserve a great vote of thanks. To my patient family, Joan, Dale, and Irene, to whom this work is dedicated, I give once again my heartfelt thanks.

Frederick H. Armstrong

A London and Port Stanley Railway passenger train prepares to leave its London terminal on Bathurst Street in the 1920s. At the urging of Sir Adam Beck, the city began operating the line in 1915 and electrified it. However, the popularity of the automobile led to the eventual termination of the L&PS in 1957. Courtesy, UWO

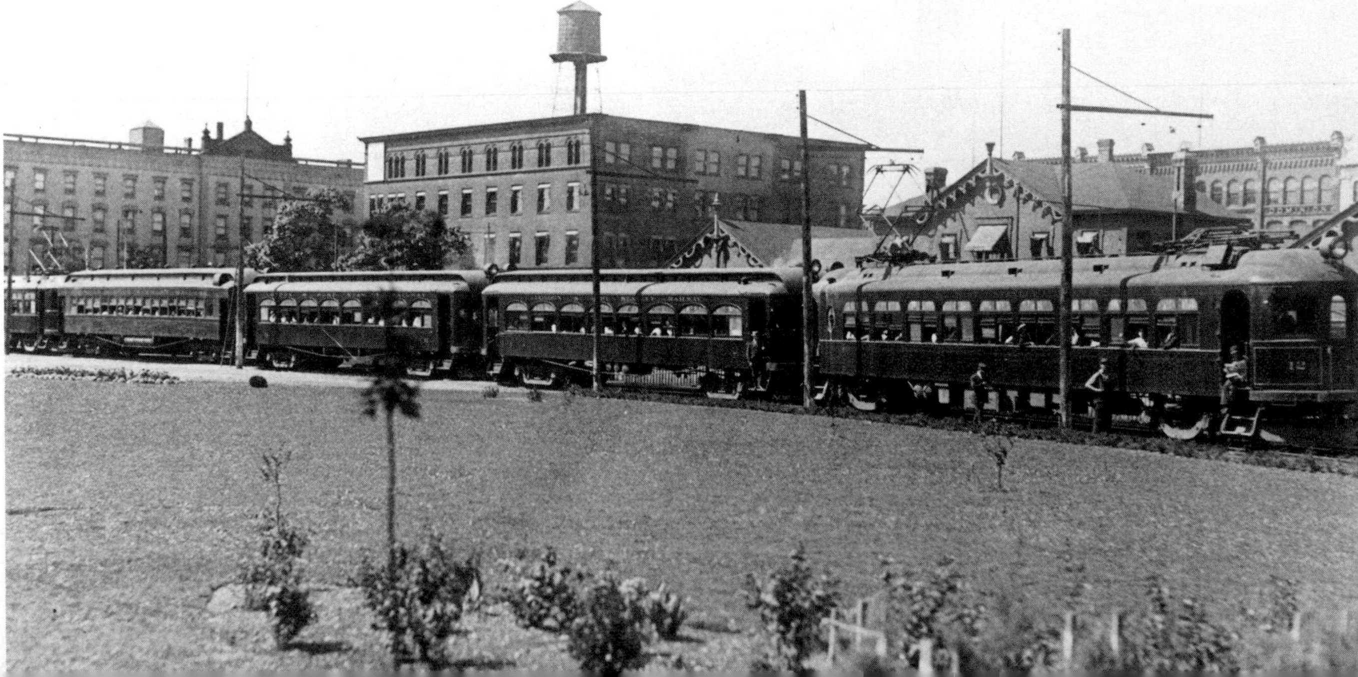

PHOTO RESEARCHER'S ACKNOWLEDGMENTS

As well as thanking many of those noted by the author, I would like to extend my thanks to several other individuals, especially my wife Kathryn Lutman, and the photographers who showed so much patience with the work: Alan Noon, Walter Eldridge, David Hallam, James A. Hockings, and John Tamblyn. In addition I would like to thank: Ken Sadler, city clerk, City of London; Ken Smith of the *London Free Press;* Christopher Severance, Joanne Reynolds, and Peter Mitchell of the London Historical Museums; Karen Niece, Harriet Walker, and David Smith of the Museum of Indian Archaeology; Kenneth D. Pommer of the London Police Force; Nancy Poole, Paddy O'Brien, and Barry Fair of the London Regional Art Gallery; Marsha O'Neill and Fran Stephenson of the London Visitors Convention Bureau; the staff of the Picture Division at the Metropolitan Toronto Library; Guy Fortier, Ken Macpherson, and Arthur Murdoch of the Ontario Archives; Patricia Chalk and Serge Sauer of the University of Western Ontario geography department; Lori Stewart and Clarke Leverette of the U.W.O. Library; Maurice Stubbs and Catherine Elliott Shaw of the U.W.O. McIntosh Gallery; and Michael Baker. As well I would like to thank Robert Windebank, Lillian Davis, Sheila M. Stevenson, Margaret Stotesbury-Leeson, Donald Pierson, and Victor Aziz.

John H. Lutman

This circa 1910 view of London's Springbank Park and its famous pavilion commemorates the school picnics held in June each year through the 1930s. Students from London Public Schools were transported to the park by streetcar to enjoy sack races, baseball, relays, and a free lunch provided by the Board of Education. Courtesy, UWO

Index

PARTNERS IN PROGRESS INDEX

GENERAL INDEX
Italicized numbers indicate illustrations.

THIS BOOK WAS SET IN
CENTURY, TIMES, AND AVANT GARDE TYPE,
PRINTED ON 70 POUND BASKERVILLE GLOSS,
AND BOUND BY
D.W. FRIESEN & SONS LTD